GEORGE SANDYS

Poet-Adventurer

GEORGE SANDYS, 1632

by Cornelius Janssen

From the portrait in the possession of Lt.-Colonel George Sandys, of Graythwaite Hall, North Lancashire

[*Frontispiece*

GEORGE SANDYS

Poet-Adventurer

A
STUDY IN ANGLO-AMERICAN
CULTURE IN THE SEVENTEENTH
CENTURY

RICHARD BEALE DAVIS

LONDON: THE BODLEY HEAD
NEW YORK: COLUMBIA UNIVERSITY PRESS
1955

PUBLISHED IN GREAT BRITAIN
BY JOHN LANE THE BODLEY HEAD LIMITED
AND IN CANADA
BY OXFORD UNIVERSITY PRESS

Printed in Great Britain

CONTENTS

		page
	Preface	9
	Introduction	15
I	Heritage	19
II	Education and Marriage	28
III	Constantinople and Cairo	44
IV	Jerusalem and Naples	68
V	Virginia Adventurer, 1612–21	91
VI	Colonial Official: the Massacre and its Consequences	119
VII	Colonial Official: the Active Life, 1622–5	163
VIII	The Translation of Ovid's *Metamorphoses*	198
IX	Courtier and Sacred Poet	227
X	Colonial Expert: Last Years	254

APPENDICES

A	George Sandys at Corpus Christi, Oxford	269
B	Sandys' Marriage	271
C	Belon as a Typical Example of Sandys' Use of Sources	275
D	Sandys' Travelling Companions from Cairo to Jerusalem	276
E	The Will and Epitaph of Cicely Sandys	278
F	Sir Edwin Sandys and the Virginia Company	279
G	"Liberalism" in the Virginia Company and Colony	280
H	Sandys and the King's Privy Chamber	283
I	Sandys and the Milton-Ovid Script	286

Bibliography	287
Index	311

Illustrations

ILLUSTRATIONS

GEORGE SANDYS, 1632, by Cornelius Janssen, from the portrait in the possession of Lt.-Colonel George O. Sandys of Graythwaite Hall, North Lancashire *frontispiece*

facing page

EDWIN SANDYS, Archbishop of York, and his Wife, Cicely, from the portrait in the National Portrait Gallery, London 32

The Jamestown Massacre, 1622, from the Engraving by Theodore DeBry, in *Historia Americae*, 1634 128

Jamestown in 1622, an engraving enlarged from a portion of the DeBry engraving and appearing in L. G. Tyler, *The Cradle of the Republic*, 1907 144

Jamestown Island about 1624, drawn by H. Chandlee Forman in 1937, and first appearing in his *Jamestown and St. Mary's* in 1938 192
Reproduced by kind permission of the author and the Johns Hopkins University Press

GEORGE SANDYS, probably in the 1630's, by Cornelius Janssen, from the portrait in the possession of Lord Sandys of Ombersley 224

The Church at Boxley, Kent, in which George Sandys is buried, through the courtesy of the Rev. T. E. Prichard, former Rector 264

PREFACE

SOME DOZEN years ago in a conversation concerning neglected figures of early American history and literature, my friend the late Professor Armistead C. Gordon of the University of Virginia suggested that George Sandys deserved a full-length study. Not long after that conversation I began my investigation of Sandys among secondary sources, and within a year had published a preliminary and tentative sketch of his life and work. Two other bibliographical studies of his writings were published before my research was interrupted by the War and three years in the armed service. Since 1946 I have worked fairly steadily on the project. Besides the present work, I have been able to prepare several shorter essays on special phases of Sandys' activities which did not seem to fit too well into a biography. Also in collaboration with Professor Fredson Bowers I have completed a bibliographical catalogue of Sandys' writings printed in England before 1700.

The greater part of this work was made possible through the grant of a fellowship by the John Simon Guggenheim Foundation. This enabled me to spend a year in major English and American libraries working solely on Sandys. In addition, a grant-in-aid from the Henry E. Huntington Library enabled me to spend two months working with that fine collection of rare books and manuscripts. To the Trustees of both corporations I am most grateful. Again I am indebted to the Guggenheim Foundation and to the University of Tennessee for financial assistance which has made possible this publication.

Much of the research in secondary materials and of the actual writing in this study was done in the libraries of the universities of Yale, Virginia, South Carolina, Tennessee, and Texas, and in the Huntington Library, and to their staffs I am greatly indebted for patient and willing assistance. In this country I have examined manuscript materials and/or rare books of the Renaissance period in such libraries as the Pierpont Morgan, the New York Public, the Houghton at Harvard, the William A. Clark of the University of California at Los Angeles, the Folger Shakespeare, the Union Theological Seminary of New York, the Virginia Historical Society, and the Library of Congress. Invariably I have met with courteous and cordial assistance.

In England I was equally fortunate. In every way possible I was aided by the officers and staffs of the British Museum, the Public Record Office, the Victoria and Albert Museum, the Literary Enquiry Room of Somerset House, and the libraries of Lambeth Palace, the Bodleian, Cambridge University, the Advocates of Edinburgh, Corpus Christi College at Oxford, and Trinity and Magdalene Colleges at Cambridge. I am particularly indebted to Mr. J. W. Wallace-Hudrill, Fellow and Librarian of Corpus Christi, for allowing me to examine the Fulman manuscript history of the college, and to Mr. F. McD. C. Turner, Fellow and Librarian of Magdalene, who gave me access to the invaluable Ferrar Papers. Through the latter I had the rare privilege, while I examined the Ferrar Papers, of being locked for (the daylight hours of) several days in the Pepys Library.

To many individuals I am greatly indebted for advice, documents, or other assistance. At the University of Virginia, in addition to Professors Gordon and Bowers, I owe much to Mr. John C. Wyllie, Curator of Rare Books, for advice and the loan of rare items. For many years Dr. Louis B. Wright of the Folger Shakespeare Library has encouraged this project. Professor William A. Jackson of the Houghton Library and Miss Eleanor Goehring of the University of Tennessee Library have helped particularly in certain bibliographical matters. Professor Alexander McElwain of Boston University was most generous in turning over to me valuable copies of documentary materials relating to Sandys which he had gathered over several years. Professor George B. Parks of Queens College has made helpful suggestions as to Sandys' place in the literature of travel.

In England Professor J. Leslie Hotson initiated me into the mysteries of the indices of the Public Record Office. Without him I should have been lost. To him I am grateful also for many clues leading directly to Sandys documents. Mr. Esmond S. de Beer was generous with his own notes on the sources of Sandys' *A Relation*, and gave valuable advice as to further pursuit of similar materials. Lt.-Colonel George O. Sandys of Graythwaite Hall, North Lancashire, supplied me with family genealogical materials and photographs of portraits of the earlier George Sandys, and showed his interest and encouragement over several years. Colonel Arthur Hill, Lord Sandys of Ombersley, gave permission to photograph a portrait of George Sandys at Ombersley and to have certain volumes in the Ombersley Court library examined. To Archdeacon D. M. M. Bartlett of Richmond, Ripon; to the Rev. J. S. Purvis of the Borthwick Institute, York; to the late Rev. George W. Gillingham of Ombersley; to the Rev. Thomas E. Prichard, formerly of Boxley; to

Miss Elizabeth Brunskill of the York Minster Library; and to Mr. Richard Holworthy of the County Record Office, Maidstone, I am indebted for various items of information or copies of documents. Without the expert knowledge and interested assistance of the late Miss Lucy Drucker dozens of copies of seventeenth century documents used in this study would not have been possible.

Finally, in a customary fashion which is nonetheless a most sincere acknowledgement of a debt, I thank my wife, Lois Bullard Davis, who accompanied me on most of my travels in search of materials, transcribed documents, and collated editions of Sandys' writings.

University of Tennessee
Knoxville
January 1955

Richard Beale Davis

Mr Smith likewise moved . . . Virginia . . . might be now preserued, by divulginge fame and good report, as she and her worthy Vndertakers did well deserue, . . . to haue a faire & perspicuous history, compiled of that Country. . . . And to haue the memory and fame of many of her worthies || though they be dead to liue and be transmitted to all posterities . . . wherevnto were it not for suspition of flattery he would wish also the names of many her other worthies yet livinge and some of them now present in Court, might haue also their hono^{ble}: and good deservingę com̃ended to eternall thankefullnes, for that our inhabilities had as yet no trewer Coyne, wherewith to recompence their paines and merrite. . . .

Court for Virginia of 12 April 1621 [Susan Myra Kingsbury, ed., *Records of the Virginia Company of London*, I, 451–2]

INTRODUCTION

THE MAN of the Renaissance has in our age received a remarkable amount of attention, partially at least because we feel a real kinship with him. In another period of enormously expanding physical and intellectual horizons we admire and sympathize with his mixture of sharp realism and sometimes rather vague idealism, his eager search for Truth in its manifold forms, his courage and tenacity in the face of the unknown future, and perhaps above all his almost subconscious yearning for spiritual reassurance

This man of the Renaissance has been studied as he manifested himself in the Latin nations, the Low Countries, and England, in his role of artist, philosopher, scientist, antiquarian, philologist, politician, explorer, warrior, and theologian. We often prefer him when he plays most or all these parts at the same time, for then we see more quickly the complexities and simplicities of his civilization.

Very rightly the genius with head and shoulders above his fellows has not been the only actor on this great stage whose quality has been examined, for the lesser figure usually is the more representative and therefore the more revealing. One learns about the period in England from a variety of biographies—of a choirmaster who set *Comus* to music; of a busy printer and bookseller; of a travelling preacher; or of a circle of brilliant but even then relatively unknown scientists.

Less than the great artist and more than the busy bookseller is the man, often eminent for one or a number of reasons in his own time, who has been largely forgotten but who actually summed up in his career the characteristic if not the major accomplishments of his race and time. Such a figure is George Sandys. The present volume is the first attempt at a full-length study of this complex and significant individual.

First he is the traveller looking at men and nations. Few persons of even his vigorous and roving age had his opportunities to observe the vanities of this world. For in Asia, Africa, and America had he been, in courts and cabins, among Moslem sultans and red Indian chiefs. He had grown up under Elizabeth, travelled under James, and worked as government official under James and Charles I. Of Egypt he gave archaeological descriptions, and there he had collected curious objects.

In Constantinople he looked at the Turk with a searching and critical eye, and sought—within limits—to find out what had made the Infidel what he was. In America he had explored rivers, observed the aborigine in his native forests, sent home accounts of primeval curiosities, and dreamed of finding the Northwest Passage. Folk lore and folk custom always fascinated him. Heir of the Middle Ages as well as son of the Renaissance, he was reminded by most of what he saw that man is frail, that the law of the universe is mutability.

Poet and scholar always accompanied observer in Sandys. His quotations from classical literature in his travel account, his translations of Ovid's *Metamorphoses*, his paraphrase of the more lyrical Scriptures, and his handful of original poems show fine feeling, innovations in technique, and real erudition. Member of the Great Tew circle of Lord Falkland, he spent many years of his life as one of the chief ornaments of that learned and talented company.

But above all George Sandys is of interest for his connections with America and the founding of the British Empire. He is quite clearly the best-known and the ablest of English Renaissance belletristic authors who spent any appreciable time in what is now the United States. In the Virginia colony he translated most of the fifteen books of his Ovid, and he published the whole as the product of the New World. Even more important is his role in laying colonial foundations, for he was director of industry, collector of revenue, chief adviser to the governor, model farmer, and military raider in a crucial period in Virginian and English colonial history. With his kinsman Governor Wyatt he stood for representative assembly and merchant company rather than royal rule, courtier though he was. And in the years after his return to England he served as Privy Council expert on colonial affairs and as personal representative of the colony in a new struggle against direct monarchical control.

Sandys, then, is a striking example of the well-rounded Renaissance man in his role of colonizer and empire-builder. This study, already noticed to be the first to deal with him at any length, can be and is only relatively and tentatively critical as to certain aspects of his place in literature. It does outline his public and private career, it assembles a considerable number of new facts, and it traces in some detail the relation of Sandys' writings to their direct sources and general backgrounds. The present writer has been fortunate in locating in many different places primary documents which augment and alter previous brief treatments of his subject. New material has been discovered on Sandys' college life at Oxford; proof has come to light that he was married, and unhappily, thus explaining from one point of view at least his subsequent career; a new letter indicates where he was and what he was doing at a particular time, and many legal documents "locate" him in various places at specific times; a list of his travelling companions and his own name in the register of the monastery in Jerusalem add further proof of the accuracy of his "Travels"; and a few more original poems have been located and added to his canon. Most rewarding at least to the writer was to bring together the scattered record of Sandys' activities in the Jamestown colony, for his name and work appear more often than anyone has heretofore noticed.

These materials and the biography itself will, it is hoped, supply at least a great portion of the background for further and more definitive studies of colonial American history generally and of Sandys as artist and public official. To make the primary and secondary materials here used most easily available to scholars in many fields, generous and even heavy annotation accompanies the text. The study furnishes bases and suggests trends, but it offers no final conclusions regarding two important matters: (1) Sandys' exact place in the development of English verse, especially of the heroic couplet, and (2) his exact part (including the nature, extent, and motivation of his apparent "liberalism") in one of the major phases of England's first experiment in empire, the battle between interested parties, merchant company and monarchy, between colonial planter and home-office administrator, for control of government or voice in government. Much remains to be done. Any one of a number of studies necessary before drawing final conclusions would occupy as much time and printed space as this whole book. Research should be made into Sandys' couplet form in its relation to that of his predecessors, contemporaries, and successors, and into the influence of his poetry and prose on Milton. A scholarly edition of *A Relation* should be prepared. And, to determine his governmental attitudes, a re-examination should be made of the political situation regarding Virginia both in England and America, 1618–42, perhaps approached through a study of the British Parliament's politics and political parties in the same period. These and other questions are raised here, for their answers would throw light on the whole stage on which he acted.

Actually the task has already begun, for two complete studies of certain phases of Sandys' literary work have just been completed in American universities. These have proved to be extensions, and not contradictions, of matters discussed or projected in this biography. They lie outside its immediate province. They etch in fine literary details, but they do not alter the picture.

For the general historical reader who would know something of at least one of the types of men who were our earliest economic and political leaders this volume should be of some interest. Here is a poet-adventurer. Forthright, honest, quick-tempered, resourceful, shrewdly analytical, he is individual evidence that England could give of her best in laying the foundations of the world she was to dominate two centuries later. Sandys' varied life, his intellectual and moral character, his creative and critical mind, compel our admiration. They also afford us one of those rare flashes of insight into why we are what we are.

I

HERITAGE

ON THE surface the Renaissance Englishman is an intense individualist. Yet if a probe is made in a particular case, the great 'original' often proves to be but a somewhat exaggerated example of the recurrent traits of a vigorous family. Stimulating as the mighty events of the age may be in determining his actions, what he makes of himself bears quite clearly the impress of family character. George Sandys is a case in point. In ideas he usually does not agree with his father the prelate or his most distinguished brother the politician. But in actions and in interests he is a true branch from the same tree.

On 2 March 1577/78, the Archbishop of York sat in his study in the palace at Bishopthorp with a copy[1] of the Bishops' Bible he had helped to translate on the table before him. He had just recorded the birth, at four o'clock that morning, of his ninth child and seventh son, probably named after its godfather, George Clifford, Earl of Cumberland.[2] It had

[1] This copy is preserved at the Hawkeshead Grammar School, North Lancashire, which Archbishop Sandys endowed. A copy of his entry is included in Br. Mus. Add. MSS. 45866 ("The Notes of Charles Sandys for a Biography of Archbishop Sandys"). References to the flyleaf on which the birth dates of the children appear may also be found in T. R. Nash, *Collections for the History of Worcestershire* . . . (2 vols, London, 1782), II, 223; Alexander Brown, *Genesis of the United States* (2 vols., Boston, 1897), II, 992; and J. H. Pleasants, "Sandys of Furnace Fells, Lancashire," *Virginia Magazine of History and Biography*, XXIX (April 1921), 243. Lt.-Col. George O. Sandys of Graythwaite Hall, a trustee of the Hawkeshead School, assures me that the Bible is still preserved.

[2] Or possibly after the archbishop's long-dead brother, George Sandys, or the Archbishop's grandfather of the same name (in Pleasants, "Sandys of Furnace Fells," pp. 228–30). The prelate's brother was killed in battle on the field of Musselburgh in 1547. The child's greatgrandfather was living at Furnace Fells, North Lancashire, in 1513. That George was named for his godfather George Clifford, Earl of Cumberland (see below) seems most probable. Of the nine children whose baptism is recorded in the Archbishop's Bible, all save the first two, Samuel and Edwin, have one godparent bearing the same Christian name as the child. *E.g.*, Myles (b. 1563), his uncle Myles Sandys; Margaret (b. 1566), Lady Margaret Russell; Thomas (b. 1568), Sir Thomas Lucy Knt. (cf. Shakespeare.). Anne (b. 1570) had two godparents named Anne. For these entries see Brown, *Genesis of the U.S.* II, 991–2.

been five years since the birth of another child,[3] and this was to be the last. His two older sons[4] were already at Oxford. Providing for the seven living children[5] would be troublesome, but the good prelate knew how it could be managed.

In fact, the Archbishop had already a reputation[6] for a voracious appetite for "fruits and fees," especially in the form of landed property for himself and his family. This appetite was not unusual in an Elizabethan churchman,[7] and he shared it with all his secular contemporaries. But in Edwin Sandys' case it was to increase exceedingly and, according to his enemies, scandalously. In the next decade, as he felt the pressure of encroaching age and youthful family forcing him, he devoured Yorkshire lands in large quantities, often by what seem to us dubious methods. What he did for his children was not to enhance his fame in the eyes of posterity. And what he did for his youngest son, at least, was to affect profoundly and perhaps deleteriously the whole course of the younger man's life. But whatever Edwin Sandys did here or elsewhere he did for the best, under the eyes of God.

The Archbishop's story is the key to much in his son. The future churchman was born in North Lancashire in 1516 or 1519,[8] of a family of country gentry prominent[9] in the Furnace Fells neighbourhood since the fifteenth century. About 1533[10] he entered St. John's College,

[3] Henry, born in 1572.

[4] Samuel and Edwin, though the Fulman MS. history of Corpus Christi College (see below) shows them "battelling" at a later date, Edwin entered Corpus in 1577 and Samuel, the elder, presumably earlier (the Fulman MS. shows Samuel still there or back again in 1580).

[5] James, his only child by his first wife, his cousin Mary Sandys, had died of the plague while the family were in exile between 1554 and 1560. A younger son, William, also died young (b. 1565). He is not mentioned in the will (see Pleasants, "Sandys of Furnace Fells," p. 232).

[6] See John Ayre, introduction to *The Sermons of Edwin Sandys* (Cambridge, 1892), pp. xxv, xxvii.

[7] See, *e.g.*, M. M. Knappen, *Tudor Puritanism* (Chicago, 1939), p. 241, and the account of William Cole given below.

[8] W. A. J. Archbold, in his biographical sketch of Edwin Sandys in the *D.N.B.*, gives 1516 as the probable date. John Ayre, *Sermons of Edwin Sandys*, p. i, mentions 1519.

[9] The best history of the family is that of E[dward] S[eton] Sandys, *History of the Family of Sandys*, (2 vols., Barrow-in-Furness, 1930). An earlier history is that of Comley Vivian, *Some Notes for a History of the Sandys Family* . . . (London, 1907). There are a series of very good sketches, somewhat outdated, by J. Hall Pleasants, "Sandys of Furnace Fells, Lancashire," as noted above.

[10] John and J. A. Venn, *Alumni Cantabrigienses* (Cambridge, 1927), Pt. I,

Cambridge, already becoming a stronghold of the Reformation.[11] Advancing rather rapidly through four academic degrees, he was in 1542 Proctor of the University and in 1547 Master of St. Catherine's Hall. By 1553 he was Vice-Chancellor, and with this eminent academic position came the opportunity to prove his convictions. On Edward VI's death he unhesitatingly took his stand on the side of Protestantism, preaching a sermon before the University and the Duke of Northumberland which committed him unequivocally. The sermon was printed, Mary was proclaimed, and Sandys was at once a fit object for punishment. He was almost a full-fledged martyr, and Foxe's story of his courage in affliction is quoted with relish by later ecclesiastical writers.[12] Certainly he bore himself like a man. He did not flinch or compromise. He accepted his imprisonment in the Tower and Marshalsea without complaint. When he was offered release on the condition he remain in England, he declined. Finally he obtained it without provision and immediately crossed to the Continent, taking along his wife[13] and young son. Here he joined the group of exiles who were to be influenced profoundly by the Geneva, Strasburg, and Zurich groups, and who in turn were to be the forerunners in England of the church puritans. Cox and Grindall he saw much of. Going to Zurich after the death of his wife and son, [14] he lived for a time in the house of Peter Martyr.[15] It was here, while he sat at dinner, that the news came of the death of Queen Mary. Soon he was back in England, and almost immediately received preferment. In fairly rapid succession he was Bishop of Worcester, then of London, and in 1576 Archbishop of York.

But Edwin Sandys' life is not a simple story of faithful Protestantism and consequent ecclesiastical reward. His personality and his convictions brought him enemies all along the road. His attitude towards marriage for the clergy, for example, including himself, was an irritant in a nation by no means entirely converted from the Popish idea of celibacy. One of his first and longest quarrels was at Worcester, when his new second

vol. IV, 19, gives no date of matriculation. 1532 or 1533 is suggested by Ayre, p. i.

[11] Ayre, p. i.

[12] *E.g.*, John Ayre, pp. ii–xvi.

[13] His relative Mary Sandys. See note 5 above.

[14] See note 5 above.

[15] Sandys followed Martyr to Zurich from Strasburg in 1558. See Christina H. Garrett, *The Marian Exiles* (Cambridge, 1938), pp. 283-4, where Edwin Sandys' career in exile is summarized.

wife[16] was ridiculed by[17] a prominent parishioner of obvious Catholic leanings who had been Secretary of State under Queen Mary.[18] But the marriage of the clergy, of which even Elizabeth did not approve, Sandys defended in sermons both in England and on the continent.

Sandys' theological position was acknowledgedly difficult. Though he had the exile's natural leaning to "Germanical doctrines," he was quite conscious that he had the dignity of his office to maintain. He opposed vestments and making the sign of the cross, among other things. Yet in a debate-conference on conformity in Whitgift's day he upheld the Church's position against the puritan delegates, and he constantly fought the encroachments of the secular government on church property. He was certainly not simply "an obstinate and conscientious puritan at a time when those in authority wished that men with Romish leanings should be treated indulgently,"[19] for he was threatened by the puritan Dering[20] as well as by the papist Bourne.[21] His courage was that of his own conviction. "When Gods cause cometh in hand, I forget what displeasure may follow," he once replied[22] to the Archbishop of Canterbury who had reprimanded him.

That he was a lover of the "fruits" of his office has been touched upon. He seems to have declined for a time promotion from the see of Worcester to that of London because he felt that the income of the latter diocese would actually be less than what he already was receiving. In York particularly he was accused,[23] even by his own dean, of providing

[16] Cicely Wilford or Wilsford, daughter of Sir Thomas Wilford of Hartridge in Kent. She became the mother of seven sons and two daughters. It should be noted that she was the sister of one of Edwin Sandys' fellow-exiles, a second Thomas Wilford (see Christina H. Garrett, pp. 283, 332–3 and note 31 below). Her two brothers, Sir James and later Sir Thomas, became famous soldiers with strong anti-Papist feelings (see A. F. Pollard's article on the two in the *D.N.B.*).

[17] Ayre, p. xviii. Sir John Bourne was the offender.

[18] Though the quarrel involved other things such as property and an altar-stone ordered to be removed.

[19] Summarized in this fashion by W. A. J. Archbold, "Edwin Sandys," in *D.N.B.* John Strype, *The Life and Acts of John Whitgift* . . . (3 vols., Oxford, 1822), I, 546–7, quotes extensively and convincingly from the preamble of Archbishop Sandys' will to demonstrate that Sandys' theology was not puritan, but moderate Anglican.

[20] Knappen, p. 240.

[21] See above and note 17.

[22] John Strype, *The Life and Acts of Matthew Parker* (3 vols., Oxford, 1821), III, 44, letter of 24 Oct. 1560. Also see Strype, *Whitgift*, I, 545.

[23] Ayre, pp. xxvi–xxvii.

for his family out of the revenues of the archdiocese. This Sandys categorically denied, declaring that he had merely granted leases[24] to his sons which he had to grant to someone, and that he was justified in giving to his own children rather than to strangers. There is every evidence that he was sincere, and convinced of his own honesty and integrity in the matter.

His learning was generally admitted. Beginning his career as university fellow and administrator, he continued to evidence his scholarship in his sermons, his translations for the Bishops' Bible, and in his various pastoral epistles and other letters. His sponsorship of Richard Hooker for the Mastership of the Temple and his founding of the Hawkeshead Grammar School are also more than tokens of his interest in things of the mind.

The archbishop's belligerent stubbornness in supporting his own ideas is matched only by the astute diplomacy he could combine with the former when he chose. In the same letter [25] in which he bluntly refuted Archbishop Parker's accusations he so well demonstrated his own faith in and loyalty to his superior that he removed any sting the earlier part of the letter may have inflicted. Though on principle he declined to fill an advowson, as Burghley personally urged,[26] before it fell due, the double role of adviser-suitor he here and always played with the Lord Treasurer kept them on excellent terms. With the Queen it was the same. He opposed her openly and sometimes violently on matters of images,[27] vestments, and marriage, and declined absolutely[28] to alienate Bishopthorp and Southwell from the archdiocese at her command. Yet soon after his return from exile he preached a sermon[29] at York which delighted her and later, in conference with her concerning one of her

24 Br. Mus. MS. Lansdown 50. f. 34 contains Lord Burghley's notes on "Grants by ye Archbi[shop] of York/ to his sons./xxxi/May 1586." This MS. contains twenty-six items ranging in value from £200 down to £20 annually. The annual rent is, of course, but a small fraction of the income. The eldest living son, Samuel, received by far the largest share (6 leases), followed by Edwin (4 leases) and Myles (5 leases but inferior in value to Edwin's). The younger sons, Thomas, Henry, and George received two leases each.

25 Strype, *Parker*, I, 156 and III, 41–4.

26 Ayre, p. xxiv.

27 H. Robinson, *Zurich Letters* (Cambridge, 1846), 1st series, p. 98. In this matter, of course, he was merely a typical Marian exile.

28 Ayre, pp. xxii, xxvii.

29 Archbold, "Edwin Sandys," *D.N.B.*

prospective marriage[30] alliances, showed himself a skilful courtier. Though he himself once said that he ran the risk of losing his bishopric in his oppositions, he usually won, and was steadily promoted.

Such was the father who was at the height of his career, already an archbishop, when his son George was born. The boy's mother, his father's second wife acquired after the exile, has left almost no record of her personality save the tone of her will,[31] written twenty-two years after her husband had passed to his reward. She was born Cicely Wilford,[32] only daughter of the second marriage of Sir Thomas Wilford of Hartridge in Kent, a man of some means and wide connections.[33] To her personal supervision the Archbishop by his will entrusted the upbringing of his three youngest sons, Thomas, Henry, and George. Potentially her part in George's life is considerable, for her husband died before the boy was eleven.

George's older brothers and sisters, too, were an interesting group. There is evidence that the brothers played a considerable and quite definite part in his future, particularly the three oldest, Samuel, Edwin, and Myles. All three were knighted,[34] Myles eventually becoming a baronet,[35] and all three were at various times members of Parliament. Samuel and Myles were to remain country gentlemen of some wealth

[30] Martin A. S. Hume, *The Great Lord Burghley* (London, 1898), 339–40. The conference concerned the Alençon affair. The Archbishop also seems to have suggested to the Queen, through Burghley, that it was politically necessary that Mary Queen of Scots be beheaded (see his letter of 5 September 1572, quoted in *The Edinburgh Review*, XCI, June 1827, 196–7, in a review of Henry Ellis' *Original Letters Illustrative of English History*).

[31] Here she shows herself merely as a woman of strong family affection with a practical eye in money matters (see the abstract in Pleasants, "Sandys of Furnace Fells," p. 234).

[32] Sir Thomas Wilsford (see note 16 above) of Hedinge, one of the executors of her will, was her one full brother. She had two older half-brothers and eight half-sisters. Her portrait, with that of her husband the Archbishop, may be seen in the National Portrait Gallery. See note 16 above.

[33] Through the Wilfords, for example, comes George Sandys' kinship with Sir Dudley Digges, whose grandfather Leonard Digges had married Cicely Sandys's sister (see "The Rev. T. Streatfield's Collections Relating to Kent," Br. Mus. Add. MSS. 33,894, f. 24).

[34] Samuel, at Whitehall, 23 July 1603; Edwin, at Charterhouse, 11 May 1603; Myles (or Miles), at Charterhouse, 11 May 1603 (see Brown, *Genesis*, II, 995; Pleasants, "Sandys of Furness Fells," pp. 235, 236, 242).

[35] On 25 November 1612 (Pleasants, p. 242). Myles is not to be confused with his uncle Myles Sandys of Latimers, Master of the King's Bench; nor with his cousin (grandson of Myles of Latimers), Sir Myles Sandys of Gloucester,

and considerable eminence in the counties[36] in which they settled. Edwin had a really distinguished career. The lives of all three and the lives of some of their children cross the life of the younger George, even in the public records, many times. These three seem to have shared with his mother the parental responsibility, for they appear as financial and personal, even marital, advisers.

His two sisters, Margaret and Anne, married respectively Sir Anthony Aucher and Sir William Barne,[37] and through both marriages connected their family with the Lovelaces, who with the Sandyses were to have a significant part in the establishment of the American colonies. Of George's brothers William, Thomas, and Henry, not a great deal is known.[38]

When the Archbishop's youngest son came to be christened, there were present as participants,[39] in addition to the family, three notable persons. George Earl of Cumberland and William Lord Eure stood as godfathers, and Catherine Countess of Huntingdon as godmother. The

M.P., who died in 1636 aged 36 (see E. S. Sandys, Pedigree E). The names Edwin, Myles, Samuel, and George appear many times in the family and public records, and during the Elizabethan and Stuart periods. The individuals will be distinguished as carefully as possible.

[36] Myles lived at Wimberton, or Wilburton, Isle of Ely, and married Elizabeth, daughter of Edward Cooke of North Gray, Kent. His father had "left" him the five leases (Br. Mus., Burghley Papers, 1586, Lansdown MSS. 50 f. 34) noted above, and there are evidences that he married well. Samuel, as eldest son, had been given six valuable leases (Burghley Papers) and had married so well that it was with his wife's dowry, it is said, that he bought the fine estate of Ombersley (which the Archbishop had owned and left, in the form of an annuity, to his wife Cicely. See Pleasants, "Sandys of Furnace Fells," p. 233). At Ombersley he established his residence, though like his brothers he owned fine manors in Yorkshire.

[37] See Pleasants, "Sandys of Furnace Fells," p. 242, or E. S. Sandys.

[38] William, born 1565, died young, as noticed above. Henry, born 1572, was to enter Oxford at the same time as George (see Chapter II below), but little more is known of him. Thomas, born 1568, lived his adult years in London, married the daughter of Robert Tyas, Clerk Comptroller of the Wardrobe, and became a member of the Virginia Company. He left numerous issue, including an eldest son, Robert, who married Alice Washington, and a second son George, to whom his uncle of the same name later showed some attention (see E. S. Sandys, Pedigree C, and Henry and Richard St. George, *Visitation of London . . . 1633, 1634, 1635* [2 vols., London, 1883], II, 228). Both Henry and Thomas were members of the Virginia Company.

[39] They are listed, opposite the name George Sandys and his date and time of birth, in the Bishops' Bible at Hawkeshead.

two peers were members[40] of the Council of the North, and the peeress was the wife of the President of the same governing group. Thus the leaders in State and Church were present for the Christian baptism of this seventh son.

Two[41] of these sponsors are of particular interest as personalities and as personages, and one at least may have had some influence on his young godson's later thought and action. Catherine Countess of Huntingdon was the wife of the man who was the chief Protestant claimant, after Elizabeth, to the throne, a man called in his own day and since a zealous puritan.[42] The Countess herself, daughter of the able Duke of Northumberland[43] who took the field against Mary in favour of Lady Jane Grey, was sister-in-law of "Queen Jane," and through her own sister Mary the aunt of Sir Philip Sidney. She and her husband represented not only present political power, but the union of politico-religious ideas of which the Archbishop approved. The Countess lived on until 1620, and may have read the first of the books which were to make this godson's name in Stuart literature.

But the fascinating one of the two is George, third Earl of Cumberland. When he attended this christening he was still a young man just under his majority, though already married and an M.A. of Trinity College, Cambridge.[44] He was then still living most of his time at

[40] See G. C. Williamson, *George, Third Earl of Cumberland* (Cambridge, 1920), pp. 12–13, 14.

[41] William Lord Ewer or Eure (1529–93/4), as far as extant evidence goes least important in George Sandys' story, was Warden of the Middle Marches in the reigns of Edward VI, Mary, and Elizabeth, and one of the commissioners to deal with Scotland in 1587. His life has one thing much in common with George Sandys': in 1541 he was contracted in marriage at the age of eleven, the bride being only four, to Mary daughter of George, Lord Darcy. In his case the contract was set aside.

[42] Henry Hastings, Earl of Huntingdon (1535–95). See the article on him by T. F. Henderson in the *D.N.B.* and the "Hastings Papers" in the Henry E. Huntington Library.

[43] Her father had been Chancellor of Cambridge in 1553 when Archbishop (then Dr.) Sandys was Vice-Chancellor at the time Queen Mary had to be proclaimed. Sandys stood his ground in opposition and went to the Tower, but the Earl of Northumberland proclaimed her at Cambridge with tears, it is said, running down his cheeks. Submission did him little good, for shortly after he himself went to the Tower and his execution.

[44] He was born in 1558. For details of his life, see the interesting biography by G. C. Williamson, *George, Third Earl of Cumberland* (Cambridge, 1920), a study based largely on original documents.

Skipton Castle in Yorkshire with his mother, the Dowager Countess.[45] Within ten years, however, he was to make his way at court, become a voyager and buccaneer, and fight furiously against the Armada. He was a colourful figure, winning the Queen's favour[46] early, and showing himself in the lists and on the quarterdeck a man of magnificent courage and knightly ability. Fitting out expeditions at his own expense, and sometimes borrowing his ships from the Queen, he had considerable success against the Spaniard. But somehow prizes and treasure always slipped through his fingers. Though he began life with a vast property, the spirit of adventure and gallantry had led him at his death in 1605 into a thousand-pound debt. But living or dead, he was one of the Elizabethan symbols of the thirst to do and to see the strange and the new. George Sandys, growing up in the Earl's own Yorkshire with the great man's fame always before him, may well have felt the urge to follow in the adventurous footsteps of his godfather.[47]

[45] When she died in 1581 he and his wife began to spend most of their time not spent at court at Brougham Castle.

[46] He wore the Queen's glove, encrusted with jewels, like a plume in his hat (see the miniature by Nicholas Hilliard, and the portrait by an unknown artist in the National Portrait Gallery, date about 1588).

[47] Forty years later the Earl's daughter, Anne Clifford, then Countess of Dorset, spent a day (9 January 1617) at Knole reading, or having read to her "Mr Sandys's book . . . about the Government of the Turks." (See V. Sackville-West, ed., *The Diary of Lady Anne Clifford*, London, 1923, p. 47.)

II

EDUCATION AND MARRIAGE

BUT THE path of adventure would open before George Sandys only after he had undergone many of life's more ordinary experiences. The first of these, after parental care, was schooling. Since he was able to enter the university within a year of his father's death, he had already, almost surely,[1] attended one of York's two schools, probably[2] St. Peter's,[3] within the shadow of the Minster. Already almost a thousand years old,[4] St. Peter's in Archbishop Sandys' period at York was flourishing. The school had an able headmaster, John Pullen; and, since the Council of the North was resident in and near York, many of its members[5] sent their sons to study there.

George Sandys may have spent the impressionable years from his seventh to his eleventh birthday at St. Peter's. The little we know would indicate that it was a lively place. Pullen, a Cambridge graduate, held the mastership from 1575 to 1591. The curriculum, textbooks, the daily life of the scholars, however, remain unknown, except as we surmise from the few extant records of later date[6] or of similar schools.

[1] Though of course he may have had a tutor, such as his father's chaplain, at home.

[2] The Archbishop Holgate Grammar School, founded within the sixteenth century, also existed at York. Student records (according to the administrative authorities of both schools when the present writer visited York in 1947) for St. Peter's and the Holgate School for this period do not exist. A boy of George Sandys' social and ecclesiastical standing, however, was more likely to have attended St. Peter's. There were other Yorkshire schools which he may have attended at Beverley, Howden, and especially at Ripon (see Arthur F. Leach, *Early Yorkshire Schools* [2 vols., Yorkshire Archæological Society, Record Series, 1899 and 1903]) but there seems no good reason why he should have travelled farther than to the best of them so close to Bishopthorp.

[3] For a history of St. Peter's School, see Angelo Raine, *History of St. Peter's School: York* (London, 1926).

[4] Its "official" founding date is A.D. 627.

[5] Raine, pp. 79, 82–3.

[6] A list of textbooks surviving as the inventory of a York stationer who supplied the school, John Foster, twenty-five years after Sandys' time, shows: "25 Gramers . . . Eleven Terences . . . 27 Pueriles Confabulatio . . . 8 Ovid de Tristibus . . . 9 Isocrates 3 Orations . . . 5 Ovid Fastorum . . . 20 Tullii Pro

Late in the year 1589 George Sandys ended his schoolboy days and became at the age of eleven a gentleman of the University of Oxford. His father had been dead a year, and his mother was his guardian. On 5 December his name was entered[7] in the register of St. Mary's Hall just below the signature of his brother Henry, who was matriculating at the more mature age of sixteen.[8] Both boys are described as sons of an archbishop, Henry giving his birthplace as London and George his as Yorkshire. They appear to have transferred[9] within a few days to nearby Corpus Christi College. At least the evidence is that they had their tuition[10] within the walls of Corpus and should be associated with its intellectual and social life. That they were entered as Gentlemen-Commoners may explain this shift in colleges,[11] for only six men of this classification were allowed by statute to live within the walls of Corpus. George may have studied there until he was ready for the law courts six years later, but Henry went on to London in 1590 to become a member of the Middle Temple.[12]

Certainly Corpus Christi was the natural place for the two sons of the Archbishop. Just a few years before their brothers Samuel and Edwin had preceded them in the college. Edwin, friend and pupil of Richard Hooker, had proceeded B.A. in 1579 and M.A. in 1583, had held a fellowship in 1578–80, and had been granted the B.C.L. in the year Henry and George entered. Most important in certain respects, the President was that staunch Protestant and fellow-exile of their father's, William Cole.[13]

Archia Poeta . . . 3 Demosthenes Orationis . . . 1 Cato" (see Raine, pp. 91–2).

[7] See Andrew Clark, *Register of the University of Oxford* (4 vols., Oxford 1887–9), II, Pt. II, 174.

[8] The ages of those around them on the register range from eleven to twenty (and occasionally to thirty and thirty-six). There is one other matriculate aged eleven on the same page. Most students entering, however, were between fourteen and eighteen. Entering St. John's College this same year, at the age of sixteen, was George Sandys' future friend William Laud.

[9] Most authorities simply state that George was a member of St. Mary's Hall, but Anthony Wood, *Athenae Oxonienses* (5 vols., London, 1813–20 [original edition 1691–2]), III, 98, who gives St. Mary's Hall as their original college, says that "both, as I conceive, received their tuition at Corp. Ch. coll. How long George tarried, or whether he took a degree, it appears not."

[10] See Appendix A for evidence.

[11] See Appendix A for reasons why this was true.

[12] Foster, *Alumni Oxonienses*, Early Series, IV, 1309.

[13] See Thomas Fowler, *The History of Corpus Christi College* (Oxford, 1893),

Though student life at Corpus was perhaps not so strenuous as it had been before the Reformation,[14] the scholar still had little time for relaxation. By statute all Fellows and Scholars[15] had to attend the University and college lectures in Greek and Latin, which took place each day, and on the Greek alone were to be examined three evenings a week.[16] Though the ordinary Scholar may have been excused from theological[17] lectures, he attended long and pedagogical chapel services each day, and he was obliged to participate in disputations in logic, natural philosophy, metaphysics, and morals.[18] And most demanding

pp. 124–60, and Christina H. Garrett, *The Marian Exiles*, p. 123. Cole was elected President in 1568. The story of the pro-Catholic Fellows' refusal to elect him, of the turning out of some of the old Fellows for new Protestant ones, and Cole's triumph, is an interesting example of religion and politics at Oxford. Cole, the first married President of Corpus, throughout his thirty years there continued to have bitter enemies among the older Fellows and good friends among the younger ones and among the students. Though he seems, like Archbishop Sandys, to have been too great a lover of the fruits of his office (and less scrupulously so than the prelate), he also appears to have been an able administrator and excellent scholar who inspired in others his reverence for learning. His only published work, other than a few letters, is his part in the translation of the Geneva Bible.

[14] See Fowler, pp. 37–59.

[15] Presumably this included the Gentlemen-Commoners, for in the Fulman MSS. (see Appendix A) Henry and George are designated as Scholars under the term "Discipuli."

[16] One of the significant questions here is whether or not George Sandys acquired any knowledge of Greek during the Oxford years, or earlier or later, for his later published works, relying on Latin and perhaps on Italian, French, and Spanish sources, give no real hint (see discussions of his travels and translations in Chapters III, IV, and VIII below). The Founders' stipulations as to what Latin authors should be "taught," or lectured upon, were probably followed in Sandys' time. Those specified for in-term lectures daily were Cicero, Sallust, Valerius Maximus, Suetonius, Pliny's Natural History, Livy, Quintilian, Virgil, Ovid, Lucan, Juvenal, Terence, and Plautus. Vacation lectures thrice weekly were to include the *Elegantiae* of Laurentius Valla, the *Attic Nights* of Aulus Gellius, the *Miscellanea* of Politian. Noticeably omitted are Horace and Tacitus. It is interesting that almost all of these authors are alluded to by name, and used as reference, in Sandys' first published book, his travels.

[17] Fowler, p. 40. Sandys' tremendous interest in Theology, manifest in his published (and one known unpublished) work, was simply typical of the learned man in his day.

[18] Again by early sixteenth century statute. That these rigid requirements had been modified slightly in the Elizabethan period is probable.

of all, he had to work diligently and steadily under the eye of the Fellow or tutor.[19]

The younger Sandyses missed Hooker, who had departed in 1584, though his fame as a lecturer was still very much alive.[20] And they missed the fine scholar and future President of the College, John Rainolds, who in 1586 had resigned his fellowship for a university lectureship in controversial theology and retired temporarily to Queen's. If George did stay until 1595, he witnessed the visit of the Queen to Oxford in 1592,[21] and saw his college's head, William Cole,[22] conspicuous among those who greeted her at Godstow. Most exciting to a boy of fourteen must have been this glimpse of the glories of a reign and a sovereign already past their prime.

It is of course impossible to say what Oxford did for a youth whose only certain connection with it is his matriculation at the age of eleven. The same youth grew, however, into a gentleman famed for his learning in the classics and foreign tongues. Wood[23] has emphasized the idea that Sandys came back from his travels (1610–12) a scholar, but he admits that Sandys had already "a zealous inclination to all human learning."[24] Certainly the foundations of this erudition must have been laid at Corpus Christi.

[19] If he actually moved to Corpus, George Sandys probably shared a room—his being the truckle bed—with his tutor. Such was the arrangement at the College from the beginning of the century, at a period when other colleges placed three or four men in one room (see Fowler, p. 50). In the early sixteenth century, at any rate, the Scholar kept the room in order.

[20] See Fowler, p. 152. They almost surely knew Hooker personally as he was a friend of their brother Edwin and was appointed to his Mastership of the Temple through their father's influence.

[21] Disputations, plays, and sermons were among the delights provided. Students were warned, under pain of imprisonment and other dire penalties, not to make "outcries or undecent noyse" outside in case they "could not gain admittance to the play houses." Sandys' father's friend Burghley was present. (See C. E. Mallet, II, 150–4 and Charles Plummer, ed. *Elizabethan Oxford: Reprints of Rare Tracts* [Oxford, 1887], pp. 173–273.)

[22] He may also the next year have heard much of the arbitration of Cole's dispute with the Fellows regarding college leases (see Fowler, pp. 343–4).

[23] In *Athenae*, III, 97–8, he says "The author upon his return in 1612 or after, being improved in several respects by this long journey, became an accomplished gent. as being master of several languages, of fluent and ready discourse and excellent comportment."

[24] *Ibid.* Corpus Christi's fine library, praised by Erasmus, must have been a useful and fascinating place to Sandys.

However long he had spent in the university, by 1596 the eighteen-year-old boy was continuing his education elsewhere. On 23 October of that year, the *Minutes of the Parliament of the Middle Temple*[25] reveal, admitted to membership was "Mr. George, sixth son of Edwin Sandys, archbishop of York, deceased, specially; no fine,[26] by request of Mr. Sandis, late Treasurer,"[27] and George's uncle. Thus the youngest member of a family followed a tradition set by many relatives, for *Sandys* is one of the most frequently recurring names in the records of the Middle Temple.[28] His course of study is more uncertain to us in the Court than it was at Oxford.[29] Though men were now, after several years' study, being formally called to the Bar in certain instances, there is no proof that any of the Archbishop's sons attained the rank of Utter Barrister.[30] The older sons certainly[31] had legal training, probably in

[25] Edited by Charles T. Martin (4 vols., London 1904–5), I, 368. See also E. A. Jones, *American Members of the Inns of Court* (London, 1924), pp. xii, 191–2.

[26] That is, without entrance fee.

[27] Myles Sandys of Latimers, Bucks., Master of the King's Bench, fifth son of William Sandys and younger brother of the Archbishop, had been until a few months earlier the chief executive officer of the Middle Temple (that is, "Treasurer"; see Charles T. Martin, *Minutes*, I, 365 and Nash, *Collections of Worcestershire*, II, 220) and was still exercising a prerogative he had used many times before in behalf of his own four sons and four of the older sons of the Archbishop (Martin, *Minutes*, I, 230, 270, 303, 311, 312, 318, 320, 325, 364, 365). His four sons, Edwin, William, George, and Henry (see E. S. Sandys, Pedigree E) all appear to have been knighted. His three daughters, Bridget, Hester, and Elizabeth married respectively Sir Nicholas Hyde (later "Chief Justice of the King's Bench"), Sir Thomas Temple, and Edmund Conquest.

[28] Anthony of Hawkeshead (probably the younger brother of the Archbishop) was admitted in 1564; the four sons of Myles, Edwin in 1579, William in 1589/90, George and Henry in 1593–4; four older sons of Archbishop Edwin, Samuel (called not by name but "son and heir apparent of the Archbishop") in 1579, Thomas in 1588, Edwin in 1589, and Henry in 1596. Thus all of George's brothers who lived to maturity, save Myles, preceded him in the Middle Temple.

[29] He may have been a member for the sake of convenience, perhaps in order to live in London near his brothers. Whether he actually ever had chambers in the Court one cannot say, though the records indicate that his brothers did (see Martin, *Minutes*, I, various pages as quoted in note 27 above).

[30] Or for that matter, of the grades between. During Elizabeth's reign (1574–1602) there were 241 calls to the Utter Bar at the Middle Temple (see J. Bruce Williamson, *History of the Temple, London* [London, 1925], p. 244).

[31] For the records show three (Thomas being the exception among the older brothers) in residence, with the names of the persons with whom they were "bound" (see Martin, *Minutes*, I, pages as in note 27 above).

EDWIN SANDYS, ARCHBISHOP OF YORK, AND HIS WIFE CICELY

From the portrait in the National Portrait Gallery, London

Sir Edwin's case[32] a most serious course over a considerable length of time. It is probable that they considered a limited residence and reading among the Benchers a necessary part of the education for life of country gentlemen who managed[33] their own estates, or for public service as Members of Parliament.[34] Beside George's entry of admission is no indication as to the occupancy of any quarters,[35] though he may have been in residence. Beyond the entry there are three other doubtful, but not improbable, indications of a legal education. One is his propensity to litigation.[36] Another, perhaps more probable, is the interest in law he displays in his published writings.[37] Most convincing is his employment in his last years as legal agent of the Virginia Colony and the colonial governor. From the very fact of his admission, at any rate, it seems most likely that he was in residence (or in lodgings near by) for a year or two and read law with more or less seriousness.

At the end of Elizabeth's reign the Inns of Court were gayer places than Oxford in which to pursue learning. Regulations against elaborate costumes and boisterous behaviour had repeatedly[38] to be enacted. There were even some luxuries. Food, even as early as Sir Thomas More's day,[39] had been much better in the Inns of Court than at

[32] See Sir Edwin's parliamentary and business career discussed in Chapter V below, and in Appendix E.

[33] The Public Record Office contains dozens of Chancery Proceedings entries in which these brothers and their estates were involved.

[34] And all were engaged in various commercial enterprises, such as the Virginia Company, in the administration of which knowledge of law was more than useful. Also the Law Courts were a step up the ladder to preferment at court (see, *e.g.*, C. T. Prouty, *George Gascoigne, Elizabethan Courtier Soldier and Poet* [New York, 1942], p. 22).

[35] Actually a goodly percentage of the "clerks" (or lowest rank among the Members) were unable to find rooms within the Temple during Elizabeth's reign (see J. Bruce Williamson, *History of the Temple*, pp. 244–5, 277). His several relatives still active at the Inn would have helped him to a chamber had he so desired.

[36] A most doubtful one normally, but Sandys' evident relish in dispute, as evidenced in his suing of his relatives and relations-in-law, of his neighbours in Virginia, and of two or three booksellers may be indicative. See below.

[37] See his discussion of the 'Laws of the Turks' in *A Relation of a Iourney . . .* (1615 ed.), pp. 62–3, and his allusions to the law in his commentaries on Ovid's *Metamorphoses* (Oxford, 1632 ed.), *passim*. Once at least in *A Relation* (p. 62) he alludes with bitterness to loopholes the law allows. His interest, of course, may be primarily antiquarian, or simply Renaissance omnivorous curiosity.

[38] See J. B. Williamson, pp. 206, 212–14, and Martin, *Minutes*, *passim*.

[39] Williamson, p. 118.

Oxford. George Sandys' later alleged habits of "wasteful spending," if he had them at all, are more likely to have been inspired here in London than in Oxford.

As for instruction, it was primarily oral and practical, for the great body[40] of legal literature was not yet in existence. From the earliest times the Law had been taught as a craft, the apprentice working with and learning from the master. In Elizabeth's day the younger gentlemen had to attend and in more advanced stages to argue in the moot courts in the Inns of Chancery,[41] and in and out of term to attend readings. All this was good discipline if it were taken seriously.

That George Sandys did not remain any great length of time, certainly nothing approaching the seven years necessary for a Call to the Bar or other qualification, would appear to be borne out by a study of the circumstances of another significant event in his life, his marriage. This seems to have taken place not long before or after his admission to membership in the Middle Temple.

It is curious that the existence of the determining factor in Sandys' life should have been up to the present time unknown to biographers,[42] for the principal clue has appeared many times in print in accounts of Archbishop Sandys. The good parent, anxious to secure the prosperity of his family, had made financial agreements of varying kinds. What he could bequeath himself had to come, of course, from his rents on church properties within his gift, but if he could join to them by marriage others adjacent, so much the better. In the case of his son George he took a long view and made a long bargain. Involved in the agreement are cross-currents of politics and religion.

In December 1584/85 one John Norton of Ripon made his will and died.[43] Son of the patriarch of the pro-Catholic rebellion of 1569–70,

40 Although such things as Dyer's *Reports* and Plowden's *Commentaries* had appeared from members of the Inns of Court and had gone through several editions before the end of the century (see J. B. Williamson, pp. 246–9).

41 See J. B. Williamson, pp. 184, 285. Certainly no member could have a chamber in the Inn unless within three years of admission he "do exercise moots and have been made an 'Inner-barrester.'" This implies, of course, tremendous preparatory work before that time.

42 See Appendix B (I) for a summary of earlier statements.

43 The will is dated 12 December 1584 (District Probate Registry, York). He died on 4 January 1584/85 (see P.R.O., Inquisitions Post Mortem, Court of Wards, Inquisitions, Vol. 21, no. 39, or another copy, with writ, c 142/208/236).

Richard Norton, he had been like his father [44] and brothers attainted, gaining his freedom[45] in 1572 only "on his composition." Norton had been twice married, and at the time of his death had one daughter twenty-one years of age, herself married, and a second four years of age. He was anxious especially to do all he could to make this second child secure, for she would grow up in a world in which her family were looked upon with suspicion as papists or at least would-be papists.[46]

Already two of Norton's most valuable properties in Ripon and Givendale[47] were held of Edwin Archbishop of York,[48] and by mutual consent or course of law his younger daughter Elizabeth became the prelate's ward. Though they might not inwardly agree in theology, churchman and country squire could agree to their mutual material advantage. Their respective wills, they decided, should so condition the disposal of certain property that the marriage of two of their children would be a matter of economic necessity. Norton's statement,[49] which came first, leaves his younger daughter little choice.

> Whereas by articles made and indented betwixt me, the said John Norton, of the one part and the most Reverend Father in God, Edwin, by permission and providence Lord Archbishop of York of the other part, a marriage is agreed by the Grace of God betwixt George Sandys, one of the younger sons of the said Lord Archbishop, and Elizabeth Norton, youngest daughter[50] of me

[44] Richard Norton (1488–1588). He died in exile.

[45] See W. A. Archbold, "Richard Norton," in *D.N.B.*

[46] Actually not at all unusual in Yorkshire, the great stronghold of recusant elements during most of Elizabeth's reign.

[47] Spelled variously Geendale, Gevendale, Givendale. His other properties were held of the Crown. See his will.

[48] Of his manor of Ripon.

[49] Abstract of "The Will of John Norton of Ripon in the County of York, Esquire" (District Probate Registry, York), 12 December 1584. Spelling, except proper names, has been modernized. This will was proved 10 June 1585 "by Margaret, the relict." Norton's son-in-law John Salmon [or Sawman] had entered a caveat against probate of the will on 10 January 1584/5 (see in the District Probate Registry, York, Exchequer Court of York, Craven Act Books, 1579–88). On 21 January a sequestration of his goods was granted and an "inventory of goods exhibited by William Norton of Ripon the younger, gent., Margaret his relict and Robert Freare." Evidently his lands were not affected.

[50] By his second wife, Margaret, daughter of Christopher Redshaw [or Readshaw], esq. of Owston. (See "Pedigree of Norton, Baron Grantley, of Grantley Park," in Joseph Foster, *Pedigrees of the County Families of Yorkshire* (London, 1874), I, "The West Riding," *n.p.* Elizabeth was baptized at Ripon on 30 October 1580 (see Ripon Cathedral Register examined by the present writer in June 1947).

the said John Norton, and meaning the said marriage shall take effect do in consideration thereof give to the said George and Elizabeth (if the marriage take effect) and to the heirs of their two bodies lawfully begotten, and for default of such issue to the said Elizabeth and her heirs, all my lands and tenements, hereditaments, rents, reversions and services in Givendale and Sawley in the County of York, and if the said marriage breakes in default or by reason of disliking of the said Elizabeth then I will this legacy to her for the said lands and tenements shall be void.

In consideration of the said marriage to be held and solemnized I give the said George and Elizabeth £1,000 and if the said marriage break or by default or disliking of the said Elizabeth then I give the said George £300.[51]

Within a year after Norton's will was probated, the Archbishop had filed with his friend Burghley, the Lord Treasurer, a list[52] of his leases to his sons. This included two[53] to his youngest, George, both in Yorkshire, one at Muncton and one in North Grange near Ripon. In another year, on 1 August 1587, Edwin Sandys made his own will. This document[54] gives the Archbishop's side of the contract.

. . . I do signify and declare that if it shall please God that Elizabeth Norton daughter of John Norton late of Rippon in the county of York, esquire deceased, and George Sandys my youngest son shall hereafter fortune to marry together, that then Thomas Spencer and Thomas Porter[55] shall assure all such messuages, lands and tenements as John Salmon and Anne his wife did hereafter assure and convey[56] unto the said George Sandys and Elizabeth Norton and heirs of their bodies lawfully begotten. I will that the said Elizabeth Norton be discharged of her wardship and value of her marriage which

[51] The will continues: "To John Salmon and Ann [Norton's daughter by his first marriage] his wife, all my lands in Thorpe in his occupation, and also 200 pounds. The rest of my goods I give unto Margaret, my wife, whom I make Executrix." His witness was Thomas Darbie.

[52] See Chapter I, note 24, above.

[53] Of the value of £20 and £50 annually.

[54] A copy is in the Diocesan Registry, York, signed by Edwin Sandys. What is here given is a rather full abstract. A briefer abstract is included in Pleasants, "Sandys of Furnace Fells," pp. 233–4. Spelling has been modernized except for proper names. The Torre MS., York Minster (abstract of Mr. Alexander McElwain) shows that in the will later a "Nest of Silver pinked [bowles?] double gilt wth a cover" and "a small square salt double gilt" were the father's only bequests of personal property to George. George did receive, with Henry and Thomas, a share in an annuity granted out of the manor of Ombersley. See Chapter VI, note 107, below.

[55] See note 69 and Appendix B (III) below.

[56] See note 49 above. Salmon, who had contested probate of the will, had evidently now agreed on certain things with the Archbishop.

belongs to me, and further I will that if said George Sandys and Elizabeth Norton do marry together then they shall have paid unto them £300. If said Elizabeth Norton refuse to marry George Sandys at the age of 15 years,[57] the said Elizabeth Norton shall pay to my executors for her wardship and marriage all the charges which I have been put to by reason of said Elizabeth in respect to her wardship. If George Sandys refuses to marry said Elizabeth before his age of 17 years then said Elizabeth shall have assured unto her all the messuages, lands, and tenements by said Thomas Spencer and Thomas Porter.

So were matters set when George Sandys entered Oxford in 1589. From the very terms of the will the marriage could not have taken place in the university years, but it may well have occurred, as mentioned above, just before or more probably a year or two after his admission to the Middle Temple. The exact date[58] has not been determined, but it must have been several years before George's twenty-first birthday.

The sole evidence of this fulfilment of the Archbishop's wishes lies in the legal records of the period, in the conveyances of leases and lands, in suits to recover jurisdiction over property, in a patent from the King. It is a story of disagreement between husband and wife, of strong family persuasion on each side, of mutual recrimination, and in the background the differences in religious sympathy and a hint of rebellion against a compulsory union. It is, of course, the tragic but not unusual result of childhood agreements of marriage made by well meaning parents.

The story must be pieced together. Evidently the marriage in fact was over by 1606, for about 1609 Elizabeth Sandys' relatives brought the whole matter to record by trying to "recover" her "rights" in alleged "joint" property, on the basis that the defendant deserted her three years before and had made no allowance for her maintenance.[59] The history of the marriage is reviewed, including quotation from and

[57] Coming of age, as far as marriage was concerned, seems to have been twelve for the female and fourteen for the male (see Chilton L. Powell, *English Domestic Relations, 1487–1653* [New York, 1917], p. 15).

[58] See Appendix B (II).

[59] This is a suit of about or before the year 1609 (for an approximate "countersuit" obviously of somewhat the same period is dated 3 November 1609), only one sheet of which (the Duplication) survives, in very bad condition, and curiously is included in much later Chancery Proceedings (P.R.O., Chancery Proceedings, C. 2/Charles I/G. 61/138). Sir William Gascoigne, William Norton, and William Calverley were the complainants. Of these certainly

reference to the Archbishop's and John Norton's wills. The Archbishop knew well, the plaintiffs stated, that the defendant "should have great advancement, as well in money, as in lands to the value of £3000 or more"[60] if the marriage took place. The plaintiffs also stated that the two parents had come to an agreement in November, 26 Elizabeth [1584?], that "the said Elizabeth should have a joint estate with the defendant in the same leases, & she to enjoy them in case of defendant's death."[61] The defendant, instead of making over the leases his father[62] granted him to his wife,[63] had assigned them to strangers, and when he reached the age of twenty-one entered "into a wasteful course of spending"[64] and very carelessly neglected his own estates. As the result, though Elizabeth behaved[65] "dutifully and respectfully [*sic*]" towards her husband, "discontent and dislike" grew between them. Though Elizabeth gave him no just cause, about three years[66] before this suit the defendant deserted his wife and went to live in southern England. Before and since that time he granted to Sir Myles Sandys his brother, at the latter's instigation, leases so that Elizabeth "should take no

Gascoigne and Norton were her "cousins german" as they claim in the document (see J. Foster, "Pedigree of Norton, Baron Grantley," *Pedigrees of the County Families of Yorkshire*, "West Riding," [London, 1874], I, *n.p.*). Calverley was probably the father of Walter Calverley, protagonist in the drama "A Yorkshire Tragedy" (see *D.N.B.*). The Calverleys had been lords of the manors of Calverley and Pudsey, Yorkshire, since the twelfth century. William Calverley was almost surely a Norton relative, for almost all the families in this part of the county were related.

60 This is the wording of the abstract, a slightly condensed and modernized version of the original which is, as noted above, in very poor condition. Many words and phrases are obliterated or missing.

61 Here lies, perhaps, the crux of the whole series of litigations. Evidently an agreement was reached and formulated a month before John Norton made his will. If it did include the stipulation of a "joint estate," which the wills of the two men may imply, George Sandys' subsequent course of action would appear to be in defiance of it.

62 For 21 years. This implies that Elizabeth's own property had been made over or "assigned" to her husband.

63 The charge reads that George did not make them over to her "within a year of his marriage nor at any time since."

64 The exact words of the original are used here, and in the two quotations immediately below.

65 "as complainants have heard" is inserted here.

66 The allusion may possibly be to the period of Sandys' travels, 1610–12. If so, the date of separation was as late as 1609 and the date of this litigation 1612. In general other circumstances would make 1609 as the date of this litigation the more probable one.

advantage" in case he died first. This same Sir Myles was the real cause[67] of the separation, the plaintiffs believed. They concluded by stating that George had made no yearly stipend for Elizabeth's support, nor had he, as he promised,[68] caused the lands to be reassured to Elizabeth and to him by the two[69] who had held them according to the Archbishop's will. The plaintiffs denied that Elizabeth had money independently.[70]

There are other documents[71] which add proof that they were married before 1602 and that many of the actions alleged in this Replication are true, but space prevents their consideration here. Soon after Elizabeth's relatives had sued her husband, he in turn entered complaint[72] against the same three gentlemen[73] for recovery of a title to a certain Yorkshire property, formerly John Norton's, which Sandys felt they had fraudulently secured from a previous owner. This document is interesting in that it seems to indicate that his wife's relatives were recovering her property for her by one means[74] or another, and in that it gives a glimpse of George's attitude toward what had happened in his marriage. All

[67] There is no clue to this allusion beyond the obvious one of family interference.

[68] In fact, they say he "utterly refuses" to cause the lands to be reassured.

[69] Thomas Porter and Thomas Spencer.

[70] Or that the lands "bought of Salmon [Elizabeth's brother-in-law] in Thorpe were bought as given in the answer." Since the answer has not survived with the Replication, the reference remains obscure.

[71] See Appendix B (III), for condensed abstracts of these documents.

[72] The date here appears on the document—3 November 1609 (P.R.O., Chancery Proceeding, c. 8/15/92). Here Sandys refers to himself as "George Sandys of Canterbury, gent." Evidently he had removed to the "south parts" and was living with his Wilford or Sandys relatives in Kent.

[73] Plus Cuthbert Pudsey, who was involved in the deal.

[74] In this case they had gone to a former owner's heir who had promised to confirm the property to George (he says) and persuaded her to confirm it to Elizabeth's relatives for her. The property was sold to William Norton, who gives "divers bonds" of £600 for "the only use of the complainant's wife." George acknowledges that the "Common Lawes of the Realm" will not recover it for him, but that "in all equity" the property belongs to him. (Years later [see "George Sandys *v.* William Stansby": the 1632 edition of Ovid's *Metamorphoses*, *The Library*, 5th series, III (December 1948), 197] he again enters on another matter a plea in equity, acknowledging that the common law will not help him.) In their answer, Gascoigne, Norton, Calverley, and Pudsey point out that they are within the law, and that at any rate George was given "valuable consideration" to give a deed of release to the property to this same group. They can see "no colourable reason" for his claim.

this surreptitious conveyance happened, Sandys states, when he had been in London on urgent business, "from whence he hasted back with as much expedition as he could."[75] Rather bitterly he states that this underhand procurement of title was done at the instigation of his own wife, "who out of the guilt of her misdemeanours & evil carriage of herself toward complainant, her husband, has plotted that course to gain the whole benefit thereof forever."

So the story goes. George Sandys' name appears only once more as a principal in these affairs, in 1613[76] when he and Sir Myles were given a "Pardon of Alienation" by King James confirming them in title to lands according to the indenture of 24 June 1605.[77] According to this Myles and George and George's heirs forever should enjoy the property "without impediment, molestation or vexation of us, our heirs or successors or any our Justices, escheators, sheriffs, bailiffs or ministers or those of our heirs or successors, by reason or pretext of the same alienation." This appears to have been George's last move in the dispute. Despite the King's patent, Elizabeth Sandys seems to have gained control[78] of the property and disposed of it to her own advantage. There is not one whisper in the later records of George Sandys' personal and public life to indicate that he was ever married; yet as late as 1662 the eighty-two year old Elizabeth Sandys was involved in chancery, now with the descendants of her relatives and partisans, regarding the income from this property.[79] Though she rather pathetically excused what amounts to extortion on the ground of dire necessity, this final case seems to tip the scales of the whole matter in favour of her husband. She appears as a grasping old woman, perhaps poor now, but if so one

75 Evidently expecting something of the kind? This may also raise the question as to whether Sandys did maintain residence in Yorkshire after *c.* 1606.

76 P.R.O., Patent Roll 11 James I, Pt 36, No. 77 (18 June).

77 See Appendix B (III) below. The "alienation" was the conveyance by Spencer and Porter to the two Sandyses, which was done, it is here stated, without the King's approval. He now approves it fully. The real reason for the document, however, would appear to be an attempt to strengthen George's claim to the property.

78 By the end of the seventeenth century, and probably at this period at its beginning, the courts would generally decree maintenance (in the form of property) in case of separation if the separation were the husband's fault (see W. S. Goldsworth, *A History of English Law* [12 vols., Boston, 1927], V, 312–13, VI, 646). Though proof that separation was Sandys' desertion of his wife is only by implication, the fact clearly existed and may have been grounds for restoring Elizabeth's property to her.

79 See Appendix B (IV) for a summary of the documents in the case.

who has run through considerable capital, and in her maturity has probably been more guilty of prodigal spending than her husband ever was in his youth.

The court records show more, however, than a marriage ending in separation. Where George was living at various times before he left England in 1610, and something of his character, are made evident. His official and actual residence through 1605 appears to have been Ripon[80] in Yorkshire, where he and Elizabeth lived surrounded by her relatives.[81] In other words, after his stay at the Middle Temple he lived the life of a country squire, though the wasteful spending[82] he is accused of doing after his twenty-first year may have taken place in London. Actually his extravagance may have been nothing more than expensive lodgings or a town house and several months in the city, which Elizabeth, country bred, did not enjoy. And the discontent which grew between them may have had other causes. One can never forget, for example, that the staunch Protestantism of the Sandys family in the reigns of Elizabeth and James is in sharp contrast to the definite Popish sympathies of the Nortons[83] and their kin. And the Archbishop had not endeared himself to local families by his leasing of church lands, or diverting those of recusants, to his family. Whether there is even a hint of accusation of marital unfaithfulness in George's reference to "the guilt of her

[80] In one 1605 document (P.R.O., Close Roll, 3 Jas. I, Pt. III, M 2d) he appears as "George Sandys of Ripon co. York esq.," though in the other of the same year he is referred to as "George Sandys of London, esq." The only conclusion is the obvious one that he, like other English gentlemen, spent part of the year in London and maintained an additional residence there. In the same two documents his brother Sir Myles is in one instance "of London" and in the other "of Claybury, co. Essex."

[81] Though it should be recalled that other Sandys brothers had estates in Yorkshire. None of them, of course, gave Yorkshire as an official residence during his mature years.

[82] All due allowance must be made, of course, for legal name-calling here and when George speaks of Elizabeth.

[83] The Nortons had intermarried with Gascoignes, Stapletons, and Mallorys (see J. Foster, "Pedigree of Norton, Baron Grantley," I, *n.p.*), all of whom appear in the Sandys' chancery suits. These strong groups in the sixteenth century had, with other Yorkshiremen, given various indications of Romish sympathy (see above). One John Norton was executed in 1600 for harbouring the priest Thomas Palaser (see *Sacra Ritum Congregatio Sectio Historica Westmonasterien. Beatificationis seu Declarationis Martyrii Venerabilium Servorum Dei Thomae Palaser, Sac. Saec., Jonnis Norton, Laici, Jonnis Talbot Laici in Odium Fidei, Uti Fertur, Dunelmi in Anglia, Die 9 Aug. 1600 Interfectorum* [Br. Mus. No. 20010. i. 8]).

[Elizabeth's] misdemeanours & evil carriage of herself" toward her husband, it is difficult to say.

That she used some powers of persuasion to get various deeds into her hands from one Francis Tunstall is evident in the complaint of William Tunstall.[84] Yet one may be doing Elizabeth's moral character a grave injustice to summarize by saying that from the evidence she appears to have been in the 1600–18 period no better than she ought to have been. Even that she was more than normally litigious in a litigious age also cannot be stated with certainty. The final impression is the most definitely unpleasant—of the old woman who has outlived her generation (her grandfather Richard lived to be a hundred) and squandered considerable property, taking unfair advantage of the grandson of her relative.[85] But even then she may have been merely a woman who had been hardly dealt with in what was still a man's world.

At any rate, by November 1609 the persons and the rolling pasture lands of Yorkshire had ceased to be a part of George Sandys' life, for one then finds him referring to himself as a "gentleman of Canterbury."[86] Thus early he was identified with the county of Kent in which he was to die. Hereafter Kent, Oxfordshire, and London would be his English residences.[87]

[84] See Appendix B (IV), below. William Tunstall brought her into court in 1662. Francis was his grandfather, who had "befriended" her in 1618 and earlier.

[85] Or "connection" (see *Visitation of Yorkshire* [Harleian Society, 1881], p. 328).

[86] P.R.O., Chancery Proceedings, c. 8/15/92, 3 November 1609. He probably was living with his Wilford or Sandys relatives. His uncle Sir Thomas Wilford of Hedding in Kent had died *c.* 1604, but the latter's son Sir Thomas had married Elizabeth, daughter of George Sandys' brother Sir Edwin. Sir Edwin himself was established near by in Kent. It is probably worth noticing here that a George Sandys had been, in 1595, granted for life the keeping of the Blockhouse at Gravesend with a fee of £26 a year and five acres of land (see *Calendar State Papers, Domestic, 1595–1597*, p. 149 and P.R.O., S.P. 12/Eliz 255/No. 34). This sinecure, easily handled by a deputy, could have been granted to the son of Archbishop Sandys through the influence of his uncle Sir Thomas Wilford, at that time lieutenant of Kent. Sir Thomas also superintended the admiralty works in Dover Harbour, and in 1593 was governor of Camber Castle (see A. F. Pollard, "Sir Thomas Wilford," in *D.N.B.*). The grant is signed by Lord Admiral Howard. George probably spent much time, too, at his mother's residence of Woodham Ferrers, Essex, "Edwin's Hall," where Cecily Sandys lived until her death on 5 February 1610/11. See E. S. Sandys, *The Family of Sandys*, I, 180–1.

[87] That his connection with Ripon and Yorkshire was definitely severed is

The effects of this marriage, however, once its existence is realized, are evident all through George Sandys' life. The desire to escape from the property litigation, as well as from the memories of the marriage, was probably an impelling motive in his travels beginning early in 1610, and in his later personal part in American colonization. The marriage, never dissolved, and an estranged wife who outlived him many years, explain at once his living with his nieces in the country, his solitary lodgings in London, and his manner of life in Virginia. And it may well indicate why there is no love poetry[88] in his extant published writings.

In 1610 Sandys was thirty-two, restless and eager to escape for a time from his surroundings. He had shown himself a persistent disputant in litigation, a characteristic which was to develop as he grew older. Whether he had shown poetic or scholarly ability by then is more difficult to decide. Almost half the years of his life were gone. Along with his marriage, the material wealth his father had so carefully planned had for the most part been swept away. Always hereafter he would look at life in sober disillusionment. Yet, true son of the Renaissance that he was, with his cynicism he combined an immense curiosity to see the world, a willingness to aid his country to an empire, and romantic love of the past in architecture and in literature.

evidenced in the reference to him in the 1617 Tunstall-Mallory indenture (P.R.O., Close Roll, 4 April, 15 Jas. I, c. 54/2325), in which he is "George Sandys, late of Ripon, co. York, Esq."

[88] If one excepts his sensuous *Paraphrase upon the Song of Solomon* (1641) and "A Dream," which is apparently his (see below, Chapter VIII, and Richard B. Davis, "George Sandys and Two 'Uncollected' Poems," *Huntington Library Quarterly*, XII [November 1948], 105–11).

III

CONSTANTINOPLE AND CAIRO

AT THE beginning of May 1610, Sandys began his travels by crossing the Channel to France. A desire to escape the litigious consequences of his wrecked marriage was certainly not the only motive impelling him to the journey. By this day such a tour as he planned was a well-established English tradition. It was thus that the talented young gentleman rounded out his education and prepared himself for a life of public service. In his own family his brother Edwin had already preceded him on the Continent and had written his observations[1] on certain conditions in the countries of Western Europe he had visited. Both journey and account had been in the orthodox travel tradition. George would follow his brother's example, though his quite different interests and itinerary resulted in a very different sort of record.

Although he was older than the average gentleman making an educational tour, the pattern[2] of his travels is fairly typical. He kept a journal,[3] he lived with ambassadors and consuls at various places, he

[1] *Europæ Speculum* [or *A Relation of the State of Religion . . . in the Western partes of the world,* the original title] had first been published without Edwin's consent in 1605 in London (it was written in 1599).

[2] The English traveller, like his Continental contemporary, followed the procedure of a definite system. From Wynkin de Worde's time to Sandys' a whole literature had developed, not only of travel, but of advice to travellers (see Russell H. Barker, "George Sandy's [*sic*] *Relation,*" *Transactions of the Wisconsin Academy of Sciences, Art and Letters,* XXX [1937], 253–73, and Clare Howard, *English Travellers in the Renaissance* [London, 1914], pp. 20–49). Hieronymus Turlerus' *De Peregratione* (Argentorati, 1574), translated into English as *The Traveiler of Jerome Turler,* was frankly a manual for the traveller, and others followed it rapidly. The development of the individual (*i.e.,* virtù) and his increase in usefulness to the state are two of the principal reasons for travel. For a bibliography of the books of advice to travellers see Clare Howard, pp. 205–9.

[3] Cf. Fynes Moryson, *An Itinerary . . .* (orig. ed. 1617, 4 vols., Glasgow, 1907), III, 373–4: "Let [the traveller] . . . write these notes each day, at morne and at even in his Inne, within writing Tables carried about him, and after at leasure into a paper booke, that many yeers after he may looke over them at his pleasure." Moryson's series of 'Precepts for Travellers' is most illuminating concerning the Elizabethan traveller generally.

observed the strength and weakness of men and nations. He gathered curios in Egypt, and perhaps many books in Italy. When he returned home, he composed from his notes a coherent narrative,[4] embellishing his account with classical quotations and the records of other travellers from Herodotus to his own contemporaries.

And since the embellishments are often indistinguishable from personal observation and action, his actual journey and his literary method in producing a book of travels cannot be considered separately. Many of his sources can be pointed out. Though in his composition he undoubtedly kept his reading public in mind, the multiplicity of classical allusion[5] woven into the text and the very selection of subject matter are strong evidences of his personal tastes, for his method differs considerably from that of earlier English travellers.[6] That his book went through nine editions within little more than a half century would indicate that what he produced was as appealing to the reading public as it was interesting to him.

In the Dedication of the work, to Prince Charles, Sandys shows clearly that he was fully conscious of the tradition of public service in which he travelled. All due allowance must be made, of course, for the conventions of the noble patron and the travel book generally. Even then, there can be no doubt of the author's sincerity. The reader of Sandys' book should follow the Dedication closely, for here the author states point by point his aims[7] in writing and in making the journey.

> SIR,
>
> The Eminence of the degree wherein God and Nature haue placed you, doth allure the eyes; and the hopefullnesse of your Vertues, win the loue of all men. For Vertue being in a priuate person an exemplary ornament; aduanceth it selfe in a Prince to a publike blessing. And as the Sunne to the world, so bringeth it both light and life to a kingdome: a light of direction, by glorious

[4] *A Relation of a Iourney begun An: Dom: 1610. Fovre Bookes Containing a description of the Turkish Empire, of Ægypt, of the Holy Land, of the Remote parts of Italy, and Ilands adioyning*, LONDON, Printed for W: Barrett. 1615.

[5] See Chapter IV, below.

[6] Compare his immediate predecessors, Fynes Moryson (who travelled before Sandys but did not publish until 1617), Thomas Coryat (1611), William Biddulph (1609), John Cartwright (1611), Sir Anthony Shirley (1601 and 1613), Henry Timberlake (1603). Only the first of these, Moryson (*An Itinerary*) combines effectively travel, formal geography, and history as Sandys does. In other things such as style and narrative method, however, he differs considerably from Sandys. For some further summary of Sandys' method, see Chapter IV below.

[7] One should also observe in reading the book how much Sandys goes beyond these avowed aims.

example; and a life of ioy, through a gracious gouernment. From the iust and serious consideration whereof, there springeth in minds not brutish, a thankfull correspondence of affection and duty; still pressing to expresse themselves in indeuours of service. Which also hath caused me, (most noble Prince) not furnished of better meanes, to offer in humble zeale to your princely view these my doubled trauels; once with some toyle and danger performed, and now recorded with sincerity and diligence. The parts I speake of are the most renowned countries and kingdomes: once the seats of most glorious and triumphant Empires; the theaters of valour and heroicall actions; the soiles enriched with all earthly felicities; the places where Nature hath produced her wonderfull works; where Arts and Sciences haue been invented, and perfited; where wisedome, vertue, policie, and ciuility haue bene planted, haue flourished: and lastly where God himselfe did place his owne Commonwealth, gaue lawes and oracles, inspired his Prophets, sent Angels to converse with men, aboue all, where the Sonne of God descended to become man; where he honoured the earth with his beautiful steps, wrought the worke of our redemption, triumphed ouer death, and ascended into glory. Which countries once so glorious, and famous for their happy estate, are now through vice and ingratitude, become the most deplored spectacles of extreme miserie. . . . Those rich lands at this present remaine waste and ouergrowne with bushes, receptacles of wild beasts, of theeues and murderers; large territories dispeopled, or thinly inhabited; goodly cities made desolate; sumptuous buildings become ruines; glorious temples either subuerted, or prostituted to impietie; true religion discountenanced and oppressed; all Nobility extinguished; no light of learning permitted, nor Vertue cherished: violence and rapine insulting ouer all, and leauing no security saue to an abiect mind, and vnlookt on pouerty, Which calamities of theirs so great and deserued, are to the rest of the world as threatening instructions. For assistance wherein, I haue not onely related what I saw of their present condition; but so far as conueniency might permit, presented a briefe view of the former estates, and first antiquities of those people and countries: thence to draw a right image of the frailty of man, and mutability of what so euer is worldly; and assurance that as there is nothing vnchangeable saving God, so nothing stable but his grace and protection. Accept great Prince these weake endeuours of a strong desire: which shall be alwaies deuoted to your Highnesse all acceptable service; and euer reioyce in your prosperity and happinesse.

Thus his note is serious,[8] and so it remains throughout the work. The purpose of his writing is both practical and pious. The present states of these once mighty nations stand as "threatening instructions." Yet one feels that the poet and philosopher in Sandys is more interested in his

[8] This, of course, is the conventional note for the traveller. He must not admit his pleasure in the journey for its own sake.

second kindred point, "to draw a right image of the frailty of man and mutability of what so euer is worldly."

The journey began with a graphic illustration of the frailty of man, for Sandys reached Paris at the time[9] of the assassination of Henry IV. Here he observes characteristically that the obscure varlet who murdered the king shows "that there is none so contemptible, that contemneth his owne life, but is maister of another mans." The soldiers drawn secretly into the city, the general unrest, and the threat to "those of the Religion" made it an exciting time. The significance of this event in changing the history of Europe he did not of course realize.

The remainder of France and upper Italy, already so familiar to his fellow-countrymen,[10] Sandys ignores. At Venice he began his account and his sea journey, probably after a several weeks' stay. Regarding the city he says nothing, yet he came there at the interesting period of Sir Henry Wotton's first embassage. The republic, at odds with the Pope, was the one famous place in Northern Italy in which King James maintained a representative, for religious, political, and commercial reasons. Here Wotton carried on [11] an active campaign to convert the ruling class to Protestantism. Here liberals such as Fra Paoli Sarpi, who had probably translated Sir Edwin Sandys' *Europæ Speculum* into Italian, lived, and wrote. And here young Englishmen about the Ambassador studied languages, gathered Latin and Italian books, and admired the physical beauties of a sophisticate culture.

Though Sandys does not say so, it is probable that for several weeks he was one of the group of eager young minds in the coterie of the busy diplomat.[12] Certainly Wotton kept open house[13] for English visitors,

[9] 14 May 1610.

[10] "daily surveyed and exactly related" (*Relation*, p. 1), he says. Other travellers, since 1600 alone, who had described French and/or Italian travels, include Sir Robert Dallington, *A View of Fraunce* (London, 1604); ——, *A Survey of the great Dukes State in Tuscany*, in 1596 (London, 1604); Lord Herbert of Cherbury, *Of Travellers: From Paris* (London, 1608); Thomas Coryate's *Crudities* (London, 1611). For a convenient list of others see E. G. Cox, *A Reference Guide to the Literature of Travel* (2 vols., Seattle, 1935–8), I, 95–7.

[11] See Logan Pearsall Smith, *The Life and Letters of Sir Henry Wotton* (2 vols., Oxford, 1907), I, 64–100, and also Horatio Brown, ed., *Calendar of State Papers, Venetian, 1610–1613*, (London, 1905), *passim*.

[12] He does mention later the ambassador in Constantinople and the consuls with whom he resided in other cities, but since he deliberately begins his story with the embarkation from Venice, he may easily have omitted what to the modern reader would prove a most interesting association.

[13] Logan P. Smith, I, 60. Wotton entertained, for example, Tom Coryat,

and probably presented a man of Sandys' family connections to the Doge himself. Wotton and Sandys had many things in common, including an admiration for Elizabeth of Bohemia and a genuine personal affection for Prince Charles.[14]

Egypt and the Holy Land appear to have been Sandys' original goals, and for centuries Venice had been the port of embarkation for the Near East. Earlier there had sailed annually a pilgrim ship[15] to Palestine, but before this period it had ceased operating. Sandys embarked on an English merchant ship, the *Little Defence* of London, on 20 August. Sailing nine hundred miles along the east coast of the Adriatic, called at the time the Gulf of Venice, he was interested in the history and present industries of Dalmatia and various islands passed. The ship actually touched at only one spot in this considerable distance, but Sandys, in the tradition of the guidebook, pointed out anything of possible interest to his reader whether he had seen it or not. On 2 September the ship entered the harbour of Zacynthus (or Zant), and fired her guns in salute as she passed the castle guarding the entrance. In what becomes an habitual fashion, Sandys summarizes the history of the place and then goes ashore. His pattern of exposition and description here he is to follow later in visiting more important places. The three religions of the inhabitants, the government by Venice, a local wedding and its peculiar customs, the murder of an English sailor who seeks to evade the duty on a little bag of currants, the inscription on the supposed tomb of Cicero, are topics discussed with a good deal of human interest but little humour, and interspersed with appropriate Latin-English poetical quotations, classical and otherwise, the English of which is his own translation. Sandys' marginal note quite frankly admits that Zuallardo's "Itin. *1*. I"[16] was the source for his account of the Cicero tomb, but if he had other literary sources he does not mention them. Here and frequently elsewhere he creates a fine flavour of an

who made an enthusiastic acknowledgement in his *Crudities* (original ed. 1611; the edition used here was printed [2 vols.] in Glasgow, 1905, I, 332). Wotton lived in the Canareggio district, near the present railway station.

14 See Richard B. Davis, "Two New Manuscript Items for a George Sandys Bibliography," *Papers of the Bibliographical Society of America*, XXXVII (3rd quarter 1943), 215–22, and Logan P. Smith, *op. cit.* II, 293–5.

15 Fynes Moryson, *An Itinerary* . . . (4 vols., Glasgow, 1907), I, 447.

16 Giovanni Zuallardo's *Il Devotissimo Viaggio di Gerusalemme* . . . [original edition 1586] appeared in many editions in the later sixteenth century, for example, in 1587 and 1595. For Sandys' later use of this book, see below Chapter IV.

admixture of local gossip and personal observation, though in other passages, usually of historical summary, the flavour is not so pleasantly fresh.

After twelve days, on 14 September, he embarked on another English ship, the *Great Exchange*, "bound for Chios, and then for Tripolis." Fair winds brought them quickly down the coast of the Peloponessus, passing by the Strophades, where he tells the story of the harpies, quoting partly from Vergil. And regarding them he makes the kind of allegorical comment he was to develop later[17] in his Ovid, when he asks, "And what are these Harpyes, but flatterers, delators, and the inexpleably couetous? who abuse, deuoure, and pollute the fame of miserable Princes, blinded in their understandings."[18]

The ship thrust between Capes Malio and Cerigo, sailed by the island of Cytherea, and then into the Aegean. Here Sandys pauses to tell the story of Aegeus, Theseus, the Minotaur, and the ship with black sails. Passing by Delos he again indulges his fondness for classic myth, discusses the oracles and quotes Plutarch on their cessation. In three days from the time of embarkation, a very fast passage, they arrived at the island of Chios.[19] Here he was entertained in the city of Sio by a friendly English consul. This land had but recently, in 1566, fallen to the Turk. In Chios Sandys first met the Mediterranean Greeks, who, indifferent to form of government or master, were usually looked upon somewhat contemptuously[20] by the western European. Sandys shows his interest in folk custom in describing them:

> . . . The inhabitants for the most part are *Turkes* and *Grecians*; those living in command, and loosely: the other husbanding the earth, and exceeding them infinitely in number. They are in a maner releast of their thraldome, in that vnsensible of it: well meriting the name of Merry *Greeks*, when their leisure will tollerate. Never Sunday or holyday passes over without some publike meeting or other: where intermixed with women, they dance out the day, and with full crowned cups enlengthen their iollitie . . . The streets do almost all the night long partake of their musicke. And whereas those of *Zant* do go armed into the field to bring home their vintage; these bring home with songs and reioycings. . . . The women celebrated of old for their beauties, yet carry

[17] In the 1632 edition, of which about half the pages are taken up with such commentaries on Ovid's myths.

[18] *A Relation*, p. 9.

[19] Or Sio.

[20] See Samuel C. Chew, *The Crescent and the Rose* (New York, 1937), pp. 61–3, 133–5.

the same: I will not say undeseruedly. They have their heads trickt with tassels and flowers. The bodies of their gownes exceed not their arme-pits: from whence the skirts flow loosely, fringed below; the upper shorter than the neather; of damasks or stuffes less costly, according to their condition.[21]

At near by Smyrna[22] the traveller was saddened by contemplating the city's former glories now defiled by her Mahometan master. The principal commodity of this port, "cotton wool," he describes, marvelling that so much of it can be compressed into small spaces. Then he is ready for a third ship and a new stage of his journey.

The desire now laid hold of him, Sandys says, to see the city of Constantinople.[23] Taking with him as interpreter a Greek who spoke a little broken English, he engaged passage on the bark *Armado* of Simo, a little island near Rhodes. The "Patron," or Captain, and the crew were Greek, and the little ship laden with sponges. It was to be rough travelling.

The *Armado* sailed on 20 September,[24] putting in the first night at Mitylen, or Lesbos, where Sandys comments on the products of the island, quoting and then translating Horace[25]

Here underneath some shadie vine
Full cups of hurtlesse Lesbian wine
Will we quaffe freely. . . .

The following day the winds were contrary, and the open seas too rough for this small vessel "no bigger, and in proportion to a Graves-end tilt-boate."[26] Yet rowing under the shelter of the land, the crew made some headway. For three days they were thus weatherbound, moving only a little way each night to a different harbour so as not to be surprised by brigands or pirates. On the fourth day they proceeded on the voyage, arriving that night at Tenedos,

21 *A Relation*, p. 14.

22 It is not entirely clear whether Sandys actually visited Smyrna. He may be reporting merely from oral or printed sources, and the cotton from observation at Chios. Cotton was one of the principal commodities shipped to England from this region. See *Calendar of State Papers, Venetian, 1607–1610, 1610–1613, passim.*

23 Since he had to wait fifteen days anyway for his ship to sail, he thought he might get another ship later still and spend his time profitably by visiting Constantinople.

24 The text gives November (p. 15), but later returns to September reckoning.

25 Sandys gives *1. 1*, Ode 17 [correct, ll. 21, 22].

26 *A Relation*, p. 17.

In sight of Troy, an Ile of wealth and fame,
Whilest Priam in his princely state abode,
Now but a bay, and an unsecure rode[27]

The next day, after some hours' further sailing, the ship approached a famous spot. The traveller persuaded two or three of the crew to go ashore with him, "desirous to see those celebrated fields where once stood Ilium the glory of Asia, which hath affoorded [sic] to the rarest wits so plentifull an argument."[28] Here he made his first archaeological explorations, though he dared not stray far from the shore. He gazed at the site of Troy on the plain beyond the promontory on which he stood. Into the account of what he saw Sandys brought memories of the Rape of Helena, of Achilles and Ajax and all the glorious host, and he presented in his own couplets translations from Homer, Ovid, J. C. Scaliger, and Alciatus.[29] Quite rightly he disagreed with the Frenchman Belon's[30] location of the Homeric Troy. The ruins of the later city are not, he observed, exactly as they were a century earlier in Belon's time, for they "are lessened daily by the Turkes, who carried the pillers and stones into Constantinople to adorne the buildings of the Great Bassa."[31]

Soon the little vessel sailed past Lemnos, and in a short time entered the Hellespont. As he passed Sestos and Abydos, Sandys dragged forth the ghosts of Hero and Leander, but described the fortifications and mountains along the shore as he saw them. At "Callipoli," or Gallipoli, he went ashore to visit the "Franke consul," an Augustinian friar, in hope of some refreshment after his weary voyage. Not finding the official at home, he was forced to return aboard ship, as the inhospitable Turks

[27] Sandys' translation of "Vergil's *Aeneid, 1. 2*" [he says], *A Relation*, p. 19. It occurs, Book II, ll. 21–3.

[28] *A Relation*, p. 19.

[29] Professor Warner G. Rice, in "English Travelers in Greece and the Levant" (*University of Michigan Essays and Studies in English and Comparative Literature*, X, 1933, pp. 226–33), is probably correct in pointing out that Sandys' literary association of poets and myth with classical places was not made as he visited, but when he had returned home and was writing his account surrounded by his library. It is by no means proved, however, that the travel notes did not actually contain references made from memory—or from books he carried—to classic literature. Coryat (see S. C. Chew, *The Crescent and the Rose*, p. 60 n.) carried volumes of Belon and Gillius with him. Sandys may well have had an anthology of the poets such as *Corpus Omnium Veterum Poetarum* (see Chapter IV, note 67 below).

[30] For Sandys' use of Belon and of sources generally, see text and notes below and Appendix C.

[31] *A Relation*, p. 22.

had no inns. On the way back he was derided and scoffed at by the common people. His introduction to the main territories of the Mahometan empire was thus none too pleasant.

On 27 September the ship entered the Propontick Sea, anchoring that night on the south side of the island of Marmora. While most of the crew washed sponges, Sandys and his interpreter scrambled up a steep slope just ashore and made their way to the town to purchase food. In the evening they returned to find most of the crew dead drunk, the Patron lying wet, writhing, and speechless on a rock. A comedy of errors, though a dangerous one, ensued. A blind man, then on the way to the Patriarch to complain because his wife would not lie with him, laid about him vigorously with a stave. The Patron, finally aroused by the clamour, seized a scimitar and likewise swung wildly to the four winds. His crew all leapt into the sea. He pursued the Greek interpreter as far as a steep cliff side, and then turned on Sandys, who was armed only with stones. Fortunately for the traveller the drunken sea captain stumbled on the way, fell, and lay in a stupor for two hours. Alarmed at the situation, Sandys resolved to return to the town, but the recovering Patron, being informed of the way he had used his paying guest, kissed the traveller and promised good behaviour.

The next day the ship came to anchor just below the customs house for Constantinople. The sea-weary wanderer crossed the harbour of Galata, "ascended the vines of Pera,"[32] and soon reached the house of the English ambassador. Here he rested his fatigued body, and for four months observed first hand the customs of the Turks.

Sir Thomas Glover, the plenipotentiary in whose hospitable residence Sandys found himself, was one of England's early and able career diplomats. "A man full of spirit, able both to defend and offend, if our neighbours should go about in any way to wrong us,"[33] as an East

32 The location of the residence of the English ambassador at least since Edward Barton's time (see Sir Richard C. Temple ed., *The Travels of Peter Mundy* [Cambridge, 1907], p. 47 n. 3). William Lithgow (*The Totall Discourse of the Rare Adventures and Painefull Peregrinations* . . . [original ed. 1614, 1632, Glasgow, 1907], p. 125) says "Perah [or Galata] . . . is the place at which the Christian ships touch, and where the Ambassadours of Christendome lie." He says the Roman Emperor's, the French, the English, the Venetian, and the Holland ambassadors live there, and that with the last he has often conversed. Sandys (*A Relation*, p. 36) states, however, that the German Emperor's ambassador was the one foreign diplomat allowed to live within Constantinople proper.

33 Ralph Preston to the E. I. Co., 1 January 1614, *Letters Received by the East India Company from Its Servants in the East* (introduction by Sir William Foster,

India company resident official characterized him. Glover was in 1610 in his last year as ambassador. Born of a Polonian[34] mother and English father, he lived much of his boyhood in Constantinople and spoke the Slavonian tongue perfectly. He spent his later youth in England, but returned to Constantinople about 1592 as secretary to Ambassador Edward Barton and continued in the same capacity under Henry Lello.[35] In 1606 he was knighted by King James and appointed Lord Ambassador[36] in succession to Lello. Though in 1611 he was recalled to England under something of a cloud, he eloquently defended[37] and cleared himself before the Privy Council, and was later frequently consulted as an expert on Turkish affairs. He was a versatile man. As an English archer in a great tradition Sandys saw him shoot Turkish arrows through thick steel targets in a remarkable display of strength and skill.[38] As purchasing agent for English noblemen collecting Greek "antiques" he personally and by means of agents examined statuary and "monuments" through much of the Levant. And as representative of his king and the merchant company, he was a stout champion of English interests. Sandys' comment on him might have been made by any traveller who had enjoyed his flowing hospitality:

> . . . And to give [him] . . . no more than his due, for this place none can be more sufficient; expert in their language, and by a long experience in their nature and practices; being moreouer of such a spirit, as not to be danted. And surely his chiefest fault hath been his misfortune; in the too violent, chargeable, and successlesse solliciting of the restitution of the Prince of Moldauia,[39] (whom adversity hath rather made crafty then honest:) whose

Vol. II [London, 1897], p. 261). For further evidence of Glover's aggressive action on behalf of his countrymen and the consequent respect in which he was held by the Turk, see William Lithgow, *The Totall Discourse . . .*, pp. 60–1.

34 See Lithgow, *The Totall Discourse*, pp. 126–7.

35 See Sir William Foster, ed., *The Travels of John Sanderson in the Levant . . .* (London, 1931), pp. 11, 162 n. 188, 219.

36 Under the new and extended charter of "The Governor and Company of Merchants of England Trading in Levant Seas," in 1607. See *The Travels of Peter Mundy . . . 1608–1667*, I, 171.

37 See *Calendar of State Papers, Venetian, 1610–1613*, p. 494 (Item 767).

38 *A Relation*, p. 64.

39 Stefano Janiculo, who termed himself Prince of Moldavia (or Bugdania, as it was sometimes called), had appeared in England in Queen Elizabeth's time to solicit aid in recovering his principality from the Turk. He returned to the Levant in 1601 and stayed at the English Embassy. After capture by and escape from the Turks and various adventures in other countries, he was in 1608 again in Constantinople. Glover sponsored him "with more zeal than discretion,"

house doth harbour both him and his dependents: being open also to all our Nation: a sanctuary for poore Christian slaves that secretly fly hither, whom he causeth to be conveyed unto their countries, and redeemeth not a few with his mony.[40]

Glover's was evidently an interesting household. The Prince's entourage, Christian refugees of all kinds, travellers to and from the Near and Far East, all mingled here. Crop-eared William Lithgow, the Scottish wanderer who published his observations[41] a few months before Sandys, was probably the latter's fellow guest. Curious persons and happenings connected with the household Sandys sometimes mentions casually as he describes the city, its people, or its history.

Though he had admitted that going to Constantinople at all was not a part of his original plan, Sandys actually spent more time there than in any other one place. His living quarters must have been comfortable and the city fascinating. Here was the seat of the greatest of contemporary empires. Although in power, some observers felt, it had passed its zenith, its government, its military organization, and the history of its rise would interest the English reader as much as its physical environment, for the western European still lived under the shadow of a potential Mahometan invasion. And in the city itself the most obvious of "threatening instructions" and symbols of the mutability of worldly glory existed in the physical remains of the once mighty Roman Empire of the East.

almost all contemporaries observe. In 1612 the "Prince," despairing of realizing his claims, turned Turk, and Glover never recovered more than half the enormous sums he had invested in Janiculo's future (see Foster, ed. *Travels of John Sanderson*, pp. xxxv–xxxvii, 269 n.). Though Sandys in 1615, when his book was published, probably knew that Janiculo had gone over to the Turk, he comments only as the 1610 observer, who saw the Ambassador eaten out of house and home by Janiculo's retinue.

40 *A Relation*, p. 85. Compare also William Lithgow, who was in Constantinople in 1610–11 (*Totall Discourse*, pp. 126–7). Lithgow's *A Delectable and True Discourse* (London) had appeared as early as 1614.

41 In 1614. See note 40 above. Lithgow's observations superficially parallel Sandys' quite closely. Similar or the same places, the history of the city, the customs of the Turks, the Mahometan religions, etc., are described, but in less detail and with no attempt at realization of their significance. Lithgow (*Totall Discourse*, p. 125) states that he spent twelve weeks of 1610–11 in the Ambassador's house. Since Sandys did not depart until late in January 1610–11, they almost surely met there. Fynes Moryson (*An Itinerary* . . . [4 vols., original ed. 1617, Glasgow, 1907], II, 90–102, 161) gives an outline guide-book description of Constantinople after his visit in 1597, but makes almost no observations on history and customs.

Sandys begins his account in the guide-book tradition by summarizing the history of the city. As usual, he uses ancient authors, contemporary commentators on ancient authors, and contemporary observers as his sources.[42] When he turns from books to what he saw, the narrative comes alive. In his description of the Mosque of Sancta Sophia, for example, he gives details of structure and decoration, and incidentally shows aesthetic appreciation, superior to anything in the work of other contemporary [43] English travellers.

> . . . A long labour it were to describe it exactly: and having done, my eyes that have seene it, would but condemne my defective relation. The principall part thereof riseth in an ouall: surrounded with pillars, admirable for their proportion, matter, and workmanship. . . . The roofe compact, and adorned with *Mosaike* painting: an antique kind of worke, composed of little square pieces of marble; gilded and coloured according to the place that they assume in the figure or ground: which set together, as if imbossed, present an inexpressable statelinesse, and are of marvellous durance: numbered by Pancirollus[44] amongst things that are lost: but divers in *Italy* at this day excell in that kind: yet make the particles of clay, gilt, and coloured before they be neiled by the fire. The rest of the Church, though of another proportion, doth ioyne to this with a certaine harmonie. . . .[45]

He goes on, sometimes relying on Antonius Menavimus,[46] but scornfully denying the veracity or accuracy of Belon's exaggerated account[47]

[42] Sandys usually mentions his source, if at all, only by the surname of the author. On this passage, for example, he acknowledges use of "Zosimus" (. . . *Comitis et Exadvocati Fisci Historiae* . . . [Basileæ, 1576?], probably pp. 32 and 238, for *A Relation*, p. 29); "St. Augustine's *De Civitate Dei*" in the edition of "Ludovicus Vives" (one Latin selection at least was as early as 1522; there was an English edition of Vives' version in 1610, *St. Augustine, of the Citie of God*, which Sandys may have used for his source, *A Relation*, p. 29, *St. Augustine*, p. 4); "Pausanias" (. . . *hoc est* . . . *Descriptio*, 1613, p. 41 for Sandys' *Relation*, p. 29). Location of work and page have been made, of course, by the present writer.

[43] Cf. the accounts of Fynes Moryson, *An Itinerary*, II, 94. Peter Mundy used Sandys' description as his source, or quoted directly (see *Travels*, pp. 30, 192–8.

[44] *Rerum Memorabilium Jam Olim Deperditarum* (Ambergae, 1599, also 1607, 1612). The exact reference has not been located in the editions examined.

[45] *A Relation*, p. 31.

[46] His *Trattato di Costumi et Vita de Turchi* . . . (Florence, 1548, and later editions) does not appear to have been published in a Latin version, though Sandys here uses the Latin form of his name (which may be after all only a convention).

[47] For Pierre Belon, on Bellonius, see Appendix C below. Sandys gives book and chapter of Belon's *Observations*.

of the number of the church's doors. Next he describes the "Proud Pallace of the Tyrant" and the Seraglio,[48] then the tombs of the Sultans. At every turn in the crooked streets he remembers the ancient Romans who lived here and built some of these edifices. At one open space surrounded by buildings, "like that of Smithfield,"[49] he recalls the horse-races in the Hippodrome, on this very spot where the Turks now play every Friday a game called *Giocho di Canni*, "which is no other then Prison bace vpon horsebacke." The Christians enjoy seeing the Turks make terrible and fatal falls in this sport, he soberly informs the reader. Then he gives the Latin and Greek inscriptions[50] on the obelisk and column[51] which stand in this place, and mourns that the remains of Constantine's palace are now but a stable for wild beasts.

The city, with its narrow winding streets, rooftops covered with exotic flowers, and magnificent harbour, has been subject to the most terrible fires known in the world. From the time of Basilicus, when the great library of 120,000 volumes was destroyed,[52] to the year 1607, when 3,000 houses were consumed on the fourteenth of October, the city has been so cursed. And Sandys had seen a snow storm from the Black Sea break and ruin, even in September, branches of great trees. Add to fires and storms the plague and the sceptre of a Tyrant, "with the insolencie of slaves: and then ô New Rome how are thy thus balanced profits and delights to be valued!"[53]

After a brief description[54] of the Bosporus and the countryside about

[48] A folded engraving of the Sultan's Seraglio appears in all editions of *A Relation*, usually at page 32, where a space was left for it.

[49] *A Relation*, p. 34.

[50] Though Sandys does not mention it, he copied these inscriptions from Georgii Dousa, *De Itinere Suo Constantinopolitano, Epistola. Accesserunt veteres Inscriptiones Byzantio et ex reliqua Graecia* . . . [Leyden, 1599], pp. 38–9, where even the grouping of quotations is similar.

[51] An engraving of the column covers all but one (type) line of p. 35 of *A Relation*. Exactly the same figure, though on a much smaller scale, appeared in Petrus Gyllius, *De Constantinopleos Typographia* (Lugduni Batavorum, Elzivir ed. 1632) on the title-page, and in his *De Bosporo Thracio* (Lugduni, 1632) [there were earlier (*e.g.*, 1562) and larger editions of these works which probably also included the illustration]. Mr. Esmond S. deBeer informs me that it also appears in Busbecq's . . . *Legationis Turcicæ Epistolae Quatuor* (1605), p. 48.

[52] An infinite loss, says Sandys (p. 37). He mentions that the Odysseys and Iliads of Homer, written on the inner skin of a dragon, were there contained.

[53] *A Relation*, p. 38.

[54] The most interesting part of which is a tale from recent events, the thrilling escape of a Hollander, Hadrian Cant, from the prison of the Black Tower on one side of the straits.

Constantinople, Sandys turns to the history of the Turks. Drawing probably from many sources,[55] he traces quickly yet comprehensively the various individuals, reigns, and dynasties, and goes on to an analysis of Turkish policy in government. The army of Moslemized sons of Christians, its organization and equipment, he describes with the clear eye of one who had seen it. Their navy he held in contempt, as had most Europeans since the battle of Lepanto. He concludes the discussion of the Turkish forces by observing that "Thus is the Great *Turke* served by those whom he may advance without enuie and destroy without danger."[56]

The Mahometan religion is presented with somewhat less Christian scorn than one usually finds in Renaissance accounts. Perhaps because he was the son of an archbishop, he was interested even in the form of the service and in their fast days. He shows that in some respects their ideas parallel those of Christianity and in others of the Stoics and other pagans. But "their opinions of the end of the world, of Paradise, and of hell; exceede the vanity of dreames, and all old wives fables."[57] It is a tempered, judicious account.

The laws and manners of the Turks are to the traveller and his readers matters with which, in the light of the European political situation in their day, they know they should be concerned. And here Sandys appears to be relying largely on his own observations. He deals less with the spectacular criminal punishments than do other English observers, and more with the civil law (incidentally thus giving evidence of his own legal training).[58] He is not the merchant nor the preacher, but the cultivated traveller with an almost twentieth-century sociological interest. Anecdote or detail illustrates a national characteristic.

Sandys shows typical Renaissance interest in the texture of materials, colour and cut of costume, furniture and interior decoration. Some of their foods he found most palatable. As for drink, despite the *Koran*,

55 For possible sources on the Turks, see S. C. Chew, *The Crescent and the Rose*, pp. 200–1, etc. and E. G. Cox, *A Reference Guide to the Literature of Travel*, I, 201 ff. Almost all of these sources mentioned in these two, and others, have been examined. Sandys may have used such English works as Richard Knolles *The Generall Historie of the Turkes* (London, 1603), a great compendium of information, but exact parallels are difficult to find. It is probable that he used Knolles, if at all, to suggest continental Latin sources, ancient and recent, for Knolles has a long list of them.

56 *A Relation*, p. 51.

57 *Ibid.*, p. 58.

58 See Chapter II above, pp. 32–4.

they preferred English beer[59] above everything else. And he gives one of the earliest references to coffee, one which Robert Burton and Francis Bacon, among others, borrowed[60] from him:

> . . . Although they are destitute of Tauerns, yet have they their Coffa-houses, which something resemble them. There sit they chatting most of the day; and sippe of a drinke called Coffa (of the berry that it is made of) in little *China* dishes, as hot as they can suffer it: blacke as soote, and tasting not much vnlike it (why not that blacke broth which was in vse amongst the *Lacedemonians*?) which helpeth, as they say, digestion, and procureth alacrity: many of the coffa-men keeping beautifull boyes, who serve as stales to procure them customers. . . .[61]

The Turkish lady, her great black eyes, red nails, and strange dress, he delineates in words and then pictures in an engraving. He describes the magnificent public baths, and hints with some relish at the abominations practised there. For the slaves, treated as cattle, he has the usual western European's compassion. Folk customs in marriages and funerals he still notes with care, and the flower-decked graves of the middle-classes bring him to translate two lines of Persius:

> *Lie earth light on their bones, may their graues beare*
> *Fresh fragrant flowers: let spring-tide still liue there.*[62]

Of the Turks' knowledge of philosophy, physics, and astronomy Sandys thinks little. Their poetry and music are somewhat better. "Printing they resist; perhaps for fear lest the vniversality of learning should subuert their false grounded religion and policy; which is better preserved by an ignorant obedience." The Turkish tongue, its vocabulary and character, is illustrative of the nation's history. A discussion of their

59 *A Relation*, p. 66. Alcoholic beverages were allowed only in ambassadors' houses. Though wine is forbidden all Mohametans, Sandys says, "now to that liberty they are growne (the naturall *Turke* excepted) that they will quaffe freely when they come to the house of a Christian: insomuche as I have seen but few go away vnled from the Embassadors table." Curiously, though Sandys probably actually was a witness to such a situation, his words are almost a translation of Dousa, p. 35, who in speaking of some Turkish official, refers to him "qui cùm ad prandium Oratoris Angli accessisset, tantum vini exhauriebat, vt mero sapitus . . ." etc.

60 See R. R. Cawley, "Burton, Bacon, and Sandys," *Modern Language Notes*, LVI (April 1941), 271–3.

61 *A Relation*, p. 66.

62 *A Relation*, p. 71. Sandys as usual gives the Latin lines in the margin.

trades and arts, their universal laziness and, where Christians are concerned, unscrupulousness, rounds out the sketch of the people in general.

The person of the young Sultan and his Court, as they appeared in the year 1610, are described as though by an eye witness. Of the Court in its room of white marble, where the Sultan receives ambassadors, there is an exotic picture.[63] But the traveller seems more interested in the polyglot population of the great city than in the person and palace of its ruler, perhaps because the common people permitted of closer scrutiny.

Constantinople's seven hundred thousand[64] Turks, Jews, and Christians lived in groups more or less to themselves. Pera, where the Ambassador's house was located, was largely a city of Grecian Christians, for no Jews were allowed to have more than business establishments there. The Greeks, almost as scattered throughout the world as the Jews, had interested Sandys earlier along the Adriatic and Aegean, and now he proceeds into an analysis of their folk character. They are worth considering, he argues, for they once were

> . . . a nation . . . so excellent, that their precepts and examples do still remaine as approved Canons to direct the mind that endeuoureth vertue. Admirable in arts, and glorious in armes; famous for government, affectors of freedome, every way noble. . . .[65]

Behold, how are the mighty fallen. Carefree, untrustworthy, they are symbols of the shiftless. Their costumes are picturesque, however, their feasts sumptuous, and their women very handsome. Their debased language still preserves traces of its former dignity, and their ecclesiastical organization is much more palatable to the Protestant than is the Roman.[66] Their funeral customs also are worth observing, and bring forth recollection of the obsequies for Achilles and Archemorus. "But enough of the Grecians,"[67] the traveller concludes, realizing that the account of Constantinople must not consume all his volume.

[63] Though this may be from Sandys' observation, it is much like Dousa, p. 25.

[64] Sandys seems to have got this figure from Giovanni Botero, *Le Relationi Vniversali* . . . (Venice, 1596), p. 106.

[65] *A Relation*, p. 77

[66] Lord Falkland, in a later complimentary poem to Sandys, referred to this passage when he mourned the unenviable position of the Greek church, caught between the infidel and Rome (see S. C. Chew, *The Crescent and the Rose*, p. 134, and Sandys' own *A Paraphrase upon the Psalmes of David*, 1636, commendatory poems preferred to the text).

[67] *A Relation*, p. 85.

At the end of January Sandys embarked on the sturdy but slow *Trinity* of London, bound for Alexandria. A three-day wait for clearance at customs was spent watching a country wedding on the near-by shore and an unsuccessful attempt of Christian slaves to escape in a captured galley. At last, with patience and bribery, the English ship got under way. Sticking to the east coast of the Aegean, she passed Mitylen, Samos, Icaria, and Patmos,[68] Coos, and Rhodes. The history of the last, its Colossus and its association with the knights of St. John, Sandys records,[69] though evidently the ship did not put in there. Off this shore they expected pirates, but were happily deceived. Three nights later, amid lightning and tempest, they discerned the coast of Egypt. The next morning they anchored at Alexandria.

Before he takes his reader ashore, Sandys gives an extended account of Egypt's history, topography, and inhabitants. For his purpose he found fewer Renaissance sources than he had for Greece and the Levant. He relied on a mixture of the ancient geographers, the few near-contemporaries he could find, and on his own observation.[70] Curiously, his antiquarian interests are much stronger here than they were in Grecian territory, if his absorption in the history of the Nile, the pyramids, mummies, and ancient Egyptian religion are indicative.[71]

Beginning with the usual brief sketch, of Egypt in general, he follows it immediately with a treatise on that timeless topic, the Nile. Relying

[68] *Ibid.*, p. 89. Sandys, of course, is interested in St. John and the Book of *Revelations*, citing St. Augustine as authority concerning St. John's miraculous grave at Ephesus.

[69] He cites as sources, giving book and chapter, [Joannes] Zonaras' *Annales* [many editions, 1587 being one] and Pausanias' *Corinthiaca* [many editions exist].

[70] Strabo, Pliny, Plutarch, and Herodotus are acknowledged, as are Leo Africanus, Alpinus, Diodorus Siculus, Belon, Choerilus, Christophorus Helvicus, Isocrates, Claudius Ptolemæus, Salanicus, Statius Pompinius. They are often acknowledged once but used many other times. Edward Webbe (pub. 1590) and Henry Timberlake (pub. 1603) were among the Englishmen who preceded Sandys in Egypt, and William Lithgow (in 1612) immediately followed him. Webbe is a mere repeater of old wives' tales of fishes twelve feet long in the Nile, etc. Timberlake gives little except an interesting discussion of of artificial incubation. Lithgow, whose work appeared the year before Sandys' even though he travelled later, devotes considerable space to the Nile and the Pyramids, but nothing approaching Sandys'.

[71] There was an immense interest in these things in England before and after Sandys' time. See S. C. Chew, *The Crescent and the Rose*, pp. 83–9, and R. R. Cawley, *The Voyagers and Elizabethan Drama*, pp. 11–82.

considerably on Leo Africanus,[72] Strabo,[73] Pliny, and Herodotus but including his own observation, he describes the river, its branches (he saw only four, though Herodotus and others claimed to have seen many more), and deltas. "But amoungst the hidden mysteries of Nature, there is none more wonderfull, then is the ouerflowing of this River," he observes, thereby agreeing with all previous commentators. The river in ancient times, he notices, rose seventeen cubits,[74] but the year he was there it rose twenty-three. He makes the usual conjectures as to the cause of the annual swelling, citing the explanations[75] of ancients and moderns. He tells of the "vulgar" experiment by which earth from the Nile bank, kept in a "private place," will by its increasing weight foretell the approach of the flood. "Proceeding without doubt from the humidity of the Aire, which hauing a recourse through all passable places, and mixing therewith, increaseth the same as it increaseth in moisture."[76] Then he turns to the strange creatures inhabiting the river. The hippopotamus, or river horse, he describes from others' accounts. The crocodile, however, he had seen, and on its habits and appearance he expatiates, including the familiar story of the parasitic little bird the Troculus, which picks the monster's teeth; and the "Icnumon" which darts into the crocodile's open mouth, glides into its belly, and gnaws until it destroys.[77]

[72] Probably in the Latin version of Florian, 1556, or one of the many "copies" and later Latin editions of it. It had been translated into English by Sandys' later friend John Pory in 1600. He uses Leo for all Egypt, not simply the Nile.

[73] Isaac Casaubon's edition of Strabo, . . . *Strabonis Rervm Geographicarvm* . . ., ([Genevae] 1587, and others), he may have used (for Casaubon's commentaries would have been useful). Much of his material on p. 131, for example, the pyramid and sphinx, was probably extracted from Strabo, XVII (1587, pp. 956–7), Pliny XXXVI, 2, and Herodotus (though he may quote these latter two second and third hand). He also mentions Ptolemy as an authority on the river. There were many Latin editions of all these latter writers available.

[74] And he illustrates this by a full-page engraving of Father Nilus, with seventeen children playing about representing the annual rise. Sandys' source for this drawing seem to have been ultimately an engraving of G. B. de Cavalieri (*c.* 1560), but may have come more directly from L. della Vaccaria's *Antiquarum Statuarum urbis Romae . . . icones*, 1584 (see E. S. de Beer, "George Sandys's Account of Compania," *The Library*, 4th series, XVII [March 1937], 465).

[75] Anaxagoras, Aeschylus, Euripides (in verse), Lucan (in verse), Lucretius (in verse), Diodorus Siculus, and others.

[76] *A Relation*, p. 99. Francis Bacon used this in *Sylva Sylvarum* (see R. R. Cawley, *Unpathed Waters* [Princeton, 1940], p. 243).

[77] See R. R. Cawley, *The Voyagers and Elizabethan Drama*, p. 63, who points out that Sandys quoted the description of this creature almost word for word from Diodorus.

From physical features of the Nile valley he turns to the history of Egypt. Fossil remains[78] disprove, Sandys contends, the Egyptians' claim to be "the prime nation of the world," for certainly Egypt was still a sea when other parts of the earth were already inhabited. Though not the first nation,

> The *Ægyptians* first invented Arithmeticke, Musicke and Geometry; and by reason of the perpetual serenity of the aire, found out the course of the Sunne and the starres, their constellations, risings, aspects, and influences; dividing by the same the yeare into moneths, and grounding their diuinations vpon their hidden properties. Moreouer from the *Ægyptians, Orpheus, Museus*, and *Homer*, haue fetcht their hymnes and fables of the Gods: *Pythagoras, Eudoxus*, and *Democritus*, their Philosophie: *Lycurgus, Solon*, and *Plato*, the forme of their governments: by which they all in their seuerall kinds haue eternized their memories . . .[79]

Their hieroglyphics are explained and then illustrated in an engraving. Human interest stories, such as that of Cleopatra being carried to Caesar "trvst up in a mattress,"[80] are attached to a chronological outline of Egyptian history. Sandys brings the account through the various dynasties to the Turkish conquest, commenting grimly on the harsh rule of the present Bassa. The Egyptian Moors he did not admire, for "A people breathes not more savage and nastie; crusted with dirt, and stinking of smoke, by reason of the fuell,*[81] and their houses which have no chimnies." The real Egyptians, however, were the "Copties," who were Christians. These naturally interested the Protestant a great deal, and he observed with regret that lately they were being converted to Popery "by the industry of the Friers." The wonders of Alexandria, the lighthouse of ancient days, Lake Marseotis, the Labyrinth, and the Pillar of Pompey complete the lengthy introductory matter in this book. Then for the first time[82] he brings the reader ashore with himself.

Customs officers levied a tenth of all goods and a half per cent of all

[78] Fossils and the earth's strata always interested Sandys. See the 1632 edition of his Ovid, Book XV, p. 497, where he comments in the margin that he has seen the residue of ancient seas on mountain tops in America.

[79] *A Relation*, p. 104.

[80] *Ibid.*, p. 106.

[81] *Ibid.*, p. 110. His marginal note opposite the asterisk is "*Stercus bovinum* [in some later editions, *hominum*]."

[82] Sandys' organization here is psychologically inferior to that of Book I, when he brought himself and his reader ashore before he launched into a discussion of the nation being visited. I have followed his order, partly to show his method.

money before they permitted the visitor to go on to the house of the French consul, where he was to reside. Sandys describes this "Vice-Consul," Paulus Marcitus, in an excellent example of his laconic prose. And for an English Protestant, characterizes quite tolerantly.

> . . . The Vice-consul keepes a table for Merchants, he himselfe a Magnifico, lesse liberall of his presence, then industrious of pleasure; yet rather stately then proud; expecting respect, and meriting good will: that was a Priest, and would be a Cardinall, with the hopes whereof, they say, he feasteth his ambition.[83]

This gentleman provided Sandys, and others of the group[84] with which he was to continue, with a Janizary as protector and guide. On 2 February, mounted magnificently on camels and asses, they started for Cairo. As they journeyed Sandys noticed a ruin over in the distance, a troop of passing soldiers, the ferry crossing, the many tolls paid, the arrival at Rosetta late at night. Two days here, and the party embarked on a river boat, a "Jerbie," which they had hired with its crew of seven for twelve dollars. They ate fish, gazed curiously at the miserable mud huts of the poor along the banks, and watched sympathetically (but did not offer to help) their wretched Moorish crew pushing the craft off the shoals in which the river abounded. Five days of this, and then Cairo, where they were grateful to be entertained without charge by a hospitable English merchant.

Though on the whole Constantinople seems to have interested Sandys more, Cairo and its teeming life fascinated any Renaissance visitor. At least one picturesque celebration occurred during his visit, the feast of little Byram, a sort of Passover in which sheep were slaughtered in private houses, the doors besmeared with blood, and pieces of flesh distributed among the poor. He recalled how one beggarly Moor who tormented the party of Christian sightseers was justifiably and severely punished by another Moor of better sort. He attended an Armenian Christian service, and watched a caravan go out to relieve another returning from Mecca.[85] The street shows charmed him: talking

[83] *A Relation*, p. 115.

[84] Sandys speaks here of "we," no longer including merely, presumably, the Greek interpreter of his Turkish tour, but other travellers.

[85] He spells the name of the city 'Mecha.' At this point, rather stiffly and artificially, Sandys describes Mecca (*A Relation*, pp. 124–5), bringing himself up short with, "But to digress no further." The account is brief, and the exact source has not been located. Earlier (pp. 123–4) he gives a brief description of Mt. Sinai, also almost surely derivative.

ravens, climbing dogs and goats, dancing camels, and even solemn asses taught such tricks that "to . . .[them] *Banks* his horse would have proved but a *Zany*."[86]

As had other travellers,[87] he discusses the artificial incubation of eggs as he saw the process demonstrated in Cairo. And like other Europeans, he enjoyed the fruit—oranges, pomegranates, lemons, figs, and something which must have been a banana.[88] The chameleon, scuttling everywhere about the city, did not, as others had said, change to all colours, but did show a predominance of the colour when placed on green or yellow. Finally, the crown of Cairo's interesting things was the Castle upon the rock overlooking it. "Such is this Citie, the fairest in *Turkie*, yet differing from what it was, as from a body being yong and healthfull, doth the same growne old and wasted with diseases."[89]

Before departing forever from "the most excellent of countries," Sandys visited the Pyramids and Sphinx. His party crossed the Nile, journeying past the place where arms and legs appear on Good Friday,[90] and then twelve miles across an open plain to the foot of the Libyan Deserts. There stood the Pyramids. The history of the great monuments Sandys borrowed from Strabo and Pliny.[91] In summing up the reasons for their having been built, he touches his recurrent theme:

> . . . Besides, they [the Pharoahs] considering the frailty of man, that in an instant buds, blowes, and withereth; did endeuour by such sumptuous and magnificent structures, in spite of death to giue vnto their fames eternity. But vainely . . . [92]

[86] *A Relation*, p. 126. Banks' well-known juggling horse could tell an Englishman from a Spaniard, Thomas Nashe said (see R. B. McKerrow, ed., *The Works of Thomas Nashe* [5 vols, London, 1904–10], II, 230; III, 21).

[87] See note 70 above for Henry Timberlake, *A True and Strange Discourse of the Trauailes of two English Pilgrimes . . .*, (London, 1603 or 1608), who also describes the process and results.

[88] *A Relation*, p. 121. "Plantains, that have a broad flaggy leafe, growing in clusters, and shaped like cucumers, the rind like a pescod, solid within, without stones or kernels, to the taste exceeding delicious (this the *Mohametans* say was the forbidden fruit . . .)."

[89] *A Relation*, p. 122.

[90] *Ibid.*, p. 127. This "miracle" Sandys disdainfully explains away immediately.

[91] Strabo (probably in Casaubon's ed., see note 73 above), 1587, Book XVII, pp. 555–6. Pliny existed in many editions, though available was the translation of Philemon Holland, *The Historie of the World . . . of C. Plinus Secundus* (2 vols., London, 1601), Book XXXVI, Chapter 12, p. 577. Particularly did Sandys use the geographers on pp. 127–8, 131.

[92] *A Relation*, p. 129.

But the greater part of the discussion of the Pyramids is of heat and sweat and dead air rather than of glorious antiquity, and is surely Sandys' own.[93] First he ascended the Great Pyramid with much difficulty, and from the summit drank in the wonders of that silent plain spread far before him. On descending, he entered the passage to the tomb, though not until his Janizaries had fired their arquebuses into it to frighten forth any skulkers. For surer footing, and probably because of the heat, he removed his shoes and most of his clothing. Stooping and creeping, he descended a steep incline for a hundred feet, not daring to go deeper. At this level, finding that he could not enter one foul-smelling chamber, he ascended another way, "as on the bow of an arch," one hundred and twenty feet. Stooping along an entry, he came to a handsome little marble chamber with a strong sepulchral odour, from which he retreated hastily. Finally, after ascending again for a hundred and twenty feet, he entered a large and "goodly" marble chamber[94] containing a tomb, "vncouered, empty, and all of one stone: breast high, seuen feete in length, not foure in breadth, and sounding like a bell."[95] Here once, he thought, lay the body of the builder.

The Sphinx, or Colossus, he describes briefly, and then considers the ruins of the ancient city of Memphis five miles southeast of the figure. He asks himself and the reader

> . . . But why spend I time about that that is not? The very ruines now almost ruinated: yet some few impressions are left, and diuers throwne downe, statues of monstrous resemblance: a scarce sufficient testimony to shew vnto the curious seeker, that there it hath bin. Why then deplore we our humane frailty?
>
> *When Stones, as well as breath*
> *And names, do suffer death*[96]

Sandys had meant to visit the sepulchres containing the mummies, but the high price of guards and the fear of Arabs then holding a religious festival in the vicinity prevented him. He had seen many of the embalmed bodies, however, in Cairo. He describes partly from

[93] It is a circumstantial account in homely English narrative prose, and is much more detailed than that of any previous English traveller (or continental one that I have examined).

[94] See the note on the various chambers in the Great Pyramid in Horace L. Jones, ed., *The Geography of Strabo* (8 vols., London, 1917–32), VIII, 92–3.

[95] *A Relation*, p. 130.

[96] *Ibid.*, p. 132. Sandys gives the Latin two lines of Ausonius in the margin opposite his translation.

hearsay the tombs themselves, the coffins rank on rank, the funeral linen, the condition of the bodies. Within the bellies of the mummies were little figures of their gods in stone or metal, "some of the shape of men, in coate-armours, with the heads of sheepe, haukes, dogs, &c. others of cats, beetles monkies, and such like. Of these I brought away diuers with me."[97] Though he does not mention it, Sandys later presented many of these little figures to John Tredescant,[98] the great collector, through whom they found their way into the original Ashmolean Museum. But methods of embalming he explains in detail,[99] and again shows his intense interest in funeral customs by his account of an Egyptian burial.

Less than a month altogether Sandys spent in Egypt, for on 4 March he set out overland for Jerusalem. It was to be a hazardous and arduous journey. His particular party was composed of four Englishmen and three Italians,[100] of whom one was a priest and another a physician. Attired as pilgrims, they attached themselves to a great caravan. The four Englishmen hired three camels and their keepers, and secured ample provision, including goatskin bags of water, for the "voyage." They

97 *Ibid.*, p. 133. This description of the little figures is illustrated with an engraving of seven of them.

98 See John Tradescant (or Tredescant), *Museum Tradescantianum* (London, 1656), p. 42, under the heading "VII./variety of Rarities." Among curios from India and other strange lands are

> The Idol *Osiris. Anubis*, the sheep,
> the Beetle, the Dog, which the Egypti-
> ians worshipped. Mr. *Sandys*.

Of the five, four at least are depicted in the engraving on page 133. The authorities of the Ashmolean do not find these figures surviving among their present collections. In the commentaries on the Ovid (1632 edition, p. 334) Sandys mentions "Barking *Anubis*, fained to haue the head of a dogge, and so figured in his statues; whereof I brought one out of *Ægypt*, taken out of the belly of an inbalmed body."

This Tradescant catalogue is an interesting little volume which lists many Virginia items Sandys may have presented. Sandys' name is not included in the roll of "Principall Benefactors" of the Museum, though the King and Queen, Sandys' cousin Sir Dudley Digges, his friends Archbishop Laud, Lord Falkland, Captain West (see chapters on Virginia below), and Sir Kenelm Digby are.

99 Bacon and others borrowed from Sandys' account here (see R. R. Cawley, *The Voyagers and Elizabethan Drama*, p. 29).

100 The names of the Italians and Englishmen are listed in the recently discovered register of the monastery at Jerusalem (see Appendix D).

rode two to a camel, in cradles with linen coverings above, the whole conveyance proving very uncomfortable.

The seven western Christians found themselves in the midst of a motley multitude of ancient Jewish women going 'home' to die, negro slaves, merchants of all nations, and Turkish soldiers. They began travelling at night, starting at ten or twelve o'clock and pitching camp at seven in the morning. Everywhere they paid tribute or customs duty. One tribal chieftain even invited himself into their tent and devoured a great part of their provisions.

In a short time they were at the edge of the main desert, where the whole caravan, consisting of a thousand horses, mules, and asses, and five hundred camels, was assembled. Much as he disliked riding on the beast, Sandys paused to pay tribute to the camel:

> . . . These are the ships of Arabia; their seas are her deserts. A creature created for burthen. Six hundred weight is his ordinary load; yet he will carry a thousand . . . Their pace is slow, and intollerable hard; being withal unsure of foot, where neuer so little slipping or vneuen. They are not made to amend their paces when weary, with blowes; but are encouraged by songs and the going before of their keepers. A beast gentle and tractable . . . About their necks they hang certaine charmes included in leather, and writ by their Deruises, to defend them from mischances, and the poison of ill eies. . . .[101]

On 10 March the caravan entered the greater desert of Arabia Petrea. One night the rear of the straggling column, in which the Christians rode, was assailed by Arabs, who swooped down quickly and carried away all they could lay hands upon. These desert marauders, the children of Ishmael, Sandys paused to describe, and with them that wanderer of the waste places, the ostrich. Then the caravan continued, stopping for rest at brackish wells of water, and moving as before usually at night. On the seventeenth they rode into a pleasant country and pitched camp under the walls of the City of Gaza. They had entered the Holy Land.

101 *A Relation*, p. 138.

IV

JERUSALEM AND NAPLES

BEFORE PROCEEDING farther into Palestine, Sandys paused to give his usual condensed history[1] of the country he was about to visit, including an outline of its topography and a discussion of its Biblical, classical, and mediaeval periods. Though in his day it was inhabited principally by Moors and Arabs, it was traditionally the home of the Jew. Therefore Sandys here discusses the Hebrew race, giving a thoughtful and relatively unprejudiced[2] essay on the Jew in Renaissance Europe and the Mohametan empire—his religion (including his attitude towards Christ), his dress, language, and social customs. The Jews are

> . . . a people scattered throughout the whole world, and hated by those amongst whom they live; yet suffered, as a necessarie mischiefe: subiect to all wrongs and contumelies, which they support with an invincible patience. Many of them haue I seen abused; some of them beaten: yet neuer saw I *Iew* with an angry countenance. They can subiect themselves vnto times, and to whatsoeuer may aduance their profit. In generall they are worldly wise, and thriue wheresoever they set footing.[3]

For a few days Sandys and his companions resided in Gaza,[4] though none too comfortably. They lived in miserable Christian houses with doors so low as to prevent surprise attack by the Mohametan masters of the country. Even from these, fortunately not until they were about to depart anyway, they were thrust by the rapacious Spahis, who seized some of the "very necessaries" among their provisions. Rejoining the

[1] Sandys' acknowledged sources here are the Bible, Josephus, and Christophorus Helvicus (*Theatrum Historicum Sive Chronologiæ Systema Novum* . . . [Giessæ Hessorum, 1609], is one edition). He probably used also his sources for Jerusalem and its environs (see below).

[2] Certainly for his day.

[3] *A Relation*, p. 146. Sandys also continues the tradition that "They are generally fat, and ranke of the savours which attend vpon sluttish corpulency" (pp. 148–9), a passage Sir Thomas Browne uses in his essay, "Enquiries into Vulgar and Common Errors—that Jews stink" (in *Pseudodoxia Epidemica*, G. Keynes, ed., *The Works of Sir Thomas Browne* [6 vols., New York, 1928], III 47), as a point of departure.

[4] *A Relation*, p. 150.

caravan, now dividing as it proceeded, they followed the coast northward to Ascalon, Cane Sedoe, Rama, and finally to Joppa. At Joppa, though they had been previously excused by certificate from paying toll, a sheik of the Arabs entered their tent and greedily devoured most of their remaining viands, demanding also a present before one was offered. Here, however, they met the guide sent by the Pater-Guardian at Jerusalem to conduct pilgrims—at a price—to Jerusalem. Under his direction they climbed through mountain country and then rode rapidly across more level plateau. Soon they were opposite the North Gate of Jerusalem, but there no Christians were admitted. A short time later, at the West Gate, they were greeted by two Franciscan friars and led to the monastery, where all Christians were supposed[5] to lodge.

Sandys' account of Jerusalem was to the average seventeenth century reader the most interesting part of *A Relation*. Though the more sophisticated person such as Lady Ann Clifford[6] might prefer the government of the Turks, the monuments of Egypt, or the glories of Greece, the middle-class citizen could read and appreciate the description of the places he had known by name ever since he could remember, places which many of his mediaeval ancestors had visited in person. Sandys appears to have been quite conscious that his guide to the city would seem fresh only to the Englishman who understood no tongue save his own:

> Although diuers both vpon inquisitions and view, haue with much labour related the site and state of this Citie, with the places adioyning (though not to my knowledge in our language[7]) insomuch as I may seeme vnto some, but

[5] Some Protestant travellers felt themselves in an awkward situation, *e.g.*, Lithgow, p. 210 and William Biddulph, *The Travels of certaine Englishmen into Africa, Asia . . . Palestina, Jerusalem* . . . [London, 1609], p. 119). They made the situation worse by scorning or deriding Catholic ritual.

[6] See Chapter I, p. 27n above.

[7] Evidently Sandys is entirely sincere. The principal earlier English travellers of his generation whose accounts were printed before his and who visited Jerusalem before he did were Edward Webbe (1590); Henry Timberlake (1603); and William Biddulph (1609). Christianus Adrichomius had been translated into English in 1595 by T. Tymme under the title of *A Brief Description of Hierusalem and of the Suburbs thereof, as it florished in the time of Christ* . . . (London). Lithgow travelled after Sandys but published before him (in 1614). Webbe and Timberlake are very brief. Biddulph devotes many pages (115–43), to Jerusalem, dividing his discussion of things he saw into "Apparant Truths," "Manifest Untruths," and "Doubtfull Things." He spends so much time refuting Papist "absurdities" as a good Protestant should, that he gives little or no real

to write what hath bin written already: yet notwithstanding, as well to continue the course of this discourse, as to deliuer the Reader from many erring reports of the too credulous deuote, and too too vain-glorious: the one

Seminat in vulgus nugus— *Do toyes diuulge—*

The other charactred in the remainder of the Distiche:

—auditague lingua,
Auget & ex humili tumolo producit olimpum. Bapt. Mant. 1.3

. . . —Stille adde to what they heare
And of a mole-hill do a mountaine reare:

I will declare what I haue obserued, unswayed with either of their vices.[8]

Thus Sandys took an objective and therefore temperate view. There is nothing of Lithgow's or Biddulph's anti-Papist ranting against shameful idolatries, nor is the simple credulity of the older continental writers present. He uses Adrichomius and Zuallardo considerably,[9] and other sources he mentions as he goes along; but he relies principally on his own experiences. Occasionally he is moved emotionally. Usually he eyes everything critically, though he takes care not to spoil a fine early-church tradition or beautiful ritual by scoffing at what other Englishmen considered scandalous Popery. The combination of all this, with the fact that he gives detailed and accurate description of dozens of sacred places, made Sandys, for the rest of the seventeenth century, the English traveller of most authority on Palestine.[10]

Not a small part of the attraction of the Jerusalem and Palestine section is the series of elaborate engravings of landscapes, buildings, and floor-plans appearing in this Book III. The Temple and Holy Sepulchre, famous places such as the Mount of Olives, and a variety

description. Adrichomius Sandys apparently used in the original (*Theatrum Terræ Sanctæ et Biblicarum Historiarum*, 1587 etc. See notes below). Tymme had attempted to Protestantize Adrichomius' account (see *A Brief Description*, p. ¶ 2v), but the book remains an outline guide to the supposed city of Biblical times, not to that of Sandys' own day.

8 *A Relation*, p. 154.

9 Giovanni Zuallardo's *Il Devotissimo Viaggio di Gerusalemme* . . . (Rome, 1587), appeared in many editions in the later sixteenth century. Sandys used Zuallardo for material, for example, on pp. 176–7 and on 210. For his use of Adrichomius, see note 13 below.

10 Thomas Wright, *Early Travels in Palestine* (London, 1848), makes such a statement, but adds that Sandys often erred on the side of credulity. Wright evidently did not read *A Relation* carefully. The number of editions of Sandys, and the number of authors of the later century who used him (see below) is good evidence of the truth of Wright's statement regarding Sandys' popularity, however.

of views of the city are included. There are twenty-two of these illustrations of the Holy Land, all of them drawn from Zuallardo.[11] The plates are not tied to the text by numbers on particular buildings or places, however, as is the case in travel-books which adhered more strictly[12] to the outline—and guidebook—tradition.

Sandys began his discussion of Jerusalem with a close paraphrase[13] of Adrichomius' Latin opening sentence on the same subject, but rapidly

[11] Sandys' engravings are not printed from the Zuallardo plates, though they are almost the same size. Although all Sandys' figures in this section come from this one source, he did not by any means use all Zuallardo included. Comparing Sandys, 1615 ed. and Zuallardo, 1587, the illustrations are as follows: Jerusalem, S, p. 158, Z, p. 131; Temple of the Sepulchre, S, p. 161, Z, p. 186; Platform of Sepulchre and Mt. Calvary, S, p. 162, Z, p. 184; Mount Calvary, S, p. 164, Z, p. 203; Interior of the Sepulchre (?), S, p. 165, Z, p. 189; Sepulchre (3 figures), S, p. 166, Z, p. 207; Way between Jerusalem and Bethlehem, S, p. 175, Z, p. 223; Platform of Temple and Monastery in Bethlehem, S, p. 178, Z, p. 230; Altar of Nativity, S, p. 179, Z, p. 241; Combination altar and figures, S, p. 180, Z, pp. 232 and 234; Desert of St. John Baptist, S, p. 183, Z, p. 252; Mountain of Juda, S, p. 184, Z, p. 249; Jerusalem, S, p. 185, Z, p. 139; Alceldema, S, p. 187, Z, p. 142; Sepulchre of "Zaccary," S, p. 189, Z, p. 152; Jerusalem, S, p. 190, Z, p. 159; three figures in one, S, p. 191, Z, pp. 148, 149, 150; Jerusalem, S, p. 194, Z, p. 164; Bethany, S, p. 196, Z, p. 177; Mont Olivet, S, p. 198, Z, p. 171; Chapel of the Ascension (2 figures), S, p. 199, Z, p. 174; Jerusalem, S, p. 201, Z, p. 123. Latin titles for the pictures Sandys has usually anglicized, though not always. Anyone familiar with Zuallardo of course recognized the plates at once. It was a superficial comparison of plates and a few lines that induced an antiquary in the later seventeenth century (see Appendix D below) to declare Sandys' whole account derivative.

[12] *E.g.*, see Fynes Moryson, *An Itinerary*, II, 1–20.

[13] Sandys, p. 154, begins his paragraph, "This Citie, once sacred and glorious, elected by God for his seate, and seated in the midst of Nations: like a diadem crowning the head of the mountaines. . . ." The Latin of Adrichomius begins "Ierusalem, civitas Dei electa, sancta, & gloriosa, fundata in montibus sanctis, loci eminentia. . . ." Tymme's translation (p. 1) begins "Ierusalem the elect Cittie of God, holy and most glorious, built upon the holy mountaines, excelling all the citties of the world. . . ." Sandys acknowledges his indebtedness to Adrichomius, in another matter, in a marginal note on this same page. These same phrases should be compared with the opening words of Michele Zappullo's *Historia di quattro principali Città del-Mondo, Gerusalemme, Roma, Napoli, &. Venetia* . . . (Vicenza, 1603), p. 1: "*Gervsalem Citta Reale, Metropoli nobilissima, e da Dio eletta Santa, e gloriosa, tipo ouer figura della celeste patria: sita in eminente luogo della Palestina* . . ." (much of the remainder of this paragraph is 'identical' with Sandys'). A more ancient description, perhaps of one of the church fathers, is probably the ultimate source.

proceeded to an outline of the city's past and present appearance. Inevitably he laments a glorious antiquity succeeded by an inglorious present. Then he returns the reader to the West Gate which he had just been entering, on Maundy Thursday, when he interrupted his journal to introduce the city. The party now proceeded to the monastery of the Franciscans. There they were greeted by the Pater-Guardian, Gaudentius, "a reverent old man, of a voluble tongue, and winning behaviour," and his staff of thirty or forty. Here the four Englishmen were entertained theoretically without charge, but when eight days later they presented "one hundred dollars" to the monastery, they were informed that they had scarcely paid for their food. "A costly rate for a monasticall diet," Sandys remarks, but he does explain the Franciscans' charges by telling of the Turks' extortions from the brotherhood. Though he was undoubtedly somewhat sympathetic, frequent allusion by the friars to those monetary persecutions as "motiues to charity" grew very tiresome.

The monastery was supported by the "offerings" of pilgrims and by annual allowances from the Papal, the Spanish, and the Florentine states. It also had another source of income which afforded some amusement to the cultivated traveller. For the sum of thirty "Sultanies" to the Pater-Guardian, any one might become a Knight of the ancient order of the Holy Sepulchre. Once these knights had to be of gentle blood, but now nothing but the money counted. While they were in Jerusalem the four Englishman saw an apothecary from Aleppo dubbed knight. His investiture Sandys describes most solemnly, but there is in the dryness of the description almost an ironic humour.

In order to celebrate properly Easter in Jerusalem, on the same day they arrived the little company went into the Temple of the Sepulchre, each carrying his own pillow and carpet in preparation for a stay of several days. Here, in one of his rare moments of indignation, Sandys vehemently regrets that the enemies of Christ, the Turks, are lords of this sepulchre, and on the most solemn church festivals sit "under a Canopie, to gather mony of such as do enter." Then he gives an intricate floor plan of the Temple, and describes the resting place of "Godfrey of Bullein," and the architectural details of the building. At the sacred tomb itself, Sandys was deeply moved, he says, and did then "dictate this hymne[14] to my Redeemer":

[14] Compare the sincere fervour of Sandys' poem here with Lithgow's mocking and bitter versified farewell to Jerusalem (directed at the Franciscans, *op. cit.*, p. 256). This is one of Sandys' few extant original poems (as opposed to his translations and paraphrases).

Sauior of mankind, Man, Emmanuel:
Who sin-lesse died for sinne, who vanquisht hell.
The first fruites of the grave. Whose life did giue
Light to our darknesse: in whose death we liue.
O strengthen thou my faith; correct my will,
That mine may thine obey: protect me still.
So that the latter death may not deuore
My soule seal'd with thy seale. So in the houre
When thou whose Body sanctifide this Tombe,
Vniustly iudg'd, a glorious Iudge shalt come
To iudge the world with iustice; by that signe
I may be knowne, and entertained for thine.[15]

From the Sepulchre and the moment of spiritual exultation Sandys continued about the enclosure, examining everything of interest. The college of the Knights Templar reminded him of the scene of his legal training, for he notices that

. . . The Temples in London belonged vnto them: where in the Church (built round in imitation of this) diuers of their statues are to be seene, and the positure used in their burials.[16]

Miraculous stories of St. Helena and the true cross Sandys tells objectively, prefacing them with his usual unobtrusive "they say." He then describes the Pater-Guardian's washing and kissing of the pilgrims' feet, which he did "with all outward shew of humilitie." The ceremonies of the three days, the anointing of Christ's image on Good Friday, the procession with the cross on Saturday, and the service at the door of the Sepulchre on Sunday, are passed over briefly. At noon on Easter Day the group departed from the Temple after having spent three nights on its cold stones.

The description of the various sects[17] of Christians celebrating at Jerusalem is a study in comparative ritual if not in comparative religion. And the one thousand people from all Christendom on the three continents crowded into the Temple for these services must have been indicative even to English Protestants of what a united Christianity might be.

15 *A Relation*, p. 167.
16 *Ibid.*, p. 168.
17 *Ibid.*, pp. 170–4. The groups were the Grecians, Armenians, Coptics, Abyssinians, Jacobites, Georgians, Maronites, and Nestorians, besides the western Christians.

On Easter Monday the party rode to "Emaus" and on the day following to Bethlehem. Much of the account of Christ's native city, particularly the step by step description of places and things, Sandys[18] drew from Adrichomius and Zuallardo. After a night at the monastery of Bethlehem, he enjoyed the ride towards the Mountains of Judea. At one place along the route he was moved by the beauty of nature.

> . . . Ouer this on a little flat, stands the ruines of a Monastery, on the South side naturally walled with the steepe of the mountaine: from whence there gusheth a liuing Spring, which entreth the rocke, and again bursteth forth beneath the mouth of the Caue; A place that would make solitariness delightfull, and stand in comparison with the turbulent pompe of cities. . . .[19]

That night he was back in Jerusalem, and the next day the party set out to view the sights of the city itself. The Garden of Gethesemane, the spot where Stephen was stoned, the pool of Bethesda, the Temple (on the site of Solomon's), the Dolorous Way, and the Church of St. James were only a few of the places visited. The Dead Sea they saw only from Mount Olivet. On the Mount itself Sandys spends some space, for it was "So famous in sacred histories, and so often blest with the presence of Christ, and apparition of angels."

But the time for departure had come, and the Englishmen bargained with muleteers to carry them to "Tripoly." They tipped the "Frier-servants: and that not niggardly, considering our light purses and long iourney." The Pater-Guardian earnestly enquired as to the amount they had bestowed upon his brethren, who had taken vows of poverty, and should turn over the money to the order. Excommunication was the penalty for failure to do so, "yet the lesse feared [Sandys] . . . supposed, then detection." "The *Pater-Guardian* would needes thrust vpon vs severall Certificates, which returned him as many *Zecchines*: he desired that we would make their pouertie known, with the dignity of those sanctified places, as a motive to relief, and more frequent pilgrims."[20]

Leaving behind the friendly Italians who had accompanied them from

[18] The epitaphs on Paula (the Roman lady and abbess) which Sandys attributes to St. Jerome, he seems to have drawn also from Adrichomius, pp. 42, 43.

[19] *A Relation*, p. 183. Sandys is describing the site of John the Baptist's cave.

[20] *A Relation*, p. 200. Lithgow (p. 254) carried a similar request to King James himself when he returned to England. James was most gracious, saying that the order had never requested help from him for this purpose, "and if they had, he would have supported their necessity."

Cairo, on 1 April[21] the four Englishmen set out from Jerusalem. This time their fellow-travellers included the apothecary recently dubbed Knight of the Holy Sepulchre, a Portuguese, a German, and a Frenchman, all bound like themselves for Tripoly.[22] As the route from Jerusalem to the coast they took a way they had missed in coming. The second day of the journey, however, they had to leave the regular road for fear of a nearby encampment of the terrible Spahis. The party remained in hiding during the greater part of the day and struck out again when night fell, riding without hats so that they would not be discovered to be Christians. Rain fell in torrents, and flashes of lightning were their only illumination. When the rain intermitted, the air swarmed with "sparkles of fire, borne to and fro with the wind, by reason of the infinite swarmes of flies that do shine like glow-wormes, to the stranger a strange spectacle."[23] An hour after midnight the skies cleared, and they crept silently past a camp of sleeping Spahis. A little farther along, too fatigued to keep to the backs of their mules, they tumbled to the ground in a pleasant glade and slept until sunrise. It was a night to be remembered.

Mount Carmel and its friars, Memnon's sepulchre and classical myth, and the city of Acre and its historical association with the English Richard I were all commented upon. At Acre, a port where English ships loaded cotton, they stopped for four days, hoping that a large body of merchants would accompany them to Nazareth fifteen miles away. Evidently they did not get to Christ's childhood home, for Sandys gives only a second-hand account of it which he seems to have borrowed from Adrichomius.[24]

On 8 April the party embarked on the English ship *Trinity* for the voyage up the coast to Sidon. A terrific storm came up, and to describe it Sandys translated Ovid's famous lines on a tempest at sea, lines he was to use again later[25] in his life. "But distemperature and horror is

[21] Cf. note 100, Chapter III above, and Appendix D, below. The entry of Sandys' name in the registry at Jerusalem (on 1 April) was evidently on day of departure rather than on day of arrival.

[22] On the Syrian coast, not be confused with the African Tripolis.

[23] *A Relation*, p. 203.

[24] *Ibid.*, pp. 206–7. Adrichomius, 1600 ed., p. 141.

[25] From the *Metamorphoses*, Book XI. There are two later versions of this same passage, in Sandys' translations of the Ovid in the 1626 and 1632 editions (see Richard B. Davis, "The Early Editions of George Sandys's Ovid: the Circumstances of Production," *Papers of the Bibliographical Society of America*, xxxv [4th quarter 1941], p. 274).

more then the danger, where mariners be Englishe, who are the absolutest vnder heauen in their profession; and are by forreiners compared vnto fishes," he comments with real national pride. By four in the afternoon they made out Sidon, though the heavy seas prevented the ship's entering the harbour. Some of the party (probably including Sandys) were so sick that they begged to be set ashore in a skiff, a feat performed "not without perill."

Landing in Phoenicia recalled Carthage, Dido, and Aeneas, and Sandys used Ausonius, Appian, and Vergil in his brief discussion[26] of this ancient land and its contributions to civilization. He quotes "Dionysus" concerning the Phoenicians as former Egyptians who introduced navigation and astronomy. Sandys' translation is one of his better attempts at this stage of his poetic experimentation:

These earst from the red Gulph remou'd. Who durst
On seas by new-found wayes aduenture first,
First taught to fraught ships with chang'd merchandies:
First starres obserued in the charactred skies

Also from Lucan, he observes, they gave "Arithmeticke and letters"

Phœnicians first exprest (if fame be true)
The fixt voice in rude figures. Memphis knew
Not yet how streame-loud Biblis to prepare;
But birds and beasts, caru'd out in stone, declare
Their hierogliphicke wisedomes:

Tripolis (as he now calls the Syrian city), Biblis, and Beritus he describes briefly, and then gives greater attention to the ancient Sidon. He follows the description of the last with a curiously lengthy characterization of the Emir of Sidon, an enemy of the Turk of sufficient strength to be, as Sandys hints, a potentially valuable ally for Western Christendom.

[26] Sandys himself names the three as sources. Appian of Alexandria's . . . *Romanorum historiarum* . . . (*e.g.*, Lugduni, 1588, Sandys' reference is to be found on page 1 of this edition) appeared in many Latin versions in the sixteenth century, and was translated into *English* as *An Auncient Historie and exquisite Chronicle of the Romanes Warres* (London, 1578). The fact that the English version says Carthage was built fifty years *after* the fall of Troy, while Sandys and the Latin version say fifty years *before*, is one of many indications that Sandys used Latin versions of almost all his sources. Ausonius' *D. Magni Ausonii . . . Opera* . . . (Lugduni, 1575, Sandys' reference is to be found in this edition, p. 27) was also available in several editions (1605, 1608, 1611, etc.).

Since two of the pilgrims and the ship had gone on to Alexandria, Sandys and the remainder, with a company of English merchants, returned by land towards Acre. Damascus they refrained from visiting because of the multitudes of fierce Spahis then in that city. Tyre they did see, however, and he discusses the shell-fish which supplied in former times the Tyrian purple to the world. From this ancient city they journeyed through varied country on down to Acre. Here the party rested a few days before taking ship. When they did embark they were headed west towards home.

Book Four begins on a note of exultation at the prospect of return to the traveller's beloved native land. The paragraph is one of the happiest examples of his prose style:

> Now shape we our course for England. Beloued soile: as in site
>
> . . . *wholly from all the world disioynd*:[27]
>
> so in thy felicities. The Sommer burnes thee not, nor the Winter benums thee: defended by the Sea from wastfull incursions, and by the valour of thy sonnes from hostile inuasions. All other Countries are in some thinges defectiue, when thou a provident parent, doest minister vnto thine whatsoeuer is vsefull: forrein additions but onely tending to vanity, and luxury. Vertue in thee at the least is praised; and vices are branded with their names, if not pursued with punishments. That *Vlysses*
>
> *Who knew many mens manners, and saw many Cities*:[28]
>
> if as sound in iudgement as ripe in experience, will confesse thee to be the land that floweth with milke and honey.[29]

The sailes "now swelling with the first breath of May," the ship passed on the right Cyprus, sacred to Venus. After many days against contrary winds, they made out Crete, then known as 'Candy,' which like Cyprus called up rich classical associations.[30] Approaching Zante they were frightened by the sails of five supposed pirates, and were immensely relieved when they turned out to be English. Later they watched the flagship of the little squadron give chase to what was probably a real pirate. By then they were passing south of Sicily and leaving

27 The Latin, Vergil, Eclogue I, is given in the left margin.

28 The Latin, Homer, *Odyssey*, Book I, is given in the left margin.

29 *A Relation*, p. 218.

30 Sandys uses Pliny and others here. The ship evidently did not put into any port on Crete, though Sandys does describe (p. 226) country dancing on the island as though he had seen it.

Malta behind on the left, though they had originally hoped to be set ashore at Messina. At just the moment when Sandys was reconciled to the tedious voyage round to England, the wind changed and blew so fiercely that the ship had to put about and go in at Malta. This Sunday, 2 June, they entered the harbour of Valetta, saluting the city with eighteen guns.

In six days the ship was cleared and ready to sail, but no entreaty could get Sandys aboard again. Always a poor sailor, he says, he preferred "all hazards and hardnesse whatsoeuer" to so long a voyage at sea. So he was left alone on a little promontory overlooking the city, without provision, and having no idea what to do with himself. After a few hours a local official, apparently an immigration officer, happened by and informed him that on the next day he would have to go to the lazaretto. There he was to be isolated for thirty or forty days to protect the city's inhabitants from possible infection. He was in despair,

> . . . But behold an accident, which I rather thought to be a vision, then (as I found it) reall. My guardian[31] being departed to fetch me some victuals, laid along, and musing on my present condition, a Phalucco arriueth at the place. Out of which there stept two old women; the one made me doubt whether she were so or no, she drew her face into so many formes, and with such antick gestures stared vpon me. These two did spread a *Turkie* carpet on the rocke, and on that a table-cloth, which they furnished with the choicest viands. Anon another arriued, which set a Gallant ashore with his two *Amarosaes*, attired like Nymphs, with lutes in their hands, full of disport and sorcery. For litle would they suffer him to eate, but what he receiued with his mouth from their fingers. Sometimes one would play on the lute whilst the other sang, and laid his head in her lap; their false eies looking vpon him, as if their hearts were troubled with passions. The attending hags had no small part in the comedie, administring matter of mirth with their ridiculous moppings. Who indeed (as I after heard) were their mothers; borne in *Greece*, and by them brought hither to trade amongst the vmarried fraternitie . . .[32]

At length the gentleman, who turned out to be a French captain, came to Sandys and entreated him to partake of the banquet, an invitation which Sandys' stomach persuaded him to accept. The women grew too familiar for either of their liking, Sandys avers. Because they pitied him in his hard lodging, both the captain and the courtesans tried to persuade him to go with them to the city that night, though in doing so they were risking a death penalty to themselves. While they urged,

[31] Presumably the immigration officer.
[32] *A Relation*, p. 227.

however, the "Guardian" returned with a Maltese whose father was English. At length the captain and the women departed, the latter violating all rules of modesty by stripping themselves on the way to shore and leaping into the sea. The captain interceded for Sandys the next day. He was soon admitted to the city, and for three weeks was entertained in the house of the Maltese who had visited him on the rock.

There were many things on Malta to interest Sandys. He discusses at length the Knights of St. John, their fortifications and organization, the escaped slaves of the Mahometans, and a festival he witnessed. But he was probably relieved when, on 24 June, he was permitted to depart.

He set out in a little Neapolitan felucca, rowed by five men and not twice as big as a wherry. The voyage began about sunset (to be on guard against the Turks). They reached Sicily early the next morning. Sicily, queen of the Mediterranean islands, was of course a fit subject for historical exposition and mythological allusion. The traveller recalled its Greek, Roman, and Carthaginian associations, its great Epicharmus in comedy, Theocritus in the pastoral eclogue, Empedocles in philosophy, and Euclid and Archimedes in mathematics. On 25 June the little ship rounded Cape Passaro, passing close under the cliff called Muro del Porco, a great place for tuna fishing. Here Sandys pauses to tell two or three lurid tales of tainted human flesh being barrelled and sold as tuna.[33] Soldiers who ate one shipment of it broke out in loathsome ulcers. This may be the explanation of the pox, Sandys suggests,[34] for various authorities have said that contagion and not the impurity of women is its real cause.

Syracuse, his first landing place, brings the usual flood of classical allusion.[35] One day there, and the ship put to sea again, arriving at

[33] *A Relation*, pp. 238–9. Bacon borrows the account from Sandys almost word for word (see R. R. Cawley, *The Voyagers and Elizabethan Drama*, pp. 363 and 363 n.). Most of these tales Sandys recites but does not accept as truth, for they came to him "onely by relation."

[34] Sandys gives Scaliger, Exercise 181, Section 19, as his principal authority. 'Proof' lies in that the West Indians, who were accustomed to cannibalism, were those who had the disease. Sir Thomas Browne, in "Of the Blackness of Negroes," touches on the same theme, which he may have got through Sandys, as he did so many other things (see R. R. Cawley, *The Voyagers and Elizabethan Drama*, p. 363).

[35] Sandys mentions Strabo, Seneca, and Diodorus the Sicilian as source for accounts of Archimedes' engineering skill and the past and present appearance of the city.

Catania before night. Though he had wanted to climb Mt. Aetna, Sandys had to content himself with the view of it for a whole day as they sailed thirty miles along its fringes. He does describe the volcano, bringing in allusions to Empedocles, and quoting from Lucretius, Vergil, and Silius Italicus. Then the ship turned into the haven of Messina. This old city evidently charmed the traveller. Its ancient statues and Roman fountains still gushing are the first of the important remainders of Latin civilization he comments upon. And its fashionable ladies and gentlemen promenading in the evening along the Marine are among the examples of its pleasant and gracious life in his own time. He does not too much approve of their theatres, for the women's parts, acted by women, are "too naturally passionated."

Scylla and Charybdis, near Messina as they sail north, of course evoke comment and literary allusion. Sandys points out, however, that actually they are twelve miles apart and not at all the hazard they have been reputed to be. Rather, he suspects, there have been many Charybdises "occasioned by the recoiling streams." Then he turns to the volcano of Stromboli, called by the Roman Catholics the jaws of Hell. In this latter connection he is reminded of a wild tale passed on to him by an old Englishman he met in Naples, of an English merchant named Gresham who nearly made the Devil's acquaintance on this spot.[36] Sandys repeats the story with his usual appreciation of the folk legend.

For a day the little craft lay becalmed at Scylla. Sandys' travelling companions he now mentions as Spaniards, who were very harsh to him,

> . . . (for in these parts they detest the English, & think vs not Christian) but when vpon demand I told them I was no *Lutheran*, they exceeded on the other side in their curtesie. One of thē had bin in the voyage of eighty eight, and would say that it was not we, but the windes that ouerthrew them. . . .

On 3 July they sailed again, landing that night at Aupage. The dangerous tarantulas, very common in this part of Calabria, fascinated the traveller. But no people disgusted Sandys more than the savage Calabrians, who were worse in thievery and murder than any infidels he had seen. Fearing to travel overland, the party continued in their small craft, pulling it up on a beach at night, and sleeping in their clothes on the sand. Food was little better than lodging, tuna, onions,

[36] *A Relation*, pp. 248–9. This is a good example of the type of tale Sandys continues to gather and relate in the 1632 edition of his Ovid. See Chapter VIII below.

cucumbers, and melons being the ordinary diet. Sandys appears to have been more amused than offended by one ignorant Calabrian who

> . . . hearing that I was an *English* man, came to me, and would needs persuade me that I had insight in magicke, for that Earle *Bothel*[37] was my country man, who liues at *Naples*, and is in these parts famous for suspected negromancy. He told me that he had treasure hidden in his house: the quantitie and qualitie shewne him by a boy, vpon the coniuration of a Knight of *Malta*: and offered to share it betweene vs, if I could help him vnto it. But I answered, that in *England* we were at defiance with the diuell, and that he would do nothing for vs.[38]

On 6 July they landed at Paula, the next day at Belvidere and then at Liscare. On 8 July they crossed the bay of Salerno; that night, reaching a small village, they slept in the local chapel. The next morning, on reaching the Cape, Sandys was reminded of the Sirens who were supposed to have lived there. Near Capri he remarked on the salubrious climate of the famous isle. Everywhere now were reminders of the Roman empire. By noon, having run before the wind all the way, the craft arrived at Naples.[39]

[37] Francis Stewart Hepburn, fifth Earl of Bothwell, a stormy petrel of Scottish politics, died in extreme poverty in Naples in 1624.

[38] *A Relation*, p. 250. This is one of the rare places in all Sandys' prose where there is even a hint of the humorous.

[39] Mr. Esmond S. de Beer, in "George Sandys's Account of Campania," *The Library*, 4th series, XVII (March 1937), 458-65, has given an excellent discussion of Sandys' sources and method in the remainder (he covers pp. 251–304) of the travels. Though Sandys must have visited the places he says he did, his account here is largely derivative, apparently in greater proportion than in the Turkish, Egyptian, and Palestinian portions. For all but three passages of any moment Mr. de Beer has found sources (p. 461). He illustrates in parallel columns how Sandys borrows a phrase, sentence, or fact first from one source, then from another, but ingeniously moulding the materials into his own condensed, balanced structure. Sandys' principal sources in this section were (1) J. C. Capacius (G. C. Cappaccio) *Neapolitanæ historiae . . . tomus primus* (1607); (2) S. Mazzella, *Sito, et antichita della Citta di Possvolo, e del svo amenissimo distretto, con la Descrittione di tutti i luoghi notabili, e degni di memoria, e di Cuma, e di Baia, e di Miseno, e degli altri luoghi conuicini* (1606, or earlier editions of 1591 or 1595); (3) Franciscus Schottus, *Itinerarium nobiliorum Italiae regionum, urbium, oppidorum, et locorum* (1601 or 1610 ed.); (4) an anonymous 'Relatione di Napoli,' dated 1 April 1579, presumably first printed in *Thesoro politico* (1589; there are several later editions, *e.g.*, 1602 and 1610, the latter with a parallel Latin translation).

Sandys' engravings illustrating this portion of the book are all derivative,

Now Sandys was in real tourist country. Other contemporary Englishmen, such as Fynes Moryson[40] in 1594 and William Lithgow[41] in 1614, visited the same places. Continental Europeans had in the preceding generation written many guidebooks[42] for the traveller in this particular region. Though he occasionally inserts a story or gives a description which has the colour of personal experience, Sandys here in Italy allows his account to become almost a mere guidebook. The urbanity of his style, however, saves its literary quality.

An elaborate history of Naples and an account of its present state introduce the reader to Campania. "*Naples* is the pleasantest of Cities, if not the most beautifull," he observes in describing its physical features. He was impressed by the handsome faces and fine clothing of all classes, for silk was everyday wear for even the wife of the meanest artificer. Quoting the Latin and more recent Neapolitan poets on almost each spot visited, Sandys demonstrates the richness of literary and historical association in this region.[43]

Vesuvius, the grotto of Pausilype, and the Lake of Agnano astonished him, despite his knowledge and use of ancient sources on these works

from various sources. Schott, Mazella, Cappaccio, and probably G. Braun and F. Hohenberg, *Civitas orbis terrarum* (1576–1618), LXV, are among them. These sources owe much to each other or to common ancestors. In many cases it is impossible to determine the exact source.

[40] *An Itinerary*, I, 225–8; III, 455; IV, 74–103, etc. Moryson's account of Naples is even more like a guidebook than Sandys'.

[41] *Rare Adventures*, pp. 350–3. Lithgow is much more brief than Sandys. Neither Moryson nor Lithgow uses the classical allusion as Sandys does (here more frequently than before.)

[42] Many of which he used, of course. See note 39 above.

[43] In this section Sandys quotes and translates from Alcadinus, Appian, Athenæus, Augerianus, Ausonius, Borgius, Cicero, "Corona Pighius" (actually S. V. Pighius, via Schott, was the source), "Dion," Donatus Franciscus, Eustatius, Flaminius, Franciscus Vivius, [Gabriel] Altius, Homer, Horace, Juvenal, Lucan, Martial, Ovid, Petronius, Pomponius Lætus, Pontanus, "Portacel," Propertius, Prudentius, Rota, Rutilius Numantianus, Sannizarius, Scaliger, Seneca, Sidonius, Silius Italicus, Tullius Laura [or Laurea], and Vergil. Alcadinus, Eustatius, Vivius, Pomponius Lætus, and Tullius Laura were at least second hand from Mazzella (I used the 1591 and 1606 editions). Most of the others are to be found in such a compendium as *Corpus Omnium Veterum Poetarum Latinorum Secundum Seriem Temporum . . .* (Geneva, 1611; Ben Jonson's autograph is on the flyleaf of the copy in the British Museum) or such as *Delitiæ. CC. Italorum Poetarum, Huius Superiorisque Aevi illustrum, Collectore Ranutio Ghero . . .* (1608), or in some of his other guidebook sources mentioned above.

of nature. Like others before and after him, [44] at Charon's Cave he tried the experiment of thrusting a dog in the vaporous mouth

> . . . which we no sooner had thrust in, but without crying, or otherwise struggling then if shot to the heart, his tongue hung out, and his eyes setled in his head, to our no small amazement. Foorthwith drawne out; starke, to our seeming without shew of life, we threw him into the lake; where anon he recovered, and swimming to the shore, ran crying away as fast as he could, to the not farre distant *Osteria*: where they get no small part of their living by shewing this place vnto forreiners. And it is a sport to see how the dogs thereabout will steale away, and scud to the tops of the mountaines, at the approach of a stranger . . .[45]

From the Cave of Charon the traveller went on to Vulcan's Court, where volcanic fires and smoke rose continually. The rich minerals of this fertile soil interested him most. But he could not resist telling a Faustian tale of a Neapolitan student who sold himself to the devils dwelling in this entrance to the lower world, concluding with the comment,

> . . . But if this be hell, what a desperate end made that vnhappie *German*, who not long since slipt into these fornaces? or what had his poore horse committed, that fell in with him, that he should be damned; at least retained in Purgatory? The matter that doth nourish these subterranean fires, is sulfure and Bitumen. But there it is fed by the later, where the flame doth mixe with the water, which is not by water to be extinguished: approoued by the composition of those *ignes admirables* . . .[46]

A near-by amphitheatre recalls gladiatoral combats, which Sandys illustrates by an engraving of the statue[47] of a gladiator with an amphitheatre in the background. He likewise recalls the story of Androcles

[44] Compare, for example, Moryson's *An Itinerary*, I, 242 and Lithgow's *Rare Adventures*, pp. 353–4.

[45] *A Relation*, p. 267. Sandys cites the experience of "Corona Pighius" (see Esmond S. de Beer, p. 460 n.) in exploring the cave without loss of consciousness, and concludes that the vapour is effective only close to the ground, and especially upon downward looking creatures such as dogs. For proof that he is generally correct in this belief, see the discussion of the Grotto del Cane in H. M. Smith, ed., *John Evelyn in Naples* (Oxford, 1914), pp. 28–30.

[46] *A Relation*, p. 269. Cf. *John Evelyn in Naples*, pp. 28–30.

[47] *Ibid.*, p. 271. This statue, in Sandys' time called 'Commodus,' was preserved in the courtyard of the Farnese Palace in Rome (now in the Naples Museum). Sandys' view of it is copied from an engraving by G. B. Cavalieri (*c.* 1560), or from a copy of Cavalieri (*e.g.*, that in L. della Vaccaria, *Antiquarum statuarum urbis Romae . . . icones*, part three [1584]). See Esmond S. de Beer, p. 464.

and the lion. Puteoli, Cicero's Villa, the Lake of Avernus, and the ruins of Cumae are typical tourist spots which elicit comment and allusion. Baiæ, celebrated by the poets from Horace to the Neapolitans of Sandys' own day, receives attention, though chiefly as "an egregious example, that . . . the works of mens hands [are] as frail as the workmen."[48] Thus for days Sandys wandered about the countryside around Naples, "clothed with Natures most rich and beautifull tapestry."[49]

Dissuaded from departing overland from Naples because of the "insalubrious season,"[50] Sandys embarked on a felucca for Neptune.[51] The little vessel was almost lost in heavy seas in the Bay of Putzol, but Sandys was rescued by a French fisherman and carried to Prochita, a small island fourteen miles from Naples. In a day or two he continued up the coast, eventually reaching the ancient town of Neptune. A night's stay here, and he was on the road to Rome. He and a guide acquired in Neptune rode first through an extensive wood and then across a great champagne rich in wines and grain. In the heat of the day they rested at a small inn, and in the cool of the evening rode into the Eternal City.

Any Protestant Englishman in Rome was in grave danger of the Inquisition. Sandys stayed therefore only four days—as long as he dared. Even in this time he might have been in trouble but for "the faith and care" of Nicholas Fitzherbert,[52] an Oxonian who had years before come to Rome as secretary to Cardinal Allen. During the precious four days Fitzherbert showed Sandys the ancient and modern wonders of the city. Then the traveller moved on to Siena, Florence, Bologna, and Ferrara, but on their Renaissance glories he makes no comment.[53] Embarking

[48] *Ibid.*, p. 292.

[49] *Ibid.*, p. 300.

[50] *Ibid.*, p. 301.

[51] Or Nettuno, a few miles from Anzio.

[52] Attainted in 1580 for his activity in raising money for the college at Rheims, by 1587 he was in Rome as Cardinal Allen's secretary. After the death of Allen he quarrelled with Parsons, who became leader of the English Jesuits there. Nicholas Fitzherbert in his old age was anxious to return to England, and entered into negotiations with Sir Henry Wotton at Venice with this end in view. He was used as a means of sending money to English prisoners of the Inquisition (see Logan P. Smith, *Life and Letters of Sir Henry Wotton*, I, 65, 442). Fitzherbert's book on Oxford, . . . *Oxonienses in Anglia Academiae Descriptio* . . ., had been published in Rome in 1602. Sandys' tribute to Fitzherbert incurred no danger for the latter from the Inquisition, for the expatriate had died in 1612.

[53] "Hauing seen *Florence, Bolonia,* and *Ferrara,*" is all Sandys says. Of Rome he gives no description because its features were already well known.

on the river Po, he returned to Venice, here ending his account where he had begun it.

There is no indication how long he remained in Venice. The attractions of the lively English colony[54] and fine libraries may have kept him several months. It may have been here at this time that he collected the Latin and Italian volumes he was to use not only in *A Relation* but also in the later commentary on Ovid's *Metamorphoses*. That he returned to England a widely read man, learned in many languages, would seem more logically attributable to a stay in Venice than to all his wanderings through the Mediterranean world.

At all events he was probably back in England by March 1612, when his name appears among the adventurers in the third charter of King James to the Virginia Company. Between that date and its publication three years later, Sandys prepared his work. His method is of interest because it differs somewhat from that of other travellers of his time.

He certainly began with the journal or diary he himself[55] kept. On this chronological frame he built from varied materials. Keen observation, careful reporting, and unusual interest in folk habit had made his notes rich to begin with. To them he added the accounts, as we have noticed above, of the ancient geographers, the church fathers, and the best observers among his older contemporaries and immediate predecessors of the Continent. As final decoration he embroidered into the text the always apt quotations from Latin authors, decoration which is in effect a far more integral part of the book than some of the historical summaries and second-hand descriptions. But all these elements which went into the work must be considered in some detail.

A Relation has in common with its immediate English predecessors among travel books little more than some of the places visited and certain recorded reactions natural to travellers from the same island kingdom. With particular Continental books, however, even at first glance, it has more kinship. Belon, Busbecq, Botero, Dousa, and Gyllius, it is true, though he used them extensively, have few resemblances beyond

[54] Sir Dudley Carleton (1573–1632) was then Ambassador at Venice. Sandys may have been one of the English gentlemen who were permitted to see the "Jewels of the Sanctuary and armoury of Ten" at the request of the English Ambassador (23 September 1611; see *Calendar of State Papers, Venetian, 1610–1613*, No. 337). Carleton was to be an official of the Privy Chamber and later Secretary of State in Sandys' own time at court.

[55] This is obvious especially in the places where his excursions are haphazardly taken within the vicinity of a particular city. Here his order is peculiarly his own.

generally similar fold-in maps and certain data. But Zuallardo's *Il Devotissimo Viaggio* . . . (1587) supplied some facts and all the plates for Sandys' Book III. Isaac Casaubon's edition, with commentaries, of Strabo's . . . *Rerum Geographicarum* . . . (1587) furnished facts and employed classical quotations and marginal notes giving sources somewhat as Sandys did. Mazella's *Sito, et Antichita Della Citta Di Pozzvolo* . . . (1606) uses classical quotation and reference even more like Sandys'. And Capaccio's *La Vera Antichita* . . . (1607, Italian) or *Neapolitanæ historiæ* . . . (1607, Latin) employed many Latin quotations and epitaphs, marginal notes, illustrations (in several cases identical), and even a condensed, balanced style immediately reminiscent of Sandys. Sandys almost surely owed certain ideas of form to Capaccio and perhaps to others of these Italian guidebooks he had open before him as he wrote.

The verses he employs, varying from one line to twenty-nine, are borrowed from poets of many kinds ranging chronologically from Homer (in Latin) to the sixteenth century Julius Caesar Scaliger. The formidable list includes, in addition to those already mentioned in the account of Campania,[56] Agathius, Alciatus, Alphaeus, Altius, Callimachus, Choerilus, Claudianus, Dionysius, Euripides, Eustatius, Flaminius, Hermesianax, Lucretius, Maninus, Mantuanus, Menander, Muretus, "Paul. Partaroll," Persius, Plutarch (in *Moralia*), Pope John XXII, St. Jerome (for the epitaphs on Paula's tomb), "Sibylline Prophecies," Valerius Flaccus, and Tzetzes. The more obscure names are usually those of Neapolitan or other Italian poets of the sixteenth century. Sandys occasionally found them already quoted in his guidebook sources, particularly in Capaccio and Mazzella.[57]

In addition to poets and writers of guidebooks, ancient geographers and historians, church fathers and classical philosophers, Sandys drew from such varied authority as Avicenna, Cassiodorus, Christophorus Helvicus, Dictys Cretensis, Diodorus Siculus, Josephus, Leo Africanus, Pancirollus, and Vives. It is not remarkable therefore that, soon after

[56] See note 43 above. Of course many of the thirty-five poets quoted in the Neapolitan part of Book IV were also quoted in other parts of *A Relation*. *E.g.*, Homer, Horace, Juvenal, Lucan, Ovid, Scaliger, Seneca, and Vergil are to be found in all parts of the volume.

[57] In Mazzella's *Sito, et Antichita Della Citta di Pozzvolo* . . . (1606), Pomponius, Vivius, Alcadinus, Eustatius and others of Sandys' 'sources' are quoted and a score of the others referred to. Sandys probably kept by him, too, one or more of the compendiums, or anthologies, of old poets or modern, such as *Corpus Omnium Veterum Poetarum Latinorum* . . . (Geneva, 1611), in which one volume the majority of the quotations he uses are to be found.

the publication of the first edition of *A Relation*, its author's reputation as one of the learned men of his day was firmly established.

Though the account is heavily weighted with these references, actually Sandys' prose is a real achievement. As the reader has noticed from the examples quoted above, it is condensed and balanced, with an easy rhythm[58] peculiarly its own. This laconic style, dignified in itself, is particularly suitable for the expression of an author who aims at giving a simple yet scholarly account. Sandys' narrative sentence has not the liveliness[59] of those of Lithgow or Coryat, but he attempted something quite different from what they produced.

The place of the poetic quotations in the text and the quality of Sandy's poetic translation are worth further comment. Even less than in his models the Italian guidebooks does Sandys introduce any verse for itself. The lines are carefully and aptly chosen, fitting well into the prose body of the account and quite often providing most felicitous climaxes for discussions of particular situations. They are by no means a mere parade of learning, therefore, though no English predecessor of Sandys had used them to anything like the extent he did.

As poetry Sandys' translations of the Latin usually leave much to be desired. Almost always he renders the classical measure in the decasyllabic couplet. As he did later in his Ovid, he translates as literally as possible, keeping his English version of one Latin line within the compass of one English line. The result is the stiffness Dryden was later to complain of in Sandys' Ovid. Very occasionally, as in a few of the passages quoted above, he achieves real poetry. The place of these translations in the development of Sandys' couplet will be discussed in a later chapter. In passing one may add only that Sandys included here many selections[60] from Ovid's *Metamorphoses*, the couplet translations of which are interesting and perhaps significant as examples of the first stage in the development of the Ovid toward its final form in his 1632 edition.

[58] As noticed above, it may owe something to Capaccio or other Italian writers of guidebooks.

[59] The homely, virile vernacular of Coryat and Lithgow (often loose in structure) is replaced by a still virile but more stately sentence, not stiffly literary, but capable of carrying a heavier burden of ideas and information in less space than the form these two travellers had used.

[60] Professor W. G. Rice, "Early English Travelers to Greece and the Levant," pp. 227–8, makes some comparison of these early versions of Sandys' Ovid with the 1626 edition, and concludes that the frequent use of Ovid in the 1615 *Relation* may have suggested the translation of the whole work to Sandys. For further discussion of this matter, see Chapter VIII below.

Sandys' enormous interest in folk ways and folk lore has been referred to several times. Wherever he went the traveller was keenly observant of wedding and funeral customs, of dress, and of manners, and frequently gives them as much space as he does the description of a city. An anecdote illustrative of local superstition or legend he passes along to his reader with gusto. It is apparent that he enjoyed a tall tale for itself and at the same time was conscious of its significance as characteristic of a people or place.

The accuracy of Sandys' observation was the quality most frequently commented upon by later writers[61] interested in travel, but the variety is equally noteworthy. Out-of-the-ordinary bits of information and description turn up most unexpectedly. The traveller's genuine[62] archaeological interest, which is partly the Renaissance curiosity about everything, manifested itself in collecting statuettes as well as in viewing Troy or climbing among the Pyramids or the ruins of island palaces. Commerce and agriculture, governments and armies of his own time were equally as intriguing. Yet despite all this diversity of detail, the themes of "threatening instructions" and the "frailty of man" announced in the Dedication hold the book together and give it a unity which is more than the thread of the narrative of a planned journey.

Nothing in any earlier English travel book[63] could approach in attractiveness the fine copperplate illustrations contained in Sandys' volume. Zuallardo had supplied those in Book III, but engravings in other books came from various sources, such as the Neapolitan travel-books for many of those in Book IV. And perhaps some, such as the plate[64] of the Sphinx and Pyramids in Book II showing European travellers in the costume of the day riding in front of these ancient monuments, may have been drawn from Sandys' own description. To

[61] *E.g.*, see Thomas Fuller, *The History of the Worthies of England* (1840 ed., London), III, 434; John E. Bailey, *The Life of Thomas Fuller* (London, 1874), p. 484, and Peter Mundy, *The Travels of . . . in Europe and Asia . . .* (Hakluyt Society, Vol. I, 1907), pp. 30 n., 192 n. Or among recent commentators, S. G. Chew, *The Crescent and the Rose*, p. 43.

[62] Both Warner G. Rice, pp. 226–33 and Samuel G. Chew, p. 42 feel that he is much more interested in the present than the past, and Professor Rice seems to feel that there is no genuine interest in classical antiquity (see note 29, Chapter III above).

[63] Most of them are content with a frontispiece and/or maps. A few use crude woodcuts or engravings.

[64] Page 128. There are apparently six Europeans and three native guides in the picture.

the dignity of its Dedication and avowed tradition-of-service aim, its accurate observation of famous places, and its scholarly tone and ornament, Sandys shrewdly added that which would catch the eye.

He evidently intended it to sell, and it did. In 1621 appeared the second edition, which shows in the correction of errata and alteration of verse translation[65] a careful revision but which in pagination and format is almost identical with the first edition. The 1627, 1632, and 1637 versions are little more than reprints of the earlier editions, with essentially the same pagination. In 1652 appeared an edition with the same plates but entirely new pagination. This in turn was the basis for the reprint editions in 1658, 1670, and 1673. In addition to the nine complete English editions, much of the Turkish and Palestinian sections appeared in *Purchas His Pilgrimes* . . . in 1625,[66] and the whole book in Dutch editions in 1654[67] and 1665[68] and a German edition in 1669.[69]

As a source book its use was enormous. Francis Bacon[70] in *Sylva Sylvarum*, Sir Thomas Browne[71] in various places, Robert Burton[72] in the *Anatomy*, Abraham Cowley[73] in "The Plagues of Egypt." Thomas Fuller[74] in *A Pisgah-Sight of Palestine*, Ben Jonson[75] in various places

65 A comparison page by page of the 1615, 1621, 1627, 1632, 1637, and 1673 editions reveals that no changes of importance occur after the 1621 except a complete rearrangement, in 1627, of a couplet on p. 264 of this and the 1615 and 1621 editions. There are many changes in phrase and complete line between 1615 and 1621: *e.g.*, on pp. 33, 83, 84, 90, 91, 98, 137, 151, 228, 236, 240, 266, 273, 280, 293, 299, 303. The spelling in the 1673 is considerably more modern than in the others. Other differences, however, appear to be proofreader's or typesetter's oversights or errors, auditory or visual.

66 Pages 1274–1333. Chapter VIII. *A Relation of a Iourney begunne*, Anno. Dom 1610 *written by Master George Sandys, and heere contracted.* Parts of it also appeared later in 1705 in John Harris, *Navigantium atque Itineratium Biblioteca* . . . (London).

67 Amsterdam. *Sandys Voyagien*. . . . The engraved title page gives 1654, the letter-press 1653 as the date. There is also a Utrecht 1654 edition.

68 Amsterdam.

69 Frankfurt. *Sandys Reisen* . . .

70 See R. R. Cawley, *The Voyagers and Elizabethan Drama, passim*, for some of the examples of Bacon's use of Sandys.

71 See Cawley, *Voyagers, passim*, and Cawley, "Sir Thomas Browne and His Reading," *PMLA*, XLVIII (1933), 430, note 31, etc., for Browne and Sandys.

72 See Cawley, *Voyagers*, p. 160, and Cawley, "Burton, Bacon, and Sandys," *MLN*, LVI (No. 4, 1941), 271–3.

73 See Cawley, *Voyagers*, p. 39 n.

74 *Ibid.*, p. 163 n.

75 *Ibid.*, p. 122 n.

(including "Every Man out of His Humour"), and John Milton[76] are only a few[77] of those who drew from *A Relation* in the century in which it appeared. Other travellers, such as Peter Mundy,[78] incorporated long passages from it into their own accounts, usually giving Sandys due credit.

A Relation of a Iourney has a significant[79] place in the Elizabethan travel literature tradition. Before its appearance there were two principal types of writing in the genre: on the one hand was the diary, up to and including the work of Tom Coryat. On the other was the treatise, such as the work of Thomas on Italy, Giles Fletcher on Russia, Wotton on Christendom, Knolles on the Turks, whether as history or politics or both; and Edwin Sandys, John Barclay, and Purchas (*his Pilgrimage*) in the special treatise of religion and manners. Fynes Moryson and Sandys are almost parallel[80] in working out the full combination of travel and formal geography and history, but Sandys further adds the continuous flow of literary allusions. In other words, Sandys brought to maturity the cultivated travel-narrative. After him Thomas Herbert and Blount and Evelyn seem a natural continuation.

[76] For Milton's indebtedness to Sandys' *Relation*, see Douglas Bush, *Mythology and the Renaissance Tradition* (Minneapolis, 1932), pp. 256, 259, 272, 274; Frank A. Patterson, Gen. Ed., *Works of John Milton* (New York, 1931–8), I, 9; II, 22, 59; III, 22; George W. Whiting, *Milton's Literary Milieu* (Chapel Hill, 1939), pp. 94, 109, 119; and Cawley, *Voyagers*, p. 254 n.

[77] Others, with the parallel material mentioned by R. R. Cawley in *The Voyagers*, are Bacon, Benlowes, Dekker, Phineas Fletcher, Lower, Marston, and Shirley.

[78] See Sir Richard C. Temple, ed., *Travels of Peter Mundy* (Vol. I, Cambridge, 1907), *passim*.

[79] For much of the observation made in the following paragraph I am indebted to Professor George B. Parks of Queens College, New York, whose work on the Elizabethan travellers is continuing in a history of Elizabethan travel literature.

[80] Moryson's *An Itinerary* was first published in 1617, but his travels had occurred many years before Sandys'. He "wrote at leasure" between 1609 and 1617 (see *An Itinerary*, I, XIV).

V

VIRGINIA ADVENTURER, 1612–1621

Little evidence remains, documentary or otherwise, to indicate the manner, not to mention the detail, of Sandys' personal life during the years elapsing between his return from his Mediterranean travels and his embarkation for Virginia. The legal matters already mentioned involving his permanently estranged wife, the publication of two books, and his activities in the Virginia and Bermuda companies are all that we know positively about him. Certain surmises of other activities may reasonably be made, however, from such things as the implications of the subject matter and dedications of his books, or from the verses addressed to him by a more famous poet.

The learned and undoubtedly weary traveller reached his native and "Beloved soil" to be confronted first with the probably not unexpected news of the death of his mother, who had survived the Archbishop by more than twenty-two years. Her legacy to this youngest son was small, perhaps partially because she thought there was little likelihood of his surviving his dangerous journey. George shared with the brothers closest to him in age, Henry and Thomas, the oldest son Sir Samuel being the residuary legatee and executor. Along with his brothers and brothers-in-law he received a black cloak and a ring of four "angells in weight," and like his brothers certain pecuniary benefit—"To my son, George Sandys £200, if he return with life within one year if I be then dead."[1]

There can be little doubt that George settled in southern England. The majority if not all of his closer kin were now there or in the Midlands. His mother's relatives, including his uncles and cousins, and his brother Sir Edwin and his family, lived in Kent.[2] His brother

[1] This is the wording of an abstract of "The will of Cicely Sandys, widow of Archbishop Sandys," from records of the Prerogative Court of Canterbury, 15 Wood, Somerset House, London. See Appendix E.

[2] See Chapter II above, notes 72, 86, and Chapter VI, p. 119 below. Margaret, daughter of Sir Samuel Sandys, probably married Sir Francis Wyatt in 1618 (see articles on Sir Francis in *D.A.B.* and *D.N.B.*), and may have settled immediately at Boxley Abbey in Kent, though her husband did not inherit the estate until 1624.

Thomas had established himself in London and was rearing a family, including a son named George.[3] His brother Henry, who may have taken Holy orders,[4] married into a Northamptonshire family and apparently lived near his wife's relatives. His brother Sir Myles, evidently very close to him in personal and in business relations,[5] lived at Wimberton, Isle of Ely, and in 1614 with Sir Francis Bacon represented the University of Cambridge[6] in Parliament. Sir Myles had become a baronet in 1612.[7] The oldest brother Sir Samuel resided primarily at Ombersley in Worcestershire, representing the county in Parliament in 1615 and 1620 and serving as its sheriff in 1618.[8] And Sir Samuel's daughter Anne, born in 1594, was probably married during this period to Sir Francis Wenman of Carswell, Oxfordshire.[9] Proof exists that George Sandys spent much time with his nieces, the sisters Margaret Wyatt and Anne Wenman, in the period after his return from America. It is entirely possible if not probable that the habit of visiting them was formed in these earlier years.

[3] See Henry St. George and Richard St. George, *The Visitation of London, Anno Domini 1633, 1634, and 1635*, Vol. II, edited by Jos. J. Howard (London, 1883), p. 228, for the offspring of the Archbishop, with Thomas Sandys' progeny. Thomas had married Margaret, daughter of Robert Tyas of the Wardrobe. Their second son was George, probably the George Sandys who received his B.A., 1624/25; M.A., 1628 from Sidney College, Cambridge, and was Rector of Wellersley (or Willersley, see PRO.E 334/19/pt. 1, Book of First Fruits, 4 January, 1630/31) from 1630–c. 1642 (see John and J. A. Venn, *Cambridge University, The Book of Matriculation and Degrees, 1544–1659* [Cambridge, 1913], p. 589).

[4] Mr. Malcolm Sands Wilson of New York City has supplied the present writer with considerable data concerning his supposititious ancestor, the Reverend Henry Sandys or Sandes, possible sixth son of the Archbishop. See also Malcolm Sands Wilson, compiler, *Descendants of James Sands of Block Island* (privately printed, New York, 1949), pp. 66 ff. For Henry's wife and children, see E. S. Sandys, *The Sandys Family*, I, 343, Additional Note 143.

[5] See Chapter II, notes 67, 80, above, and (George's letter to Sir Myles) Chapter VI, p. 119 below.

[6] See John Chamberlain to Sir Dudley Carleton 14 April 1614 (in N. E. McClure, ed. *The Letters of John Chamberlain* [2 vols., Philadelphia, 1939], I, 525), and *Virginia Magazine*, XXIX (April 1921), 242.

[7] 25 November (see *Virginia Magazine*, XXIX [April 1921], 242).

[8] Sir Samuel also held manors in Essex and in Yorkshire. See *Virginia Magazine*, XXIX (April 1921), 235, and T. R. Nash, *Collections for the History of Worcestershire* (2 vols., London, 1782), II, 222.

[9] See E. S. Sandys, *The Family of Sandys*, Pedigree C, and Comley Vivian, *The Sandys Family*, pp. 186–7. Listed here also are the other children of Sir Samuel Sandys.

That he was spending most of his time in London seems obvious, too, for his two books of this period were published there, he attended the meetings of the Virginia Company, and his dedication to Prince Charles in 1615 and the familiar lines addressed to him by Michael Drayton in 1621 would indicate that he was well acquainted in the court group within the city. His wife was gone from his personal life. Apparently his contemporaries of these years saw him as a sober, erudite gentleman of excellent family and some political connection, a man devoted to reading in the ancients and to composing or translating into English verse. His recorded travels had shown him resourceful in the unexpected and dangerous situation, and evidence now lost had demonstrated that he could wield his pen effectively in prose political propaganda as well as in picturesque narrative.

Most of the extant information regarding George Sandys during the decade after his return from his Mediterranean tour comes from the records of the joint stock company promoting colonization in America. He appears to have had connections with the Virginia Company of London and its sister group, the Bermuda Company, for at least ten years before the records show him active in their councils. By 1607 a "George Sandys, gentleman,"[10] is listed among the persons to whom the "Second Virginia Charter" was given by James I. Among others also listed here are his brothers Sir Edwin and Sir Samuel, Henry and Thomas,[11] and his nephew Richard Sandys.[12] In 1612, when the "Third Charter" was granted,[13] the name of George Sandys appears among the "Esquires"[14] on the list of stockholders. It was the policy of the leading spirits of the Company to persuade as many of their own blood relations, connections, and friends as possible to take out shares

10 See Brown, *Genesis*, II, 219. On later charters his name appears, usually in close proximity to that of his brothers Henry and Thomas, as "George Sandys, Esq." Several other brothers are listed in this 1609 charter, but Thomas and Henry appear in one place as "Esquires," and George some spaces below them with the simpler "Gentleman." Though another George Sandys may be the person referred to, in the light of this George Sandys' subsequent relation to the Company, it seems likely that he is the man named.

11 Actually a Thomas Sands, "gent." was listed by Captain John Smith (*General Historie* . . . [2 vols., Glasgow, 1907], I, 90) as one of the "first planters" who set out in 1606 for the Colony. If this is George's brother, he returned to England, probably before 1617 (see E. S. Sandys, *The Family of Sandys*, I, 235).

12 "Son of Sir Edwin Sandys," Brown, *Genesis*, I, 214.

13 12 March, 9 James I (1612), Brown, *Genesis*, II, 553.

14 Brown, *Genesis*, II, 546, 549 n.

in the Company, and thus to have voting privileges.[15] George's brother Sir Edwin, who began to take a leading part in the Company's affairs early in its history,[16] undoubtedly was instrumental in the affiliation, or taking out of stock, by the rest of the family. At any rate, as late as 1618 George Sandys' membership in the Company was held by virtue of one share, to the amount of £12 10*s*.[17]

To understand George Sandys' part in the story of the two merchant companies which were to lay the foundation of English colonial empire, it is necessary to follow for a space the story of the development of the Virginia Company of London and the activities of George's brother Sir Edwin in that development. All this is discussed ably and at length elsewhere.[18] Here only its essential outlines will be given.

In 1606, when the Virginia and other settlements were projected by the English, world conditions were much more favourable for colonization than they had been in the preceding generation in Raleigh's day. Though the Sagadahoc planting in Maine in 1606 was abandoned as a failure, the similar plantation in Virginia, first established with a fort at Jamestown in 1607, soon gave evidence that it might become permanent. The first charter of 1606, a royal one, was superseded in 1609 by a second, under which the government of the colony was vested in a corporation known as the "Treasurer and Company of Adventurers and Planters of the City of London for the first colony of Virginia," commonly known as the "Virginia Company."[19] Credit for the improvements in government contained in this charter, as well as for its actual

[15] Minimum holding for membership was a share of £12 10*s*, which entitled the holder to full voting privilege and 100 acres to be patented in Virginia (under stipulated conditions).

[16] See the lists of members in Susan Myra Kingsbury ed., *Records of the Virginia Company of London* (4 vols., Washington, D.C., 1906, 1933, 1935); Brown, *Genesis*, both volumes; and W. F. Craven, *Dissolution of the Virginia Company* (New York, 1932), pp. 146–7. The last work discusses this method of gaining and maintaining control of elections within the Company. Sir Edwin's brother-in-law, his daughter's father-in-law, etc., are among those who appear to have subscribed for stock under his sponsorship.

[17] Kingsbury, III, 88. "A Complete List in Alphabetical Order of the Adventurers to Virginia, with the Severall Amounts of their Holding [1618] (Manchester Papers, PRO, No. 241, List of Records No. 58).

[18] Primarily in C. M. Andrews, *Colonial Period of American History* (4 vols., New Haven, 1934), I, 98–109 and Craven, *Dissolution*. See Appendices F and G below for observations as to certain potential weaknesses in these two interpretations.

[19] See Andrews, I, 103.

phraseology, is usually given to Sir Edwin Sandys,[20] who had been actively interested in colonization and had been a member of the royal council for Virginia from 1606.

Sir Edwin's new company had at its head an official called a Treasurer, instead of a Governor, as he was termed in other commercial empire-building corporations of the period. This officer, who under the same title had earlier been appointed by the Crown, had now to be elected by a majority vote of the members. Eventually this share-holding body consisted of 659 individuals and 56 London merchant companies. The 1609 charter had made it a joint-stock company,[21] the powers of government being lodged with the Treasurer and a council but not with the Company as a whole. Sir Thomas Smith, the greatest English merchant of his day, was during this period[22] Treasurer of the corporation.

In Virginia itself the struggling colony, under resident governors[23] Sir Thomas Gates, Lord de la Warr, Captain George Percy, and Sir Thomas Dale, had alternated between despair and hope. Once, desperate and starving, the whole body of settlers had embarked for England, only to meet a relief fleet at the mouth of the James. On the whole, however, the colony prospered and set its feet firmly in the soil of the New World.

By 1612 all interested parties of the Company in London seemed to feel the need for a further broadening of the charter. The colony apparently was past the experimental stage. The resulting new charter of 1612 covered such matters as (1) an extension of the boundaries of Virginia to include the Bermuda Islands, (2) the setting up of four great courts or sessions a year, when "the generality" might have a greater voice than ever before in the government, (3) a grant of greater power to colonial courts in apprehending and punishing offenders, and (4) a permission to the Company to hold one or more great lotteries a year to raise badly needed funds.[24] These new policies or extensions of authority were generally good; but certain evils came with both the 1609 and 1612

[20] Andrews, I, 102; Brown, *Genesis*, I, 47.

[21] For a discussion of this and similar companies, see W. R. Scott, *The Constitution and Finance of English, Scottish and Irish Joint-Stock Companies to 1720* (3 vols., Cambridge, 1910–12).

[22] He was appointed Treasurer by the 1609 charter, but the same charter authorizes the election by members. See Brown, *Genesis*, I, 232. He served by election until 1619.

[23] And/or lieutenant-governors.

[24] See Andrews, I, 116; or Kingsbury, I, 71–8. See the latter for a discussion of the organization and business of the Company.

charters, evils inherent in the joint-stock system such as manipulation of voting in the great courts through sale and transfer of stock. And for good or bad, the tremendous increase in powers invested in "the generality" was to lead ultimately to a shift in the character of the company's leadership and control.

Until 1612 Sir Thomas Smith as Treasurer and Sir Edwin Sandys, powerful in the Company as well as in Parliament, had worked together in an apparently entirely amicable fashion. Situations then developed, however, in which Smith, Sandys, and other leaders of the corporation were in violent disagreement, a discord which was to lead finally to the dissolution of the Company. In the years between 1612 and 1618 there had been growing dissatisfaction in the Company's handling of Virginia affairs, apparently with the feeling that the colony was growing too slowly,[25] and also involving alarm at the rapidly developing one-crop (tobacco) economy, suspicion of personal profit as the sole motive on the part of the Magazine adventurers,[26] and general feelings that the governing officials had simply been lacking in interest in the undertaking. As often happens in such corporations, the small stockholders were the first to be alarmed for their investment. These men turned to the leaders who had supported the Company primarily through a strong interest in public service,[27] particularly to the Earl of Southampton,

[25] Andrews, I, 127. There were, of course, a complexity of reasons here, including personal rivalry on the part of Smith and Sandys and others; dissatisfactions with resident colonial administration; and perhaps a sincere belief (on the part of many or the majority) that Sir Thomas Smith was too much interested in other projects to devote sufficient time to the Company. See Craven, *Dissolution*, Chapters II, III, IV, VI; Andrews, I; Kingsbury volumes I and II; Brown, *Genesis*, II (particularly the letters of Gondomar, the Spanish ambassador, and of John Chamberlain).

[26] Craven, pp. 41–2. The "magazine" and other subsidiary joint-stock groups at the beginning invested ostensibly because the Virginia Company itself could not afford further advancement of capital to supply foods, farm implements, clothing, etc. These smaller companies were made up of men who invested their private funds, and naturally who would look first of all for safeguards for the investment. The system continued under Sir Edwin Sandys' administration and, as George Sandys warns in one letter (quoted below), continued to cause trouble.

[27] *E.g.*, see Craven, p. 42, who admits that they were the group within the the Virginia Company most interested in public service. The present writer's examination of the extant letters among the Ferrar Papers at Magdalene College, Cambridge, impresses him with this attitude in the Sandys group. For the letters are personal and confidential, not designed for propaganda purposes at the Company courts.

Sir Edwin Sandys, Sir John Danvers, and Nicholas and John Ferrar.[28] In 1617, definitely disappointed in the financial report of the officials, these five with others demanded[29] an audit of the officer's accounts. They secured the appointment of Sandys, Danvers, and certain others for this purpose. Many bitter disputes arose over this checking of accounts, and certainly the personal element became a strong one in the future conduct of the Company's business.[30]

At all events, by 1618 there was a strong demand for "reforms" of various kinds, some of them being actually a return to earlier theoretical policies of the Company which had never been worked out in practice or in most instances even attempted. Sir Edwin Sandys is usually given credit as the originator of these ideas, or at least as their principal advocate.[31]

Various instructions and ordinances[32] sent to Virginia with resident Governor Yeardly set forth these ideas in detail. The original document authorizing an enlarged Council of State and an elected House of Burgesses which together were to constitute the General Assembly does not

[28] For biographical notices of these men, particularly in relation to the Virginia Company, see Brown, *Genesis*, II. There are sketches in *D.N.B.* and much documentary information in Kingsbury, and the Ferrar Papers of Magdalene College, Cambridge.

[29] Brown, *First Republic*, 267–8. Sir Edwin Sandys was at this time elected "assistant treasurer" and Robert Johnson, "deputy-treasurer" (see Brown, *First Republic*, p. 267). Brown, *Genesis* (II, 993) states that Sandys in actuality was director of the Virginia Company in place of Smith from 1617 until his formal election in 1619.

[30] J. H. Lefroy, ed., *The Historye of the Bermudaes* (London, 1882), p. 128, gives Smith's side of the controversy. The court records printed in Kingsbury, I and II, are full of the dispute. Each side felt that it was not being fairly dealt with. Sir Thomas Smith displayed something of the typical arrogance of the merchant prince in his aggrieved manner, presumably sincere, at this "impugning of his honor."

[31] Professor Craven, pp. 49–50 states that "the company endeavoured to clear the deck for action, and prepare the way for application of those economic policies whereon [Sir Edwin] Sandys in after years laboured to build a prosperous and thriving colony." See also Brown, *Genesis*, Kingsbury, and Andrews.

[32] These instructions included the so-called "Great Charter," which gave the colonists directions regarding the internal organization of the colony (see Craven, pp. 52–6). The "Great Charter," actually "Instructions to Governor Yeardley," appears under date of 18 November 1618, in Kingsbury, III, 98–109. As Professor Craven points out (pp. 73–5, 32–56), this does not contain the "Ordinance and Constitution for a Council and Assembly in Virginia," which was separate. A copy of this ordinance survives in "An Ordinance & Constitution for Council and Assembly in Va.," 24 July 1621, Kingsbury, III, 482–4.

survive, but it also appears to have been a part of the general programme of the reformers.

For the moment, in 1618, the two factions united to support the passage of bills representing the new policies, but the truce or surface agreement did not last long. In 1619 Governor Yeardley, the choice of Smith for the colonial position the year before, broke with his former sponsor permanently, with apparently good reason. Yeardley was now championed by Sandys, who felt that the Governor had been shabbily treated.[33] And the now long-standing question of the accuracy of Smith's accounts, always rankling, broke out again in virulent fashion in the courts.

Much of this preceded, or was background for, a political election in which the factions aligned themselves clearly, and thus made the break an open one. The break came, however, not in the Virginia Company proper, but in its subsidiary, the recently organized Bermuda, or Sommers[34] Island Company.

For various reasons the Virginia Company sold its rights to the Bermuda islands soon after it secured them, in 1612, to a subsidiary joint-stock corporation composed of its own members.[35] The undertaking prospered and was in 1614 reorganized as a formal joint-stock company, the charter to "The Governor and Company of the City of London for the Plantation of the Somer Islands" being issued on 29 June 1615.[36] Though now legally distinct from the older company, in practice the Bermuda Company was one and the same with the Virginia Company; the Treasurer of one, Sir Thomas Smith, was also first Governor of the other. Courts were the same in form and met on the same day in the same place.

In this situation the first open trouble was born. Daniel Tucker,[37] a protégé of Sir Thomas Smith, was appointed resident governor of Bermuda in 1616, but he soon gave offence to the powerful Earl of Warwick[38] by imprisoning a kinsman of the nobleman. Warwick, a

[33] See Sir Edwin Sandys to the Earl of Southampton, 29 September 1619, Kingsbury, III, 216–9.

[34] Spelled variously Sommers, Somers, Summers.

[35] Called "The Undertakers for the Plantation of the Sommers Islands" (see Andrews, I, 119).

[36] Andrews, I, 120; J. H. Lefroy, ed., *Memorials of the Discovery and Early Settlement of the Bermudas* (2 vols., London, 1877), I, 83–98.

[37] See Brown, *Genesis*, II, 1033, for a biographical sketch of Tucker.

[38] See Brown, *Genesis*, II, 980–3. Robert Rich, Earl of Warwick, powerful

member of the Company, demanded that Tucker be dismissed. Smith hotly refused. And here not only Sir Edwin Sandys but his brother George[39] entered the scene. This was in April or May 1619. Tucker resigned or was simply not reconsidered at the end of his term. Sir Thomas Smith supported for governor a Captain Southwell, and Warwick had nominated Captain Nathaniel Butler,[40] perhaps the man who had been George Sandys' travelling companion[41] in Egypt and in the Holy Land. A third candidate was George Sandys,[42] evidently supported by his brother and the friends of that remarkable man.

Butler, writing[43] some time later, indicated the sources of political support for all three aspirants:

> . . . but the competition especially rested betweene one Captain Southwell, who mediated by the letters of great courtiers and fauorites; Mr. George Sands, who stood very fayre, and likely, by the strength of his brother Sir Edwin, a popular man, a great speaker, and of wise estimation in their Courts; and one Mr. Nathaniell Butler, fauored by diuers of the Lords of the Company, and in especially long known to the Earle of Warwicke, and by him well affected . . .[44]

For various reasons, the account continued, "Mr. Sands . . . desisted wholy from standeinge for the place."[45] Actually the way was cleared

freebooter, speculator, and colonizer, was interested in colonization and exploration all his life. He was a member of the Virginia and Bermuda companies.

39 In 1618 George Sandys had held two shares in the Bermuda Company for some time. (See lists of "Adventurers in the Summer Isles," by "Tribes," in Captain John Smith, *The Generall Historie*, I, 370, under "The General History of the Bermudas, 1593–1623.") George Sandys is shown under Tribe 4 [Pembroke's Tribe].

40 For sketches of Butler, see *D.N.B.* and Brown, *Genesis*, II, 836–7. Later he came to Virginia during Sandys' stay there and made himself generally troublesome. See below, Chapter VI.

41 See Chapter III, note 100, above, and Appendix D.

42 For an account of George Sandys' nomination and subsequent withdrawal see Brown, *Genesis*, II, 994; Craven, pp. 85–6; Lefroy, ed., *History of the Bermudaes . . .*, pp. 120–2.

43 Butler is now generally considered the author of (J. H. Lefroy, ed.) *The History of the Bermudaes*, though John Smith was once believed to have written it.

44 Lefroy, ed., *History of the Bermudaes*, p. 120.

45 *Ibid.*, p. 127. See also Craven, pp. 85–6, for a discussion of the motives. All accounts agree that George was sacrificed, as he had originally been proposed, for Sir Edwin's political purposes, but there exists no known contemporary direct proof that this is true. Professor Craven, p. 85, says "[Sir Edwin] Sandys took advantage of these differences between the two most

for the election of Butler by the desire of the Sandys faction to elect Sir Edwin Treasurer of the Virginia Company, and for this purpose to secure the support of the Warwick group of noblemen in the two corporations. The fact that George Sandys had been a strong contender for the Bermuda post, as admitted by his successful rival, would appear to indicate that he had something more to offer than his brother's backing. The words used two years later in George's nomination for the Virginia treasurership indicate that he was respected for more than his erudition, presumably for something we might today call administrative ability. The Renaissance Englishman may often have combined ability to compose verses, to bow before his king gracefully, and to manage 'business' realistically, but he was usually not chosen as an administrative official because he was a facile poet or a sound scholar. What George Sandys had done during those years between 1612 and 1619 which gave him the respect of his contemporaries as a man of level head and sound judgment in practical affairs we should like to know. Certainly he had done something.

Sir Edwin's political sacrifice of his brother and coalition with the Warwick faction was, however, only partially successful from the Sandys faction's point of view. Sandys was elected Treasurer[46] of the Virginia Company and his friend John Ferrar deputy, and Butler became resident governor of Bermuda, but through some political slip on Sandys' part,[47] or change of heart on Smith's, Smith was re-elected Governor of the Bermuda Company. Thus the friction remained, as every Londoner interested in colonization knew. John Chamberlain the news-gatherer wrote to Sir Dudley Carleton:

> . . . the Virginia Company have displaced Sir Thomas Smith and made Sir Edwin Sandys their governor. But the matter is little amended, when the

powerful men in the company [Smith and Warwick] to enter his brother, George Sandys." That these two were the most powerful figures *from the Company's point of view* remains to be proved, and even Butler, as noted above, indicates Sandys' power in the group.

46 Smith had declined to be considered, perhaps (see note 47 below) fearing defeat. The election took place 28 April 1619 (Kingsbury, I, 212).

47 This failure of the coalition is not satisfactorily explained either by Craven (p. 87) or by Andrews (I, 122), though the latter discusses the situation in some detail. It may have been, of course, that the lesser duties of the smaller group Smith felt he could continue to perform. If so, Smith's election apparently shows that Sandys' election in the Virginia Company was permitted or brought about partially at least by a group who still felt some loyalty to or respect for Smith as a leader in colonial enterprise. There are several other possible explanations, including a slight difference in the personnel of the two companies.

next court, or meeting, they confirmed Sir Thomas Smith in the presidentship of the Bermudas. . . .[48]

Though the matter was "amended"[49] in another year or two, the situation in 1619 resulted in further trouble and bad feeling.

The election of Sandys did not change policies, for he had been making them for at least two years past. It did, however, place the carrying out of the 1618 "reforms" in the hands of a new, and less experienced but more enthusiastic, group of officers. At the Quarter Court of 9 June 1619, new statements of the several offices and standing laws and orders of the court were set down and ratified.[50] Sir Edwin Sandys was the "moving member"[51] of the committee which had proposed these regulations. After their adoption he and his colleagues introduced the use of the secret ballot for the election of Treasurer and Deputy and principal colonial officers,[52] and turned their attention to mapping out economic policies for the colony. The policies may have combined Sir Edwin's and the average Jacobean investor's public and personal interests,[53] interests which as far as Sir Edwin is concerned

[48] 8 May 1619, P.R.O. 14/109, 18 (quoted here as in Thomas Birch, *Court and Times of James I* [2 vols., London, 1849], II, 159–61); also to be found in Norman E. McClure, ed., *The Letters of John Chamberlain* . . . (2 vols., Philadelphia, 1939), II, 236. Chamberlain was definitely not pro-Sandys, for in the next sentence he states that he would "hardly tell how to resolve," if the choice between the two men were put before him.

[49] See Craven, p. 88 and Kingsbury, III and IV. Actually the change in the administration of the Bermuda Company did not come until Sir Edwin Sandys was out of office, for he was officially Treasurer of the Virginia Company for only one year.

[50] Kingsbury, I, 224. George Sandys was among those present at this session of the Court. For a discussion of these new regulations see Craven, pp. 90–104.

[51] "Moving member" on the grounds that these were the policies he hereafter fought for, while certain other members of the committee later fought against them (cf. Craven, p. 90). Professor Craven (p. 92) gives Sir Edwin credit for all these plans (published in 1620 as "Orders and Constitutions . . ." [see note 52 below]); at the same time he points out that many of them had been advocated in various pamphlets and other "literature" for years.

[52] This document, "Orders and Constitutions, partly collected out of his Maiesties Letters Patents, and partly ordained vpon mature deliberation, by the Treasvror, Counseil and Companie of Virginia, for the better governing of the Actions and affaires of the said Companie here in *England*, residing. *Anno* 1619, and 1620," affords interesting insight into the organization of a joint-stock company. It is reproduced in Kingsbury, III, 340–65.

[53] According to Professor Craven (p. 93) who appears to overestimate the personal or selfish motive. Sir Edwin's personal pecuniary investment is only

appear largely public. Whatever the complexities of motives producing them Sir Edwin's outline of their points is fairly simple, for he concentrated on remedying the defects resulting from previous maladministrations. The defects were (1) the rapid deterioration of the company land, (2) the inordinate growing of tobacco to the exclusion of other profitable and necessary commodities, and (3) the small number of colonists who had been sent over in recent years.[54]

The most urgent necessity appeared to be for a rapid increase in population. The public lands, from which came the bulk of the Company's profits and the support of all officials, had to be settled. And a labour supply which might produce varied commodities had to be obtained. Sir Edwin set about to increase emigration by a flood of alluring pamphlet,[55] book, and ballad[56] propaganda directed at pros-

moderately large (those of his kinsmen are even smaller) and his letters to his intimates the Ferrars or to others regarding Virginia affairs show an essentially, if not entirely, "patriotic" and perhaps altruistic attitude towards the colony and his own work for it. Professor Craven does state (p. 93) that "To [Sir Edwin] the success of Virginia was measured by the degree in which it served the interests of English trade," but he goes on to say that this "in no way eliminated the motive of personal gain." Of course this must be true, but the apparent implication here and elsewhere of personal gain as a major factor in Sir Edwin's work appears unjustified. Even in Sir Edwin's reports to the adventurers, when to procure passage of necessary legislation he holds out the prospect of financial return for additional investment in a subsidiary stock, the "full picture" (including Professor Craven's) shows that he felt—or knew—all this was necessary to establish for his country a new and well-peopled kingdom.

54 Summarized in Craven, pp. 93–4. See also Kingsbury, I, 266–7, 350–3, 519; III, 103–4, 146–7, 564, 598, etc.

55 Such items as (1) the Rev. Patrick Copland's sermon, "Virginia's God be thanked, or A Sermon of thanksgiving for the happie success of affairs in Virginia this late year . . .," of 18 April 1622, London, printed by order of the company 1622 (see reference in Kingsbury, I, 155); (2) John Donne's "A sermon vpon the viii. verse of the I. Chapter of the Acts of the Apostles . . ." printed in London the same year (Kingsbury I, 161); or (3) Edward Waterhouse's "A Declaration of the State of the Colony and Affaires in Virginia," [after the massacre,] 1622. An earlier one appeared in 1620, "A Declaration of the State of the Colony and Affairs in Virginia" (reprinted in Kingsbury, III, 307-340).

56 *E.g.*, the anonymous "Good Newes from Virginia," a black-letter broadside of March 1623 (reproduced in facsimile with bibliographical notes in *A Selection of Extremely Rare and Important Printed Books and Ancient Manuscripts*, Catalogue 77 of William H. Robinson, Ltd. [London, 1948], p. 103. It is also reprinted in the *William and Mary Quarterly*, 3rd series, VI [July 1948], 351–8. See below, Chapter VI, note 50). Of course the Virginia colony had before the

pective settlers. Sandys was so successful[57] that his enemies later charged him with luring persons to their deaths by these lying papers.[58] Sturdy husbandmen, labourers, children, maidens, and some criminals were among those going to Virginia, though Sir Edwin always fought against transportation of the last of these groups.

The labourers especially were designed to eliminate the second great weakness of the colony's economic structure. They were gradually to wean the colonists away from tobacco to a diversification of crops, particularly emphasizing those commodities for which England was now dependent upon foreign countries. Naval stores, iron, silk, fruit, and salt, imported from all over the world, Sandys hoped might be grown or developed in Virginia. As hopes these were not new or original in the colony's history, but Sir Edwin's insistence on actually attempting the projects represented the most intensified effort that had yet been made. In 1619–20, definite steps were taken to develop a successful iron industry, to produce silk-worms and silk, and to grow vineyards of grapes to be made into wine. In the same period plans were formulated for obtaining cordage and linen from native plants and pitch and tar from Virginia trees, and for establishing sawmills and shipbuilding. Such were the principal features of the policies of Sir Edwin Sandys, the Earl of Southampton, and the two Ferrars, John and Nicholas, successively deputies in the Company, in the two years immediately preceding George Sandys' embarkation for the colony.

George himself had witnessed personally, as a member-adventurer attending the courts of the Company, much of his brother's struggle. For Sir Edwin's efforts were a real and continuing fight against heavy odds. Justified or not, the natural resentment of Sir Thomas Smith and his friends at imputations of at least carelessness in accounting, and the later enmity of the Warwick faction, partly because of the Virginia Company's firm stand against English pirates in Virginia, had already made Sir Edwin's a hard road. Supported by his perhaps too conscious

days of Sandys' domination of policy often used "come-hither" pamphlets, and it and other American colonies continued to do so long after this time. *E.g.*, see Alexander Whitaker's *Good Newes from Virginia . . .* (London, 1613), dedicated to Sir Thomas Smith. For an interesting article on this sort of writing, see Howard M. Jones, "The Colonial Impulse, an Analysis of the 'Promotion' Literature of Colonization," *Proceedings of the American Philosophical Society*, XC (May 1946), 131–61.

[57] See Craven, p. 96.

[58] See Kingsbury, IV, 176, 179 ("Parts of Drafts of a Statement touching the Miserable Condition of Virginia, May or June 1623").

feeling of rectitude,[59] he was unyielding and frequently undiplomatic in presenting his proposals. Whenever his enemies found a minor crack in his armour, they thrust in the knife, and only bode their time until weariness or a great catastrophe might throw Sir Edwin off guard, or at least at their mercy. Meanwhile, and despite all this, the Sandys administration accomplished a number of things.

George Sandys was present at the quarter court of 9 June 1619,[60] at which the auditing of Sir Thomas Smith's books was discussed, and again on 13 July[61] when Smith's son-in-law, Alderman Johnson, and the latter's 'scandalous' subsidiary joint-stock magazine, were brought into the open by the auditors. His name does not appear again until the quarter court of 3 November,[62] when Sir Edwin reported on the number of persons then in Virginia on various public lands and spoke of the proposal to send over one hundred "maids young and vncorrupt" as wives to make the farmers more content. At this court also were discussed the limiting of tobacco and the encouragement of growth of useful commodities. George also attended the preparative court of 15 November and the "Great and Generall Quarter Court" of 17 November.[63] It was at this latter that Sir Edwin spoke feelingly of the sharp decline in recent years in diversified agriculture in Virginia. Among other things he proposed (1) that the number of persons on public lands be increased to 300 (100 each on the Governor's, the Company's, and the College's); (2) that 100 young persons be sent as apprentices to these; and (3) that 100 young maids be sent as wives. Perhaps rashly, he also promised not to leave the Company one penny in debt for anything to be performed in his year as Treasurer. George was again present on 22 November[64] and 1 December,[65] when the preceding matters underwent further discussion. His name does not appear again on the lists until 11 May 1620,[66] and then again at the quarter court of

59 *E.g.*, see Sir Edwin's letter to the Earl of Southampton, 29 September 1619 (Kingsbury, III, 216–9) in which he gives his motives for demanding the audit of Sir T. Smith's accounts; also his evidently sincere letter to John Ferrar of 3 December 1621 (Kingsbury, III, 529).

60 Kingsbury, I, 224.

61 *Ibid.*, I, 243.

62 *Ibid.*, I, 255. The list of those present often ends "with others," but since George Sandys' name never appears in the Minutes themselves, as a participant in discussion or legislation except when it also appears in the lists, it is unlikely that he is one of the unnamed at other courts. Another reason for this conclusion is that his social rank placed him well up the list of members. Presumably those unnamed are the small merchants and "generality."

63 *Ibid.*, I, 265.

64 *Ibid.*, I, 274–6.

65 *Ibid.*, I, 276–9.

66 *Ibid.*, I, 338–44 and Randolph MSS., Virginia Historical Society.

17 May.[67] On the latter date he heard read the King's nomination of four men, his brother's enemies largely, one of whom was to succeed Sir Edwin in office. Then he saw the whole matter deferred by the Sandys faction, who asserted half-boldly that his Majesty had been misinformed. Sir Edwin's enemies by this time had reached the King, but they still lacked grounds for much action. Sir Edwin was unanimously requested by this court to hold his place until the next date at which an election could be made.

But the quarrel was by now very much in the open. George Sandys was present to hear most of the rapidly warming debate. On 23 May[68] Sir Edwin felt it necessary to justify himself before the extraordinary court "against certain aspersions cast by enemies." On 31 May[69] George listened to the discussion of the problem of the Bermuda Company's relation to the Virginia Company in matters of a common defence against pirates and Spaniards, a discussion attended by the strong implication that Sir Thomas Smith, still governor of the smaller company, would not willingly co-operate.

On 22 June His Majesty's Council for Virginia, of course Sandys controlled, issued a printed "Declaration of the State . . . in Virginia."[70] It was a strong statement, answering "aspersions" cast on Virginia by "ill disposed mindes, guiding their Actions by corrupt ends." Also, however, it made promises of supplies to be sent to Virginia in 1620, and certain significant new regulations regarding private patents. For each share of £12. 10s., the adventurer was to receive upon the first division 100 acres of Virginia land, and as much more upon a second division if the first grant had been "peopled." Also 50 acres (to be doubled

67 Kingsbury, I, 345–58.

68 *Ibid.*, I, 359–64. The Brewster-Argall affairs were among other things discussed at this court.

69 *Ibid.*, I, 364–8. A week later, 7 June 1620, Sir Edwin Sandys wrote to the Marquis of Buckingham (Kingsbury, III, 294–6), begging that nobleman's intercession with the King on Sandys' behalf. In this letter Sir Edwin accused the Smith faction of so desiring to enrich themselves that they were willing to risk extirpation of the colony rather than fail to gain their own ends. His conscious personal rectitude is evident also here (p. 295): "It was the saying of a wise man, that One good man dooth never hate another. Seeing therfore this extreme hatred of me by Sr Thomas Smith, dooth argue a great defect of Goodness in the one: let tryall I beseech discover the partie that is at falt . . ."

70 *Ibid.*, III, 307 ff. Copies of the pamphlet are now in the British Museum and in the Bodleian, Cambridge University, Harvard, John Carter Brown, Henry E. Huntington, Newberry, and New York Public libraries. Listed also are present adventurers and sums adventured.

similarly) for every person the adventurer transported at his own cost, as an inhabitant, before 24 June 1625.[71] Later, during and after his stay in Virginia, all this matter of grants was to interest George Sandys greatly.

On 20 June George heard Alderman Johnson and the Earl of Southampton in a hot and bitter exchange.[72] He seems not to have been present, however, at the great quarter court of 28 June [73] at which the "Trial Charter" was confirmed, and at which the Earl of Southampton, Sir Edwin's friend and ally, was elected[74] to succeed Sir Edwin as treasurer. George's name does not appear in a court until November,[75] by which time he seems to have become active, though perhaps not publicly, in the affairs of one or both companies. Governor Nathaniel Butler of Bermuda, writing to Sir Nathaniel Rich of the now definitely-aligned Smith-Warwick faction, began uneasily:

> I already find that the unhappy distance grown between the two earls [Southampton and Warwick?] yours pacing[76] with them, and the violences of Sir E. S. have had their influences upon this climate, insomuch that having invited Sir Ed. two several times to write somewhat it hath produced an (uncivil) nothing. Yet (if I be not much deceived) he hath clapt on his brother George and his passionate friend Sir John Danvers[77] by their letters to grope me in mine answers, if not some others besides.[78]

[71] The immigrant had to live in Virginia three years "at one or seuerall times, or die after he is shipped for that voyage" for this contract to be binding. See Chapter VI for George Sandys' use of these authorizations in making his own claims to land in the colony.

[72] Kingsbury, I, 373–8.

[73] *Ibid.*, I, 378–8.

[74] This followed the Earl's statement that the King had not wished to interfere in the election, despite his previous nominations of four men. In effect it was a Sandys victory, for Sir Edwin continued for some time to make the real decisions in policy. The election was hailed generally, however, as one which might improve the whole situation.

[75] Preparative court of 13 November 1620, Kingsbury, I, 415–30.

[76] The word in the MS. original is "paseing."

[77] (1588–1655.) See articles on Danvers in *D.N.B.* by Sidney Lee and in Brown, *Genesis*, II, 874. Danvers, member of the Virginia Company, and later Gentleman of the Privy Chamber to Charles I, was finally a regicide. He was one of the most ardent supporters of Sir Edwin Sandys in the Virginia Company. With the aid of Edward Collinwood he was later to copy the Virginia Company records before they had to be turned over to the Royal Commission. His first wife was the mother of George Herbert (she had been married twice before, and died in 1627). He appears later in George Sandys' life, for the two were fellow-members of the new commission for Virginia appointed by the King, 17 June 1631.

[78] P.R.O., GD. 15/1/284 (*Historical MSS. Comm. 8th Report*, Appendix, Pt. II,

These letters, presumably to friends in Bermuda or possibly pamphlet propaganda against Butler's administration, have long since disappeared. Evidently, however, George's pen had already shown its usefulness in controversy.

On 15 November[79] George saw four books presented to the Company to be sent to the College at Henrico in Virginia, but his name does not appear again among members present until January. At the latter court[80] he passed over two shares to his nephew-in-law Sir Francis Wenman,[81] shares assigned to George by Thomas Sandys. Also at this time the first move was made in certain matters which were to concern George Sandys personally. The Earl of Southampton began by stating that Sir George Yeardley's three-year term as resident governor in Virginia would expire in November, and that Sir George desired to relinquish the post.

> His Lo^p: therefore proposed vnto the Company a gentleman recommended vnto him for his many good parteϱ (namely S^r ffrancis Wyatt) who was well reputed of, both in respect of his parentage, good education, integritie of life and faire fortunes (being his ffathers eldest Sonne) as also for his sufficiency otherwise, being deemed every way without exception fittinge for this place who was likewise desirous to take this charge vpon him if the Company would please to accept of his willingnes to doe them service . . .[82]

Two days later,[83] in a court made up almost entirely of the

366, item 284). This is from the printed version of his letter of 23 October 1620. Butler still believes in Southampton but is evidently antagonistic to Sir Edwin personally.

79 Kingsbury, I, 421–9.

80 Of 29 January 1620, Kingsbury, I, 435–7.

81 Wenman, Weyman, Wyneman, or Weyneman, of Carswell, Oxfordshire, who had married Sir Samuel Sandys' daughter Anne, will appear later in this story. The move here was probably to get another member of the Sandys family into the company as a voter. The permission to pass these shares to Sir Francis Wenman was not fully confirmed until 10 February, according to Brown, *First Republic*, p. 393.

82 Kingsbury, I, 436. Southampton went on to say "Notwithstanding . . . [he] praied the Company not to neglect the nomination of some other if they could thinke of any one or more sufficient persons of qualitie that would willingly vndergoe this waightie burden of government: who might togeather with this gentleman aforenamed stand for the election ~~of~~ [*sic*] § at § the next Quarter Courte."

83 31 January 1620/21. (Kingsbury, I, 440.) Actual members of the Sandys family named as present at this court were Sir Samuel, Sir Edwin, George and Sir Francis Wenman, as well as Sir Francis Wyatt. At the court at which Wyatt was nominated Sir Samuel and Sir Francis Wenman are not listed among those present.

Sandys-faction adventurers, Sir Francis Wyatt was elected[84] resident governor of Virginia and also member of his Majesty's Council for Virginia.

Thus the Sandys faction in the Company introduced a prominent connection of the Sandys family[85] into the Virginia colony. Sir Francis Wyatt had married Margaret,[86] daughter of Sir Samuel Sandys of Ombersley. The heir of a strongly Protestant, liberal Kentish family, he was the great grandson of the sonneteer of Henry VII's reign, the grandson of the leader of Wyatt's rebellion in Queen Mary's time, and the son of George Wyatt, a scholarly and quiet gentleman much interested in theories of politics and government.[87] Sir Francis was himself a liberal member of Parliament, a versifier of some ability,[88] and evidently then and later a generally popular man. He appears to have been a good choice.[89]

[84] The election, by secret ballot, went without other nominees, though two votes against Sir Francis were cast.

[85] Andrews (I, 168 and 168 n.), who generally presents an unfavourable picture of Sir Edwin in the Virginia Company, is doubtful that family ties or influence were determining factors in this election or in that of George Sandys later. It was quite clear, however, that the choice of Wyatt was a Sandys-faction appointment. George Thorpe (who had been nominated for the governorship himself by Sir George Yeardley) wrote to Sir Edwin from Virginia in 1621: "I am not a litle glad . . . that you were able to make soe nere a frend soe worthie governor thereof. . . ." (Kingsbury, III, 462). Apparently Sir Francis was not to be (with George Sandys) the first member of the family to be resident in Virginia, for there is evidence that David Sandys, a cousin of Sir Edwin and George, was a clergyman there by 1620 (see *Virginia Mag.*, XXIV [April 1916], 144, and Kingsbury, III, 269, ltr. of Sir Edwin Sandys to John Ferrar). And of course the Thomas Sandys mentioned above (note 11) as being in Virginia in 1607 may have been George's brother.

[86] She was born in 1592 and married in 1618 (see *D.A.B.* and *D.N.B.* articles on Sir Francis Wyatt).

[87] See the Wyatt MSS., now (1947–8) on deposit in the British Museum, the property of the Earl of Romney, through whose courtesy I have examined them. Several manuscripts in George Wyatt's autograph exist; they include family genealogical records, a long letter of "Instructions on Government from George Wyatt to his son Francis then Governour in Virginia," verses on certain psalms, a treatise on warlike strategems, miscellaneous poems, and a Latin versifying of the *Song of Solomon*. See also J. Cave-Browne, *The History of Boxley Parish* . . . (Maidstone 1892), pp. 147 ff.

[88] See sonnets and other pieces among the "Wyatt MSS.," and among the commendatory poems in the published writings of George Sandys.

[89] Most of the invective and marshalling of data against the Virginia Company was directed at the administration at home. No really effective or valid

For the remainder of both their lives, Sir Francis and his uncle-in-law George Sandys, not too far apart in age,[90] were to be closely associated personally and politically. So close and harmonious is their political association that it is often impossible to distinguish, in the official documents in which either or both may have had a hand, which man's ideas are being presented.[91] The official record of their work together begins about this time of Sir Francis' election to the governorship, with the statement of the appointment of the two to several committees of the Company.

Whether George Sandys had already been selected for colonial office by party leaders or whether he was chosen to continue in a type of labour in which he had already demonstrated uncommon ability, within three weeks[92] after Wyatt's election George was assigned to two important committees of the Company. One of these was a group asked to consider a treatise[93] by Captain John Bargrave concerning the government of Virginia. Bargrave, a minor Virginia planter, definitely aligned against the Smith faction[94] and evidently personally quite eccentric, has been called a "persistent constitution monger."[95] He was taken seriously and treated courteously, however, for a committee of ten, including Wyatt and Sandys and Deputy Ferrar, were "desired to meete vpon Monday the 26: of this present moneth, to consider thereof and to certifie to their next Court their opinions touching the same."[96] Since no

charge seems ever to have been made by the Smith-Warwick faction against Sir Francis Wyatt as governor.

90 Sir Francis was born about 1588 (see W. F. Craven, "Sir Francis Wyatt," in *D.A.B.*, though the writer in the *D.N.B.* states. *c.* 1575).

91 This is evident in the Virginia Council's official letters sent back to the Company in London, and in George Sandys' attempt to have the Virginia Company's charter renewed in 1639–40–1.

92 On 22 February 1620/21. Kingsbury, I, 444.

93 See Brown, *Genesis*, II, 824. For the text of Bargrave's "A Form of Policy for Virginia," which may be the document referred to, see Kingsbury, IV, 408–35 (under date "Before December 7, 1623").

94 See Craven, pp. 279–80.

95 Andrews, I, 176 n. Professor Andrews cites, using Bargrave himself as authority, five treatises by Bargrave on the government of Virginia before the summer of 1622 (see also Kingsbury, IV, 408–35; 435–6). A fragmentary copy of an additional one is now in the Huntington Library. All seem to have been fairly similar. Though "usually" favourable to the Sandys faction, Bargrave implies or states that the King should take over the government of the colony. Bargrave was a 'devote' believer in the divine right of Kings (Andrews, I, 186 n.).

96 Kingsbury, I, 444.

statement concerning the document appears, the report was probably unfavourable.[97]

The second committee was certainly a more important one, for it concerned the colony's one real money crop, tobacco. An already existing tobacco monopoly, along with the import duty on the commodity, had been granted in 1620 to a group of speculators headed by Sir Thomas Roe. In July 1620 the Virginia Company had entered a strong protest against the monopoly and its limitations. For a time, however, Virginia sent its tobacco to Holland so that Bermuda might export to England the total weight permitted to both colonies. This was, of course, a very unsatisfactory long-term policy. Perhaps because several of the adventurers were also members of Parliament, the two companies decided to look to that body for relief,[98] and a petition was planned.

> It was therfore ordered that a Committee should be appointed for drawing the said peticon and for this purpose nominated S[r] ffrances Wyate m[r] George Sandys and m[r] Deputy fferar who are desired to take some paines therein and to make it in substance agreeable to that w[ch] S[r] Edwyn Sandys had deliuered vnto them.[99]

For the background for George Sandys' next and most important appointment one must turn back a moment. In 1619 the Virginia Assembly had petitioned[100] the Treasurer and Council in London to appoint a resident sub-treasurer for the colony in order that the planters might pay their annual rents to him directly and promptly, and in the form of commodity rather than money, of which they had none. On 12 April 1621, the Company court in London, almost certainly considering this petition but not mentioning it, proposed[101] a new resident officer for Virginia, an officer necessary for a variety of reasons. It was stated that in time past governors of Virginia had failed to follow the directions of the Company in the planting of staple commodities, to

[97] The press of other business, such as getting Sir Francis Wyatt and his new council ready for the voyage, may have been the reason for a tacit putting aside of the matter.

[98] Kingsbury, I, 443. See also Craven, pp. 228–9, and Brown, *First Republic*, p. 464. Also they felt that they might find redress "as of many other monopolies of like nature which the lower house had called into question and by his Ma[ts]: gracous pmission intended vtterly to extinguish."

[99] Kingsbury, I, 443.

[100] H. R. McIlwaine, ed., *Journal of the House of Burgesses of Virginia, 1619–1658/59* (Richmond, 1915), p. 7.

[101] Kingsbury, I, 449–50.

the great detriment of the colony and discouragement of the settlers. Therefore it was moved that an officer might be sent thither "in the qualitie of a Treasurer," not only to take the collection of all rents and duties (of which £1,000 was already due the Company) as his personal obligation, but also to take as his peculiar charge the fulfilment of all the directions and commandments of the Council at home, or else to give sufficient reason to the contrary so that the adventurers in London might be better informed and satisfied as to the conduct of affairs in Virginia. The motion was vigorously applauded as of the greatest consequence.

Then came a nomination from the group of leaders of the Company, a nomination which was to be "considered" until the next meeting of the court. Since the Sandys faction at least for the time ruled internal affairs of the Company almost without opposition, the nomination was tantamount to election.

> It pleased my Lo: of Southampton to propose a gentleman, well knowne vnto them all, as a man very fitt to take that charge vpon him namely m^r George Sandys who indeed was generally so well reputed of, for his approued fidelity sufficiency and integrity: as they conceaved a fitter man could not be chosen for that place and therevpon agreed to his elec̃con; referring him to the former Committees to be further treated and concluded with concerning the same.[102]

The next preparative court of 20 April outlined the manner of maintenance for this official, along with that for the Marshal, who held another newly created position. For the maintenance of the Treasurer, 1,500 acres of land and 50 tenants were allotted to his office. Of the tenants, 25 were to accompany the Treasurer at once and 25 were to go over the year following. The Treasurer was also to have the passage of "his owne family,"[103] not exceeding ten persons, at the Company's charge. According to former precedents, the Company also would allow him £150 toward furnishing himself for the voyage.

102 Kingsbury, I, 450. At the preparative court of 30 April (Kingsbury, I, 453) further allusion is made to George Sandys in this capacity: "And for the said place of Treasurer because m^r Sandys was in like manner [to the Marshall] proposed whome all men conceaved to be every way sufficient, to take that charge vpon him. . . ."

103 Kingsbury, I, 454. This refers to his retinue of servants, skilled labourers, and perhaps overseers. There is no evidence of "personal family" in blood or marriage. The "Marshall," also had been allowed 1,500 acres and 50 tenants for his office. The Governor's allowances were, of course, greater. These allowances were made in lieu of salary (cf. Kingsbury, I, 464–5).

On 2 May a formal vote[104] was taken whereby George Sandys became Treasurer and Captain William Newce Marshal for Virginia. At the same time they were both elected to his Majesty's Council for Virginia in London as well as to the Council of State in Virginia. From this time until he sailed George Sandys was busy in his own and in Company affairs. On 11 June he attended, now as a Councillor, the lengthy session of the preparative court, where so many of the increasingly familiar problems were discussed. The great question was to find a new source of income to replace that from the lotteries, abolished by an "order in council" of 4 March.[105] But commodity crops, a canvass for a new subsidiary joint-stock company to provide apparel, the offer to set up a glass-furnace, and the matter of grants of private patents, were among the other things considered.

Such discussions continued at the general quarter court of 13 June. And at this time Sandys saw a fellow poet and gentleman of standing elected Secretary for the colony to succeed another man of letters, John Pory.[106] This was Christopher Davison,[107] second son of Queen

[104] Three negative balls were cast against both Marshal and Treasurer, though there was no other candidate for either office. Two negative notes had been cast in Sir Francis Wyatt's election as Governor. Probably these came from Smith-faction adherents still attending Company courts.

[105] Craven, pp. 149–50, 183–4. The lotteries had fallen into disrepute, probably through the aspersions of Sir Edwin Sandys' enemies. The withdrawal of licence was explained as made because of the complaint of Parliament.

[106] For various reasons Pory's work as secretary was not considered satisfactory (Kingsbury, I, 478). He wrote interesting and ingratiating letters home to Sir Edwin Sandys and others, but later developments bore out the suspicions entertained by Sir George Yeardley in Virginia and Sir Edwin in London that Pory was secretly an ally of the anti-Sandys faction. For more of Pory, see *D.N.B.* and below, Chapters VI and VII.

[107] See Kingsbury, I, 489, for his election. He was one of four nominees. His position was in power, prestige, and perquisites distinctly inferior to that of Marshal or Treasurer. See *D.N.B.* under "Francis Davison" for some account of Christopher and other members of his family. The new Virginia secretary had been a student at Gray's Inn in 1597 and may have known George Sandys, nearby in the Middle Temple, since that time. Davison returned home shortly after his arrival in the colony, for on 7 October 1622 his return to England, including his alleged reasons for so doing (to petition for recompense for loss of tenants and to inform the Company regarding the state of the colony), was discussed (Kingsbury, II, 109). From Davison's statement to the court of the Company, we know that George Sandys acted as Secretary while he was gone. George Sandys says in a letter of 28 March 1623 (Kingsbury IV, 67 and below, Chapter VI) that "Mr Secretary" would not have been allowed to return to

Elizabeth's secretary of state, and brother of the poets Francis and Walter. At the same session Sandys was appointed with Davison, Wyatt, Danvers, Sandys' cousin Sir Dudley Digges, his brother Sir Edwin, and others to a committee[108] to study a new treatise on the defects of the plantation and how they might be remedied. This type of committee work was growing familiar.

Twelve days later the general court met again,[109] called primarily to consider the matter of a Captain William Norton and the Italians who were to be sent with him to Virginia to make glass and beads. Though the Company had agreed at a previous session to transport and "furnish" eleven persons for this work, it now found that the £150 necessary to do so was nowhere available. George Sandys, however, desiring to further a project so intimately connected with his own duties as director of industry, offered to accept the Italians in place of certain of those tenants who were to be allowed him by the Company. Therefore the cost of the group of skilled labourers would be no more than the furnishing and transportation of two of their wives and three of their children. The committee in charge of the matter agreed willingly to this proposal, even assuring Sandys that the men would be his own servants until the Company gave him "valuable consideraĉon for them." For their part the work men covenanted within three months to have a glass furnace set up.[110] Though this solution of the problem was decided upon at this time, later on, with George Sandys' hearty approval, the Company withdrew[111] its agreement with him on grounds

England had he been worth anything to the colony. Davison's name appears on an official document of 23 October 1622 as Secretary of the colony (Kingsbury, III, 697), but the official signature might have been added after his return to Virginia. He was back in Virginia before 4 April 1623 (Kingsbury, IV, 101, 115–6) and died there between 1 December 1623 and February 1624 (see Brown, *First Republic*, p. 568). Among other work as a poet, Davison had translated certain of the Psalms into English verse (the *D.N.B.* article cites Harleian MS. 6930).

[108] Kingsbury, I, 490. John Smith, Gibbs and Wrote were the other members of the committee.

[109] *Ibid.*, I, 498–9.

[110] Kingsbury, I, 499. They also agreed to make glass and beads for the Company in the condition of tenants "att halfe for the space of Seaven years," for which space they were to have a monopoly on the manufacture of round glass, drinking glass, and beads. The Governor and Council were to limit the output of beads, of course designed for trade, for obvious reasons. Captain Norton was to supervise the work.

[111] Kingsbury, I, 500–1, 2 July 1621.

that an individual should not profit by an undertaking[112] planned for the Company as a whole. Later the Company compromised, when it again could not find the necessary funds, and instituted another "joint-stock" to furnish capital for the enterprise.[113] As matters finally turned out, Sandys was to give to this particular project more of his close personal attention than to any other industry of the colony.

On 6 July George Sandys borrowed £20 from the Company, perhaps an advance for furnishing himself for the voyage. On 10 July he attended a court at which the Lady de la Warr asked that a commission might be granted whereby Sir Francis Wyatt, George Sandys, and others might look into the amount and condition of her late husband's properties which were placed under the supervision of Mr. Rolfe in 1611. On 12 and 16 July the press of heavy business continued. On the latter date five subscription rolls, including that for the glass-furnace group, were offered. That is, members were invited to invest in small joint-stock enterprises which would supply the colony with items the Company could not finance in itself. The clothing magazine, the transportation of maids-for-wives, and a shipyard were among the projects thus sponsored.

All this should have been an ominous sign to the little group of officials now ready to embark. They were to introduce some projects and enlarge already established older ones in an ambitious programme, and yet the Company at home was already so near bankruptcy that it could not finance even the matters necessary for bare existence, such as the magazine of clothing and other supplies.

On 24 July George Sandys attended the Virginia Company's court for the last time.[114] Shortly before the first of August he embarked on the

[112] The agreement had also contradicted a former order of "13 June last."

[113] Finding on 12 July (Kingsbury, I, 511) that the costs of furnishing and transporting were £80 more than the £150 estimated, the court voted to release Captain Norton from his contract and to leave it free for private adventurers, no more being done at this time. On 16 July a "joint-stock" of individuals was formed with a capital of £400 to further the glass works, the Company taking one-fourth of the stock (Kingsbury, I, 514–5). Sir Edwin and the Earl of Southampton set a good example by subscribing £200 each to the several projects undertaken at the same time. In November (Kingsbury, I, 511–7) the glassworks rolls closed at £500, and the magazine of supplies at £1,800, but the other three remained open for some time longer. See also Craven, pp. 191–2.

[114] Kingsbury, I, 521. His name does not appear after this, though the next meeting was on 27 July.

ship *George*, William Ewens master.[115] This 150-ton vessel had contracted to sail by "the directest course"[116] for the port of "James Citty in the Kingdome of Virginia."[117] The passengers presumably included, besides Wyatt and Sandys, Christopher Davison, Secretary; Francis Bolton and Haut Wyatt, the Governor's brother, clergymen; Dr. John Pott, physician; Mr. William Claiborne, surveyor, and certain of their "families."[118] With them went commissions for new appointments to the Council in Virginia from among the colony's residents, for the Company had learned of the deaths of three former members just as the new officials were about to sail.[119] With him Sir Francis carried a long list of "instructions to the Governor and Council of State in Virginia"[120] from the Virginia Company, a document signed by the

[115] Land patents testify that George Sandys sailed on the *George* (see Chapter VI, below, and Nell M. Nugent, *Cavaliers and Pioneers* . . . [Richmond, 1934], I). For evidence that the ship sailed in July, see Kingsbury, III, 639. Brown, *First Republic*, pp. 426–7, states that 7 or 8 August was the sailing date.

[116] She had agreed to sail with the first wind from the Isle of Wight and Port of Cowes about 1 July (Kingsbury, III, 465 ff., I, 506).

[117] *Ibid.*, III, 465. Another ship, probably the *Charles*, sailed in consort (Brown, *First Republic*, p. 427). According to word brought by the *Marmaduke* before 27 February 1621/22 (Kingsbury, I, 605–6), eight ships including the *Tiger*, which had been driven from its course and attacked by Turks, had arrived since summer in Virginia, and a ninth ship, the *Sea-Flower*, was daily expected. All did arrive safely (Kingsbury, III, 582 and 639–40). The nine must have been the *Eleanor*, of 30 tons, which had sailed in May; the *George*, *Charles*, *Marmaduke*, and *Temperance*, in July; and the *Warwicke*, *Tiger*, *Sea-Flower*, and *Flying Hart*, in August, for these are the only ships listed which could have arrived at that time (*ibid.*, III, 639).

[118] A total of 120 persons (*ibid.*, III, 640). The Marshal, Sir William Newce, appears to have sailed with his servants in another ship, for George Sandys writes of his having arrived at the beginning of October [1621] (see below, Chapter VI, and Kingsbury, IV, 22). He died by April 1622 (Brown, *First Republic*, p. 511), two days after the reading of his first patent. Sir Francis Wyatt's wife arrived a year after her husband. John Pountis, appointed "Vice-Admirall," was probably already in the colony, as were certainly the Company's "deputies" for the College and for the Company land, Mr. Thorp and Mr. Thomas Newce.

George Sandys had eight of his personal and at least one of the Treasurer's Plantation servants with him in the *George* (for a list of their names see E. D. Neill, *Virginia Carolorum* [Albany, 1886], p. 17). "The Instructions to Governor and Council of State in Virginia" referred to below state specifically that twenty-five of Sandys' tenants assigned to him as Treasurer are accompanying him (Kingsbury, III, 472). Some may have sailed on the companion vessel, probably the *Charles*.

[119] Kingsbury, I, 520, 16 July 1621.

[120] *Ibid.*, III, 468–82.

Earl of Southampton, Sir Edwin Sandys, and nine other members of his Majesty's Council, including George Sandys himself.[121] The forty-seven points of this "charter" begin with religion, and include such matters as conversion of the Indians, oaths of allegiance, limitation on tobacco and the growth of other commodities,[122] the making of an accurate map of the region, and the duties of the newly appointed officials. Paragraph 10, primarily concerning the new Treasurer, is the longest and strongest in its direct order:

> And for as much as ther hath ben in theise late yeares great fault or defect in nott putting in execuc̃on our orders of court and counsell for the setting vpp & vpholding those staple Comodities wch are necessarie for the subsisting and Encrease of the Plantation wch hath happned in part by the ou^{r} Chargeing the Governor wth toe much buissnes, wee haue vppon espetiall approuement of the industry and sufficiency of George Sandis esq^{r} as also for his faithfullnes and plenarie intelligence of o^{r} intendments and counsells here (wherevnto hee hath from time to tyme bein priuie, not only elected and athorised him to bee Treasurer in Virginia, butt also committed to his spetiall and extreordinarie care ye execution of all o^{r} orders Charters and instructions tending to the setting vpp, Encrease and maytaininge of the said Staple Comodities: Wee therfore requier you that vpon all such occationes wherin the said master [* * *] shall have occation to bee Employed, you give him all such countenance, help and power in the execution therof, as you would doe to the Governor himselfe if he were personallie present. And that ꝑuition bee [* * *] made for convenient transporting him from place vpon all those occations . . .[123]

Other stipulations specifically relating to the duties of the new Treasurer deal with sawmills, cornmills, mulberry tree planting for silkworm culture, iron works, and the glass furnace. An order of precedence is set in case of the death or mishap of the Governor.[124] This lists the Lieutenant-Governor, the Marshal, the Treasurer, the two Deputies, and then the other members, such as the Physician, in the order named.[125]

121 George Sandys was the only one of the colonial officials to sign this document. Since Wyatt and Newce, as members of the Council at home as well as in America, also were eligible to sign, it may be presumed that George Sandys had a considerable hand in its composition.

122 All, of course, typical Sir Edwin Sandys' policies.

123 Kingsbury, III, 472.

124 *Ibid.*, III, 479. Actually the Council was authorized to elect any *one* of their body to succeed, but in case there was an unexpected tie vote, the officers should succeed in the order shown.

125 Official documents of the Council in Virginia are usually signed first by the Governor, then by Francis West (as Lieutenant-Governor) and by Sir

The iron works are stressed as the most important project, and then the others are carefully described.

With such ordered policy sailed the little group which was to govern the colony during a stormy period. The same administrators were to see the failure and end of the independent Virginia Company and were to succeed themselves under a royal charter as officials of a Crown colony. Both Wyatt and Sandys were to be connected with British colonial enterprise in England or in America for most of the remainder of their lives—more than a score of years. At the moment of embarkation, however, they were enthusiastic but colonially inexperienced Jacobean gentlemen facing a new adventure.

George Sandys' last months in England had probably been busy with more than the affairs of the Company and his personal estate. In 1621 appeared a second edition of *A Relation of a Iourney,*[126] a re-setting but not an actual revised text. It may have gone through the press under the author's eye.[127] And in the same year appeared what is called a second edition of *The First Five Bookes of Ovids Metamorphosis,*[128] a little volume which Sandys probably was seeing through the press in the months before he sailed. Though the 1621 is called "the second edition," "Ovides *Metamorphosis Translated into English verse* by Master GEORGE

George Yeardley (as a former governor), then by the Marshal, the Treasurer, the Deputies, the Secretary, the Physician, etc. (see Kingsbury, III, 483, for official list of the Council of State for Virginia *in this order* of precedence). Actually Sir William Newce died so soon after landing that his name appeared only a time or two. The name of Davison, who died early and made a voyage to England even during his term of office, appears infrequently. West and/or Yeardley were not always present. George Sandys is usually the third signer. Naturally a military officer such as the Marshal (commander, under the Governor, of all forces) outranked Sandys. In influence and real significance, even had he lived, it is unlikely that Newce would have approached Sandys, for it is to the Governor and Treasurer that the Company most frequently refers or appeals. And George Sandys was the brother of Sir Edwin, the most powerful figure in the Company at home.

126 Again printed by William Barrett. A re-setting of the 1615 ed., with some variation in catchwords, etc. (see Fredson Bowers and Richard Beale Davis, *George Sandys: A Bibliographical Catalogue of Editions Printed in England to 1700* [New York Public Library, 1950]).

127 There is no evidence as to exact date of appearance. A comparison of this edition with those of 1615, 1632, and 1637 shows certain differences in printer's ornaments, etc., among them, but there is no real proof or indication of author's revision.

128 "Imprinted for W. B." Sandys' name does not appear on the title page or elsewhere in this edition. For more of this edition, see Chapter VIII below.

SANDES" was not entered in the Stationers' Register[129] until 27 April 1621, and there exists no other evidence than the title page to this *1621* of a previous edition. Evidently printer and/or author had it entered to protect the author's interest while he was away from England.

At any rate, Sandys was known as a translator and poet as well as the learned traveller before he set out for the New World. Apparently the Ovid was well known in London literary circles. Soon after Sandys sailed,[130] Michael Drayton addressed to him the now fairly familiar lines[131] concerning it:

And (worthy GEORGE) by industry and use,
Let's see what lines *Virginia* will produce;
Goe on with Ovid, as you have begunne,
With the first five Bookes; let your numbers run
Glib as the former, so shall it live long,
And doe much honour to the *English* tongue:
Intice the Muses thither to repaire,
Intreat them gently, trayne them to that ayre . . .[132]

[129] Arber reprint of *Stationers Register*, IV, 53.

[130] Probably in the winter of 1621/22 (see W. J. Hebel and others, *The Works of Michael Drayton* . . . [5 vols., Oxford, 1932–41], V, xxviii, 214 and 214 n.). The poem is, generally, in the tone of the weary disillusion of the unsuccessful court poet. James's popularity was at its nadir at this time (Hebel, ed., V, 214–5), and Drayton uses most of his lines hinting at or asserting royal ingratitude. The poem contains 108 lines.

[131] They are quoted many times in accounts of the colony, of colonial literature, and of Anglo-American literary relations. The address is "TO MASTER GEORGE SANDYS Treasurer for the English Colony in Virginia."

[132] Less familiar are the concluding lines of the poem, which show more of the temper of the poet and the problems of the colonist he addressed:

If you vouchsafe rescription, stuffe your quill
With naturall bountyes, and your skill,
In the description of the place, that I,
May become learned in the soyle thereby;
Of noble *Wyats* health, and let me heare,
The Governour; and how our people there,
Increase and labour, what supplyes are sent,
Which I confesse shall give me much content;
But you may save your labour if you please,
To write to me ought of your Savages
As savage slaves be in great *Britaine* here,
As any one that you can show me there.
And though for this, Ile say I doe not thirst,
Yet I shall like it well to be the first,
Whose numbers hence into *Virginia* flew,
So (noble *Sandis*) for this time adue.

VI

COLONIAL OFFICIAL: THE MASSACRE AND ITS CONSEQUENCES

AT THE END of the summer,[1] in October, the *George* dropped anchor off Jamestown. It had been a long voyage. Sandys, a poor sailor ten years before in the Mediterranean, had discovered at least one way of forgetting his miseries. "[A]mongst the roreing of the seas, the rustling of the Shroude, and Clamour of Saylers,"[2] he had translated two more books of his Ovid. Though he intended to continue his poetry, at landfall he had put it aside for a concentrated attention on the pressing tasks before him.

The new governor and resident treasurer had a few weeks to spend in studying the colony's situation before they assumed control of affairs. They found "James Towne"[3] a brick and timber village[4] with palisades

1 H. R. McIlwaine, ed., *Journals of the Virginia House of Burgesses, 1619–1658/9* (Richmond, 1915), p. 36, and Kingsbury, III, 640, "A Note on the Shipping, Men, and Prouisions Sent and Prouided for Virginia, . . . in the Yeare 1621" [a broadside of the end of May 1622]. Of the other eight ships arriving in the autumn of 1621, probably at least one arrived with the *George*.

2 Kingsbury, IV, 66, George Sandys to Samuel Wrote, 28 March 1623. Up to the date of this letter he had not continued the translation, but expected to do so when summer heat confined him to his chamber. For this letter, see below, pp. 137–143.

3 Perhaps occasionally called "James Citie," though the latter term was usually used to refer to the "corporation" of James City, a territorial division composed of what were later James City and Warwick counties on the north side of the river, and Surry and Isle of Wight counties on the south side. Each "City" (there were four early ones) had a capital town of its own. Jamestown thus was a double administrative centre for the whole colony and for its own "corporation."

4 There was also at least one stone house in the colony, but not in Jamestown, in 1624 (Brown, *First Republic*, p. 626). For types of dwellings probably built or standing in Jamestown in this period, see Henry C. Forman, *Jamestown and St. Mary's, Buried Cities of Romance* (Baltimore, 1938), pp. 14, 49–54. This is the most recent and complete study of the site and buildings of Jamestown. By 1623, says Forman, there were four times as many dwellings as there had been five years earlier. How many of these were built by 1621, or what the original number was, is difficult to ascertain. In 1624 there were 22 dwellings

around the major settlement,[5] and a population living within the enclosure and on what is now the island of probably less than 200 persons.[6] The concentrated settlement appears to have been situated on a low bluff on the southwestern side of the peninsula connected to the mainland only by an isthmus.[7] On this peninsula, outside the town, on spots of firm ground amid labyrinthine swamps, were the houses of other Englishmen. Up and down the James on both sides, in Elizabeth City[8] on what is now Hampton Roads, and across the Chesapeake on the Eastern Shore, were scattered plantations,[9] clinging tenaciously to the waterways as their only means of communication, but so far removed

(Brown, *First Republic*, p. 621). It is hard to believe that there were six or less in 1618. Actual archaeological work at Jamestown may be said to have just begun.

[5] A "New Towne" was surveyed by William Claiborne outside the palisades in 1623, a place already divided into lots and built on by 1620 (Forman, *Jamestown and St. Mary's*, p. 59). It has never been fully determined whether palisades surrounded the whole town, as shown in the engraving of the 1622 massacre in *Historia Americæ . . .*, 1634, XIII, Latin, p. 28 (Theodore De Bry edited and illustrated parts VII–XII) and the *Scheeps-[sic] Togt van Anthony Chester Na Virginia, gedaan in het jaar* 1620 (Leyden, 1707), though these are not vertical palisades; or whether, as indicated in certain documents (*e.g.*, Brown, *First Republic*, p. 626), palisades surrounded individually the fort or forts (see Forman, p. 59) and certain grouped establishments or "lots," of a few acres in size. William Strachey gives strong evidence that in 1610 "A Pallizado of Planckes and strong Posts, foure foote deepe in the ground, of yong Oakes, Walnuts, &c." surrounded the town in a triangle (see *Hakluytus Posthumus, or Purchas His Pilgrimes . . .* [20 vols., Glasgow, 1905–6], XIX, 56–7).

[6] In March 1621 there were 843 English in the whole of Virginia; in March 1622 there were 1,240 (Brown, *First Republic*, p. 464). In 1624 there were 182 people in the town itself and 69 others in its immediate vicinity, with a total of 1,227 in the whole colony. At the same date there were 22 dwellings, 1 church, 1 merchant's store, 3 storehouses, 1 large Court of Guard (Brown, *First Republic*, pp. 621–7). The town's population had probably not changed a great deal since 1621. There were no losses *within* the town in the 1622 massacre. Numbers of immigrants in 1623–4 had presumably been placed largely on the plantations. For an excellent map showing the probable disposal of buildings in Jamestown in 1624, see Forman, pp. 63–4 (reproduced also in the present volume).

[7] By the time of the American Revolution this isthmus, in Sandys' time carrying the great highway to the mainland, had washed away, leaving an island much as it now stands.

[8] One of the four original corporations, of which "Kikotan" was the capital.

[9] For a chart showing these early settlements (and some later ones) see Lyon G. Tyler, *The Cradle of the Republic: Jamestown and James River* (Richmond, 1900), p. 120.

from each other that they were vulnerable to any reasonably sudden attack, foreign or native.

Over half the colonists were free adults, the remainder largely indentured servants and a few children and negroes.[10] A large but inexactly determined portion of the free inhabitants were gentlemen of good family, but the majority were probably farmers, skilled craftsmen, and a few labourers.[11] They owned some hogs, cattle, and goats, and perhaps a few horses.[12] Outside the city, at least, there were no fortifications adequate against a maritime enemy such as Spain, and "only houses impaled," or palisaded, against the Indians.[13]

Such a picture a census would have presented. The matters of dependence on the Company and England for many of the basic wants of food and clothing, the apparent necessity for agricultural diversification and the establishment of industry, the obvious need for the discovery of quick-money raw materials for export to England to return needed manufactured products, were as much a part of the picture and the problem as were the location and number of the people. And above all loomed the dark threat that the Company and perhaps the colony would be lost if these economic problems were not speedily solved.

On 18 November Sir George Yeardley's term as governor expired. According to the Company's instructions,[14] Sir Francis Wyatt's com-

[10] See Brown, *First Republic*, p. 627 for his summary of the statistics for 1624 though the proportions may have changed in the three years since 1621. Brown shows in 1624 a total of 1,227 persons, of whom there were 432 male and 176 female free inhabitants; 441 male and 46 female servants; 107 children; 2 Indians; 11 negro men, 10 women, 2 children, in all 23. Most of the colonists were recent comers. All the negroes, of course, had arrived in 1619 or after.

[11] Professor Thomas J. Wertenbaker's well known *Patrician and Plebeian in Virginia* (Charlottesville, 1910) minimized cavalier influence and the probability of a large number of "gentlemen" in the colony. His conclusions have been generally adopted, though a few warnings have occasionally been sounded. A thorough re-analysis of the whole problem from original and secondary materials by Mr. John E. Manahan ("The Cavalier Remounted, a Study of the Origins of Virginia's Population, 1607–1700," Charlottesville, 1947, an unpublished dissertation, Alderman Library, University of Virginia) has reasserted the older conclusion that the cavalier-gentleman tradition had sound bases, and that colonial Jamestown and the later colony in the seventeenth century were much more largely than more recent historians have admitted communities of gentle blood and cavalier sympathies.

[12] Only one horse and one mare are listed in the 1624–5 report on the colony (Brown, *First Republic*, p. 627).

[13] Brown, *First Republic*, p. 628.

[14] Kingsbury, III, 471.

mission to succeed was read on this date, "and as speedylie as convenientlie" thereafter the oath was administered to the councillors of state. Wyatt immediately called for an election and meeting of the General Assembly in order that the Company's orders and policies[15] might be laid before the planters. Then the little group of inexperienced newcomers on the Council, many of whom had previously travelled only a hundred or so miles from their native places, were ready with the help of the older settlers to begin their task. Isolated from the mother nation by three thousand miles of lonely and hostile ocean, they were as fully conscious as their predecessors in Virginia had been that

> Wee hope to plant a Nation,
> where none before hath stood.[16]

Their first communications show that they faced their task cheerfully, perhaps bolstered by the knowledge that the nine ships which had arrived during the fall had not lost a man, and had brought what seemed at the moment sufficient supplies.[17]

Complex and urgent as the colony's problems were, the new officials were compelled first to attend to pressing personal matters of habitation and of disposal of the servants they had brought along in the *George*. Wyatt's needs were met fairly easily,[18] for naturally he was to succeed

[15] The Assembly was held in November and December (Kingsbury, III, 581). Wyatt brought several documents of varying significance with him: commissions to himself and various other recently appointed officials; a copy of a treatise on the plantation business recommended to the councillors for study; instructions to the governor and Council of the State in Virginia, consisting of 37 articles (mentioned in Chapter V, above; these policies and commands were read to the Assembly); an ordinance and constitution of the Treasurer, Council, and Company in England for a colonial Council and "General Assembly," dated 24 July 1621 (Brown, *Republic*, pp. 455–6, says date 3 August; he also states, as do others, that this is a copy of an early "charter" of 28 November 1618). The names of the Council of State inserted in the last document (see Kingsbury, III, 482–4) were, in this order of precedence: Wyatt, Francis West, Yeardley, William Newce, Sandys, Thorpe, Thomas Newce, Davison, Dr. Pott, Paulet, Leech, Powell, Roger Smith, John Berkeley, Rolfe, Hamer, Pountis, Lapworth, Harwood, and "Macocke," with their offices listed after their names. There is no evidence in the "Ordinance" for the General Assembly that it is merely a copy of an earlier document.

[16] R. Rich, Gent., *Newes from Virginia* (London, 1610), p. B2 recto. Compare also George Sandys' dedication to Charles I in the 1626 edition of his translation of Ovid. See Chapter VII below.

[17] Kingsbury, III, 582.

[18] *Ibid.*, III, 584. Sir George resigned the governor's land to Sir Francis, but

to the previous governor's official residence and estate. Sandys, however, assuming a new office, found no official residence or plantation in which he and his "family" might establish themselves. Very sensibly, though perhaps in desperation, he employed his private means to settle his servants. The Council reported to England that

> . . . yt beinge a matter of . . . difficultie to find owte one the suddene such a Convenient place for the Seatinge of the Thresurers Tenantes, as in our Judgmentę we thought requisite, and that h[e] would haue much endaungered the health of his People, and been the meanes of the certai[n] losse of his next years Cropp, to haue kept them longe withowt ymployment about James Cythie, Mr Thresurer was owte of necessitie enforced to purchace for him selfe owt of his private Estate 200 Acres of Lande beinge the divident of A privat planter for the present ymployment of his People, where they are yett remayinge [*sic*]. But th[e] Land belonginge to the place of Thresurer wee purpose as soone as may be to haue allotte[d] owte and the Tenantę belonginge thervnto placed thereone. . . .[19]

Then Sandys turned to his duties as director of industry, encourager of "staple commodities" in agriculture, and collector of the Company's revenues. The first several months appear to have been spent with industry and agriculture.[20] The beginnings of activity in these matters were auspicious of good to come, for the General Assembly had received the Company's "instructions" with approval,[21] apparently indicative of the "old planters'" agreement in the programme. The Virginia Council requested more vines, trees, and seed grains from England. To set a good example in the development of simple industry, Sir George Yeardley erected a windmill,[22] and Sandys himself had by January 1621/22 begun the construction of a water mill. By this time, too, Sandys

turned over only 46 instead of the 100 tenants expected. For Yeardley's reasons, see his letter from the Virginia Council to the Company.

19 Kingsbury, III, 585, January 1621/22, Council in Virginia to Company in London. This tract has not been located among land grant records now extant, but may have been one of those confirmed to him by patent in 1624 (see below, Chapter VII, notes 118, 120, 121, 122, 123).

20 At least the Treasurer's and Council's reports of the colony's activities in this period give greater attention to these matters than to anything else.

21 Kingsbury, III, 581. The journals of the House of Burgesses for this period do not survive. This statement of approval is made in the Council's report to the Company in London, January 1621/22.

22 Presumably in his new capacity as the leading private citizen (although he was third in rank on the Council as past-governor). Yeardley was probably the wealthiest planter in the colony.

was also able to make reports of progress in the particular industries he personally supervised, the iron works under John Berkeley and the glass-works of the Italians under Captain Norton.[23]

A month or six weeks later, on 3 March, George Sandys sent home a letter[24] so sanguine that it was used for propaganda. Edward Waterhouse, in a brochure[25] designed to attract emigrants from England, referred to it at least twice, stating that Sandys gave assurance of the perfecting within the year of various industries, of the sowing of English grains, and of the planting of vines. He also gave evidence that the Treasurer had already explored both banks of the James in his search for suitable sites for the location of industries. After quoting John Berkeley, master of the proposed iron works, as authority for the statement that Virginia was a most fit place for iron works, the pamphleteer supported his contention from the Treasurer's observations:

> . . . which also by Letters from Mr. *George Sandis* the third of *March* last, was confirmed, with this farther description of the place (called the *falling Creeke*)[26] to be so fitting for that purpose, as if Nature had applyed her selfe to the wish and direction of the Workeman; where also were great stones hardly seene else where in VIRGINIA, lying on the place, as though they had been brought thither to aduance the erection of those Workes.[27]

The Rev. Patrick Copland, preaching at Bow Church in London before

[23] Kingsbury, III, 586–7. January 1621/22. The Council's letter probably went by the *George* on its return voyage (Brown, *First Republic*, pp. 462–5). It states that the Treasurer will make individual reports on the iron and glass works, presumably by a later ship. These reports may actually have been contained in the letter of 3 March (see below, notes 24 and 27) referred to by Edward Waterhouse.

[24] The letter itself is not known, but survives in reference in Edward Waterhouse's "A Declaration of the State of the Colony . . ." (reprinted in Kingsbury, III, 541 ff.) and in direct quotation in the Rev. Patrick Copland's "Virginia's God be Thanked," 1622 (see Edward D. Neill, *Memoir of the Rev. Patrick Copland* . . . [New York, 1871], pp. 58, 62–4, and *Virginia's God be thanked* . . . [London, 1622]; also Brown, *First Republic*, pp. 464–5).

[25] See note 24 above.

[26] On the south side of the James not far below the present site of Richmond.

[27] Kingsbury, III, 548. This appears, probably or surely from Waterhouse, in Samuel Purchas, *Hakluytus Posthumus, or Purchas His Pilgrimes* (modern ed., 20 vols., Glasgow, 1907), XIX, 152. Sandys and Berkeley were confident, according to Sandys' letter, that iron would be made by the next Whitsuntide (Kingsbury, I, 629, 10 April, 1622 "Court Held for Virginia"). This was probably an earlier (than 3 March) official letter.

the assembled adventurers of the Virginia Company,[28] after referring to George Sandys in other places, quoted directly from the letter:

> Have you not read what of late your worthie Treasurer doth write unto you? 'If' (sayth hee) 'we overcome this yeere the Iron-workes, Glasse-workes, Salt-workes; take order for the plentifull setting of corne, restrain the quantitie of tobacco, and mend it in the qualitie, plant vines, mulberry trees, fig trees, pomegranats, potatoes, cotton-wooles; and erect a faire Inne in James Citie (to the setting up of which I doubt not but we shall raise fifteene hundred or two thousand pounds, for every man gives willingly towards this and other public works), you have enough for this yeere.'
>
> And a little after, in the same letter, 'Maister Pory[29] deserves good incouragement for his paineful discoveries to the southward, as far as the Choanoack,[30] who, although he hath trod on a little good ground, hath past through great forests of pynes, 15 or 16 myle broad, and above 60 mile long, which will serve well for masts for shipping, and for pitch and tarr, when we shall come to extend our Plantation to those borders.
>
> 'On the other side of the river there is a fruitfull countrie, blessed with aboundance of corne, reaped twise a yeare; aboue which is the copper mines, by all of all places generally affirmed. Hee hath also met with a great deale of silke-grass, which grows there monethly, of which Maister Harriot hath affirmed in print, many years ago, that it will make silke grow-/graines, and of which and cotton wooll all the Cambaya and Bengala stuffes are made in the East Indies.'[31]

Thus the state of the colony was reported five months after Sandys arrived. Though obviously the phrasing of this letter and the earlier reports may have been designed to encourage the investor-adventurers at home, it is also obvious that the Treasurer and the rest of the Council, justifiably or not, were quietly confident[32] of a prosperous future. In less

[28] Presumably principally, if not entirely, the Sandys faction. Copland had been asked by the Company to preach a sermon of thanksgiving that the colony was prospering. It was good propaganda as well as piety to have this sermon, and the individual members of the Company needed the encouragement. The irony of the situation was, of course, that it came just as the Council in Virginia was framing its letter to break the news of the massacre (see Kingsbury, III, 611–15).

[29] For John Pory, see below, pp. 181, 2, 191–3 and Chapter VII, notes 143 and 144.

[30] The Chowan, in Eastern North Carolina (see Brown, *First Republic*, p. 463).

[31] Neill, *Memoir of the Rev. Patrick Copland*, pp. 62–4.

[32] Professor Craven (*Dissolution*, pp. 195–6) notices this optimism and admits that there seemed some basis for it. He holds, of course, that the massacre was as much or more the *result* of London mismanagement than the *cause*, in itself, of disaster in the colony. See below.

than three weeks the blow fell whose psychological effect was far worse than its physical, terrible as that was.

There had been warnings during the latter part of Sir George Yeardley's term in office that Opechancanough and his tribes of the Virginia mainland,[33] alarmed at the increasing number of ships and men arriving, might be planning a surprise attack. The colonists generally had been lulled into a sense of security, however, by the Indian king's protestations of friendship and by the absolute lack of positive evidence of hostility.[34] And the most recent instructions from the Company had ordered them to entertain and fraternize with the natives, that the savages might aid them in defence against other enemies and assist in the general conversion of themselves and their fellows to Christianity.[35] When the Indians struck on 22 March 1621/22, they actually murdered many Englishmen with whom they sat at breakfast.[36] In no case where the settlers were on the alert is there evidence that the Indians destroyed them or their plantations.[37]

A friendly Indian had warned one Pace,[38] who in turn rowed to Jamestown and warned the governor. Thus the capital and as many outlying plantations as could be warned were saved. Even as it was, the losses were frightful. Between 300 and 400 were killed,[39] including six of the Council, and most of the rest experienced "old planters,"[40] whose

[33] Below the Potomac, or perhaps the Rappahannock.

[34] For a summary of the situation, see Brown, *First Republic*, pp. 465–6 and Edward Waterhouse, "A Declaration" (Kingsbury, III, 551). At Opechancanough's request a brass tablet, commemorating the solemn peace sworn, had been fastened to one of his ceremonial oaks (Kingsbury, III, 550).

[35] Items 5–6, Company's instructions of 24 July 1621 (Kingsbury, III, 470).

[36] See Waterhouse, in Kingsbury, III, 550–1.

[37] Kingsbury, III, 555; Brown, *First Republic*, p. 468. Actually the people at Henrico even without warning were able to defend themselves stoutly, though many were slain.

[38] The famous and romantic episode appears, with considerable embroidery, in many accounts of the massacre. Waterhouse summarizes the facts (Kingsbury, III, 555), though undoubtedly he attempts a presentation of them which minimizes the damage done. According to later letters of the Company, more than one friendly Indian warned the settlers (Kingsbury, III, 673).

[39] See Brown, *First Republic*, p. 467 for a statistical summary. Wyatt and the Council said 300 (Kingsbury, III, 612) and the official list released by Waterhouse and the Company totals 347 (Kingsbury, III, 571). Both of these would naturally tend to minimize the losses.

[40] See Brown, *First Republic*, p. 467. The Virginia Council's list of Councillors slain mentioned only George Thorpe, Nathaniel Powell, John Berkeley, and Samuel Maycock. The other two were almost surely John Rolfe and

plantations were often farthest removed from Jamestown. The corporation of Henrico, with Mr. Thorpe and the College, suffered terribly, Thorpe himself losing his life; and the part of Charles City above the Appomattox was also literally wiped out. At Falling Creek, the iron works were overthrown and the tools tossed or pushed into the river. Across the river and above Jamestown many were killed. On the lower James and the Eastern Shore, where "the Laughing King" of the Indians always remained on friendly terms, there was little or no damage or loss of life.

The Governor and Council tried to bring order out of all the consequent confusion. First they drew in the remaining population by abandoning entirely many outlying plantations.[41] Palisades at Henrico and Coxendale had protected some brave defenders, who were now ordered[42] to withdraw to Jamestown. Cattle were driven into the constricted areas now to be defended. Planters resettled themselves within the reserved plantations. About 22 May, by the *Sea-Flower*, a number of letters were dispatched from the Governor and Council, George Sandys and others telling of the great calamity. Daniel Gookin sailed for home on the same date to explain the altered situation.

The Treasurer's letters again do not survive, but there is good evidence that they were read and that his comments as well as his news were pondered.

> The letters of Mr. George Sandis a worthy Gentleman and Treasurer there, likewise haue aduertised (as many others from many particular persons of note and worth) besides the Relations of many returned in the Sea-flower (the ship that brought vs this vnwelcome newes) haue beene heard at large in the publicke Courts, that whilst all their affayres were full of successes, and such intercourse of familiaritie, as if the *Indians* and themselues had beene of one Nation, those treacherous Natiues, after fiue yeares peace, by a generall combination in one day plotted to subuert their whole Colony, and at one instant of time, though our seuerall Plantations were an hundred and forty miles vp one Riuer on both sides . . .[43]

Michael Lapworth. Thorpe and Berkeley were supervisors of projects which Sandys, who had always had them under his care, had now to "manage" personally.

41 "James City, Paspahigh, Kecoughtan, New-Port Newes, Southampton Hundred, Flowerdieu Hundred, Sherley Hundred," and the plantation of Mr. "Samuel Jourdan" were the only ones to be retained and defended (Brown, *First Republic*, p. 470).

42 The commission for removing these people was issued 20 April (Brown, *First Republic*, p. 471).

43 In Waterhouse, included in Kingsbury, III, 554.

The official letter[44] from the Council in Virginia, humble and weary in its tone, broke news of the massacre, of the abandonment of many plantations, and of the destruction or forced stoppage of many cherished industrial projects.

> . . . itt hath pleased God by our manyfo[*ld*] sinns to laye a most lamentable Afflictione vppon this Plantacon, by the trecherie of the Indyans, who on the 22th of march laste, attempted in most places, vnder the Coulor of vnsuspected amytie, in some by Surprize, to haue cutt us of all and to haue Swept us away at once through owte the whole lande, had it nott plesed god of his abundante mercy to prevent them in many places, for wch we can never sufficyently magnifie his blessed name, Butt yet they ꝑvayled soe farr, yt. . . .[45]

And the wretched story follows. The Virginia Council had now to beg for bread,[46] whereas a month before they had merely recommended the shipment of seed grains. And they made recommendations concerning military fortifications and for a more concentrated and better protected settlement.

While they awaited replies from England, the Council took stock of the situation. The rank and file of the colonists were now in mortal terror of the Indians.[47] And since the time of corn planting had passed in the general confusion after the terrible day, it was necessary to obtain grain immediately by force or by negotiation. The Indian policy determined upon appears today as ruthless and unfaithful to pledged word as any attitude the savages displayed, but these men were grim and desperate:—their existence was at stake. It was decided to burn Indian villages, destroy corn as it ripened in the fields or carry harvested grain away, and generally to harass the Indians so continually that they would remove themselves far from the plantations. Often under pretext of truce or trade and in utter disregard of pledge the settlers got near the fleet-footed savages and fired mercilessly.[48]

[44] The only one of these early accounts surviving appears in Kingsbury, III, 611–15 (dated April 1622, with no day given).

[45] Kingsbury, III, 612.

[46] In the form of corn, or wheat, of course. They needed the grain partly because ships were still coming in bearing new settlers.

[47] See the hysterical letters from Richard Freethorne to friends or family at home, 5 March 1622/23 and 20 March and 2–3 April 1623 (Kingsbury, IV, 41–2, 58–62) and from William Capps, 21 March 1623 (*ibid.*, IV, 76–8).

[48] On 30 January 1623/4, the Virginia Council informed the Company what they had done in revenging themselves, concluding: "Whereas we are

THE JAMESTOWN MASSACRE, 1622

From the engraving by Theodore DeBry, in *Historia Americae*, 1634

All colonial leaders who were capable organized foraying expeditions. It is interesting and probably significant that the first of these avenging columns was led by George Sandys, who fell upon the Tappahannocks across the river from Jamestown "in two severall expeditions."[49] As the English at home heard the story in a ballad,

> Stout Master George Sandys upon a night
> did bravely venture forth
> And mong'st the Savage murtherers
> did forme a deede of worth
> For finding many by a fire
> to death their lives they pay
> Set fire of a town of theirs
> and bravely came away.
>
> From James his Towne wel shipt and stord
> with men and victualle store
> Up Nan-somond river did they saile
> long ere they came to shore
> Who landing slew those enemies
> That massacred our men
> Took prisoners corn & burnt their townes
> and came aboard agen.[50]

The Virginia Council was unprepared for the Company's reply to their bad news. Shocked at the catastrophe and despairing financially, "The Treasurer & Counsell for Virginia" placed the blame in no uncertain terms:

advised by you to obserue rules of Justice wth these barbarous and ꝑfidious enemys, wee hold nothinge iniuste, that may tend to their ruine, (except breach of faith) Stratagems were ever allowed against all enemies, but wth these neither fayre Warr nor good quarter is ever to be held, nor is there other hope of theire subversione, who ever may informe you to the Contrarie" (Kingsbury, IV, 451). Just what constituted breach of faith is difficult to ascertain. In a letter of April 1623, Peter Arundle charges that "*wee our selues haue taught them how to bee trecherous by our false dealings with the poor kinge of Patomeche that had always been faythfull to the English* . . ." (Kingsbury, IV, 89). In a letter of 9 June 1623 another planter tells of the English strategem (of Captain Tucker) who brought on purpose, to conclude a treaty with an Indian king, a butt of poisoned sack (*ibid.*, IV, 221). It destroyed about 200.

49 Kingsbury, IV, 9. Council to Company in London, 20 January 1622/23.

50 From "Good Newes from Virginia," printed as a "cosening ballad" by John Trundle (London, 1623). The sheet is reproduced in facsimile in *A Selection of Extremely Rare and Important Printed Books*, p. 103. It is also reprinted in *The William and Mary Quarterly*, 3rd series, VI (July 1948), 351–8. The verses

We haue to o^{r} extreame grief vnd^{r}stood of the great Massacre executed on o^{ur} people in Virginia, and that in such a maner as is more miserable then the death it self; to fall by the hand℮ of men so contemptible; to be surprised by treacherie in a time of knowne danger; to be deafe to so plaine warning (as we now to late vnd^{r}stand) was last year given; to be secure in an occacōn of so great suspition and iealousie as was Nenemathanewes death;[51] not to ꝑceive any thing in so opne and generall conspiracie; but to be made in part instrumente of contriving it, and almost guiltie of the destruccōn by a blindfold and stupid entertaininge of it; w^{c}h the least wisdome or courage suffised to prevent even on the point of execucōn: are circumstances, that do add much to o^{r} sorrow & make vs to confesse that it is the heavie hand of Allmightie God for the punishment of o^{rs} and yor transgressions: to the humble acknowledgment and ꝑfect amendment whereof together wth o^{r}selues, we seriously advise and invite yo^{u}; and in ꝑticular earnestly require the speedie redresse of those two enormous exesses of apparell and drinkeing; the crie whereof cannot but haue gon vp to heaven; since the infamie hath spredd it self to all that haue but heard the name of Virginia to the detestacōn of all good mind℮, the scorne of others, and o^{r} extreame griefe and shame: In ye strength of those fault℮, vndoubtedly, and the neglect of the Devine worshipp, haue the Indians prevailed, more then in yor weakness; whence the evill therefore sprung the remedy must first begin: and an humble reconciliation be made wth the devine Matie by future conformitie vnto his most iust and holie lawes . . .[52]

The London Council did include one bit of good news in this otherwise scathing letter:— that the King was soon to grant the sole importation of tobacco to the Virginia and Bermuda companies. But it also informed the desperately hungry colonists that more mouths to fill were on their way thither in several ships. And the Company was strong in its feeling that the abandoned plantations and projects at the iron works, the College and Henrico, and other places must immediately be reestablished.[53] Sandys was ordered to resettle the College tenants under

celebrate also the exploits of Sir George Yeardley, Captain Powell, and Captain Hamor. It will be noticed that Sandys is the only one of the avengers who held no military position in the colony. Perhaps the policy was in origin his. Whether the second verse here quoted refers to an expedition led by Sandys is not entirely clear, but since the leader is named in other stanzas, and this follows one in which Sandys is named, the expedition celebrated was probably his.

51 An Indian who allegedly killed several English and was himself killed by the colonists in 1621, during Yeardley's administration (see Brown, *First Republic*, p. 466).

52 Kingsbury, III, 666. 1 August 1622.

53 Though they admitted that this could not be done immediately at the Iron Works.

a new contract[54] which would incite them to harder work and greater production. The Company concluded with a deliberate exhortation to revenge, and an explanation of how to accomplish it which fitted well with what methods the Virginians had already adopted.[55] The colonists were advised to do what they had done already—to kill and burn, to bribe friendly Indians to attack Opechancanough's tribes, and to do almost anything and everything to exterminate the treacherous native enemies. "[B]ut if any one can take Opachancano himself, he shall haue a great and singular reward from us."[56]

A guarded, careful, but firm and in some instances sharp reply, written on 20 January 1622/23, was sent as an official document to the Company. Sandys himself may have written it.[57] It answers questions or accusations point by point. And in conclusion it alludes to hearsay and other report carried orally to England.

> Lastlie we Conclude wth our humble request vnto you, y^{t} you will not iudge of us by the eventꝭ of thingꝭ wch are ever vncerten especyallie in a new Plantatione, nor by reportes of branded people, some of whom have deservedlie vndergone seuerall kindꝭ of punishment nor of the malitious and vnknowinge, but rather to give Creditt to our publique informations, and then we shall Cherfullie, as we haue ever faithfully, ꝑceede to the advauncement of you^{r} designes . . .[58]

54 Kingsbury, III, 671.

55 "We haue anticipated your desires," the Virginia Council wrote in 20 January 1622/23 "by settinge vpon the Indyans in all places. . . ." (Kingsbury, III, 9.) Sir George Yeardley alone from one expedition brought back 1,000 bushels of corn and got 3,000 more by trade and force.

56 Kingsbury, III, 673. They also ordered that the Indians who had warned the settlers should be given "a good and carefull education." This letter is not signed individually.

57 Though probably not, from what he says in his letter to John Ferrar of March 1622/23 (given below). The signers of the present letter were Wyatt, "Yardlie," Sandys, Smith, "Pountes," and Hamor. See discussion in text below. The temperate tone of this letter may have been the result of Wyatt's influence.

58 Kingsbury, IV, 17. The colonists answered the reproach of vainglorious apparel with: "for apparell wee know noe excess, butt in the puristes, and had not that taxe ꝑceeded from you, wee should have thought it a floute for our povertie and nakedness . . ." (*ibid.*, p. 11). Generally, the Virginians were "in good hope y^{t} you would not haue added sorrow to afflictione, woundinge our reputationes wth such disgrasfull reproofes, vnworthie of our sufferinge *yf* not of our industrie . . ." There were sharper criticisms in answer to other accusations.

Sandys personally, however, was getting near the boiling point. Knowing that in official correspondence he could not vent his opinions of the Company's aspersions cast on him, Wyatt, and the Virginia Council generally, he most effectively said what he thought in a series of letters to friends and relatives. In these six extant letters exists the best contemporary picture of conditions in the colony during the year after the massacre. The writer, enfeebled by illness and overwork, had now achieved through experience a critical perspective of the Company's colonial policies which was not at all flattering[59] to the leaders at home, including his own brother.

The first of these letters is to John Ferrar, deputy Treasurer under Sir Edwin and the Earl of Southampton, a man in many ways more responsible for the lack of co-ordinated and planned colonization, as far as proper provision is concerned, than Sir Edwin Sandys. By this time John Ferrar had been succeeded officially as deputy by his brother Nicholas, but continued to advise if not to direct the export of provisions to the colony.

> Worthy S^{r}, be this my excuse, that I in particular write not to y^{e} generalty: I haue nothinge $wherew^{th}$ to palliat there humors; who, I too well perceaue, will both iudge and condimne whatsoeuer succedes not to theire desires, w^{th}out either enquiry of the truth or necessity of o^{r} actions. But we, whom the hand of heauen hath humbled, professe the inability of y^{e} best Counsel[*l*] & indeauors that are not supported by ye diuine assistance, neither haue theire assertions much trubled vs. y^{t} are confirmed wth innocency and habitual patience.

59 All the letters, seized with others on their arrival in England as evidence to be employed in the investigation of the Virginia Company, were used, as well they could be, in the attacks upon the programme and judgments of the Sandys' faction. For evidence that they were not so intended, see below, the quotation from Wyatt's letter, p. 160. These letters, now all reprinted in Volume Four of Miss Kingsbury's *Records*, are (with the exception of the second letter to John Ferrar) part of the Duke of Manchester Collections, and all are in the Public Record Office. For an explanation of the contents and purpose of these and other items in the collection, see Kingsbury, I, 61–3 and IV, v. The Manchester papers, gathered principally by Sir Nathaniel Rich of the Warwick faction, present the opposite side of the Virginia Company dispute from that shown in the Ferrar Papers (of Magdalene College, Cambridge), also reprinted in great detail in Miss Kingsbury's volumes. Miss Kingsbury's texts are based on the holograph letter where possible. In a few instances, she states, because the original is torn or worn, she has relied on a contemporary copy of the letter, also included in the collections of the P.R.O. Miss Kingsbury's text is here followed throughout.

Sr Willm Nuce [60] arrived here about the beginninge of October, wth a very few of weake and vnseruiceable people, ragged, and wth not aboue a forthnights prouision: some bound for 3 yeares, a few for 5, and most vppon wages of all his goods hee hath made a deede of guift to the owners of ye shippe for ye security of her hire, wch though they were sould at excessiue rates, would hardly discarge y^t^ ingagement. Aft^r^ his death 11 men were all that remained for the Company, whom for want of prouision I was enforced to sell. Three I sold to Captain Wilcocks[61] for 600 waight of Tobacco to bee paide this yeare but two of Them dyed before hee could get to his Plantation: two to Capt: Smyth[62] for 400 waight, halfe to bee paide this yeare and halfe ye next, one to Capt: Tucker[63] for an hundred in hand, and two more the next croppe if hee liued soe longe, and an other to Capt: Croshaw[64] for 200 Fower y^t^ were left one my handes, I was fayne to send to my owne plantation;[65] two of these a little aft^r^ ran away (I am afraid to ye Indians) and noe doubt the other two [2] would haue consorted wth theire companions if sicknes had not fettered them. For ye 5 men wch Sr Willm Nuce should haue deliuered me here, I was glad to take his page (dead before deliuered) & an other little boy hardly worth theire victuals. But of all that came ouer wth him I haue sent you here inclosed a list of theire names and how they are disposed of. I haue receaued your booke of debts; in the gatheringe whereof there shall be noe fault in my indeauor: although I am affraid there bee little Tobacco left wch the Magazin hath not receaued, or the merchants & seamen not gleaned for theire sackes & stronge waters. 60000 waight beinge the most y^t^ this yeares crop hath produced. As for ye Deuty Boyes,[66] they thinke much to be brought

60 Knight Marshal of Virginia, who died in April 1622.

61 John Wilcocks located his "divident" in 1621 on the Eastern Shore. As a member of the General Assembly he later signed the reply to Alderman Johnson's "Tragical Relation" (Brown, *First Republic*, pp. 420, 571, 580).

62 Roger Smith or Smyth, who had been a captain of infantry in the Low Countries, sailed for Virginia the second time in February 1621, was appointed to the Virginia Council on 24 July 1621, married the widow of John Rolfe (after March 1621/22), and was still a member of the Council on 30 November 1629 (Brown, *Genesis*, II, 1011).

63 William Tucker, member of the first House of Burgesses in 1619 from Elizabeth City, took a leading part in avenging expeditions against the Indians (for more on Tucker, see Brown, *Genesis*, II, 1034).

64 Probably Rawley Crashaw, an "old planter" who came to Virginia in 1608. He was a burgess in 1624 from Elizabeth City (Brown, *Genesis*, II, 867).

65 Was this the 200-acre plantation he had purchased soon after arrival, or the Treasurer's official plantation, or another of his own? His various grants, as far as record survives, were not patented until 1624. See below.

66 Fifty boys to be servants and apprentices, sent to Virginia at his Majesty's command, arrived on the *Duty*, of 70 tons, John Dameron master, in May 1620. The Company had expended £100 for apparel and furnishings. Some of the tobacco carried by the *Duty* on her return trip was to pay for the boys (who had in

to a backe reconinge: since they paid as much as was demaunded for thē & receaued acquitances. Yet Sr George Yardly will pay the ouerplus for those wch he reserued to himselfe: the like offer was made by Capt. Willm Powell[67] (who is now wth God) but y^t they are not able at this time to discharge it. Sr George complaines not wth out cause who I belieue hath lost this yeare two thirdes of his estate: & to giue him his dew he hath behaued himselfe very nobly in ye seruice of ye Country to his great expenses. But what I can I will doe & send you the accomptes by the Abigall.

Concerninge ye Shipwrights[68] (ye best proiecte for ye Country & most profitable for ye Aduenturers) hath fayled wth ye rest in this generall decay: wherein, if you blame vs, you must blame the hand of God, that hath taken yet away Capt: Barwicke[69] & 6 or 7 of his principall § worke § men. A hard man, yet not a little toutched in conscience that he hath conuerted the releif of his men to his particular benefit: But out of y^t wch is his (whereof I haue [3] made me a stay) satisfaction vppon proofe shalbe giuen. Those y^t remaine shall imploy theire time to your best aduantage.

The ill successe of ye glasse workes is allmost equall vnto this: first the coueringe of ye house, ere fully finished, was blowne downe, by a tempest noe sooner repaired but ye Indians came vppon vs, wch for a while deferd ye proceedinges. Then they built vp ye furnace, wch after one forthnight y^t ye fire was put in, flew in peeces: yet ye wife of one of ye Italians (whom I haue now sent home, haueinge receaued many wounds from her husband at seuerall times, & murder not otherwise to be p'uented for a more damned

all cost the Company £500). The planters repaid (or paid) at their reckoning of 3 shillings per pound, or £10 a boy, but the Company could hardly get what amounted to £5 per boy for the tobacco. The Company demanded that the planters make up the difference, and that Mr. George Sandys collect the revenues due (Brown, *First Republic*, pp. 417, 502 and Council in Virginia's letter of 4 April 1623, Kingsbury, IV, 99). He was still collecting in December 1624 (see H. R. McIlwaine, ed., *Minutes of the Council and General Court of Colonial Virginia, 1622–1632, 1670–1676 . . .* [Richmond, 1924], p. 36).

67 A member of the House of Burgesses in 1619 (from James City?). He was probably killed when taking revenge on the Indians in January 1623/24 (Brown, *Genesis*, II, 971; *First Republic*, p. 621), though his plantations in the Tappahanna territory "over against James City" are listed under his name in the census of 1625 (Kingsbury, IV, 555). He is not to be confused with Captain Nathaniel Powell.

68 Under Sandys' supervision. The Company asked him to look after Barwick and his crew, for it was from Sandys the project had in part first moved (Kingsbury, III, 650, 10 June 1622, Company to Virginia Countil). See below.

69 Barwick sailed with the 25 shipwrights in June 1622, was dangerously sick in January 1622/23, and was dead by March, two months later (Kingsbury, IV, 15, 23).

crew hell never vomited) reueald in her passion y^t Vincentio crackt it wth a crow of iron: yet dare wee not punish theise desperat fellowes, least ye whole dessigne through theire stubbornesse should ꝑish. The sumer cominge on, Capt: No§r§ton dyed wth all saueinge one of his seruants, & hee nothinge worth: The Italians fell extremely sicke: yet recoueringe in ye beginninge of ye winter, I hyred some men for y^t seruice, assisted thẽ wth mine owne, rebuilt the furnace, ingaged my selfe for prouisions for them, & was in a mann^r a seruant vnto them. The fier hath now beene six weekes in ye furnace, and yett nothinge effected. They complaine y^t ye sand will not run. (though themselues made choise thereof, and likt it then well enought) & now I am sendinge vp ye riuer to prouide thẽ wth better, if it bee to bee had. but I conceaue that they would gladly make the worke to appeare vnfeasable, y^t they might by y^t meanes be dismissed for England. Much hath beene my truble herein, and not a little my patience (f haueinge beene called rascall to my face for reprouinge them of their ryot, negligence & dissension) but, for the debt wch I am in, for their sustentation I hope ye aduenturers will see it discharged.[70] The silkewormeseede y^t came in these last shipps, are well conditioned for the most ꝑt. I haue deliuered them to ye Frenchman least they might miscarry out of our want of skill: but when y^e [4] time of the yeare shall come, I will distribute of them to such as haue the most desire & the best meanes to cherish them. Many Mulbery trees the last yeare were planted, & many vines; but the later came to nothinge out of ye trouble of ye times, or want of art & perhaps ye badness of ye cuttings: for they all grow on old stocks, and are yearely burnt downe by ye firyinge of ye woods: but the neglect of tendinge them I beleiue is ye cheife. Wherefore now wee haue taken an other order; that every plantation, (who are bonde vnto it by indenture) shall imp§ale§ two acres of grounde, and imploy the sole labor of 2 men in y^t busines, for ye terms of 7 yeares enlarginge ye same 2 acres more, wth a like increase of labore: in wch they are to build a large house of 2 storyes, well seiled, for silkewormes. by this meanes I hope this worke will goe really forwarde, & ye better if good store of Spanish or French vines, may be sent vs.

I haue hired a ship to cary ye Colledge men to theire plantation,[71] wch is now

70 For a discussion of the glass works, see Carl E. Hatch, Jr., "Glassmaking in Virginia, 1607–1625," *William and Mary Quarterly*, 2nd series, XXI (April 1941), 119–38; (July 1941), 227–38, and "A Preliminary Historical Study of Glass House Point, with a Special Emphasis on the First Attempts at Glassmaking in Virginia," U.S. Dept. of the Interior, National Park Service, Colonial National Historical Park, Yorktown, Virginia, 4 December 1940 (typescript in archives of National Park Service). Also see below.

71 In the Council's letter of 20 January 1622/23, it had been stated "The Colledg Tenat^{te}, wth much dificultie, we are now about to resettle and haue engaged our selves to supplie them wth Cornne vntill harvest, havinge strenthned them wth divers of the olde Planters vppon ye conditions wch your selves haue

vnder sayle, I pray god it succeede well; but I like not this stragelinge: & if all had beene of my minde, I would rather haue disobayed your comaunds, then subiected yͤ Collony to such disorder and hazards. For how is it possible to gouerne a people so dispersed; especially such as for yͤ most part are sent ouer? how can they repaire to diuine seruice, except euery plantation haue a Minister? how can wee raise soldiers to goe vppon the enimy or workemen for publique imploiments, wᵗʰout weakeninge them to much, or vndoeinge them by draweinge the fro their labors? wheras if wee had planted together we could haue borne out one anothers labors, & giuen both strength and beauty to yͤ Collony & all though they goe forth in sufficient numbers, what certainety is there in yᵗ, when ꝑhaps 10 of 60 will not stand to theire health [5] and a number of them dye? whereof this yeare wee haue had a miserable experience. The other day a party went vp to seat on yͤ Kinge of Apomatuckes townes, but before they could get thither, they were soe deminished by death, and weakened by sickenes, that they were fayne to giue it ouer. Such a pestilent feuer rageth this winter amongst vs: neuer knowne before in Virginia, by the infected people yᵗ came ouer in yͤ Abigall, who were poisened wᵗʰ stinkinge bere[72] all fallinge sike & many dyinge; euery where dispersinge the contagion. The fore runninge Sum̄er hath bene alsoe deadly vnto vs; I for my part, haueinge lost 19 by sickenes & 4 by yͤ Indians. You may ges in what a pore condition I am, but the extreame sickenesse I haue sufferde, the heart-breakinge to see the ill successe of your affayires, want of all thinges necessary for life, my debts in supplyinge youre scant prouisions, the Companyes not performeinge there contractes & approatchinge pouerty, I shou[ld] esteeme as nothinge, if our incessant toyle & best indeauors could but pꝛserue your good opinions: but since all wee can purchase vs but vndeseruered infamy.

Vltra Saromatas hinc libet fugere et glacialem Oceanum.[73]

wᶜʰ is oft in my minde and all most in my resolution.

It remaines yᵗ somethinge I should write of Virginia, whereof (be not offended yᵗ I speake yͤ truth) you know but little, & wee not much more,

ꝑpounded" (Kingsbury, IV, 16; also see note 53 above). Evidently they were being sent back to Henrico, according to Company instructions, from Surry, across the river from Jamestown, where they had been settled after the massacre (see Robert H. Land, "Henrico and Its College," *William and Mary Quarterly*, 2nd series, XVIII [October 1938], 494–5, 497 n.).

[72] For more concerning Duppa's "stinking beer," see Sandys' letters reprinted below and various official letters from the Council in Virginia reprinted in Kingsbury, III and IV.

[73] Juvenal, 2, lines 1 and 2. The lines in (the Loeb edition) read: Ultra Sauromatas fugere hinc libit et glacialem/Oceanum.

(for what can be discouered w^th^out meanes, or wth such an handfull of people soe dispersed?) but this I must defer vntill a time of more leasure, beinge now wholy taken vp wth full fillinge of your co͞maunds: wherefore I pray you excuse me to my particular freindes y^t^ I write not vnto them. As for y^r^ priuate affayres, I will make them myne owne, and aduance them wth my best industry: but wth all aduize you, y^t^ you aduenture not to much in ioynt stockes, nor in those proiectes wch ever fayle by ye death of ye co͞maunder & principall workemen; for ye life of one in euery § faculty § is not to be relied vppon: such is ye state of this country. As for o^r^ other crosses & the comeinge soe far short of y^r^ expectations, I had rather other should screch them, then y^t^ they should proceede from my pen, but both you and wee must submit o^r^selues to ye iudgments of god, to whose protection I co͞mende you, & rest.

Yours most assured,

G:S:

[Indorsed:] The Copy of my Letter sent to Mr. Farrer by the Hopewel.

The next letter, of 28 March 1623, was to Samuel Wrote, evidently a personal friend. A cousin of the Earl of Middlesex and early a prominent figure in the Virginia Company,[74] Wrote had in December and January 1622 spoken sharply and at length in opposition to the Sandys-Southampton policies on tobacco, had been tried for gross slander against the leaders of the Company,[75] and had been "forever excluded" from the Council and suspended from the Company for one year.[76] In the bitterness of his trial both Warwick's and Smith's followers rallied to his support, and the powerful opposition to the Sandys faction was united and crystallized.[77] All this George Sandys could hardly have known.[78] He was writing to an intelligent, and perhaps he thought independent-minded, friend who had a strong voice in the Company. It is ironical that this letter, which Wrote did not receive personally,

74 See Kingsbury, all volumes, and Brown, *Genesis*, II, 1063. Wrote had been a member of many important committees both before and after George Sandys left England. Lionel Cranfield, Earl of Middlesex, was much spoken against by the Sandys faction in 1623–4 for his conduct of the tobacco hearings (Kingsbury IV, 532). Later, in 1624–5, Sir Edwin Sandys joined Buckingham and Prince Charles in the impeachment proceedings against Cranfield.

75 Kingsbury, II, 188, 29 January 1622/3.

76 To be readmitted only on proper submission.

77 Craven, *Dissolution*, pp. 237–9.

78 Notice comparative dates of his letter and of the trial of Wrote. Exactly two months was hardly sufficient time for the news to reach him. The dispute had not even begun until 4 December.

would have almost surely have been used for the same purpose as it actually was used—against the administration of the Company.

Noble Sr

I am almost ashamed that I haue left yor lre vnanswered thus longe: but a bodie languishinge, well nigh vnto death, and a mynd distracted and broken with ill successes here, and hard Censures at home haue disabled me from all dutyes but those wch necessitie inforceth. But now I thanke God, I haue recovered my health, and a litle cured my thoughtę with the balme of my Innocencie resolving to strive against theis Torrentę of difficultyes till I passe them over, or bee swallowed vp by them: rather in that I wilbe Constant to my Course, then out of anie hope to gaine reputacon or satisfie your Concep̃cons. For their affections to this Plantacon hath so ou9 hightned eu9ie thinge that it is impossible for our Indevours to give it that lustre, wch must neede redound to the disgrace of vs, and will, I feare, to the preiudice of the Collonie. *I would to God that some one of Judgment and Integritie whom you trusted might bee sent ou9 to give* you a true Informac̃on of our proceedingę and the State of this Countrye.[80] If then it be found that Wee are faultie let the Censure and punishment light vpon the ill deserver: for my owne part I will desire no favour. But if our *want of meanes* haue frustrated yor hopes, or the hand of God, by extreame sickness, and vnheard of mortalitie hath prevented our Indevours, or if *wee haue beene inforced by some of yor Instructions to goe Contrarie to or Judgmentę?* If wee should imploy our owne or the Serveantę of others (wch would never bee endured) for future expectac̃ons; how in the meane time shall they be fed and Clothed or how shall wee give a satisfaction to their maisters? *It is not* a small proporc̃on of Corne that will feed a man, when that is his onelie sustenance. Had you no other provisions in England perhaps the land were too litle to sustaine her Inhabitantę. and for apparrell I will giue to the Magazine 10li sterling a yeare (as the rates here goe) for the Clothing of each particular Servaunt. for eu9ie labourer wee giue one Pound of Tobacco a daye, besidę his diet and 3 or 4 §a day§ to Artificers. from whence shall theis pay-

|| that some may be sent over truly to informe of the ꝑceedinge there ||[79]

|| The officers in Virginia by instructions from hence enforced to goe against theyr Judgments.||

|| Corne is their only sustenance.||

|| Apparell ||

[79] Marginal notes and indorsements are in the hand of Sir Nathaniel Rich.

[80] The idea of a royal commission to investigate affairs in Virginia seems to have been proposed by Alderman Johnson to the King before 23 April 1623. Sandys, therefore, was not the originator of the idea of an investigation (see Craven, *Dissolution*, pp. 259–61), though quite obviously what he wanted was an investigation and report from *within* the Company *to* the Company.

mentꝭ arise? *moreouꝰ so manie come ouꝰ without anie provision. and those you set out yorselues so furnished to halues (a maine Cause of* their debtꝭ and *deathes and of yor small retournes) that they make a dearth* of a plentifull harvest.[81] I protest for my owne part if I knew how to defraie the expences of the yeare, I would not set one plant of Tobacco whilst I lived in this Countrie: so much I loath it and onelie desire that I Could subsist without it. Now if anie will vpraid vs with the successe of this yeare, let them take heed least they manifest [2] not themselves to bee of the race of those Gyantꝭ wch made warre with heaven; for who is ignorant how the heavie hand of God hath suppressed vs? *the lyveing being hardlie able to bury the dead* through their owne Imbecillitie, insomuch as I am afraid wee haue not lost lesse then 500 by sicknes (with a generall weaknes of the rest) wch taken out of so small a number (*farre short of yor Coniectures*) I belieue haue *not left behind them so manie* able men in the Countrye. And by the way I would you Could hang that villaine Dupper[82] who with his stinking beere hath poisoned most of the Passengers, and spred the Infection all over the Collonie wch before the Arrivall of the Abigall were recoueꝰd. lastlie, whereas it was the onelye benifit *wch wee reapt from the treacherie of the Indians in drawing ourselues into a narrower* Circuite, whereby the people might haue beene better gouꝰned, and lived with more Comfort and securitie, publique Charges more easilie defraied, forces raised with lesse difficultie, and hazard to the Remaynder, townes in short time would haue beene forfeited, framed houses erected, Orchards planted, and groundꝭ impailed for the keeping of Cattle, staple Comodities the better aduanced, strength, beautie pleasure, riches and reputac̄on added forthwith to the Collonie: by *yor Comaunding vs to dispearse wee are like quicksiluꝰ throwne into the fire and hardlie to bee found in so vast a distance.*[83] But I can but giue you a touch of theis thinges wch perhaps were better vnwritten then not written to the full. If God spare me life I will write a particuler discourse of this Countrie, the hindrances to the Plantac̄on and waies to aduance it, with an answeare vnto Calumny meane while I

|| Complaynt yt too many come ouer and those ill prouided ||

||The lyuing hardly able to bury the dead 500 dyed by sickness not 500 able men left ||

|| Dupper ||

|| The benefitts of drawing the Colony together ||

|| much damnifyed by dispersing then these vpon Comd of ye Company ||

[81] This point quite naturally and justifiably was made much of by the opposition as evidenced in their rough notes in support of charges against the Company. See Kingsbury, IV, 160, 184.

[82] Probably James or Jeffrey Duppa, London brewer (see Brown, *Genesis*, II, 883). See also other letters below. Apparently a dysentery carried off many settlers.

[83] Phrases underlined and marginally commented upon were used by Rich in his case against the administration.

referre you to others for other particulers, and will now addresse my replie to yo[r] letter.

If I could be proud yo[r] Censure had so made me for that slothful worke wch I was ashamed to ffather. notwithstanding it begat a desire to proceede: but heare my owne Author.

———nec plura sinit tempusȝ pudorqȝ
Dicere maius opus magni certaminis vrget.[84]

Yet amongst the roreing of the seas, the rustling of the Shrowdę, and Clamour of Saylers, I translated two bookes, and will perhaps when the sweltring heat of the day confines me to my Chamber give a further assaye. for wch if I be taxt I haue noe other excuse but that it was the recreac̃on of my idle howers, and say with Alciat.[85]

Dum pueros iugulans, iuvenes dum tessera fallit
Desinet et segnes chartula picta viros
Haec nos festiuis emblemata cadimus horis.[86]

[3] As for dubius accusaçons, Custome and the meanes of the

[84] Ovid, *Metamorphoses*, VIII, 327–8, the Loeb edition (edited by Frank J. Miller [2 vols., Cambridge, Mass. and London, 1916 and 1944], I, 428). This printing is identical in spelling save that the last word of line 328 is urguet.

[85] Andreas or Andrea Alciati (1492–1550). His *Sacra Emblemata* was published in Venice in 1546. E. D. Neill, *Virginia Carolorum* . . . (Albany, N.Y., 1886), p. 46 n., thinks that Sandys actually refers to Andrew Willet's *Sacrorum Emblematum Centura una*, chiefly from Alciatus. Willet, a Puritan and chaplain to Prince Henry, died in 1621. It has not been found in the Huntington Library nor Harvard copy (which is slightly defective) of Willet, but has been located in *Andreae Alciati emblemata cum commentatis Claudi Minois I. C. Francisci Sanctii Brocensis* . . . Patuuij apud Petrum Paulum Tozzium . . . 1621. See note 86 below.

[86] Neill, *Virginia Carolorum*, p. 46 reads the Latin slightly differently as :

Dum pueras inquilanas invenes dum tessera fallit,
Desinet et segnes chartula picta vires
Haec nos festivis emblemata adimus horis.

Sandys' quotation of three lines is exactly that of the 1621 edition of Alciatus (see note 85 above), except that the third word of line 1 reads *iuglans* in the printed version. The lines appear on page 1, after some lxxx pages of Introduction. It is not the first emblem, which is on page 9, but "Praefatio ad Chonradvm Pevtingervm Avgvstanvm." There are six more lines. I am indebted to Miss Mary Isabel Fry of the staff of the Huntington Library for transcription of the passages.

man hath made me insensible of such Injuries *but more ignoble was that, though proceeding from a nobler* Person[87] who said wee held not our selues secure without the guard of a Thowsand men: when it is well knowne, that I reciued not one man in to my Plantac̃on though I had at sometymes not five that were able to beare Armes, and for the Gou9nour I my selfe was an Eye witnes, that the Councellors themselues were Constrayned to watch nightlie by turnes, vntill the Countrie allowed him a Guard of thirtie. for whose intertaignment he is yet vnsatisfied. O what a lying deuill is a mallice! And nowe alitle to degresse (for I write as thinges Come into my mynd and expect from so worthie a freind as you are a Pardon of Errours, since I haue not the leazure to read ou9 what I haue written) what a flagitious offence was that in vs to fetch of men from their dividendę who had neither food nor Munic̃on nor in Nomber able to defend themselues in the Cultivateing of the earth, or guard of their Cattle, all being slaine about them and wee vnable to supplie anie one of their wantę without the ruyne of others! must they not haue beene left of necessitie a pray either to slaughter or famyne? *or how would their weakenes haue indured the want of their ablest* men to haue gonne vpon the *Indians when out of the whole Collonie wee Could but raise* 180 (*whereof 80 were fit onelie to Carrie burthens*) to incounter 1000? wch had put all in hazard if God had not taken their heartę from them: though as valiant as lyons against one another, and as skilfull in their bowes as the Beniamites with their slinges; haueing manie *peeces besides, with Powder and Shott, and knoweing too well how to vse them,* how §am§ I touched in particuler about that ignominious proposic̃on of removeinge to the Easterne Shore, when I onelie related the Argumentę, and nomynated the Author,[88] and although the Gou9nour and my

|| Ignoble speach of a noble man ||

|| But 180 men able to incounter the Enemye whereof 80 men were fitt only to carry burthens ||

[87] Did Sandys mean this as the Earl of Southampton or his brother Sir Edwin? One of them or another person, a nobleman, of the Sandys faction may have made such an assertion in a letter to Governor Wyatt. It may have been this person that Wyatt was addressing in his letter of the period 24 October 1623–26 June 1624 (*William and Mary Quarterly*, 2nd series, VI [April 1926], 114–21), in which he defends Sandys and himself. See below. George later, in the letter to Sir Samuel Sandys, says Sir Edwin was the author of the aspersions regarding the removal to the Eastern Shore (see below, and Kingsbury, IV, 73–4).

[88] This must have been in a letter no longer extant, probably to Sir Edwin Sandys (on Kingsbury, III, 73). The Council had mentioned the need to remove the capital to healthier and more easily fortified site (Kingsbury, III, 612–13). See Sandys' letter to his brother Sir Samuel of 30 March 1623 printed below. The "proposer's" name does not appear in the Council's letters to the Company.

selfe gaue way that the place might be survaid[89] for the planting of a Partie there as better furnished with all sortꝭ of prouisions and fit thereafter for fortificac̄on: yet neuꝰ was it so much in or Thoughtꝭ (though manie ranne violentlie that waye) to quit the places wch wee held and I for my part would first haue beene torne in peeces. But I wilbe more warie hereafter what I write.

I vsed Mr Calthrope[90] at his landinge with all the Curtesie I Could and brought him acquainted with the Gouꝰnour. I proferd him the Entertainment of my house, and my owne Chamber to lodge in [4] wch he refused in that I was to bee but seldome there my selfe, in regard of my almost dailie attendance at the Councell table (for besidꝭ our owne partꝭ, wee are faine to discharge the Offices of others: if Mr Secretarie[91] had beene good for anie thing wee would never have suffred him to haue gon home, and what a pittifull Councellour haue wee of yor Doctour!)[92] I haue giuen from time to time the best Councell I am able. At the first he kept Companie too much with the Inferiours, who hung vpon him while his good liquor lasted, after he Consorted with Captaine Whitacres[93] (a man of no good

To his most worthie ffreind Samuel Wrote Esq. at London be theis deliuered.[1] [[1] Written lengthwise of

[89] On 20 June 1622 Sir Francis Wyatt did issue a commission to George Yeardley to explore the Eastern Shore with the idea of setting up a large plantation there (Kingsbury, III, 656–7).

[90] A Captain Christopher Calthropp or Colthorp was burgess from York county in 1644, 1645/46, and 1653 (see McIlwaine ed., *Journals of the House of Burgesses of Virginia, 1619–1658/59* [Richmond, 1915], pp. xvii, xviii, xxi). He patented land grants at one place or another in Elizabeth City in 1628, 1635, and 1636, and another at an undesignated site in 1636 (see Nugent, pp. 12, 26, 34, 39, 44).

[91] Christopher Davison testified to the Company while he was in London that "for the performance of his place [*i.e.*, the secretaryship] that mr Geo: Sandys had vndertaken it out of his loue to him; and further that his cominge ouer was in parte for the better Informac̄on of the Counsell, of the State of the Colony" (7 October 1622, Kingsbury, II, 109, Extraordinary Court). See Chapter V, note 107, above.

[92] Doctor John Pott. For more concerning him see the third letter to Ferrar given below (note 131), Kingsbury, all volumes, and Brown, *First Republic*, *passim*.

[93] Captain Jabez Whitaker was member of the House of Burgesses from Elizabeth City in 1623/24 and was appointed member of the council in 1626 (Brown, *First Republic*, pp. 512, 571, 580, 646). On 13 May 1623, Governor Wyatt gave him a warrant to levy every twentieth man throughout the colony and send him to Wariscoyack to aid in building a fort (Kingsbury, IV, 191). This Whitaker is not to be confused with the Rev. Alexander Whitaker, who died about 1617 (Brown, *Genesis*, II, 1050). Jabez Whitaker evidently acted at times as Sandys' deputy in collecting revenues. See below.

page in the margin—Kingsbury's note.]

example) with whom he is gone into Kicotan,[94] yet wheresoeuer he bee, he shall not bee without the reach of my Care, nor want for anie thing that I or my Credit can procure him.
I kindlie thanke you for yor Gray hound the fairest that ever I saw; yet the want of his stones haue deaded his Courage and made him altogether vseles. But I haue written too much and yet nothinge. Inopem me copia fecit. I cease to trouble you but never to loue you.

I pray you remember my best loue and wishes to worthie Mr Gibb[95]

James Cittie 28 Martij 1623

Yo^{r} assured ffreind

George Sandys.

S^{r} I pray you be intreated extraordinarilie to importune Mr John Bonovill[96] to send me two Ffrenchmen skilfull in silke-wormes and planting of Vines I will pay them 20 markę apeece for their wages by the yeare, and find them victualls, or 20^{li} apeece if they will accept of o^{r} Virginia paym^{t}, Mr Mellin[97] will take order for their passage.

I have sent you a tast of our best Tobacco by Mr Tuke.[98] if you like it I will furnish you yearelie with enough for your takeinge.
[Indorsed, by Sir Nathaniel Rich:] G. Sandys to Mr Wrott 29 M9ch 1623.

94 Capital of the corporation of Elizabeth City, Jabez Whitaker's home.

95 Probably Thomas Gibbs, Esq., active in the Virginia Company 1620-2, and on the Virginia Commission 15 July 1624 (Brown, *Genesis*, II, 896; Kingsbury, IV, 491, 494, 497). He evidently at one time served Sir Edwin Sandys as an informer regarding the Commission's proceedings (Kingsbury, IV, 224–6).

96 John Bonoeil, silk grower to the King, had written "A Treatise of the Art of making Silke. . . ." (London 1622.) A copy was presented to the Treasurer and Council and Company for Virginia by his Majesty (Kingsbury, IV, 661). Bonoeil supervised the securing of French silk-growers for the colony. For his interest, on 22 May 1622, he had been made an adventurer (for two shares) and was granted lands in Virginia (Kingsbury, IV, 634).

97 Thomas Melling's name appears frequently in the Records of the Company. He was at one time a partner of Captain Bargrave (Kingsbury, III, 524). He may also have acted as a financial agent, or banker, for Sir Edwin Sandys (Kingsbury, III, 416, 529, 604, 692). He also kept Sir Edwin informed of the course of affairs in the Company when the latter was at Northbourne, his country place in Kent.

98 See the letter to Sir Myles Sandys given below. Tuke, or Tucke, was apparently master of the Abigail. See note 125 below.

The next two letters, to George Sandys' brothers Sir Myles and Sir Samuel, repeat some of the same animadversions but also contain a considerable amount of new material. The first is to Sir Myles.

Sr

|| the dispirsing of ye colony again very pernicious ||

It is a Curtisie that addꝭ not a litle to those manie wch I haue received from you, that you vouchsafe to remember the so farre distant. A hopefull begynneing we had in this Countrie, yet seconded with all the Calamities wherwith God vseth to scourge a disobedient people, as murder, dead by diseases, and scarcitie almost vnto famyne. Yet the first had been a reformac̃on, had wee beene suffred to haue made the true vse of it. for the English throughout this wild Countrye, planted dispersedlie in small familyes, far from Neighbours, as Covetous of large pos̃sions (larger then 100 tymes their Nomber were able to Cultivate) and to lyue like Libertines out of the eye of the Magistrate, not able to secure themselues, nor to bee releiued by others, vpon anie occasion, insomuch as if they had had anie knowledge of the purpose of the Indians, the most part Could not possiblie haue preuented their treacheries: but must either haue beene beseiged in their houses (and Consequentlie famished) or Cut of as they followed their labours. Vpon this occasion wee drew the remainder Close together, whereby they might haue beene the better gou9ned, and haue added to their lyues both Comfort and securitie presentlie wee should haue begunne to fortifie Townes, to haue built framed houses, to haue planted hortyardꝭ and gardens to haue inclosed ground for or Cattle, and set vpon more reall Comodities, by wch the Collony in short time would haue growne strong, beautiful, pleasant rich and reputable *But such is the disposic̃on of those who glorie in their wisedomes. that they will rather Justifie and proceed in their Errors then to suffer a supposed disgrace by reformeing them*; So that wee are Comaunded to suffer eu9ie man to retourne to his [2] divident, though in some stronger fashion and haue our discrec̃ons and Courages Censured for doeing that wch they should haue begunne with, Who cleare themselues by the wronginge of others; obiectinge vnto vs their *Instructions, whereof manie are infeasible and the most Inconvenient, for to say the truth they knowe nothing of Virginia, nor will beleiue anie thing from vs that is not answereable to their former Concepc̃ons. But if eu9 they will doe anie good they must admit of our Informac̃ons, and suffer ther Instruc̃ons, for the most part,* to bee rather advices then Commaundꝭ. Extreame hath beene the mortalitie of this yeare, wch I am afraid hath dobled the Nomber of those wch were massacred; yet with our small and sicklie forces we haue discomforted the Indians,

JAMESTOWN IN 1622

An engraving enlarged from a portion of the DeBry engraving and appearing in L. G. Tyler, *The Cradle of The Republic*, 1907

round about vs, burnt their houses, gathered their Corne and slaine not a few; though they are as swift as Roebuckę and not to bee destroyed but by surprize or famine they now beginne to desire a peace, and after the restitucõn of their Prisoners, for whose sakes wee seeme to be inclineable thereunto and will trie if wee can make them as secure as wee *were. that wee may followe their example in destroying them* Although in particuler I haue not suffred much by the Indians, yet haue I lost by sicknes 23 [*sic*][99] of my small Nomber to the greate diminucõn of my meanes, and impaire of my last yeares profit, and had I not hired in good time the sixth part of a ship (wch Cost me aboue 140li for my share) I and the rest of my men had hardlie [3] escaped the perishing by famyne. ffor all theis disasters I have sent home as much as will pay that Sum; discharge 100l wch I owe vnto them who haue my Cropp in their possion, with 50 more wch my Cozen Myles[100] standę bound for, and to furnish me with necessityes in some poore sorte, for the yeare ensewinge, I onelie p3sume of yor favour, in that I cannot possiblie at this time in regard of my great losses and unexpected vnexpences doe otherwise, to deferre the payment of that 100l (wch is all that I owe in the world) wch you stand ingaged with me, vntill Christmas next, wch wilbee in Charge to you in regard of the Annuitie, wch out of yor bountie[101] you were pleased to giue me; at wch time whether I lieue or die it shalbee discharged. Well may I put in die, for there is few of vs that haue not knockt this yeare at the gates of death. but by the mercie of God I am now in perfect health, as is the Gou9nour and his ladie[102] (though after much sicknes)

|| A pfidious treatye ||

99 Whether on the Treasurer's official plantation or on his personal ones it is impossible to say. Since the income from both was his, he evidently thought of them as one.

100 "Cosen," usually used loosely for "relative," may refer to (1) Myles (son of William Sandys of Graythwaite), died 1651 (see *The Family of Sandys*, II, Pedigree B); (2) Myles, son of Christopher Sandys, baptized at Hawkeshead 1582 (see Pedigree B); (3) Sir Myles, 2nd Baronet, son of the Sir Myles to whom George addressed this letter, 1593–1644 (see Pedigree C); (4) Sir Myles, grandson of Myles Sandys of Latimer's and son of Sir William of Fladbury, 1600–36, M.P. Cirencester 1625. The first two were fairly distant relatives. George evidently referred to his nephew or young cousin, grandson of his benefactor when he was admitted member of the Middle Temple.

101 This may be a euphemism, for Sir Myles at one time or another secured revenues from George's lands in Yorkshire. See Chapters I and II above. Of course it may have something to do with annuity out of the manor of Ombersley granted to George by his father. See note 107 below.

102 Lady Margaret Wyatt, Sandys' niece, had taken ship from England, *after*

who recomend ther seruices vnto you. Concerning Thomas Marson[103] I haue neither seene nor heard of him since he delivered me yor letter whether he be returned for England, or dead, or gone to some remoued Plantačon I knowe not, but if he be here he shall find me readie to giue him ~~the~~ §my§ best helpe in all occasions, and that yor recomendačon is to me a Comaund. Much afflicted I am for the decaie of Sr Thomas Josseline[104] and more for the ill vsage of his old freindꝭ. hoe eu^9^ I know you so noble that you will not add sorrowe to afflic̃con nor forbeare it to Comfortt him in his miserie. Remember I pray you my service and best wishes to those that are with you, not forgetting my loue to Mr Franklinge whom I could wish here with vs I rest

yor loveing brother

George Sandys.

James citty, 30 March 1623

[4] I haue sent you by Mr John Tuke M^r^ of the Abigail a tast of our best Tobacco of this yeare if you like it I shall send you as good or better hereafter in plentie.

[Addressed:] To the right worll my especiall good Brother Sr Myles Sandys Kn^t^ and Baronet at Wiberton in the Isle of Ely.

[Indorsed in the hand of the reviewer:] G Sandys to Sr Miles Sande See here one cause of ye Massacre.

news of the massacre had reached the mother country, about 12 October 1622 (Kingsbury, III, 690).

103 Unidentified in Kingsbury, Brown (*Genesis* and *First Republic*), or McIlwaine (*Journal* and *Minutes*).

104 Josselyn, or Jocelyn, had evidently got himself tremendously in debt in affairs involving Sir Myles Sandys, who was perhaps a relative or relative by marriage of Sir Thomas. Among the William Cole Papers in the British Museum (Add. MSS. 5808.113) are "Extracts of letters from Sir Myles Sandys of Wilberton to Sir Thomas Josselyn: taken from a *Folio MS* of Papers relating to *Cambridgeshire*, which I have chiefly extracted into my 20th Volume, and lent me by my friend *Thomas Martin of Palgrave in Suffolk Esqr*" [Blicheley 29 June 1753]. Sir Myles' ardent protestations of friendship and profuse scriptural and classical quotations are interspersed with warnings to Sir Thomas that the latter cannot blame or involve Sir Myles in his transactions, and that the attempt to do so "savoureth of a devilish Spirit, whose Delight is in Lyes. . . ." Sir Myles and his friends, however, offer to pay £6,000 of Sir Thomas' debts, and Sir Myles offers to take Sir Thomas and all his family into his own house until the latter's fortune is bettered. These letters were written on 31 August and 20 September 1622. On November 1622 Sir Myles Sandys and others entered

The next letter is addressed to his oldest brother Sir Samuel.

S^r^

I humblie crave yor pardon if I have not written §vnto you§ so often as you expected, and my dutie bound me: presumeinge that the Governour[105] had acquainted you with whatsoeu9 was worthie your knowledge: We found at our Comeing over the Country in peace, but in such a peace as presaged ruyne: the people dispearsed in small familyes, farre distant one from another, and like the foolish Arcadians, exposed to the pray of whosoeu9 would assaile them, yet Could wee not reforme this mischeife, they haueing Pattentę granted from the Court in England to plant wheresoeu9 they pleased contrarie to all order, discipline, and Example: but how well *wee beganne to build (though impossible to Continew) on this prescribed foundac̃on I coniecture is not unknowne vnto you*; Neither could the Trecherie of the Indians (although foreknowne) have beene but in part prevented: who like violent lightening are gone as soone as ꝑceived. Yet *are we taxed* with indiscrec̃on and Cowardize for drawinge *theis miserable people* to places of securitie; Who had neither victuall nor munic̃on (nor Could wee helpe them wth either) nor of strength to defend themselves: *so that of necessitie they must have perished either by the Enimye, or famyne. But men that are ambitious to bee Counted wise will rather Justifie then acknowledge their Errors and impute the fault of the execuc̃on, when it is indeed in the proiect.* Wee held not our selves secure said an ignoble Noble man vnles wee had 1000 Souldiers to guard vs; what a strict affynitie is there betweene the divell and a lyer! for my owne part I receaued not a man into my Plantac̃on although at one time I was so weake that I could not arme 5 able men: and for the Governour, the Councellors themselves were constrayned to watch nightlie by turnes vntill the Countrye allowed him a guard of 30 men. Sr Edwin writes that strucke with a Panicke feare wee proposed a Romoveall of the Collonie to the Easterne shore. Indeed I writt home of such a proposic̃on and named the Proposer with his Argumentę which were hotlie mantayned by others, (and no question but [2] that place had beene better, at the first, to have seated on, in regard

He complaynes y^t^ they are taxed from drawing theise miserable people to places of security

The error in y proie^ct^ not in ye execution

An ignoble ~~ign~~ noble mans speach

suit against Sir Thomas Josselyn and others (P.R.O., C 3 Chas I/382/50). It is interesting to note that this Sir Thomas Josselyn was presumably the father or grandfather of John Josselyn (*fl.* 1638–74), who lived in New England for many years and was the author of *New England's Rarities Discovered* (1672) and *An Account of Two Voyages to New England* (1674).

105 Wyatt was Sir Samuel Sandys' son-in-law.

of fertilitie, Convenience, all sorts of provision and strength both against the Native and fforeiner) yet theis were refuted by vs in pointꝭ of Reputac̄on, being besidꝭ, as *wee alledged*, an intollerable presumption for vs to attempt *such a Change without* your Consentꝭ: howsoever wee thought *it fitt that the place should bee further survaied*, and a *Partie there seated, and this is that treason against God and man for wch wee deserve to bee* hanged. But I pray God their Contemplac̄ons doe not so ouꝰswaye our experience that all in thend Come to no thinge: who thinke euꝰie thing done as soone as Conceived (how unfeasable soeuꝰ) and so highten their proceedinges that it is impossible for our Actions to goe alonge with their reportꝭ whereby wee must of necessitie suffer in our reputac̄ons. Wee are much upraided with Sr Thomas Dale: yet (not to detract from the dead) what did he? or what is extant of his Endevours? or what Could not wee doe if wee (as hee) had

Sr Tho. Dale had 500 men fedd and apparralled out of England. They have not one for ye publiqȝ

500 men at our *owne disposure, both fed and appareled out of England?* whereas wee haue *not one* except wee hire them with our private purses, or take them Iniuriouslie from their Mrs *The Teñants they sent on that so absurd Condition of halves are neither able,* to *sustaine them*selves nor discharge their moyetie, and are so deiected with their Scarce provisions, and finding nothing to answeare their expectac̄on, that most give themselves over, and die of Melancholye, the rest running so farre in debt as keepes them still behind hand, and manie (not seldome) looseing their Crops

Comanders

whilst they hunt for their Bellyes: Nor are their Comanders much better, who haveing little perfourmed of what was promised, their meanes not worth the Collectinge, conuꝰt their mindꝭ to other Imploymentꝭ. And now least wee should growe too rich they haue sent over (without anie [3] advice from vs) a

Capt. of a ship sent ~~Ea[ch]~~ over to buyld a castle in the ayre

Captaine of a shipp,[106] with extreame charges to the Countrye, to build a fort in the Sea (I might haue said a Castle in the aire) on a shole of oister shells everie tide overflowne, and at lowe water with euꝰie wynd washt over by the surges; where when you

[106] Captain Each, "master of the Abigail" (and apparently succeeded as captain by John Tuke, see below), had offered, on the assurance of 60,000 weight of tobacco at "3d ꝑ pound [as] fraight" home to England, to carry to Virginia twelve carpenters, who with his sailors and the assistance of the colony, could build a blockhouse at Blunt Point, below Jamestown, "vpon the Oyster bankꝭ" (Kingsbury, III, 647–8, 685). This would forbid the passage of any ship up the river beyond that point, thought the Council in London. The Company had joyfully accepted his proposal. The Virginia Council's letter of 20 January 1622/23 (Kingsbury, IV, 16) doubted the suitability of the spot. On 4 April 1623 (*ibid.*, IV, 100, 236), the Virginia Council reported that Captain Each had died too suddenly even to survey the place, but that Captain Roger Smith

have pearced the vpper Crust, ther is for manie speares lengthes no bottome to bee found. *The Captaine dyed, to save his Credit, soone after.* And I feare that their too much vaine glorie and presumption at home, togeather with our sins have drawne theis afflictions vpon vs; the massacre being seconded with a gen9all sicknes, insomuch as wee haue lost I beleive few lesse then 500, and not manie of the rest that haue not knockt at the doores of death. yet with our small and weake forces wee haue Chased the Indians from their aboadę, burnt their houses, taken their Corne and slayne not a few. The great King now sues for peace, and offers a restitucon of his Prisoners: for whose sakes wee seeme to bee inclineable thereunto, and will trie if wee can make them as secure as wee were *that wee may following their Example in destroying them.* We are now of o^r^selves about to erect a ffort in as advantagious place as the other, but vpon a solid foundacon My Ladie Wyat God be thanked hath recou9ed her health and no question will Continew it, shee being of so chearefull a disposeition, w^c^h is in this Countrie an Antidote against all diseases. I am ashamed, yet enforced, to importune you once more for one yeares Rent of my Annuitie[107] before hand, this being a hard yeare. I haueing lost 23 men by sicknes, and received not one of those 25 wch the Companie Contracted to send me, haveing also paid almost 200li for my share *in the hire of a Shipp without wch both I and mine had famished*, and discharged besidę diu9s debtę in England. I will send you [4] my Acquittances by Mr Mellyn. Remember I pray you my best seruice to my Worthie and kind sister, and to my Ladie Wayneman with the rest of my Cozens.

This Capt. dyed to saue his Creditt.

Vayne glory & presump^tio^ at home haue drawne theise affliction on ye Colony

they colony inclyne to a peace but meane it not

About to erect a fort.

He had famished but y^t^ he had p^t^e of a ship

I humblie take my leaue.

yor loueing Brother.

GEORGE SANDYS.

James Cittie 30 March 1623

[Addressed:] To the right wor^ll^ my much honored Brother Sr Samuell Sandys Kn^t^ at Omberslie in Wocter shire giue theis.

[Indorsed, in the reviewer's hand:] G. Sandys to S^r^ Sa: Sandys, 30 March 1623 ~~about ye concerning the att order~~ imputing the cause of theyr ill proceedings to ye directions from hence.

found it nothing but an upper crust of oyster shells and all beneath quicksand. The workmen therefore refused "absolutely to medle wth it." This "castle in the air" idea was the sort of thing the Smith-Warwick faction cited with telling effect to prove the impracticality of the Sandys-Southampton group.

107 Again presumably from George's portion of an annuity "granted out of the manor of Ombersley" by the Archbishop to his three youngest sons, Thomas, Henry, and George. For date and other features of will, see Chapter II above.

The last two of the six letters were addressed to John Ferrar, the man who still controlled shipments of supplies for agriculture and industry. The first departs from the defensive and critical attitude and is briskly businesslike in tone. Sandys discusses the revenues and property for which he is accountable and the state of the various industries, and ends the letter with a plea that he be permitted to adventure further into the unknown West. The second letter, really a postscript of three days later, contains a harsh but discerning appraisal of the personnel of the Virginia Council.

> Worthy S^{r}, I have sent you the copy of my Letter by the Hopewel how coppied, I know not, for I have not the leasure to pervse it. N.P. Of all your depts, & the tobacco dew for the saile of their times w^{c}h belonged to Sr William Nuce[108] (of whom 3 onely are alive) I can but receive a hundred weight, w^{c}h I am ashamed to send you single Som fault I must lay vpon the tardy receait of your accounts, w^{c}h I have often importuned. I have divers under arest, & distrained on the goods of others; but the Country is so empty of tobacco, that no present satisfaction wilbe given. Let it be accounted my fault if you have it not the yeare following wth arerages, for I wil trust no more vnto promises but seaze on their crops before any be distributed. The like Counsil I gave Mr Blany[109] the last yeare (for ~~yoyr~~ §your§ informations cam too late for me) but he trusted too much vnto those who had never formerly failed him. Leifetenant Perce[110] hath tak[en] order in England to pay you the 50^{l} w^{c}h he owes.
>
> I have been at Kicotan to order your affaires in that place. Cap-

108 Knight Marshal, who had died, as noted above, soon after his arrival in Virginia.

109 Edward Blaney, Blayney, or Blaine, merchant, had been associated with Sir Edwin Sandys (Kingsbury, III, 503, 508) in the Virginia business for years before George Sandys went to America. He was the Company (or the smaller joint-stock company) factor or representative in charge of the Magazine, or Company store, in the colony. He evidently operated his store as Southern plantations or American mining companies sometimes operate theirs, on credit —in this case in expectation of a tobacco crop.

110 William Pierce, Perse, Perce, etc., was later in Sandys' time captain of the guard at Jamestown and eventually burgess and member of the Council in Virginia. He was evidently an old planter, and a prosperous one. His daughter Jane had been Rolfe's third wife. His own wife, on a trip to England twenty years after she reached the colony, boasted of her garden and fine house and of how she and her husband had gone to America with little or nothing (see Neill,

taine Nuce[111] died very poore: he had no crop of tobacco this yeare, nor hath any of the tenants a graine, hardly, of corne to sustaine them. it is aledged that most was spent in releiving of those that came thether for succor. But they lay al on the short provitions sent wth them: by wch meanes they [~~do~~] depart wth most of their corne as soone as it is reaped to discharge their borrowings & besides the Companyes tenants are planted on the barrenest places in al the Country, by reason of your affecting of cleared ground, wch is generaly worne out, & vngrateful to the planters. Captaine Whitacres[112] lost yearly his labor on the place where he was seated. Of him onely I receaved 180 waight of tobacco, wch wth 20 more, I payd to Mr Cleyborne[113] for his wages according to your agreement. He is now at Kicotan, drawne thether by Captaine Nuce a little before his death. I have disposed of things there in this manner. I have taken Captaine Whitacres bond to pay you for the tenants, together wth those wch he formerly com̄aunded, a hundred waight of the best tobacco a man, & 15 bushels of corne, (besides a like proportion for themselves) wch is as great a rate as any ~~wil~~ do give, & more then most men can make. Captaine ~~Wh~~ Wilcocks[114] pays 20 waight les a man, being compounded wth before: & Captaine Smith shal pay, if he have his, as much as the most. By this meanes you wil have a constant rent, & equal the gettings of the privat planter, the moyety for the tenant deducted: wch other wise wil com (as it hath don) vnto nothing. The tenants that belong to Captaine Nuce his place, I have suffered his widdow (provided that it be alowd of by you) to enjoy them this year: not out of charity onely, although she hath nothing left to sustaine herselfe, & her poore child (her houband [*sic*] having sould his land to

Virginia Carolorum, p. 61 and P. A. Bruce, *Economic History of Virginia in the Seventeenth Century* . . . [2 vols., New York and London, 1896], I, 328). For a sketch of Pierce, see *William and Mary Quarterly*, 1st series, IX (April 1901), 270–1.

111 Captain Thomas Newce or Nuce, brother of Sir William, was himself deputy for the Company land and member of the Council. He arrived in 1620/21 and died about 1 April 1623 (Brown, *Genesis*, II, 956).

112 See note 93 above.

113 William Claiborne, Clayborne, or Cleburne, the surveyor, who had entered the colony with Wyatt and Sandys. For his later adventurous career in Virginia, see the article in *D.A.B.* and J. H. Claiborne, *William Claiborne of Virginia* (New York, 1917).

114 John Wilcocks, who had located his "divident" by 1621 at Accomack, was a member of the House of Burgesses in 1623/24 from the Eastern Shore (Brown, *First Republic*, pp. 571, 580).

furnish himselfe for this place; she being besides a woman of good birth, & better conditions.) but partly out of right in that he livd a good part of the yeare, & partly out of necessety; they having no corne nor we able to help them w^{t}h any, the Seafloure not [2] yet arived; so that they must have famished, or by shifting abroad returnd you no proffit.[115] You may hereafter save the charge of a Deputy, who can no way advantage you ~~in~~ I have sent you hereinclosed the names of al your tenants[116] that are living; W^{t}h the times past I wil have nothing to do; but for the future I doupt not but to give you contentment. Your pinnas lies like a wrack at Elizabeth citty; w^{c}h hath brought in this year not les then 1800 bushels of corne, & yet, w^{c}h is strange, not any in the Colony so nere starving as they. I sent Nun [117] w^{t}h his fellows (of whome none deserve the name of a shipwrite) to vew her; who writ the woord that 150^{l} would not repaire her; w^{c}h was twice as much, if not more, as she cost: but one having offered to buy her, I suspected som knavery, & vpon my coming downe had her exactly serched, & found that no great matter would renew her: so that I have set both them & others vpon her. yet sailes & tackling we shal want except you supplie vs: & I doubt not but to imploy her to your better satisfaction.

The Vinerouns are placed together at Elizabeth Citty & altogether imployed about ~~silck~~ §silckwoormes§, that we may preserve the seede & send you home som silck the next yeare. for the planters are so busied about rebuildings & prepareing theyr

[115] At the Virginia Courts in London of 25 June and 6 August 1623 Sir John Danvers pleaded Mrs. Nuce's cause, based on her official request to continue on the plantation until a new deputy for the Company's lands be appointed. The court granted her request.

[116] This possibly may refer to tenants on Ferrar's personal land. Virginia Company courts, in recognition of his services as deputy, in May 1622 moved to bestow 20 shares of "old adventure" on him (Kingsbury, II, 31) but these were not confirmed until after 12 November 1623 (*ibid.*, 480), when he spoke also of lands due him because of persons he had sent over. Nugent's list of land patents beginning with the earliest extant (of 1623) does not include John Ferrar as a holder or former holder. It seems more probable, therefore, that these are the Company's lands, for which Ferrar had been responsible (before his brother succeeded him on 22 May 1622) as deputy. "Your pinnas" is also probably the Company's pinnace.

[117] A Thomas Nunne appears in McIlwaine, ed., *Minutes* (pp. 8, 45, 46), though not as a shipwright. Evidently the man referred to here was foreman of the shipwrights, now under Sandys' immediate charge. Otherwise unidentified.

grounds, that few, at this time, ether can, or wil atend them. Yet for my owne part I have set 4 to do nothing else: & ~~im~~ prepared the chamber where in I ly at Leiftenant Perses (the fairest in Virginia)[118] for that purpose. I heare the Frenchmens times com out the next yeare: you must vse the meanes to procure their stay, & send more of their quality if you would have that woorke goe realy forward.

Since my last letter I ~~have~~ sent my shallop with my servants as far almost as the fals for sand for the Glasse men, but ~~can~~ §could§ find none that would serve; & since to Cape Henry, where they lighted of that wch they like (however send us two or three Hogsheds out of England) if it be not disliked in the tryal. Al the servants are dead, wch you must supply, for the charge is intollerable to hyre them: w^{ch}, wth their provitions, lyes al vpon me, that am not able to feede my owne familie. And, to give a greater blow to our necessitys, the Tygar sent forth a trading wth M^{r}

118 At Jamestown. The location of grants or houses remains partially conjectural, though current excavations may soon give positive proof of location. According to Mr. Forman's plot of Jamestown in 1624, William Pierce's "lot" was in the "New Towne" (Forman, pp. 63–4, 79), north of the "Back Street and Mr. Blaney's." In 1623 this house was apparently new (Forman, p. 79) and contained a dining hall. Mr. Samuel H. Yonge (*The Site of Old James Towne, 1607–1698* . . . [Richmond, 1907], p. 16) shows it in the same relative position, near the property of Dr. John Pott (Pierce's was west of Pott's and east of Captain Roger Smith's). Forman's plot shows Blaney, Roger Smith, and Pott as Pierce's nearest neighbours, all of them north of the "Back Street" (which ran parallel to the shoreline perhaps $\frac{1}{8}$ mile inland). Another group of houses south of "Back Street" lay between it and the river. The census taken at Jamestown in 1624/25 (see John C. Hotten, *Original Lists of Persons of Quality* . . . [London, 1874], p. 174), evidently taken by residential groups, places Sandys in the fourth group (the first contains the names of Sir Francis and Lady Wyatt and ten other men and women, the second Sir George and Lady Yeardley and others, the third the small household of Davison's widow and the clerk Sharpless), with the persons listed as follows:

George Sands, Treasurer
Captain William Pierce
Jane Pierce [and 17 others including "Angello A Negar"]

Lyon G. Tyler, *Cradle of the Republic*, pp. 36–8, incorrectly runs the Davison and Pierce groups together as one household. Sandys thus lived in a house, or group of houses, with the Pierces when he was in town. It is almost surely this town house Sandys refers to, although Pierce had a dwelling house and later, at least, 2,100 acres on Mulberry Island (Nugent, p. 149).

Puntises[119] pinnace vnder Captaine Spilman[120] (a man warie enough heretofore & acquainted w^t^h their trecheries) is not onely returned empty, but himselfe w^t^h 26 wel armed, sufficient to have defended themselves against 500 Indians, are cut off or taken prisoners; ether by ambushes or too much credulity: for as yet we know not the certanty. the ship attempted by 60 canoues (not above five of the seamen aboard) but were dispersed by the discharge of their Ordnance. So that if the Seaflower[121] com not quickly in, there wil hardly be found a preservation against famin. And by the way, to our no little discontentment, we having w^t^h great expence set out that ship to Somer Ilands for furnishing the country w^t^h their frutes, in print[122] you have given the reputation [to another] Sic vos non vobis.

119 John Pountis (or Poyntz, Pountes, etc.), member of the Virginia Company (12 December 1618, Brown, *First Republic*, p. 295), was commissioned on 28 June 1620 a member of the Virginia Council and on 24 July 1621 vice-admiral for the colony (Kingsbury, I, 379, 383, 479, 506, 546). In 1624 he was sent by the General Assembly, as their representative, to the King and Lords of the Privy Council, that his testimony might represent the Assembly's side of the situation as opposed to that presented by the Commissioner's (see below) report (Kingsbury, IV, 474, 476, 559, 560, 584, 585; McIlwaine, ed., *Journals*, p. xxix).

120 Captain Henry Spelman, Indian interpreter and son or nephew of Sir Henry Spelman of Norfolk, England, was killed when trading with the Anacostan Indians, probably near the present site of Washington, D.C. (Brown, *Genesis*, II, 1021). An old and experienced Indian fighter, he probably should not have allowed himself to be ambushed, as Sandys says. Spelman had lived with the Indians, as a captive, in 1609–10. For a more detailed account of what happened, see Peter Arundle's letter to William Caninge of April 1623 (Kingsbury, IV, 450). Spelman wrote in 1611 an account of Virginia events of 1609–11 which was published by J. F. Hunnewell, in London in 1872, under the title *Relation of Virginia, by Henry Spelman, 1609*.

121 The *Sea-Flower* had been blown up and wrecked on 18 March, at anchor in the Bermudas, by a careless lighting of pipes near the powder room. See Miles Kendall's letter to Sir Edwin Sandys of 15 April 1623 (Kingsbury, IV, 120). Kendall saw letters from England to George Sandys in the wreckage, all "spyled" by water. The *Sea-Flower's* loss was a real tragedy, for she had aboard "500li worth of Meale and other provisions" (*ibid.*, IV, 525).

122 Possibly in the broadside of May 1622 of the Virginia Company, "A Note of the Shipping, Men, and Prouisions Sent and Prouided for Virginia, . . . in the Yeere 1621" (Kingsbury, III, 639–43), which contains the paragraph: "A small Ship comming in December last from the *Summer-Ilands*, to *Virginia*, brought thither from thence these Plants, *viz*. Vines of all sorts, Orange and Lemon trees, Sugar canes, Cassado roots (that make bread) Pines, Plantans, Potatoes, and sundry other *Indian* fruites and plants, not formerly seen in *Virginia*, which now begin to prosper very well." If Sandys' reference is

[3] Since our general latter we have vewed the place where we are now goeing ~~about~~ to erect our fort,[123] naturaly almost intrenched
about wth deepe ditches: wch, by the grace of God, shal not want our vtter most indevours in the finishing. We shal need great ordnance, whole Culvering & demy-culvering at the least. And if God shal prosper vs, we wil frame a platforme hereafter & sinck it on the opposite flat, ~~to~~ large enough to containe 5 or 6 peeces, & thereby make the passage more vnpassable for an enimy.

Qy Answer to Capt. Butler's Unmasking of Virginia[1] [[1] In pencil in modern hand —Kingsbury's note.]

For Silke gras, earths, rareties &c, it was impossible for me this year, by reason of the trobles & want of meanes to send you any. But if I can make the pinnace Navegable, & furnish her (wch I shal do the better of your healpe) you shal never [haue] occation to complaine in that kind.

It would wel please the Countrye to heare that you had tak[en] revenge of Dupper for his stincking beare; wch wth what [hath] succeed by their contagion, in my conscience hath beene th[e] death of 200. You have imployed a strange Purser:[124] a m[an] wthout witt, or out of his witts: who hath lost much & never d[e]livered a great part of his good; throwing them vpon the shore scare above the hygh water mark, wthout the informing of any, or setting any to guard them. But Mr Tucke[125] deserves your thancks, & our comendations.

specifically to the *Sea-Flower*, the printed 'document' remains unidentified. There were many broadsides on the state of affairs. Nathaniel Butler may have instigated the trade in fruits between the two colonies in 1621 (see his letters in Neill, *Virginia Carolorum*, p. 28). A second ship went from Virginia in March 1622 (*ibid.* p. 29) to obtain another supply. It is presumably to this that Sandys refers. Butler came to Virginia, says John Smith (*Generall Historie*, V, 199; "The Historie of the Bermudas," I, 392–3), on a small ship sent out "by two or three private men of the Company, and having landed her supplies [in Bermuda], was to goe for Virginia." Butler was in Virginia in 1622/23. Evidently it is to Smith's source that Sandys refers.

123 A reference to the fort to be erected at Warrscoyickë [*sic*] (see Wyatt's proclamation of 29 April 1623, Kingsbury, IV, 129), which would command the river from the shore as well as it would have from the oyster banks, at Blunt Point formerly projected by Captain Each (see *ibid.*, IV, 102; Brown, *First Republic*, pp. 511, 514, 515).

124 Unidentified.

125 Evidently the Mr Tuke of the Abigail, who apparently succeeded Captain Each as master of the ship. See several letters above.

Great are the likelyhoods of the vicinity of the South sea by a general report of the Indians: the mountaines being, as they say, not past 4 days iourny above the falls, they two days over, & rivers on the other sid there into of no great length. I [*sic*] I were furnished w^t^h meanes, I would willingly venter my life in that discovery.[126] but we want asineicos,[127] provisions & numbers of men ~~fro~~ for such an attempt: w^c^h requires a general purse, & patient expectance of proffit. And indeede theise slow supplies, w^c^h hardly rebuild every yeare the decayes of the former, retaine vs onely in a languishing state, & curb vs from the carrying of enterprise of moment. As this is in the greater, so is it in the lesse. for tis a great pitty that so goodly a territory as Martins Hundred[128] should be no better followed: by w^c^h they certainly loose what they have already ventured. who might, w^t^h a forward hand, secure that place, & raise to themselves an vndoubted proffit; besides the honour & example.

It doth greive me much that your noble disposition & burning

126 The possibility of a northwest passage to the South Seas had fired the imaginations of the members of the Virginia Company from its beginning. As an appendix to Edward Waterhouse's "A Declaration of the State of the Colony . . ." in 1622 appeared "A Treatise of the Northwest Passage to the South Sea, through the Continent of Virginia, and by *Fretum Hudson*." This proposes a route northwest from Henrico to the Virginia mountains [or through the "continent of Virginia"] to "all those Countries bordering vpon the South Sea in the *East* and *West Indies*" (Kingsbury, III, 575). Earlier in "A Declaration" Waterhouse tells of the voyage up the Potomac, which brought forth a "*China Boxe*" from among the savages, and a story of a great king who dwelt on a great sea not ten days' journey to the west (*ibid.*, III, 547–8).

127 Apparently a variant of 'asinego,' "a little ass." The *NED* quotes from T. Herbert's *Travels* (1634), p. 127 "We jogged leisurely on upon our mules and asinegoes."

128 Established in 1618 by the Society of Martin's Hundred, this 7,000-acre tract, seven miles below Jamestown on the north side of the river, is not to be confused with (John) Martin's Brandon above Jamestown (see Bruce, *Economic History of Virginia*, I, 587, and *Institutional History of Virginia in the Seventeenth Century* [2 vols., New York and London, 1910], II, 292–3, and Andrews, I, 131). The first great private venture financed by a group of individual adventurers, the tract had been abandoned at the time of the massacre. As early as 7 October 1622 the adventurers had sent out new settlers for this plantation (Kingsbury, III, 689). They either had not arrived when Sandys wrote, or were too few to cultivate the plantation properly. On 5 June 1623 the Council in Virginia, in an official letter, suggested that Martin's Hundred might be populated immediately, for its strategic position in defence against the Indians was very important. For the miseries of life at Martin's Hundred, see Richard Frethorne's letters of 20 March, and 2 and 3 April 1623 (Kingsbury, IV, 59–62).

zeale to the good of this place should incounter w^{t}h such dis-hartnings, & be burthned wth so many ingagements; but I hope ere long we shal remove the first, & free you of the latter: Wherein their shalbe nothing wanting that lies in the endevours of ~~your~~

Your devoted servant

George Sandys.

From Nuports Newes 8 April 1623

[Addressed:] To his most respected freind John Farrer Esquier at his house in St Sithes Lane

[Indorsed in another hand:] New England Newportę Newes from Mr George Sandys to Mr John Ferrar the 8th Aprill 1623 by ye Abigall.

Sr

One thing I had forgotten to informe you of. Wee haue here a verie weake Councell, few in Nomber and those for the most part either not respecting greatlye the publique, or of no sufficiencie. Sr George is taken vp with his private,[129] and attendę but the other as it were on the [ ][130] Besidę some will say that he desires not that his goũnment should be Ecclipsed by his Successors. The Secretarie and yor Doctor[131] are no more then Ciphers. Mr Puntis[132] meanes well, Capt. Hamor [133] is miserablie poore and necessitie will inforce him to shiftę. Captaine Smith[134] is fitter for Action then advice, yet honest in both.

129 Sir George Yeardley's private estates were extensive.

130 A blank space.

131 See note 92 above. Dr. John Pott, acting governor of the colony in 1629 (Neill, *Virginia Carolorum*, p. 71), was tried and condemned by Governor Harvey for stealing cattle, but was pardoned (*ibid.*, pp. 79–80). For more details of his activities in Sandys' time, see text of the present chapter below.

132 See note 119 above. On the voyage home in 1624 John Pountis died.

133 Ralph Hamor or Hamer the younger was in Virginia in 1609–14, and from 1617 until his death (Brown, *Genesis*, II, 908–9, and Kingsbury, all volumes). In 1615 "*A booke called a narracon of the present State of Virginia by Ralph Hammer*" was published in London (Kingsbury, I, 32). The actual title was *A True Discourse of the Present State of Virginia, and the Success of the Affairs There till the 18 of June 1614. . . .*

134 Roger Smith, a veteran of wars in the Netherlands, was in Virginia 1616–19, and again after 1621. With others of the new Wyatt group, he was appointed to the Council in the colony on 24 July 1621. He married Jane (daughter of William Pierce), the widow of John Rolfe, and was Sandys' neighbour in Jamestown (Forman, pp. 63–4).

Here are all, and what is worst, I know not well how wee can bee supplied in this Countrie. Capt: Mathews[135] intendꝭ wholie his Cropp, and will rather hazard the payment of fforfeitures, then performe our Injunctions Capt Tucker[136] is industrious and fit, if the Cariage of yor buisnies here disable him not in your Censure: yet I doubt not but hee will make you an honest Accompt

Mr Blanie[137] is now married in Virginia, and when he hath discharged your trust in the magazine wilbee a Planter amongst vs. he is forward in whatsoeuer Concernes the Geñall and of good vnderstandinge, Neither is Leiftenant Peirce (now Gou̅nour of James Towne) inferiour to anie, expert in the Countrie, who refuses no labour, nor stickꝭ at anie expences, that may aduantage the publique, and of a Capacitie that is not to bee expected in a man of his breedinge nor wilbe euer borne (wch Sr George Yardlie knowes) [2] by the bigg lookes of his letters[138] Theis are all that are worthie the menc̄oninge And I would you Could perswade some of qualitie and worth to Come ouꝰ for that Purpose. once more farewell.

Yours

G: SANDIS

To my worthie ffreind Jo: Ffarrar Esqꝰ at his house in St Sithes lane

[Indorsed by Sir Nathaniel Rich:] G. Sandys to M^{r} Jo: Farrer concerning the weaknes of ye Counsell.

135 Samuel Matthews, or Mathews, is shown in the census of 1624/5 as *living* in his "divident" in the "Territory of Tappahannock over against James Cittie" (Brown, *First Republic*, p. 621). In 1619/20 he had a place "3 myles beyond Henrico" (Kingsbury, III, 246). He was one of the commissioners appointed to investigate Virginia on 24 October 1623 (*Acts of the Privy Council . . ., Colonial*, I, W. L. Grant and James Munro, ed. [London, 1908]; mentioned also in Kingsbury, IV, 294). See text below for more concerning Matthews.

136 William Tucker, a member of the first House of Burgesses from the "borough" of Kecoughtan (here "Kiccowtan," corporation of Elizabeth City), was in 1623 commander of Kecoughtan. In February 1624/5, aged 36, he was living in Elizabeth City with his wife, daughter, and servants (Brown, *Genesis*, II, 1034).

137 See note 109 above. He was the Company's factor in charge of the "Magazine" or store of clothing, provisions, etc.

138 *Sic*, Kingsbury. Probably "betters." Sandys was correct in his judgment of Pierce. The latter became a leader of the colony, rising steadily in reputation and office until in 1646 he was second to the Governor on the Council. That Pierce was uneducated, as Sandys suggests, is borne out by the fact that he uses his "mark" in place of signature as witness (McIlwaine, ed., *Minutes*, p. 55).

Sandys' letters reached England at the most critical moment in the Company's history. The official Company letter to the Governor and Council of Virginia of 7 October had warned that "thingę are at the bottome, except the currant be again restored from Virginia. . . . The Companies great povertie, and many debtę keepe vs infinitly perplexed."[139] Partly as a result of petitions presented by the anti-Sandys faction, the King had in April 1623 appointed a commission to investigate the affairs of Virginia and Bermuda.[140] About 27 June the *Abigail* arrived with over fifty letters from Virginia,[141] including most of those from George Sandys which formed "a map of the Colony's misery." All his letters found their way into the hands of the commissioners, or of the Privy Council,[142] and at some time were handled by Sir Nathaniel Rich of the anti-Sandys faction.[143]

In abstracted form these and sundry other letters were read before a Virginia court of 1 July 1623, so that the Company might "consider howe to send a present supplie vnto [the colony]."[144] One can imagine how the colonial treasurer's strictures on his fellow members of the colonial council, most of them related by blood or friendship to the adventurers of the Company, were received. And Sandys' stress on straggling and dispersed plantations and insufficient provision for new colonists as major factors in Virginia's troubles may have hit certain leaders of the Company hard, for these were part of, or the result of, deliberate policies. Above all, these private observations became public

139 Kingsbury, III, 688.

140 Brown, *First Republic*, pp. 520–1.

141 Kingsbury, IV, 238.

142 The letter to John Ferrar of 8 April was sent by Lord President Mandeville to Secretary Conway on 2 July 1623, though he says a "copy" of Sandys' letter (W. N. Sainsbury, ed., *Calendar of State Papers, Colonial Series, 1574–1660* . . . [London, 1860], pp. 42, 47–8). This letter appears among State Papers, Colonial, Jas. I, Vol. II, Nos. 27, 35, in the P.R.O. The others were all part of the Manchester Papers before they found their way to the P.R.O.

143 Sir Nathaniel Rich, apparently acting for the Commission and/or Privy Council, made abstracts from the letters to Samuel Wrote (Kingsbury, IV, 159, 160, 184–5, 216, 239), to John Ferrar of 11 April 1623 (*ibid.*, IV, 161, 185–6), to Sir Samuel (*ibid.*, IV, 161), to Sir Myles (*ibid.*, IV, 239), but evidently not from the 8 April letter to Ferrar. There had evidently also been letters (no longer extant) from Wyatt and George Sandys to Sir Edwin Sandys (*ibid.*, IV, 226), which were read by the commissioners. Rich evidently prepared the case for the Commission against the Sandys administration. See his notes in the margins of the letters, as noted above, and in Kingsbury, IV, 238.

144 *Ibid.*, II, 458–9.

property, and no doubt embittered friends as well as enemies of the Edwin Sandys group. Sir Francis Wyatt, who must have received some angry or bitter letters regarding George Sandys' "indiscretions," wrote back to a prominent member of the Company:

> . . . Those letters of mine uncle George Sandys I will not excuse nor qualify, although the censures past upon him and us all, which so farre transported his penne, were bitter and provoking; their lighting into other hands then [*sic*] was intended, I cannot but exceedingly lament: But his reall service hath been faithfull and diligent and pity it wanted a subject, the publique being exhausted, and left greatly in debt, when it fell into his hands. The drawing of those generalities, as leveled onely at Sr Edwin Sandys differs little from wresling. By that justice would they lay upon him the burden of all supposed errors in the Government there, and in your[145] officers here. But I doubt not the issue of their malice wil be, the rendring of his integrity and vertue the more conspicuous, which I most heartily wish, not onely for my particular obligation, but the generall cause of goodnes. For defiling our own nest,[146] a privat advertisement to supply the vacant places of so many consailors lost was very necessary, but it might have been exprest in milder termes, which appear hard, if not mollified by a favorable construction. . . .[147]

Wyatt, if he had placed the principal blame for misadventures in Virginia in any one policy, would probably have agreed with George Sandys that unprovisioned and overhasty colonization was the major misjudgment.[148] And instead of blaming Sir Edwin Sandys for most of the colony's troubles, as the Smith-Warwick faction and certain historians since have done, he placed the onus on another figure, as the Treasurer's letters had by implication. On 4 April 1623, at just the time Sandys was writing, Sir Francis commented to his father George Wyatt, "I often wish little Mr *Farrar here, that to his zeale he would add knowledge of this Contrey.*"[149] For it was John Ferrar, with his brother Nicholas who

145 The contraction y^{r} of course appears in the original. The source for this letter (see note 147 below) does not follow Kingsbury's exact reproduction policy.

146 Evidently one of the accusations made against the Council in Virginia as a result of George Sandys' letter to Ferrar of 11 April 1623.

147 The letter is printed in the *William and Mary Quarterly*, 2nd series, VI (April 1926), 114–121. It is dated conjecturally between 24 October 1623 and 26 June 1624. I have checked this version with the original in the Wyatt Manuscripts of the Earl of Romney.

148 See his letter to John Ferrar of 7 April 1623 (Kingsbury, IV, 104–6).

149 Kingsbury, IV, 237, quoted in Sir Nathaniel Rich's notes. See also Lady Wyatt's letter to her sister of 4 April 1623 describing her voyage. She stated that

succeeded him as deputy, who certainly executed and administered the policies of provisioning and emigration.

Conscious as he was of the integral relation of Company and colony, Sandys was for the time an officer of and in the colony. His attitude had in two years' time become that which the colonial was hereafter to hold toward the mother country, a real affection combined with a certain impatience at the failure of home officials to understand his problems. English administrative officials were to learn much in the next two centuries, but never quite enough to keep abreast of the needs of the colonies they controlled. Here near its beginning is a key to the story of the mingled success and failure of the building of England's colonial empire.

Thus George Sandys' letters became inadvertently one of the significant documentary evidences of the need for a change in Company policies and/or in groups or structures governing the colony. Some of his father's belligerence and asperity was in these letters. But there can be no doubt that he was not consciously, nor perhaps in any other way, advocating a change in government. He merely wanted his friends and relatives among the adventurers to see things as they were and to act accordingly. He made no suggestions as to methods of raising funds whereby most of these conditions might be ameliorated. This was the Company's problem.

That the home government of the colony needed now to be reorganized, and replaced in personnel, was probably true, as it was in later periods of English colonial history. The mistakes of the Sandys faction appear in perspective the mistakes of intelligent beginners in any economic and political experiment. The need for financial return to investors, and the form of government under which the colony had been developed, combined with the limited facilities of the age to lead to policies which in turn led to bankruptcy and discord. It is difficult to see

Captain Each laid all the troubles of the ship, including the overload of provisions, on "the two Mr Ferrars!" Actually the whole matter of Sir Edwin's responsibility, ultimate and immediate, that is in principle and detail, for the overhasty colonization in these years, warrants a thorough re-examination. Of over-all policy there can be no doubt of his responsibility. But of immediate plan and detailed execution there is more question. From certain of his letters, for example, it would appear that the illness of his wife and of himself, and his personal affairs at Northbourne, precluded his having as dominant and direct a part in Virginia affairs as he is usually credited with having. There is evidence, of course, that he advised in some matters of general policy. See all his letters of this period in Kingsbury, III and IV, and Appendix F below.

that any individual, any other group in the Company, or the Crown itself, would have in general done better *until* the lesson had been learned from this experience. Apparently the government of Stuart England gradually came to realize this. In later years, when the Privy Council's sub-committee for the Plantations controlled the colony, one of its members was George Sandys, and others came from the old group who had learned of Empire-building in Virginia or on the Company Council. Thus the personal and general experiences of trial and error played their part in determining the more successful policies through which the British colonial empire was to develop.

VII

COLONIAL OFFICIAL: THE ACTIVE LIFE, 1622–1625

THE REMAINDER of the story of George Sandys' stay in Virginia is told through a survey of his official activities and the brief glimpses possible of his social and intellectual life. Though the massacre had increased his problems, the dissolution of the Company in 1624 affected these problems immediately very little. Therefore what he did accomplish was through steady effort from the summer of 1622 until his departure three years later.

One of Sandys' most important duties, and perhaps the most unpleasant, was the collection of revenues, usually in the form of tobacco, from the planters. As noticed in Chapter V above, £1,000 was already owing the Company when Sandys was appointed to office, this debt being one of the reasons for the creation of the position of resident treasurer. By an earlier regulation, the tenant farmer owed the Company one-half his crop. By 1622 this was modified so that each tenant settled his rent each year with twenty bushels of grain, sixty pounds of tobacco, and one pound of silk.[1] Since private plantations were just beginning to be established, the majority of the crops, and therefore potentially a considerable revenue, came to the Company from the farmers who lived on the public lands. Actually the revenue was always less than the Company hoped for and seemed to expect. John Pory said this was because the officials of the colony employed the tenants so largely at other things that it was impossible for them to cultivate the earth to the extent demanded.[2] Assignation to land already worn out was perhaps a better reason, which Sandys himself gives.[3] But undoubtedly many of the farmers, in greed or in desperation, concealed the amount of their crops and pled inability to pay. Others, who for some reason were set free of their seven-year agreement and owed the Company tobacco as

[1] Bruce, *Economic History of Virginia*, I, 233. The silk never amounted to anything. The grain, *if* collected, was used within the colony. Only the tobacco was a money crop for Company and planter. The modification in the tax was intended, of course, to encourage diversification of crops.

[2] *Ibid.*, I, 232.

[3] See letter to John Ferrar of 8 April 1623 quoted above.

payment for their transportation to the colony,[4] in some instances also attempted to evade payment.

Sandys was a strict, brusque, even pitiless collector. Well he might be, for over and over again the official letters from the Company were insistent that the Treasurer be very careful in securing all revenues due.[5] The result might have been expected. "[T]he treasurer hath generally a badd report for his hard dealings with the planters,"[6] seamen returned from Virginia observed in the spring of 1623.

But it was as promoter of staple commodities and director of industry that Sandys worked hardest. When he arrived he had under his supervision the glass works,[7] the planting of mulberry trees for silk and the introduction of fruits and grains of many kinds, particularly on the Company's lands, and the proper restricting of tobacco. Under his more general care were all other matters of agriculture and new industry.[8] Saw mills, iron works, shipyards, salt works, buildings of public utility such as the inn at Jamestown, he was to see constructed. He was also to keep on the alert for news of silk-grass, copper mines, ship's stores, and anything else which the Company might gather or work with profit. As noticed above, an auspicious beginning was made on almost all these things.

Soon after his arrival the Treasurer, with Berkeley, went to Falling Creek to select the site for the iron works,[9] and in 1622 he was asked by the Company to supervise the shipwrights under Captain Barwick, for from Sandys "at first this proiect in parte moved."[10] After the massacre it was his task to resettle the Company's tenants and collect

[4] See the case of Richard Minter, who owed the Company £100 for his furnishing and transportation and was ordered to pay it to George Sandys (Kingsbury, II, 101).

[5] *E.g.*, Kingsbury, II, 108; IV, 267–8.

[6] Kingsbury, IV, 94. See McIlwaine, ed., *Minutes*, p. 32, for an example of Sandys' collecting through his own "deputies," as Captain Whitacre. Or in another case, through Sandys' "servant" Thomas Swifte (see, Grant and Munro, edd., *Acts of the Privy Council, Colonial*, I, p. 117, Item 190). Sandys was equally careful of expenditure of the Company's revenues. See below, notes 51–3.

[7] Kingsbury, I, 500; III, 495, 587.

[8] *Ibid.*, III, 471–2, 485. Vineyards and winemaking, for example, were his problem (*ibid.*, IV, 452).

[9] See note 26, Chapter VI above.

[10] Kingsbury, III, 650; Neill, *History of the Virginia Company of London* (Albany, 1869), pp. 308–9. Barwick died, and Sandys assumed charge of this group. See letters to John Ferrar above and McIlwaine, ed., *Minutes*, p. 100.

rents from them,[11] for the deputy in charge, George Thorpe, had been among the first to be murdered. And after Captain Nuce's death in 1623 Sandys managed the Company's plantation in Elizabeth City,[12] a full-time occupation in itself.

The glassworks tried Sandys' strength and patience until their abandonment, probably in 1624. The furnace was planned primarily to make beads to be used in vital trade with the Indians for corn and game. It is probable that simple glassware was made there also.[13] But nothing ever worked properly, and the temperamental glass men were a trial scarcely to be borne. In January 1623/4 the Governor and Council noted that the success of the glassworks had not been great despite the fact that the Treasurer's "care and exceedinge charge [therein were not] wanting."[14] Apparently after this winter the project was moribund or definitely inactive.[15] At any rate, by 23 April 1625, the work was officially abandoned and Vincentio and Bernardo, two of the glass men, were allowed to return to England.[16] In June the Virginia Council explained this step, again referring to the Treasurer's labours in the undertaking:

> [the accounts] of the Shipwrightes and the glass workes geuen in by Mr George Sandys we heerwith send you, the death of one of ye princypall woorkmen,

[11] Kingsbury, III, 671. This was an order from the Company that the tenants be returned and re-settled at Henrico (see note 71, Chapter VI above). Actually Sandys may have been the one who moved them after the massacre to the section (now Surry county) across the river from Jamestown, near one of his personal plantations and his official plantation (see Land, "Henrico and Its College," p. 497, note 4). Sandys sent a statement of the accounts of the Company's tenants to London on 15 June 1625 (Kingsbury, IV, 563).

[12] Kingsbury, IV, 104. Sir Francis Wyatt to John Ferrar.

[13] See Carl E. Hatch, Jr., "Glassmaking in Virginia, 1607–1625," pp. 119–38, 227–38. Also see Chapter VI, note 70 above. The glasshouse was probably located (as an earlier one had been) on Glass-House Point, on the mainland at the end of the old isthmus about a mile from Jamestown. In the massacre period the Indians approached the glasshouse; but there is no evidence that damage was done, though the work was certainly abandoned for a time after that (Kingsbury, III, 546; IV, 23–4; William Stith, *The History of the First Discovery and Settlement of Virginia . . .* [Williamsburg, 1747], pp. 218–9, 311).

[14] Kingsbury, IV, 453. The line continues "even to the neclect & great hinderance of his own ꝑticular."

[15] In the winter of 1623/4 five persons were living at the "glass house," evidently most of them Italian:—Vincentio, Bernardo, "Ould Sheppard his son," Richard Tarborer, and Mrs. Bernardo (Hotten, p. 235; Bruce, *Economic History of Virginia*, I, 443).

[16] McIlwaine, ed., *Minutes*, p. 56.

an other beinge subiect to the falinnge sicknes, and many defects wch render the woorke vnservable, Hath moved us to Cond[e]scende to the importunate suite of the glass men of returninge for England, wch woork so longe, as there was any hope, was supported by Mr George Sandys to his great charge and hinderance.[17]

The Treasurer was also 'at great charge' after the massacre to re-establish vineyards and silk culture,[18] to superintend the shipwrights (as noted above), and generally to encourage grain production, now so vital. The needs of the colony took him and his assistants far afield. In person, and through his "servants" Thomas Swyfte[19] and Robert Poole,[20] he covered the areas of the James, the Chesapeake, and the Eastern Shore, collecting tobacco taxes or trading with the Indians—probably with beads from the glass furnace—for corn.[21] In the autumn of 1622 he sailed up the great bay into the river Potomac, visiting the colonists' "ancyent alies," the Potomack Indians. With them he concluded a new treaty, "not only to assiste us in that revenge, but to accompany us and be our guides in a warr against the Pamunkeys."[22]

Sandys was never away from Jamestown for very long on these expeditions, for his presence as a member of the Council of State was required. In the "Ordinance and Constitution for Council and Assembly in Virginia" accompanying Wyatt and Sandys in 1621 was the statement that

17 Kingsbury, IV, 564–5. Mr. Hatch thinks the reason for the failure of this second attempt at glassworks in Virginia (and in English-speaking America) was simple: "the colony was not yet adjusted to support and maintain such an industry" ("Glassmaking in Virginia, 1607–1625," p. 228). For a description of the site and the works, see Hatch, pp. 228–36. Some of the beads from the Jamestown region have been discovered in recent years (see Hatch, pp. 236–8).

18 Kingsbury, IV, 452–3.

19 Referred to as "Thomas Swyft, gent" or as "Mr Swyft" (McIlwaine, ed., *Minutes*, pp. 73, 96, 102). Evidently he was official and personal agent for Sandys as treasurer.

20 Also referred to as "gent" (*Minutes*, p. 28). Poole, "who hath been Interpreter long tyme in the colony" (*Minutes*, p. 57), was on 2 May 1625 granted permission to return to England.

21 Poole undertook one trading expedition for "Mr Thresurer" in the pinnace *Elizabeth*, exchanging beads for corn (*Minutes*, pp. 29–30). For over a tub of corn he gave ten arms' lengths of beads. For another tub he gave 13 arms' lengths. On the same expedition Captain Croshaw bought "A great Canoe with 10[,]000 of blew beades." For other "bead prices," see *Minutes*, p. 30.

22 Kingsbury, IV, 450 ff. Council in Virginia to Company, 30 January 1623/4. These Indians appear to have lived in or near the present District of Columbia. Governor Wyatt followed up Sandys' agreement in November 1623, himself visiting these friendly tribes.

"this Counsell is to bee alwais or for the most part residing about or neere the said Governor."[23] In its various capacities this body met frequently, and though prosperous and semi-private landowners like Yeardley and Matthews might absent themselves in favour of their personal concerns, a man in such a position as Sandys' could not.

The Council, although legally only an advisory body to the governor,[24] by the time of Yeardley and Wyatt was a powerful agent of government in itself. Its duties were a combination of the executive, the judicial, and the legislative.[25] From its membership came a new governor in case of the death of a Company-elected official; and along with the governor, by the individual signatures of its members, it lent its weight to orders and decrees. It was also, with the governor, the general quarterly court in which were concentrated the jurisdictions of the Chancery, King's Bench, Common Pleas, Exchequer, Admiralty, and Ecclesiastical Courts of England.[26] And in its entirety the Council constituted the upper branch of the General Assembly, a relationship roughly analogous to that of the House of Lords in Parliament.[27]

As Treasurer, and by the Company's express instructions regarding his powers when he was appointed, Sandys probably had a considerable voice in executive policy and decree. His signature appears in its proper place of precedence below the governor's on more than a dozen documents in the 1622–5 period.[28] Among these official letters, commissions, and proclamations are two which are clearly his own orders, and bear his signature first.[29] Whether it was his opinion which determined the tone and content of certain official letters to the Company, and whether the actual composition of these and other documents is his, is more difficult to determine.

23 Kingsbury, III, 483.

24 Bruce, *Institutional History of Virginia*, II, 374.

25 McIlwaine, ed., *Minutes*, Introduction, p. xi.

26 Bruce, *Institutional History of Virginia*, II, 360.

27 *Ibid.* See this also for a list of five other lesser functions of the Council of State during the seventeenth century.

28 In 1622, in January [n.d.]; in 1623, on 20 January, 4 April (twice), 8 December, 31 December (twice); in 1624 on 9 January, 28 February, 12 May, 2 December; in 1625 once, undated, 4 February, June [n.d.], and 15 June (twice). His signature is normally third or fourth, depending on whether both Yeardley (former governor) and West (lieutenant-governor) were present.

29 The Governor's, of course, does not appear. These are two commissions to Captain William Tucker to stop and examine all persons attempting to return to England in order to ascertain whether they had the proper passes (Kingsbury, IV, 445–6).

That he composed many official letters is almost certain, for Secretary Davison testified in England in 1622 that Sandys was acting for him while he was absent from the colony. It is probable that he wrote the long letter of 20 January 1622/3, for on that date Secretary Davison was either still out of the country or too ill to act.[30] This letter, which concludes with the request, quoted above, that the colony be not judged by "branded people," is a long and generally able answer to the Company's letters of 1 August and 7 October 1622. Though its temperate tone is unlike that of his personal letters, its official nature and the influence of Wyatt may account for the difference. In the points made, it agrees entirely with what Sandys stated in his personal letters. Besides taking up the Company's commands point by point, it gives a concise statement of what had been done against the Indians and what the state of industry and agricultural were ten months after the massacre. For details of these activities, it refers the Company to the letters of the Treasurer.[31]

Since Secretary Davison was apparently dead by January 1623/4, Sandys may have had a hand in many of the letters[32] after that date, though for part of that time—early 1624[33]— Edward Sharpless the Clerk, acting as Secretary, had probably done the manual composition.

[30] Sandys, penman for his brother's faction in the Company before he left England, acknowledged by Davison when in England as the person who undertook the latter's duties in Virginia for him, and acknowledging himself his work in this capacity in one of his letters given above, seems the most likely composer of the letter. On 14 April 1623 Davison wrote to John Ferrar that he had been too ill since his return to write earlier (Kingsbury, IV, 115–6). Davison's name appears in the position of signature on only one document between 7 May 1622 and 4 April 1623, that of 23 October 1622 (*ibid.*, III, 697); it is probably not a signature contemporary with the document for the evidence indicates that he was not then in Virginia. See Chapter V, note 107, and Sir Edwin Sandys' letter of 13 October 1622 to John Ferrar, which mentions that the Secretary and his wife had sailed from England the night before (*ibid.*, III, 690). Davison's name does not appear after 31 December 1623. He probably died in January 1623/4. Brown (*First Republic*, p. 502) says that Sandys wrote this letter, probably reasoning along the same lines as I have. For more of Davison, see Chapter VI, note 91, and Chapter V, note 107.

[31] These apparently do not survive. Evidently they were semi-official epistles too critical in tone to be read to the "generality." They may possibly, however, be the letters Sandys wrote to Ferrar a month or two later (reproduced above).

[32] Council letters of 17 April, 12 May, 2 December 1623, and 10 January, 4 February, and 15 June (two) 1625 bear his signature.

[33] See McIlwaine, ed., *Minutes*, p. 14, 10 May 1624 for Sharpless' trial and sentence for betraying the Council's proceedings and orders to the Commissioners.

Only three of these, written not long before Sandys left the colony, are of any length or significance.[34] The latter two, of 15 June 1625, addressed respectively to the Privy Council and to the Commissioners for the Affairs of Virginia, protest vigorously against the "late ꝑnitious contract" for tobacco, presumably that which gave Ditchfield, and other commissioners, a patent for searching and sealing tobacco. The monopoly, well ordered,

> would certainely and suddenly advaunce the Plantacione, by the presente inhablinge us for woorkes of woorth and continuance, but by convertinge the benefitt therof to theire privatt and inordinate lucre, hath giuen the Colony the greatest blow that euer it receaued, And w^t^howt spedie redress, will proue incurable, and cause this noble and hopefull Accone to be deserted. . . .[35]

These documents agree essentially on this matter with Sir Edwin Sandys' "Discourse of the Old Company" prepared a few weeks before, and afford another evidence of the essential agreement of the Virginia Council with Sir Edwin Sandys' policies for the Colony.[36] That George Sandys personally agreed with these official expressions of opinion is almost certain.

The minutes of the colony's Council, acting as general court and executive board, give evidence that the Treasurer had a good deal to say in many matters. "Mr. Sandys . . . beareth all the sway," one young

34 The first, dated 2 December 1624, gives an interesting report on victories over the Pamunkey Indians (Kingsbury, IV, 507–9). The other two, to the Privy Council and to the Commissioners of Affairs of Virginia, (*ibid.*, IV, 559–62, 562–7), include able defences of the colony's action in domestic matters, and give vigorous reasons why the pernicious tobacco contract must be overthrown. The second of the 15 June letters, in addition, protests against the wresting of certain personal privileges, evidently of the use of company tenants, from the Governor and Mr George Sandys, who were entitled to them as 'due dept and not a gift.'

35 Kingsbury, IV, 561. For a discussion of the violent reaction to the Ditchfield contract, see G. L. Beer, *The Origins of the British Colonial System, 1578–1660* (New York, 1908), pp. 141–2. Bruce (*Economic History of Virginia*, I, 278–80) shows that the apprehensions of the colonists were well founded. "The Discourse of the Old Company of Virginia" (Kingsbury, IV, 519–51, see especially pp. 541–2), prepared by the Sandys faction in April 1625 to convince Charles I of their point of view on Virginia, bitterly attacks the Ditchfield contract.

36 There can be little doubt that the Commissioners were personally profiting from the matter, but so had the Virginia Council in several matters in which they had to judge themselves.

man who had been compelled to work for him wrote home.[37] Sandys may not have borne quite all the sway in the Council, but the mild Wyatt[38] probably allowed from wish or necessity a considerable voice to his vigorous and perhaps somewhat irascible relative.

The minutes, fragmentary in early 1623, are fairly complete after that time for the years Sandys spent in Virginia.[39] They indicate, incidentally, that Sandys spent much or most of his time at Jamestown itself in these years,[40] and therefore probably in all his years in Virginia. And they give, as such records often do, the best existing picture of everyday life

[37] John Baldwin to Roger Wood, in J. H. Lefroy, ed., *Memorials of the Discovery and Early Settlement of the Bermudas* . . ., I, 264–5, and E. D. Neill, *Virginia Vetusta* (Albany, 1885), pp. 203–4. Baldwin prefaces this by saying: "he maketh vs serve him whether wee will or noe and how to helpe yt we doe not know." Baldwin was a freeman who arrived on the *Tyger* in 1622 and probably was compelled to work in a place he disliked. He is listed in the muster of George Sandys' servants (Neill, *Virginia Carolorum*, p. 17).

[38] During the 1622-1623 period, dissatisfied William Capps wrote home that the Governor "stood . . . for a Cypher [during the massacre] . . . the old smoker our . . . Gouernor, so good so carefull mild, Religious, iust, honest. . . ." (Kingsbury, IV, 76).

[39] See the Preface to McIlwaine, ed., *Minutes of the Council and General Court*, pp. v–xii and text of *Minutes*, *passim*. Among approximately 51 courts listed between 1 March 1622/3 and 13 June 1625, Sandys is named as present 34 times. Five of the lists of members of the court are fragmentary, and there is no indication that he was *not* present at others, for in one instance (4 April 1625, *Minutes*, p. 51), where the list is apparently complete without his name, he is mentioned in the proceedings as a witness present.

[40] During 1624, for example, he was present *by name* on 7 and 9 January; 7, 9, 11, 12, 30 March; 10 May; 28 June; 12 July; 10, 19, 25 October; 1, 25, 31 November; 27 December. In the same year, according to the dates of official decrees of the Council (Kingsbury, etc.) he was also present on 9 and 30 January, 17 April, 12 May, and 2 December. *The Journals of the House of Burgesses* (McIlwaine, ed.) indicate that Sandys was in Jamestown 28 February and 2 March (and at other unspecified-by-date times). The entries for the first five months of 1625 in the *Minutes* are even more frequent than those for 1624, and show Sandys' presence in all months except March. How often the court met by law and/or ordinance is not clear. By law the *General Court* was a quarterly session (Bruce, *Institutional History of Virginia*, I, 656). Probably the other sessions listed in the minutes which actually perform what might be called court duties are merely preliminary hearings by the Council. They are not distinguished in the *Minutes* as they now exist. It is worth noting that on 11 March 1623/4 (*Minutes*, p. 12) it was ordered that a court should be held every Monday "to hear Causes." There is no evidence from the *Minutes*, however, that this court was the General Court. Note Sandys' own testimony in his letters home that he was present almost daily at the Council table.

in the colony. Civil suits or hearings concerning land, tobacco, rent, and trade generally were heard in Mr. Treasurer's presence, several of these cases involving him personally or officially.[41] Sandys heard what must even then have been amusing evidence concerning the alleged abduction of Mara Buck, daughter of the deceased clergyman Richard Buck, by the Reverend David Sandys;[42] a petition by a woman falsely accused of bearing a bastard that her female accuser, standing in a white sheet (in the church) be compelled to recant before the Sunday congregation;[43] the astounding complaint by Mrs. Blaney that she had miscarried because Dr. Pott refused to give her a piece of hog's flesh to eat. The Court's opinion in this last case is worth recording:

> Y^t^ *is the opinion* of the Courte y^t^ it is no slander y^t^ Mrs *Blany* Chargeth Doctor *Pott* wth denying her a peece of fflesh, wherevpon shee miscarried, because she hath taken her oath that she thinketh in her Conscience that it was the occasion of her miscaryinge, but it no way appereth, and it is barbarows to Imagine, that he had any conceipt she had A longing to it but thought it was spent by his wiefe.[44]

And Sandys sat on the court of 1623 which heard the first breach-of-promise suit of English-speaking America brought by the Reverend Greville Pooley against Cicely Jordan, who broke her alleged troth to him and contracted herself to William Ferrar.[45] It was a complex matter, and though Sandys and others of the Council had legal training they declined to make a decision, sending the facts home to England,

> (not knowinge how to decide so nice a difference, our devines not takeinge vppon them precisely to determine, whether it be a formall and legal contract desire the resolution of the Civill Lawiers, and a speedy return thereof.[46]

The seamy side of colonial life—the beating to death of a maidservant, buggery, suicide, cattle stealing—[47] were also a part of the story. The

[41] *E.g.*, Mrs. Geny's complaint that Captain Whitaker, as Sandys' agent, had taken tobacco as rent without her consent (*Minutes*, pp. 31–2), or Luke Eden's complaints on tobacco payments which caused him to speak disrespectfully to the Treasurer (*ibid.*, pp. 20–1, 24, 57).

[42] *Ibid.*, pp. 15, 16, 18, 109.

[43] *Ibid.*, p. 31.

[44] *Minutes*, p. 59.

[45] *Ibid.*, pp. 8, 41, 42; Kingsbury, II, 519, IV, 219–20, 487; Brown, *First Republic*, pp. 563 ff.

[46] Kingsbury, IV, 220. On 24 June 1624 the Virginia Assembly passed a law against women contracting themselves to "two severall ꝑsons at one time" (Kingsbury, IV, 487).

[47] McIlwaine, ed., *Minutes*, pp. 22–3; 34, 42.

grim penalties reflect a grim age and the absolute necessity for sternness, if not harshness, among a scattered and therefore lawless people. Two men were sentenced to death for stealing a calf: one was executed, the other, who had only "received" it, was reprieved.[48] One Richard Barnes, for speeches against the Governor, was disarmed, his arms broken, and his tongue bored through with an awl. Then he was forced to run a gauntlet of forty men, who kicked, butted, and booted him out of Jamestown.[49] The most notorious case was that of Edward Sharpless, clerk of the Council, who had acted in most duties of the Secretary after Davison died. Suborned by John Pory, one of the commissioners sent from England, Sharpless sold the secrets of the Assembly and Council to the Commission. He gave them copies of petitions and other documents which the Council wished to send to England by John Pountis, to be used in defence of the Sandys administration of the Company. In indignation the Court, certainly conscious that in doing so they were in some sense defying royal authority, condemned Sharpless to be set in the public pillory in the market place at James City and "there haue his eares nayled to it, & cutt of."[50]

Though the Council for years, perhaps during its entire existence under the Company, had been judge of itself in the sense of passing on matters advantageous to its own members,[51] Sandys individually, as treasurer, refused to follow the precedent. According to instructions given to Yeardley in 1618[52] of the half-profits from the Company's lands collected by the Council, "one moiety" of varying proportion was to be employed for the entertainment, or expenses, of the Council of State residing in Jamestown, the other to go to the Company in England. When the Council asked for their 'moiety' in November 1624, Sandys stated that it was something he had not before paid, and that he saw nothing in his commission to authorize him to do so. He petitioned the

48 *Ibid.*, p. 5. Compare with Dale's stern code (Bruce, *Institutional History of Virginia*, II, 385–6).

49 *Minutes*, p. 14. For another case, see p. 12.

50 The story came to the King, probably through the Commissioners themselves. The Council, in a letter of 15 June 1625 to the Privy Council (Kingsbury, IV, 560–1) defended themselves in their action, and stated among other things that actually Sharpless lost only a piece of one ear. They commented that it "hath been so misreported & aggravated to his Ma[tie], as other thinge also hath benn, as a bloudie and barbarous Acte, and we threatned wth such fowle and iniourjous tearmes as yf we were below the Conditione of ffreemen. . . ."

51 Bruce, *Institutional History of Virginia*, II, 361.

52 18 November. Kingsbury, III, 100.

Court, therefore, that a jury of 18 persons be appointed to decide the question. This was done.[53]

The most vexing and long-drawn-out case to come before the Council and General Court, and even before the General Assembly in the 1621–5 period, was that of Captain John Martin. In this dispute the Treasurer had an active part. Martin, one of the most persistent litigants of a litigious age, was the only member of the original Council for Virginia remaining in the colony.[54] Evidently trained in the law,[55] and a stout champion of what he considered his rights, he was a thorn in the flesh of the Sandys-Southampton administration at home and in the colony. Some years before the Great Charter of 1618, Martin had been granted a patent for certain lands at Brandon, on the James. This patent, so broad in its implications that Martin was in effect lord of a feudal manor independent of the laws and enactments of the rest of the colony, was recalled by the terms of the 1618 charter, and Martin was asked to surrender the validating document. After a long fight including such incidents as the refusal of the General Assembly to seat the burgesses from Martin's Brandon and Martin's calling upon his brother-in-law, the powerful Sir Julius Caesar, for aid, the patent was given up and another in conformity with new Company policy was issued. Martin had gone to England several times to look after his "rights," and may have been the reason for Sir Julius Caesar's work in bringing about the dissolution of the Company.[56] Whether this was true or not, Martin's vociferous complaints certainly served to advertize in Virginia and in England the dissensions within the Company.[57]

[53] McIlwaine, ed., *Minutes*, p. 34. It is possible, of course, that the principal officials, such as the Governor, Marshal, and Treasurer received nothing from this "moiety," since they already had an income ultimately derived from the Company.

[54] There are several extended discussions of the John Martin case: Brown, *Genesis*, II, 943–4; *idem*, "The Case of John Martin," *Virginia Magazine of History & Biography*, VII (January 1900), 268–75; James P. C. Southall, "Captain John Martin of Brandon on the James," *Virginia Magazine of History & Biography*, LIV (January 1946); 21–67; Craven, *Dissolution*, pp. 117–20. For Captain John Smith's contemptuous attitude toward Martin, see *The Generall Historie . . .*, I, 113, 190. For copies of the documents in the case, see Kingsbury, all volumes.

[55] Brown, *Genesis*, II, 943.

[56] For Martin and Sir Julius Caesar see Kingsbury, III, 702; Craven, *Dissolution*, pp. 119–20. Sir Julius Caesar was Master of the Rolls. For further details concerning him, see Brown, *Genesis*, II, 839–41.

[57] Craven, *Dissolution*, pp. 119–20.

Late in 1623 Martin decided to return to Virginia from his most recent visit to England. Though the Company's, or Sandys faction's, power at home was definitely declined, Martin and Caesar knew that the authorities in Virginia were not likely to greet him with open arms. Through Caesar's influence,[58] therefore, the Privy Council gave Martin a warrant to the Governor and Council in the colony, ordering or requesting that he be shown respect and that he remain free from oppression.[59] To add insult to injury, when the new Council in Virginia was appointed by the King on 26 August 1624, Martin's name appeared on its list of members.

Meanwhile Martin had arrived in Virginia. He was taken aback to find that "Sir Francis Wiatt . . . and George Sandes the Tresurer . . . made noē more accounte of ye Lords Letters the^{n} if it had cō frō the meanest mē in England." And George Sandys, he further observed to Sir Julius Caesar, dared "to speake ope<ly in theyre Parliment [the General Assembly] t^{y} att all times for tenn peces givē to a secretary he could have such a Letter."[60] Martin soon showed he had learned nothing of discretion. By whispers, innuendos, and outright accusations against any individual or group which had fought his patent, he stirred up trouble. Many of his statements came to the attention of the Council, and George Sandys sat on several courts which did nothing but hear witnesses in the case. Martin made threats against those responsible for Sharpless' punishment, accused Sir Edwin Sandys of misappropriation of funds, and advised various planters not to pay the tobacco taxes agreed upon by the General Assembly.[61] He even told various persons that the fact that the ship which brought him back to Virginia went a roundabout way via Canada and was detained there for some weeks was really a plot of the Virginia Company to make away with him.[62] And he boasted about having "unhorsed the Company."[63]

[58] And bearing his signature.

[59] Kingsbury, IV, 443–4. 8 December 1623.

[60] Br. Mus. Add. MSS. 12, 496, Papers of Sir Julius Caesar, Folio 449, 8 March 1626[27?]. The official letter of the Virginia Council of 2 December 1624 acknowledged receipt of letters from the Privy Council in Martin's behalf, and said that his behaviour since his arrival showed that they were little deserved (Kingsbury, IV, 507).

[61] McIlwaine, ed., *Minutes*, pp. 21–22, 61. In 1625 he said that no governor then had the power to call a General Assembly (*ibid.*, p. 62).

[62] *Ibid.*, pp. 25–6, 28–9, 32, 33, 46. Martin asked for and obtained damages because of the ship's delay, but still was not satisfied.

[63] *Ibid.*, p. 61.

The Virginia Company itself had requested, after Martin had accepted the new patent, that he be treated more considerately in the colony. But the Council in Virginia, in a letter perhaps written by George Sandys, replied that Martin had returned the Company's favours by slandering it from the moment of his arrival.[64] A few months later, the Virginia Council in another letter which has something of Sandys' asperity in its style, bluntly informed the Privy Council that Martin was utterly unworthy of the appointment to the Council, offering proof in depositions enclosed of his unwarranted slanders and accusations and stating that he had been suspended from his office.[65] In a letter of the same date the Commissioners for Virginia were informed of what the Council had done regarding Martin, "a man of a prostituted conscyence, a sower of disentione and seditione, one from whose false accusations no innocency can be safe, disobedient to Government, and a ꝑsone exceedinge daungerous to the state and Colonie. . . ." Then the Council added boldly, "and we humblely desire he may not be restored, w^th^out our remoueall."[66] These were among the last official words of the Council while Sandys was in the colony; and that he and Wyatt were both planning a return to England may be the reason for this unequivocal boldness. Sandys' and Wyatt's parts in this Martin case present another evidence that three years after the massacre they retained a fundamental sympathy for the policies and administration of the Sandys-Southampton group in the Company.

George Sandys' exact part in the proceedings of the Virginia General Assembly is not so clear as his part in the Council-Court, for the Journals of the legislative body are more formal and less specific in detail, and at the same time much more fragmentary, than the Minutes of the smaller body.[67] But no study of any Virginia colonial official would be complete without some consideration of this first New World legislature, the official's relation to it, and the relation of both to the so-called "liberal movement" within the colony and Company. Involved in the matter too is the question of the nature

64 Kingsbury, IV, 517–18. Sandys, Governor Wyatt, and five others signed it.

65 *Ibid.*, IV, 560. 15 June 1625.

66 *Ibid.*, IV, 565. Martin lived on until after 1630, for he petitioned the King about that time (Southall, pp. 61–2). He appears to have had little influence in the colony after 1625.

67 See the volumes of *Journals* and *Minutes*, both edited by H. R. McIlwaine, referred to frequently above.

and source of this "liberalism"[68] of the Virginia legislative body.

No finally accurate measure can be taken of individual or group ideas of "liberalism," or its influence in this period of colonial expansion, until a basic survey and analysis of the "liberal" thinking and action of Sir Edwin Sandys and others in the British Parliament and in the Virginia Company is made, and the relationship of this "liberalism" to similar ideas among colonial leaders traced. But some intimation of George Sandys', and Wyatt's, part and attitude in moves—not movements—we may label "liberal" for want of a better term may be gained through a glance at the proceedings of the General Assembly and Sandys' and Wyatt's proved or probable part in them.

Certain obvious questions present themselves to any reader of the history of the period.[69] Who were the moving figures in the repeated requests for the right of assembly, the right to tax, the right to a voice in government? Was the pressure from the planters, the Council, or from the Governor? Or was it pressure at all? Finally, was this "liberalism" bound up with the policies of the Virginia Company of London?

A thorough study should be made of Sir Francis Wyatt as a "liberal" statesman, for it was during his two terms as governor of Virginia, 1621–6 and 1639–40, and in the years between while he was a member of the Privy Council's sub-committee on the plantations, that the fight for a "free assembly" was made. Certainly the whole matter of the Old Company—first of survival and then of revival—is inextricably woven into the pattern. And in the study of Wyatt's career must come George Sandys' career in its relation to the colony, for the two almost exactly parallel. The two men served the 1621–6 period together in Virginia and were fellow-members of the Privy Council's sub-committee in the 1630's. And during Wyatt's second term in Virginia, Sandys was in England the personal representative of Wyatt and the agent of the colony (for the General Assembly).

It can almost be taken for granted that the General Assembly's boldness in its dealing with Company and Crown must have stemmed in

[68] I use the words *liberal* and *liberalism* in quotation marks because, although they are the terms most frequently applied to men and movements, in the nineteenth and twentieth century sense of the terms they are inappropriate, or at least inexact. See notes and text immediately below.

[69] Partial answers for some of these questions exist, but no complete or final convincing studies of the subject appear to have been made. For a more extended discussion of factors to be considered, see Appendix G below.

part from a confidence inspired by the 'quality' of the more prominent members of the Council. The names of Wyatt, West, Yeardley, and Sandys undoubtedly bore weight.

Such are some of the factors to be considered when the basic study is made. Since this book is primarily a survey of George Sandys' career, there is space only[70] to trace the more significant actions of the Assembly with an eye to the Treasurer's part in them.

The first General Assembly of Wyatt's administration, and the second in history, met in November and December 1621, just after Wyatt's commission was read. The only record remaining of its enactments is included in the Virginia Council's letter to the Company of January 1621/22.[71] It tells little more than that the Company's policy of intensified production of "staple commodities" and the development of industry was presented to the body and met with its approval. Of the next session, from 14 February through 5 March 1623/4[72] many records in the form of official letters and laws survive,[73] but there is again no journal for the period. The extant documents do show the Virginia Assembly's part in the fight to retain the Company.

This General Assembly met at one of the hottest political moments in the colony's history. While Virginia was struggling to get on her feet after the massacre, the Sandys faction of the Company was fighting desperately to retain its control. His own apparent mistakes or those of his assistants the Ferrars had so opened cracks in Sir Edwin Sandys' armour that his enemies of the Smith-Warwick faction had leaped to the attack. By the time the Assembly convened at Jamestown the Sandys faction and even the Company had its back against a wall. In April 1623, at a moment when Company affairs were "at bottom" because of the psychological as well as financial effects of the massacre, Alderman

[70] The study of "liberalism" which seems to be needed will probably take space equal to the length of this biography and therefore cannot even be attempted here, important as it is to a full understanding of George Sandys' career in the colony. See above Chapter V, note 18, and Appendices F and G.

[71] McIlwaine, ed., *Journals*, p. 17, extracts only; Kingsbury, IV, 449. The whole letter, in more accurate form (for the *Journals* followed E. D. Neill's transcription) appears in Kingsbury, III, 581–8.

[72] McIlwaine, ed., *Journals*, pp. xxix, 21–42. There were evidently other assemblies or at least another in 1622/3, for the "Ordinances" had called for one each year.

[73] See Kingsbury, IV, 580–5, for "Laws and Orders," which also appear in W. W. Hening's *Statutes at Large* . . . (13 vols., New York, 1810–23), pp. 122–7, and McIlwaine, ed., *Journals*, pp. 21–42.

Johnson, Sir Thomas Smith's son-in-law, had submitted a petition to the King requesting a thorough investigation of the Company's affairs,[74] claiming that the colony had been prosperous for many years under the earlier leadership of Sir Thomas Smith. Johnson requested that a royal commission be appointed to enquire into the true state of the plantation in the past and present. The Company itself (*i.e.*, the Sandys faction) in extraordinary court welcomed the investigation by a petition also directed to his Majesty. The two groups appeared before the Privy Council on 17 April. After heated discussion, a commission headed by Sir William Jones was appointed[75] to investigate all questions under dispute. On 7 May the Company prepared its answer[76] to Alderman Johnson, and evidently about the same time sent letters to Virginia informing the Council there as to what had happened.[77] When the General Assembly met the following February, it drafted an answer to Johnson's assertion concerning the state of the colony during the twelve years of Sir Thomas Smith's administration, an answer signed by a group almost all of whom were witnesses personally to what they stated.[78] It was a far more effective rebuttal than that which the Company at home had drafted.

At almost the same time a more detailed document, replying to certain other charges against the condition of the colony under the Wyatt administration, was composed. This involved directly a man who had already crossed George Sandys' path two or three times. Captain Nathaniel Butler, who had probably been Sandys' travelling companion in Egypt and Palestine and certainly was the successful candidate over him in the election to the governorship of Bermuda, had come to Virginia from Bermuda in the winter of 1622/3, at the end of his term as governor, and under something of a cloud.[79] After participating in a

[74] Kingsbury, II, 373–4.

[75] Craven, *Dissolution*, pp. 267–8. The commission was approved by the Privy Council on 9 May.

[76] Kingsbury, II, 393–7.

[77] The Company's letter of 6 August 1623 (Kingsbury, IV, 262–71) indicates that the Virginia Council had been kept informed of the establishment of the commission and of its activities.

[78] McIlwaine, ed., *Journal*, pp. 21–2.

[79] An involved matter, of which there are contradictory accounts. See Sabin ed., William Stith's *History of Virginia*, p. 243; Brown, *First Republic*, p. 475–6; Craven, *Dissolution*, pp. 137–40, 254; Andrews, *Colonial Period*, I, 226–7; McIlwaine, ed., *Journals*, p. 24. Butler arrived 20 November 1624, and was welcomed by the Virginia Governor and Council, who remembered the chests of fruit and plants he had sent some time before.

fight against the Chickahominies with Captain Nathaniel Powell and indulging in other assorted actions, he returned to England, probably on the *James*, in late February or early March.[80] On the basis of what he saw, heard, and perhaps imagined, and at the instigation of the Warwick-Smith faction, he wrote "The Vnmasked face of o^{r} Colony in Virginia as it was in the Winter of ye yeare 1622."[81] Though there is considerable truth in his statement, and though he was in some matters agreeing with Wyatt's and George Sandys' expressed opinions, it is in all respects a partisan attack on the Sandys faction at home, and in many particulars on the Wyatt administration of the colony.[82] The document[83] was read or presented at the Company court of 23 April 1623. A week later a long detailed series of statements from planters who had lived in Virginia was presented at the Court in answer,[84] and on 7 May, with the reply to Johnson's petition, the Company prepared an answer[85] to be presented to the King. These replies show clearly that Butler's slanting of evidence is at least partially the result of personal and political animosity, but they also were compelled to contain damaging admissions about the state of the colony, admissions which added weight to the evidence against the Sandys administration of the Company.

Since these charges included so many aimed directly at the colony's resident administration, the General Assembly also prepared an answer[86] to them. Like that of the former planters then in England, it is a point by point attempt at refutation. Though it may prove Butler a liar in certain of his statements, it also contains damaging admissions. Its chief interest in the present study lies in the beauty of certain passages of its prose, and the possibility or even probability that George Sandys was the author of the document. It was written after the death of Davison,

80 Brown, *First Republic*, pp. 498, 500, 506; *Genesis*, II, 836.

81 Text, at least in part, in Kingsbury, II, 374–6.

82 *E.g.*, Butler charged that the Virginia government wilfully disregarded his Majesty's letters patent that the colony should be governed by English laws, and that it ignored or wilfully strayed from English law (Kingsbury, II, 376). See below for the colony's reply. As Professor Craven points out (*Dissolution*, pp. 254–6, 137–40), Butler had political grievances against the Sandys faction from his Bermuda days.

83 Miss Kingsbury (II, 374 n) locates this document in the P.R.O., State Papers, Colonial, Vol. II, No. 20, I.

84 Text in Kingsbury, II, 381–7.

85 Text, *ibid.*, II, 397–9. Professor Craven points out (*Dissolution*, p. 255 n) that originally Butler's paper preceded Johnson's appeal to the Crown.

86 The General Assembly's answer had been in preparation, Brown says (*First Republic*, p. 569), ever since the arrival of the *Bonny Bess* in September 1623.

and came from a group which at this particular time contained no other member of known 'literary' ability.[87] Above all, there is something of the style of Sandys' *A Relation* in its sentences.

For example, in replying to the charge that the plantations are located on such shallow streams that no ship can approach them, and that for the same reason diseases are rampant, the Assembly wrote:

> In this he traduceth one of the goodliest Rivers in the habitable World, which runs for many Miles together within upright Banks, till at length, enlarged with the Receipt of others, it beats on a sandy Shore, and imitates the Sea in Greatness and Majesty. It is approachable on both Sides, from half Flood to half Ebb, for boats of good Burthen; neither is there any River in the World of this Vastness, without Cranes or Wharfs, more commodious for landing. . . .[88]

And again, when Butler states that he expected to find, from the representations made in printed pamphlets of the Company, a great development of industry and staple commodity, and found little, the reply begins:

> THE time that this Informer came over, was in the Winter, after the Massacre; when those Wounds were green, and the Earth deprived of her Beauty. His Ears were open to nothing but Detraction, and he only enquired after the Factious, of which there were none among us, and how he might gather Accusations against those in the Government, being, as it should seem, sent over for that Purpose. . . .[89]

[87] For a list of the signers of the documents of this Assembly, see McIlwaine, ed., *Journal*, pp. 22, 26, 27, 39, 42. Sharpless as clerk signs the letters of the Commissioners, but evidently was not acting for the General Assembly at this time. Wyatt himself had some ability in handling prose, but it seems unlikely that the Governor in person would compose such a document *from* the Assembly. Of course the ability of the literate Renaissance Englishmen to compose good prose is frequently evident, even in the colony. See Howard M. Jones, *The Literature of Virginia in the Seventeenth Century*, in *Memoirs of the American Academy of Arts and Sciences*, XIX, Pt. 2 (Boston, 1946).

[88] McIlwaine, ed., *Journals*, p. 23.

[89] *Ibid.*, p. 24. The truth of this latter statement is borne out by the *Minutes* (p. 24) of 10 October 1624, at which evidence of Butler's search for evidence was heard by the Virginia Council:

> *Robert Sweete* gent sworne and Examined sayeth y^t^ Capt *Nathaniel Butler* was very vrgent and importunate wth this Examinate at two sevrall tymes to sett downe vnder his hande all such grevances and misbehaviours might anywyse have in his owne ꝑticuler or of any other iniuryes or iniustice done by Mr *George Sandys* Thresurer, Promising this Examinate that yf there were any

Butler's personal behaviour, in drunkenness and pursuit of lewd women in the colony, had been notorious, as this[90] and the Governor and Council's official letters testify.[91] Mild Sir Francis Wyatt in a personal letter commented somewhat drily on his former guest:

> When we were taxed by Captain Butler for disunion, he had least reason to urge it, for we all agreed in distast of him, though his usage was every way faire and courteous, as he being in our powers we could not do less. . . .[92]

But this General Assembly did more than reply to Johnson and Butler. They addressed a short petition to his Majesty, protesting their desire to continue under their present government, and requesting the King's aid in putting into effect the tobacco monopoly and in securing soldiers for the colony.[93] To the Privy Council went a somewhat similar letter, avowing the Assembly's ignorance "of the dangers and ruynes which might have befallen [them] . . . by the continuance of the former [government]."[94] Their longest document was "A Briefe Declaration of the Plantation of *Virginia* duringe the first Twelve Yeares, when Sir *Thomas Smith* was Governor of the Companie, & downe to this present tyme,"[95] evidently in preparation over a considerable period, and much more detailed in its argument than the first answer to Alderman Johnson. It concluded with a reference to the commissioners now arrived in Virginia to investigate conditions first hand.

This group, appointed by the Privy Council, was composed of Captain John Harvey, John Pory, Abraham Peirsey, and Samuel Mathews, all

> such thinge he wold remedy it in *England* or ells this Examinat should Accompt him A very villain And further this Examinat sayeth that the said Captain *Butler* hath vrged Mr *John Baynam* to the like as he hath harde Mr *Baynam* reporte[.]

90 McIlwaine, ed., *Journals*, p. 24. Professor Andrews (I, 226) refers to Butler as "a pirate under the skin" but says he was neither brute nor liar. In the latter the historian seems to be wrong. Myles Kendall refers (Kingsbury, IV, 119) to "that machauill Butler." For a more sympathetic account of Butler, see Andrews, I, 221–8.

91 *E.g.*, Kingsbury, IV, 450–30 January 1623/4. This letter states that the General Assembly is now "vnmasking of [Captain Butler]."

92 Letter referred to above dated between 24 October 1623 and 26 June 1624. The General Assembly (*Journals*, p. 25) said his principal spleen came from his not having been admitted to the Council when he came to Virginia.

93 McIlwaine, ed., *Journals*, pp. 25–6.

94 *Ibid.*, pp. 26–7.

95 *Ibid.*, pp. 28–37. "By the Ancient Planters nowe remaining alive in Virginia," follows the title.

men who had lived or were living in the colony.[96] When Harvey and Pory landed and met their confreres, the General Assembly was already in session.[97] According to a statement from Harvey himself, they found conditions much better than they had been led to expect,[98] evidently by Johnson and Butler, but also found that resentment against the two detractors had "been a breeding" ever since September. Privately Governor Wyatt thought these men were not too bad a choice for their mission, for two were personal friends of Yeardley's and two of Argall's, though he "could wish persons of more eminence and sufficiency had been sent upon this service, if the meaning be, that their judgments should ballance with the publique declaration of the generall Assembly."[99]

Harvey found the two answers to Johnson and Butler already signed.[100] On 5 March he delivered to the General Assembly his letter and order from the Privy Council of 24 October 1623,[101] and Pory "published" the Privy Council orders of July and October which related to supplies and the surrendering of its present charter by the Company, and gave assurance that the surrendering of the Charter was for reform and change and not for abolition of the government of the colony.[102] Nothing was said in these documents of the continuation of a House of Burgesses or

[96] These men are not to be confused with the Commission mentioned above headed by Sir William Jones, a group which did its investigating entirely in England. Harvey and Pory apparently came directly from England, Peirsey (or Piersey) apparently and Matthews certainly were already in the colony (see Brown, *Genesis*, II, 963, 969–71; *First Republic*, p. 556 and *passim*; Craven, *Dissolution*, p. 322). John Jefferson also was appointed but did not act. Harvey and Pory pushed the investigation.

[97] Kingsbury, IV, 476.

[98] *Ibid.*

[99] Letter dated between 24 October 1623 and 26 June 1624, *William and Mary Quarterly*, 2nd series, VI (April 1926), 114–21.

[100] Brown, *First Republic*, p. 571.

[101] Kingsbury, IV, 294; *Acts of the Privy Council, Colonial*, I, 71–2; Brown, *First Republic*, p. 572 (although he gives the date as 3 November). On 2 March 1623/4 the Commissioners had issued a declaration of their purposes to the General Assembly, asking assistance (Kingsbury, IV, 464–5). The Assembly had replied with the request for an exhibit of the Commissioners' authority (*Journals*, p. 40), to which the group replied that they had no authority to compel co-operation, etc., but that they as planters themselves asked for it. The General Assembly in turn ordered that the several plantations transport the Commissioners according to their desires, and accommodate them as well as possible (Kingsbury, IV, 41).

[102] See Brown, *First Republic*, pp. 554–6, 522–3.

General Assembly, and therefore certain historians[103] have concluded that the love of freedom impelled the composition of the next letters of the Assembly to authorities in England. Whether that be true or whether it was merely a Sandys-faction Council which was dominating affairs, the Assembly proceeded to address letters to King and Privy Council which show vital concern as to the colony's having a voice in its own government. The first of these, relating to tobacco and the need of soldiers, concluded concerning the proposed garrison:

> Wee most humblie desire that the Gouvernor[r], Counsell and General Assemblie may have a voyce in their disposall, since none at that distaunce by reason of accidents and emergent occasions can direct y[t], so advantagiously as our presence and experience. . . .[104]

The second was even more explicit, containing the statement that no change in government was desired, for since Sir Thomas Smith's time, "our slavery . . . [has] . . . been converted to freedome."[105] The Assembly begged that future governors might not have absolute authority, "but may be restrayned as formerly by the consent of this Counsell."[106] And after suggesting that governors be appointed for longer terms so that they might learn the country, the letter concluded:

> But above all we humblie intreat yo[r] Lo[ps] that we may retaine the libertie of our generall Assemblie, then w[ch] nothinge can more conduce to our satisfaction or the publique utilitie. . . .[107]

In "A Brief Declaration," noticed above as the most elaborate document of this Assembly approved to be sent home, and drawn up by "the Ancient Planters now remaining alive in Virginia," the history of the colony's first twelve years is traced. Much is made of the fact that in 1619, with the beginning of the Yeardley administration, planters were given "a hande in the governinge of themselves,"[108] by the establishment of the General Assembly, and that these liberties were ratified and

103 Particularly *ibid.*, p. 572.
104 McIlwaine, ed., *Journals*, p. 26.
105 *Ibid.*, p. 27.
106 *Ibid.*, Evidently meaning the General Assembly.
107 *Ibid.* One other evidence of the Assembly's interest in "representative government": among the "Laws and Orders" passed (Kingsbury, IV, 580–5) no. 8 states "that the Gou9 nor shall not laye any taxes or ympositiones vppon y[e] Colony, theire landes or commodities other wy[se] then by the awthoritie of y[e] generall Assemblie. . . ."
108 McIlwaine, ed., *Journals*, p. 36.

confirmed upon the arrival of Wyatt in 1621. There can be no mistaking the emphasis on self-legislation, whether that emphasis proceed from anticipations of a liberalism of a later sort, from astute politics on the part of Wyatt and Sandys, or simply from common-sense experience which convinced the colonists that distance made some measure of self-government imperative for safety and prosperity.

Apparently the commissioners were not given access to the replies to Johnson and Butler,[109] nor to the other more significant documents addressed to King and Privy Council. Through John Pory, however, they seduced the clerk Edward Sharpless into giving them copies of these documents. The Assembly was sending a special representative, Vice-Admiral John Pountis, to England to see that these documents were presented personally and directly to the "umpires" concerned. Harvey desired to get his stolen copies to Sir Nathaniel Rich before the official ones arrived so that a case against them might be prepared.[110] Sir Edwin Sandys and his colleagues of the Company were more than right in believing that their judges were also accusers.

George Sandys, who had evidently been Pory's friend in the first year in the colony, was probably as disappointed as Wyatt and the rest of the Council in this underhand dealing. The Virginia Council warned the Company at home that, contrary "to his ꝑfessed integritie," Pory had forestalled their plans,[111] and that they feared sinister intention. Pountis himself died on the way to England, and Secretary of State Conway ordered his executor to hold all papers he had carried until called for.[112] Thus the commissioners and the anti-Sandys faction won another round. The papers probably never got to royal hands, the colonists later believed,[113] apparently with good reason, though it is doubtful that their reception by James would have had any effect whatsoever.[114]

109 One of the commissioners, however, Samuel Matthews, the resident planter, had signed the two documents against Johnson's statement before Pory and Harvey arrived, and later as a burgess signed the long letter which asked that the liberty of General Assembly be retained (see Brown, *First Republic*, p. 573; McIlwaine, ed., *Journals*, pp. 22–7). The conclusion seems to be that Pory and Harvey ran the show, and that the local members of the commission were merely "ciphers," to use a favourite Stuart appellation.

110 See Harvey's letter to Rich, 24 April 1624 (Kingsbury, IV, 476–7).

111 Kingsbury, IV, 481. 12 May 1624.

112 To Sir Thomas Merry, 14 June 1624 (Kingsbury, IV, 483–4).

113 McIlwaine, ed., *Journals*, p. 42. "Petition of the Convention of 1625."

114 For the King's personal antagonism to Sir Edwin and the Sandys faction, see Brown, *First Republic*, and Craven, *Dissolution*.

There was no other official Assembly in George Sandys' time in Virginia. But in April 1625 Wyatt called for an election of burgesses to appear at James City on 10 May.[115] He was acting, as Captain Martin had said, without any authority.[116] This gathering, generally referred to as the "Convention of 1625," survives through one document, a petition to the King. It states that the planters, fearing Mr. Pountis' papers never reached his Majesty, are now sending Sir George Yeardley himself as their representative, with this petition and "relations" concerning the Smith faction as an unfit agent of government, and also concerning the pernicious tobacco contract. Sandys, who was the fourth signer of this petition, probably accompanied Yeardley to England.[117]

Sandys' place as an influential member of the Assembly, his alignment personally against individuals of the anti-Southampton-Sandys faction, and his later part in Virginia history mark him as a zealous believer in the Old Company as a colonial governmental institution, and perhaps, like his brother Sir Edwin and probably Sir Francis Wyatt, a believer in the justice of colonial self-government. To call any one of the three a liberal in the eighteenth or nineteenth century sense is simply to ignore the political philosophies of Renaissance England and Europe, as has been noted above. But theirs is distinctly a step away from monarchical personal government of a colonial empire at the moment that system was getting under way.

There is much less evidence of the activities and interests of Sandys' private life than there is of his public, presumably because he had little time for the former. He seems to have owned or operated, however, at least four plantations. As observed above, he had felt compelled to buy one of 200 acres from a private planter when he arrived in 1621, for otherwise his servants who came in the *George* with him might have starved before he might settle them where they could produce their own crop. Exactly where this was located it is impossible to say, but it was certainly close to Jamestown. Sandys' commission as treasurer assured him of 1,500 acres from which he would draw the revenues. Some of this was probably apportioned to him by 1622, but the only record remaining is of 17 January 1624/5, when "Mr Threasurer doth make

115 *Ibid.*, pp. 55–6. The Governor hoped he would not have to keep them more than 3 or 4 days.

116 McIlwaine, ed., *Minutes*, p. 62, 23 May 1925. Against the King's wishes, Martin thought.

117 Their names appear on the Council's letters of 15 June 1625 (Kingsbury, IV, 559–67). For evidence that he accompanied Yeardley, see below.

Choyse for five hundred Acres of Land at *Chapokes Creeke* opposite against *Sandy poynte* for the land dew to his office."[118] This he may have occupied earlier, or another near it, for the census of 1624/5 gives a list of those living at the Treasurer's plantation, as distinct from those living on Mr. George Sandys' plantation,[119] the latter presumably near Swan's Point and Gray's Creek down the river.[120]

The last mentioned grant, of 300 acres, was Sandys' by patent of 4 December 1624 from Governor Wyatt.[121] Another, of 400 acres, granted on the same date,[122] lay within the precincts of Archer's Hope, on the northern side of the river just below Jamestown. This larger tract, separated on its east side from Martin's Hundred by a pond, was partially at least a matter of ravines and bottoms. It was apparently called in Sandys' time, almost surely ironically, "Utopia," and in the nineteenth century still retained the name "Utopia Bottoms."[123]

118 McIlwaine, ed., *Minutes*, p. 43. This location was up the river west of Jamestown on the southern side, on Upper Chippokes Creek. There is a Lower Chippokes, near Sandys' temporary settlement of the college people in 1622 (see Tyler, *Cradle of the Republic*, map, p. 120, and text, pp. 122–124).

119 See Hotten, pp. 34–5. The muster was taken 23 January 1624/5.

120 See Nugent, p. 190, under "John Seneor," regarding Sandys' plantation's location. Also see Tyler, *Cradle of the Republic*, p. 20.

121 Nugent, pp. 1, 3; *The Researcher*, I, no. 2, 92, "Earliest Extant Land Patents of the Colony of Virginia." The 300 acres were his by virtue of his bill of adventure in the Company of £12. 10s., which gave him 100 acres, and for the transportation of "William Right William Heynes Junr William Smith & Georg Gurr" in the *Tyger* in 1621, at 50 acres for each man transported. His annual fee rent was one shilling for each fifty acres. The land was surveyed by William Claiborne, who measured 650 acres in all, 200 for "Mr. Bainham" and 150 for Edward Grindon, who later bought Sandys' holdings here and elsewhere. (This tract was sold by Sandys to Grindon, who in turn sold it to Captain George Evelin, who deeded the same to his son Marjoy Evelin in 1651 [Nugent, p. 401, under "Monjoy Evelin."]) At the time Sandys was said to be possessed of all three "dividents," which probably means that his tenants were then working all the land. Perhaps this included Company tenants [*i.e.*, The Treasurer's] before the Treasurer's plantation was granted or operating.

122 Abstracts in Nugent, p. 4; *Researcher*, I, no. 2, 93–4. For the subsequent history of this grant, see Nugent, p. 168.

123 According to Tyler, *Cradle of the Republic*, p. 149. Mr. Robert H. Land, when he was Librarian of the College of William and Mary, investigated the origin of the name "Utopia" for me. Mr. Land did not find the name Utopia in any record of Sandys' grant of patent, but concluded that if Sandys' grant was not called "Utopia," the place adjoining it was from Sandys' time. Nugent, p. 4, lists Sandys' Archer's Hope patent of 4 December 1624, and describes (p. 168) a grant to William Browning on 10 April 1646, of 650 acres which

It was apparently in his two or more plantations across the river, in the former territory of the Tappahanna Indians against whom Sandys had led the expeditions, that the Treasurer went in for farming and the development of a plantation community on an extensive scale. Primarily he must have been concerned with making a good income or modest fortune for himself, as he saw Sir George Yeardley had done, but he must also have felt that the director of staple commodities should set an example, or create something we might now call a model farm. In January 1624/5 Sandys had with him on his own plantation fourteen men and boys, besides a Frenchman, Daniel Poole, and his wife and child.[124] On the Treasurer's plantation, listed next to those on the personal plantation, were eleven men and two women, besides two of the Italians, and the wife and child of one of them.[125]

includes Sandys' old property and a strip belonging to John Utie, the latter referred to as "my plantation . . . called Utopia." Neither Dr. Earl G. Swem, Librarian Emeritus of William and Mary, nor Mr. Land was familiar with a present tract in James City County called "Utopia" or "Utopia Bottoms." The local Commissioner of Revenue, however, informed Mr. Land (communicated to the present writer on 4 March 1949) that there is now a place in the county called "Utopia," located about fifteen miles from Sandys' tract and owned by the Powhatan Hunt Club. There is also a reference to "Mr. Threars swamps" (McIlwaine, ed., *Minutes*, p. 63). Sandys sold some of the land rights due to him for transportation of servants. For example, the land due for the transportation of Thomas and John Daunsey [Dancy] and John Mott Sr and Jr, he made over to John Baynam (McIlwaine, ed., *Minutes*, p. 39, 3 January 1624/5).

124 The "MUSTER of m^r^ GEORG SAND'S, Esquire" appears in Hotten, *Original Lists*, pp. 234–5 and E. D. Neill, *Virginia Carolorum*, pp. 17–18. They are all listed as "Servants": in the *George*, 1621, Martin Turner, George Bailiffe, John Sparks, John Dancy, John Edwards, Nicholas Thompson, Rosamus Carter, John Stone, a boy; in the *Guift*, 1622, Nicholas Comon and Nicholas Eyres, a boy; in the *Bona Nova*, [n.d.] "hired servants," David Mansfield, John Claxon; in the *Tyger*, 1622, freemen, Thomas Swifte and John Baldwin; then Poole, his wife, and "a young child of theires."

125 The "Muster of those that live in ye Treasurars Plant." (Neill, *Virginia Carolorum*, pp. 17–18, and Hotten, pp. 235 ff.) lists Robert Sheaperd, who came in the *George*, 1621; James Chambers, in the *Dutie* in 1620; John Parsons, William Benge, John Evans, Robert Edmunds, John Comes, and John Tyos, in the *Marygold*, 1619; William Pilkington, Elias Longe, and Thomas Hall, in the *Bona Nova*, 1620; Margaret Pilkington and Jane Long, "weomen"; "Mr Vincencio," "Mr Bernardo," his wife and a child. Sandys may have had five persons at his plantation in Archer's Hope, near Jamestown, for in Hotten's list (p. 235—Neill omits these) are listed five men grouped after the Treasurer's plantation list, and followed after another space by the words "m^r^ Treasurers Plant. James Citty," these last words being closer to the list of dead which

A census of the physical features of plantations of 1624/5 survives along with the lists of individual humans. Evidently the report contained therein of "Mr. Sandys, the Treasurer," is of his official plantation across the river, or of that combined with his personal plantation, for the inventory of certain items would indicate that these were official or public properties. This report shows that Sandys' people in one year grew and harvested 100 barrels of corn, 30 bushels more than the next most productive plantation, and that the Treasurer had in his arsenal 1 piece of ordnance, 30 pieces of armour, 20 swords, 20 pounds of powder, 30 snaphaunce pieces, and 300 pounds of lead and shot. Fifteen goats and two swine constituted his livestock, and he had one house framed for silkworms, 2 storehouses and "other cabbens," 2 dwelling houses, a garden of 1½ acres, a vineyard of 2 acres, and 1 large fort. In addition, listed as being at his own plantation, were 1 large palisaded fort, 1 piece of mounted ordnance, 1 dwelling house, and 4 other houses.[126]

Whether the 100 barrels of corn indicates greater industry or a greater labour supply is difficult to determine.[127] Perhaps his harvest was the

follows than to the five names. At any rate the five were Zachary Cripp's, who came in the *Margaret & John*, 1621; Edward White in the *Bona Nova*, 1620; Mathew Harmon, in the *Southampton* 1622; Philip Kithly, in the *Furtherance*, 1622; and Anthony West, in the *James*, 1622. These are followed by a list of those who died during the year in the whole group of plantations "over the water," including those of Roger Smith, Edward Blaney, Samuel Mathews, David Sandys, and George Sandys. Among the dead are listed George Gurr, who was brought over by George Sandys in the *Tyger* in 1621, and just above his name, William Sand's (unidentified—see the several William Sandyses in E. S. Sandys, *The Family of Sandys*, both volumes). Two years after Sandys left Virginia, in arguing a dispute over his servants left in the colony, the Virginia Council stated that Sandys had appropriated to his own use, in 1623, 16 tenants, and that he had no order to do so from the Company (Sainsbury, ed., *Calendar of State Papers, Colonial*, p. 88, 4 March 1628). Sandys took these, perhaps high-handedly, as part of the 50 tenants promised to his office and never received. The Company had earlier acknowledged its regret that it could not supply both Wyatt and Sandys with the number promised (Kingsbury, IV, 270).

126 Brown, *First Republic*, p. 626. Brown states that these figures are from "the most reliable sources" (*ibid.*, p. 615). There is other evidence that Sandys' 300 acres were planted (Kingsbury, IV, 555). Reference is made in the *Minutes* (p. 86), on 3 January 1625/6, to the loft "at the old forte of Mr George Sandys," a place where shelled corn was kept.

127 Perhaps the official Treasurer's plantation was also cultivated by Sandys until after 1628, for he was re-appointed to the Virginia Council as late as that year. There is evidence (25 July 1627, *Acts of the Privy Council, Colonial*, Item

result of something of both. His letters quoted above indicate his troubles in provisioning his people during the terrible years immediately after the massacre, but they also indicate his real interest in the development of these lands. After he left Virginia, for several years his lands continued in production under his factor.[128] His interest in their cultivation, at least for the revenues derived from them, continued for some time.

Of creature comforts enjoyed by Sandys we know nothing beyond what certain lists of necessities for everyone, and certain inventories of ship's cargoes of clothing and provisions[129] show, except for one item in a letter of 13 October 1622, from Sir Edwin Sandys to John Ferrar. Sir Edwin complained that the ship's captain, because he was already overloaded, refused to take the many barrels of provisions for "my brother George." "Only a rundlet of Sack sent to him from my wife, wth som other things of small bulk; & a Seller of glasses wth hote waters sent to him from my Lady Aucher, he yielded to take in."[130]

Whatever its physical comforts, Jamestown could not have been too uncongenial a place intellectually for a man of Sandys' interests and education. One evidence of this lies in the letter addressed to the King by the General Assembly unmasking Captain Butler's *Unmasking*. The particular reply is to Butler's charge that they had at various times ignorantly and/or wilfully ignored the laws and customs of England.

> THE Governor and Council, whom it only concerned, replied to this; that they had followed the Laws and Customs of *England* to their utmost Skill; neither could he, or any other, produce any Particular, wherein they had failed. As to their Ignorance, they held him to be no competent Judge of those, who

190, pp. 116–7) that certain "servants" he retained after his departure in 1625 were actually then in his personal service, and that some of them were originally Company's or Treasurer's Plantation tenants that he retained for the remainder of their seven-year indenture, after his three-year period (1621–4) as Treasurer under the Company, to recompense him for the proportion of the 50 tenants originally promised, which he never received. This seems the real basis for his petitions in 1627–8 to the Privy Council and the replies from the Virginia Council (see *Acts of the Privy Council, Colonial, passim,* and Chapter IX, below). Sandys claimed that an old Company order of 9 June 1624 authorized this.

128 At least this deduction may be drawn, for in 1626 and perhaps in 1628, servants were apparently in his employ (McIlwaine, ed., *Minutes*, pp. 144, 179).

129 *E.g.*, the invoice of goods sent by John Harrison in the *Marmaduke*, 16 September 1623 (Kingsbury, IV, 278–80). There are several other such lists in the Kingsbury volumes.

130 Kingsbury, III, 690–1. Lady Aucher was one of Sandys' two sisters.

so far transcended him in Point of Learning and Ability. For he had never been bred to the Law (as was not unknown to some of them) nor yet in other of the liberal sciences. . . .[131]

These Councillors and others of the "ruling class" with whom Sandys had come into contact from his arrival in 1621 could very properly claim representatives of training in law and arts among themselves. Of the twenty members, including the governor, of the Council in Virginia appointed on 24 July 1621,[132] at least seven were almost certainly educated at Oxford or Cambridge and/or one of the Inns of Court.[133] Of the remaining thirteen it may be that several were university bred, for the records of both institutions for the period are incomplete.[134] Though Sandys did not admire Christopher Davison as a public official, he probably enjoyed literary conversation with the Secretary, who had like Sandys a legal education and was a poet and the brother of two other poets.[135] And George Thorpe, former courtier and parliamentarian,

[131] McIlwaine, ed., *Journals*, p. 25. Of course Butler was a prolific and effective expository writer on such varied matters as marine procedures and the history of Bermuda, as well as the unmasking (see *D.N.B.* article under "Nathaniel Butler"; Kingsbury, III and IV, *passim*; Br. Mus. MSS. Sloan 758; *Calendar of State Papers, Charles I, Domestic*, XXXII, 75).

[132] Kingsbury, III, 483.

[133] Actually the names of eight of them—including Sandys'—appear in the records of these institutions. Wyatt and Sandys and probably (if their identification with persons of the same name and date of flourishing listed in J. Foster, *Alumni Oxonienses*, [Early Series, Oxford, 1892], is correct) Roger Smith, Ralph Hamor, and Michael Lapworth were students at Oxford (in several of these cases the identification is already made in Foster). Dr. John Pott and Samuel Maycocke had attended Cambridge (see John and J. A. Venn, *Alumni Cantabrigienses* . . ., Pt. I [4 vols., Cambridge, 1924], III, 124, 384). Wyatt (see Foster, *Alumni Oxonienses*, ES, IV, 1690) and Davison (see *D.N.B.* under "Francis Davison" and Brown, *First Republic*, p. 453 n) had been members of Gray's Inn; a Ralph Hamor was in 1614 a member of the Inner Temple (Foster, p. 638); and of course Sandys had been a member of the Middle Temple.

[134] Councillors who possibly on the evidence of distinguished family and/or highly literate prose may have been university men were Francis West, son of Lord de la Warr, George Thorpe, former M.P. and Gentleman of the Privy Chamber, Nathaniel Powell, William Claiborne, and John Rolfe (see Brown, *Genesis*, II, and *First Republic*). For the letters of several of these men see Kingsbury, III and IV.

[135] See *D.N.B.* under "Francis Davison," and Br. Mus. Harleian MS. 6930 (containing translations into verse by Davison of some of the Psalms). It should be recalled that Davison testified to the Company in London that George Sandys undertook the secretaryship while Davison was in England out of his love for him (Kingsbury, II, 109).

student of Indian views on religion and astronomy, and deputy in charge of the college, almost surely was a congenial companion for the Treasurer when the latter made his official visits to the College lands.[136] And one must remember that Wyatt himself wrote creditable verses and showed himself a learned and sound observer of theories of government.[137]

But the colony included several gentlemen outside the Council whose cultural attainments added at least some polish to the rough exterior of this frontier society. Peter Arundle, who had taught French and is said to have published several books before he left London, concerned himself in Virginia with silkworms and interesting though querulous letters home.[138] William Ferrar, probably the brother of Nicholas and John of the London company, was a trained barrister,[139] as was the old litigant and troublemaker John Martin.[140] Henry Spelman, Indian interpreter killed by the Indians in 1622, was an able student of Indian language and customs who had written years earlier "The Relation of Virginia."[141] Charles Harmer, brother of the Greek professor at Oxford, had settled on the Eastern Shore of Virginia in 1622.[142] And among several others perhaps the most scholarly and picturesque was John Pory, secretary of state under Sir George Yeardley and in 1624–5 one of the King's commissioners sent to investigate the plantation.

136 For John Pory's and Sir George Yeardley's high opinion of Thorpe as capable official and as personal companion, see Kingsbury, III, 123, 305. Thorpe, who had great faith in the Indians, was killed with many of his household in the massacre. It was then that Sandys took direct charge of college affairs.

137 See Wyatt MSS. No. 29, now on deposit in the British Museum (property of the Earl of Romney) for manuscript verses by Wyatt, and his commendatory poem in Sandys' *A Paraphrase upon the Divine Poems* (1638). Also see Wyatt's letter to an official of the Company cited above (*William and Mary Quarterly*, between 24 October 1623 and 26 June 1624) and his official papers in McIlwaine, ed., *Journals* and *Minutes*, and Kingsbury, III and IV. Sir Francis' father George Wyatt wrote a long letter of 'instructions' to his son in Virginia, beginning "The groũd of happie governm̃et. . . ." (Wyatt MSS.) and quoting much Roman and Scriptual authority.

138 See Kingsbury, III, 534–5, 589; IV, 89, 230–1 for his letters.

139 See Brown, *Genesis*, II, 891, and A. L. Maycock, *Nicholas Ferrar of Little Gidding*, London, S.P.C.K., 1938, p. 112.

140 See J. P. C. Southall, "Captain John Martin of Brandon on the James," *Virginia Magazine of History and Biography*, LIV (January 1946), 21–67, and Brown, *Genesis*, II, 943–4.

141 Edited by James F. Hunnewell, London, 1872. For more of Spelman see Brown, *Genesis*, II, 1020–1; Howard M. Jones, *The Literature of Virginia in the Seventeenth Century*, p. 11 (and present work, Chapter VI note 120 above).

142 See *Virginia Magazine of History & Biography*, III, 273–4; XIX, 129.

Pory, protégé and disciple of Hakluyt, M.A. of Cambridge, M.P. for Bridgewater, King's emissary to France, translator of Leo Africanus, and a traveller in the Eastern Mediterranean countries, came to Virginia in 1619. Out of office in 1621, he remained in the colony, writing letters and making voyages of discovery, as Sandys testifies in one of his own letters quoted above.[143] He made himself generally useful until he sailed for England in August 1622. He was probably received cordially on his return in 1624 as a commissioner, for there was regret as well as resentment in the Council's letters to England which mentioned that Mr. Pory, contrary to his professed integrity, had suborned the Council's clerk Edward Sharpless.[144]

Pory's letters, like Sandys', show a real appreciation of the physical beauties of this new land, and an even greater appreciation of its potentialities, for Pory's were written before the massacre and Company criticism had embittered Sandys and other councillors. At any rate, Sandys must have found Pory a most stimulating companion during that first year in Virginia.

Besides these lay gentlemen, there were a number of educated clergy in the colony, among them Richard Bucke, considered an excellent preacher,[145] and Hawte Wyatt, the Governor's brother and a former student at Oxford and Gray's Inn.[146] And the colony contained at least a fair number of good books, as a recent study has shown,[147] many or most of which must have been available to Sandys in Jamestown. In 1619 Pory had written from Virginia a now oft-quoted remark, "I am now

143 See Chapter VI, note 29 above and Neill, *Memoir of the Rev. Patrick Copland*, pp. 62–4.

144 Council in Virginia to the Earl of Southampton and the Council and Company of Virginia, 12 May 1624 (Kingsbury, IV, 481). For other accounts of Pory see Brown, *Genesis*, II, 969–71; E. D. Neill, *Memoir of the Rev. Patrick Copland*, p. 63 n; "John Pory" in *D.A.B.*; Howard M. Jones, *The Literature of Virginia in the Seventeenth Century*, pp. 26–8; and William S. Powell, *John Pory: His Life Letters and Works* (unpublished University of North Carolina M.A. thesis, 1947). For Pory's fine letters to England, 1619–22, see Kingsbury, III, *passim*; for other letters of his see Br. Mus. MSS. Harleian 7000, ff. 308–80.

145 See Brown, *Genesis*, II, 835. Bucke is said to have been educated at Oxford. William Leate, Greville Pooley, Francis Bolton, Thomas White, and David Sandys were other clergymen in the Virginia colony at this time.

146 See Lyon G. Tyler, *Encyclopedia of Virginia Biography*, I, 364. Hawte Wyatt was later, until his death in 1638, to be vicar of the church at Boxley (in which Sandys was buried in 1644).

147 William S. Powell, "Books in the Virginia Colony before 1624," *William and Mary Quarterly*, 3rd series, V (April 1948), 177–84.

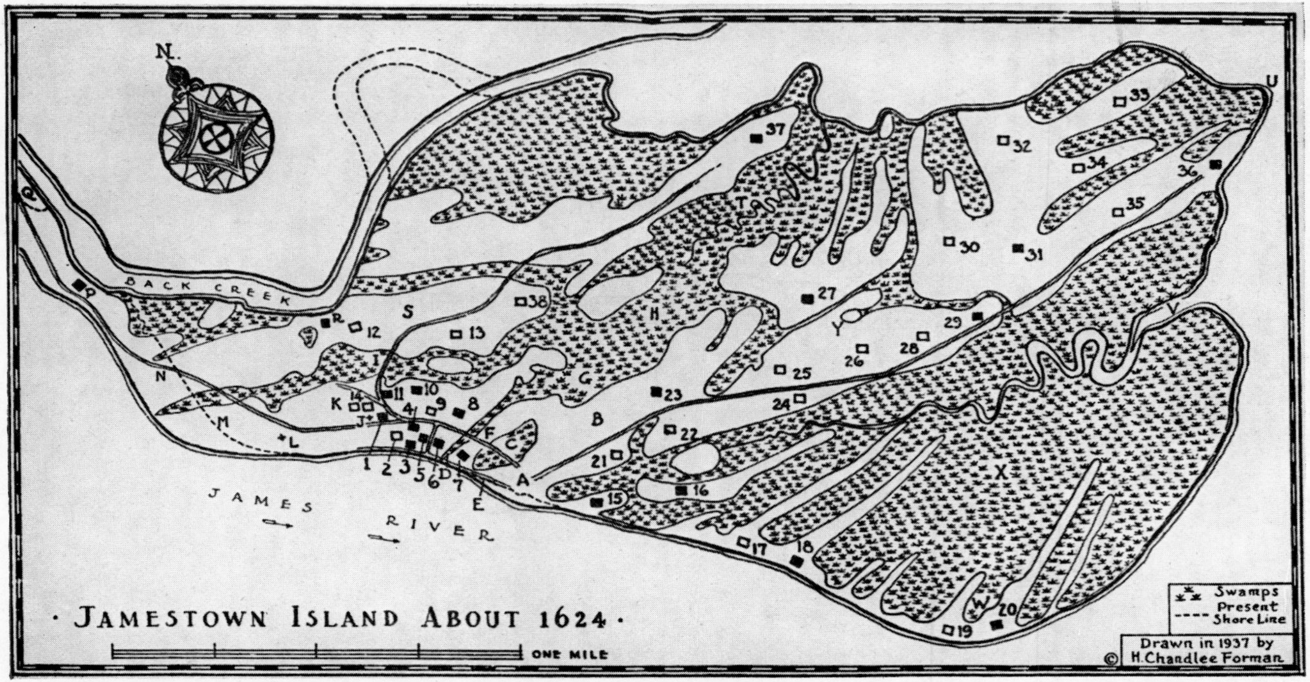

JAMESTOWN ISLAND ABOUT 1624

Drawn by H. Chandlee Forman in 1937, and first appearing in his *Jamestown and St. Mary's*, in 1938

Reproduced by kind permission of the author and the Johns Hopkins University Press

resolved wholly to mind my business here, and next after my penne, to haue some good book alwayes in store being in solitude the best and choicest company."[148]

In the little period snatched from night and repose Sandys had one book continually by him, the Latin version of Ovid's *Metamorphoses* from which he translated. Probably in his own room at Captain Pierce's, "the fairest in Virginia,"[149] or in the dwelling house of a plantation across the river, he translated the last eight books of the Ovid and prepared the whole for publication if and when he should return to England. Virginia and America could hardly enter the text of the Roman author,[150] but the dedication itself[151] and the commentaries added to the second, or complete edition,[152] show that the New World must have been much in Sandys' mind as he composed.

And probably it was from this same room at Captain Pierce's that he wrote to the great collector of natural curiosities, John Tradescant,[153] presumably concerning the wonders to be found in Virginia. As he had been a collector of curios in Egypt which found their way to Tradescant,

148 Kingsbury, III, 222. Pory to "The Right Honble and My Singular Good Lorde," 30 September.

149 See Chapter VI note 118 above; Kingsbury, IV, 106–40, and Brown, *First Republic*, p. 626. Also see Chapter V note 127 and above. There were two dwelling houses on the Treasurer's Plantation, as well as the loft for silkworms, and one dwelling house on his own plantation. The old romantic conception that Sandys kept his Ovid, his silkworms, and himself in a loft of a cabin of Pierce's at Jamestown is as far as I can ascertain without more foundation than the facts given in the present chapter.

150 Though there may be reminiscences of the storms in crossing the Atlantic in Sandys' translation of the storm scene in Book XI.

151 See Chapter VIII below.

152 See Richard B. Davis, "America in George Sandys' Ovid," *William and Mary Quarterly*, 3rd series, IV (July 1947), 297–304. Though most of the bits of information about America were added to the book by Sandys after he returned to England, it is possible, if not probable, that some of them occurred to him and were noted as he translated.

153 This is John Tradescant the elder. See Brown, *Genesis*, II, 1032; Kingsbury, III, 58. World travellers, Tradescant and his son are interesting figures. Sandys' letter to Tradescant does not survive, though it is listed as among the letters confiscated from the *Abigail* on 19 June 1623: "George Sandys to Mr John Tradesicant at my Lord Wottons house" (Kingsbury, IV, 229). There are portraits of the Tradescant family in the new Ashmolean Museum, Oxford. That Tradescant was at times at least in government employ seems evident in a warrant of the Lord Chamberlain 31 December 1635 (P.R.O., L.C. 5/134, p. 91) to deliver to him Henry VIII's stirrups and Henry VII's gloves.

so Sandys was probably a collector of those Indian and other relics listed in the 1656 catalogue of the *Musaeum Tradescantianum*.[154] His room in Jamestown may have been full of specimens of fauna and flora, seashells and native costumes, which he planned to send or take with him to England.

So the English poet, traveller, and scholar occupied himself in the tiny settlement on the fringe of the strange, uncouth new continent. He remained conscious of its sights and sounds long after his return to England.[155] The crash of trees falling under the settler's axe, the croaking of frogs, the war whoop of the Indians, the sickly sweet stench of dead men and animals in the streets of the capital, the broad river rising in unexplored mountains, the mighty green forests, the great blue bay of the Chesapeake, were memories of a rough but exciting existence. And along with these must have remained other remembrances of official duty and solemn ceremony on this edge of the wilderness. Though he did not record his impressions of this kind of event, Sandys had the same sort of poet's eye for colour and proportion that William Strachey had shown ten years or more earlier[156] in a description of life in Virginia. Strachey's picture of a Sunday in Jamestown about 1610 might easily fit a Sunday in the same spot in 1621–4, though perhaps a knight as governor did not possess quite as imposing a retinue or bodyguard as Lord de la Warr had gathered about him.

> In the middest is a market place, a Store house, and a Corps du guard, as likewise a pretty Chappell, though (at this time when wee came in) as ruined and unfrequented: but the Lord Governour, and Captaine Generall, hath given order for the repairing of it, and at this instant, many hands are about it. It is in length threescore foote, in breadth twenty foure, and shall have a Chancell in it of Cedar and a Communion Table of the Blake Walnut, and all the Pewes of Cedar, with faire broad windowes, to shut and open, as the

[154] London. Many Virginia birds, Powhatan's cloak of state, etc., are listed. Among the objects the visitor notices most easily in the new Ashmolean is Powhatan's ceremonial cloak in a large glass case on the wall of one of the exhibit rooms.

[155] See his references to geological formations, noisy frogs, possums, etc., in the 1632 edition, or in Davis, "America in George Sandys' Ovid," pp. 303–4.

[156] From *Hakluytus Posthumus, or Purchas His Pilgrimes* (20 vols., Glasgow, 1905–6), XIX, 56–7. This is the Purchas version of William Strachey's "A true reportorie of the wrack, and redemption of Sir Thomas Gates, Knight; upon, and from the Ilands of the Bermudas: his comming to Virginia, and the estate of that Colonie then, and after, under the Government of the Lord La Warre, July 15. 1610."

weather shall occasion, of the same wood, a Pulpet of the same, with a Font hewen hollow, like a Canoa, with two Bels at the West end. It is so cast, as it be very light within, and the Lord Governour and Captaine Generall doth cause it to be kept passing sweete, and trimmed up with divers flowers, with a Sexton belonging to it, and in it every Sonday wee have sermons twice a day, and every Thursday a Sermon, having true preachers, which take their weekely turnes, and every morning at the ringing of a Bell, about ten of the clocke, each man addresseth himselfe to prayers, and so at foure of the clocke before Supper. Every Sunday, when the Lord Governour, and Captain Generall goeth to Church, hee is accompanied with all the Counsailers, Captaines, other officers, and all the Gentlemen, and with a Guard of Holberdiers in his Lordships Livery, faire red cloakes, to the number of fifty, both on each side, and behinde him: and being in the Church, his Lordship hath his seate in the Quier, in a greene Velvet Chaire, with a Cloath, with a Velvet Cushion spread on a Table before him, on which he kneeleth, and on each side sit the Counsell, Captaines, and Officers, each in their place, and when he returneth home againe, he is waited on to his house in the same manner. . . .

But by 1625 Sandys was willing to exchange all that Virginia had to offer for what should be at least an extended visit to England. Though he had with Wyatt been reappointed[157] to the Council by King James in 1624 under a royal commission, he was now ready to return home. No statement of reasons is given, but the reasons themselves are not hard to find. Wyatt, who had requested permission from the Privy Council to return to England, gave as his excuse the death of his father and the necessity of settling the estate to which he was heir,[158] but the change in colonial home administration must have been at least an additional reason for the Governor's request.

Sandys' reasons may have been any one of a combination of several good ones. Apparently he felt that the office, and at least his personal function

[157] It will be noticed that this is to the Council; Sandys claimed that his tenure of office as Treasurer ended in 1624. The commission of appointment by the King, dated 26 August 1624 (Kingsbury, IV, 501) included the old Council yet living and added the names of Harvey, Mathews, Claiborne, and John Martin. See Brown, *First Republic*, 614, 639–40. On 4 March 1626, when he was in England, Sandys was reappointed by King Charles' commission to the Council under Sir George Yeardley as Governor (Sainsbury ed., *Calendar of State Papers, Colonial, 1574–1660*, p. 77). He was reappointed again in 1628 (see Chapters IX and X below).

[158] Licence to return was dated 24 September 1624 (Kingsbury, IV, 504). Wyatt for various reasons, however, was unable to leave the colony until after 8 May 1626 (McIlwaine, ed., *Minutes*, p. 102). Sir George Yeardley had succeeded him by 28 July 1626 (*ibid.*, p. 104).

of Treasurer, ended with the dissolution of the Company.[159] Politically he was certainly out of sympathy with James's assumption of control and may have wanted to go to London and look over the potentialities of the situation as it related to his personal future before he decided as to his further course. Or he may have been anxious to get his now completed manuscript of the Ovid to an English printer. Or there is perhaps a better reason, that he was in semi-official capacity to support and advise Sir George Yeardley, appointed by the "Convention of 1625" as agent or representative before the King. He apparently received permission to return to England at the Council meeting of 25 April 1625, for a fragmentary line regarding him survives: "*Yt is ordered yt Mr Threar goinge for England*[.]"[160] This was the same date on which authorization was given to call for an election of burgesses to meet on 10 May, at which assembly Sir George Yeardley was 'elected'[161] the colony's representative before the King, though the choice was probably made earlier by the Council.

Whatever the reason in Sandys' case, Yeardley and Sandys appear to have sailed together soon after 25 June 1625[162] and to have reached

[159] Governor West and the Council testified in March 1628 that Sandys had before his going away refused to execute his office of Treasurer, saying he had nothing to do with it (Sainsbury ed., *Calendar of State Papers, Colonial, 1574–1660*, p. 88).

[160] "Minutes of the Council and General Court," *Virginia Magazine of History and Biography*, XXIII (January 1915), 16. The same line is not included in the McIlwaine edition of the *Minutes* (p. 56), though the entry which follows this in the *Virginia Magazine* is present in McIlwaine, that concerning "Vincentia and Bern[ardo]," two of Sandys' glassmen, being granted permission to sail for England. A letter to the present writer of 12 November 1948, from Mr. Leslie W. Dunlap, Assistant Chief, Division of Manuscripts, Library of Congress, states that the words regarding the Treasurer appear, crossed out with a wavy line apparently contemporary, in the manuscript "Court Book" from which the *Virginia Magazine* and the McIlwaine "Minutes" were printed. Many such lines or phrases have been crossed out in the book, but there is no further evidence in other entries from April through July 1625 that allude to George Sandys, either in the ordinary record or in the crossed-out portion of the "Minutes."

[161] McIlwaine, ed., *Journals*, p. xxx. No record of the "election" of Sir George Yeardley survives. His selection may have been made privately and unofficially by the Council on 25 April and confirmed by the "Convention" assembly of burgesses in May.

[162] Brown, *First Republic*, p. 642, says Yeardley carried the petition of 25 June 1625 to the King and Privy Council. This petition appears in the *Virginia Magazine of History and Biography*, XV (1907), 360–2, under date of June 1625,

London before 1 September. Sandys the poet-adventurer had another dangerous and perhaps thrilling escape, from Turkish pirates, on the way home.[163] On 1 September Secretary Conway wrote to the Turkey Company to express in the King's name, the sense he had of the equity and humanity with which Sir Francis Wyatt, Governor of Virginia, "or some other principal person returning from thence," was treated by the Turks.[164] This could refer only to Yeardley and/or Sandys. That Sandys was at least with Yeardley when overtaken at sea is borne out by three hitherto unexplained[165] lines of his later autobiographical poem, "Deo. Opt. Max." The storm mentioned may have been on the voyage either way, but the encounters with pirates and perhaps the Salian Moors, seemingly successive events, must have occurred on the voyage home. Sandys' account of his varied life concludes with a list of the dangers from which the Almighty has rescued him and with an expression of gratitude to his Maker. For him has God

> Preserved from swallowing Seas; when towring Waves
> Mixt with the Clouds, and opened their deep Graves.
> From barbarous Pirats ransom'd: by those taught,
> Successefully with Salian Moores we fought.
> Then brought'st me Home in safety. . . .[166]

and gives George Sandys as third signer. On 24 October 1625 the Privy Council wrote to the Governor and Council of Virginia that the "present miserie and wants of that Collonie . . . haue bene related at large both to his Majestie and this Boarde. . . ." (*Acts of the Privy Council, Colonial*, I, *1613–1680*, item 154, p. 92). Sandys' signature appears in no extant documents in Virginia after this date, 25 June 1625.

163 No previous biographical study of Sandys has noticed this episode.

164 Sainsbury, ed., *Calendar of State Papers, Colonial, 1574–1660*, pp. 74–5. The letter is dated September 1625. The originals (in the Levant Company's Papers, S.P. 105/109, No. 49, Public Record Office) have been checked and found to supply no further details.

165 All the autobiographical references in "Deo. Opt. Max." except these and possibly an adventure in "those darke Seas where horrid Winter reigns,/and binds the stubborne Flouds in Icie chaines," can be identified in *A Relation* or in his letters included above. One other reference to "That false Sidonian Wolfe" and his "cruel Litter" is obscure but covered in part in *A Relation . . .* (1615), Book III, 211–2.

166 First printed by Sandys in 1636 in *A Paraphrase upon the Psalmes of David*, p. 243.

VIII

THE TRANSLATION OF OVID'S *METAMORPHOSES*

SANDYS RETURNED to England at the right moment. For a time he may have intended going back to Virginia,[1] but here at home was an opportunity he may long have awaited.[2] Certainly he knew that his brother Sir Edwin had not been in the good graces of James I. But for George Sandys at least the new king was another matter. Already two editions of *A Relation* had appeared dedicated to Charles as prince. The *Metamorphosis* was now completely translated. Its publication, with a dedication to King Charles, might in the new reign open interesting avenues to preferment.

Sandys must have seen his sovereign crowned on 2 February 1625/6,[3] and also must have noted with satisfaction that the first Parliament of Charles's reign included his brothers Sir Edwin, Sir Myles, and Henry, his cousins Sir Dudly Digges and Sir Thomas Wilford, and his relative by marriage Sir John Finch.[4] He was well aware that a new king would

[1] His reappointment to the Virginia Council on 4 March 1626 and 22 March 1628 (Sainsbury, ed., *Calendar of State Papers, Colonial, 1574–1660*, pp. 77, 88) would perhaps indicate this. Also see Chapter X, pp. 256–7 below for more of the letters of Governor West and the Virginia Council of 1628 concerning "his two years absence from the colony and his purposing not to return" (*Virginia Magazine*, VII [January 1900], 259–60).

[2] The first recorded indication of Sandys' planning to return to England is in the Virginia Court Record of 25 April 1625 (see Chapter VII, note 159 above). James I had died on 5 March. It is barely possible, though hardly probable, that Sandys' was a hurried decision made immediately upon receipt of the news of James's death. The sailing time between England and Virginia was usually much longer than seven weeks, though not always.

[3] Samuel R. Gardiner, *History of England . . . 1603–1642* (10 vols., London, 1904–9), VI, 49.

[4] See Thomas Rymer and Robert Sanderson, edd., *Foedera . . .* (20 vols., London 1703–35), XVIII, 517, 553–6. For more of Digges, see Chapter IX below. Finch had married the sister of Sir Francis Wyatt and was later Lord Keeper. Sir Thomas Wilford or Wilsford, son of Sandys' half uncle Sir Thomas, had married a daughter of Sir Edwin Sandys (see "Sir James and Sir Thomas Wilford," article by A. F. Pollard, in *D.N.B.*). Charles I was much more favourably disposed to Sir Edwin Sandys than his father had been (see Thomas Birch, *Court and Times of Charles I* [2 vols., London, 1848], *passim*).

make many new appointments. His own qualifications for general government or royal household post were obvious. He knew the troublesome colonial problem first hand, he had been Charles's loyal literary suitor for more than ten years, and he had influential political and social connections.

Sought or unsought, modest preferment came to him. During the next fifteen years Charles recognized his abilities as civil servant, poet, and accomplished gentleman. Apparently the recognition as gentleman and poet came first. Though no documentary evidence remains as to the date of Sandys' appointment as a Gentleman of the Privy Chamber to the King, it seems most likely to have been within the first two years after his return to England. Anthony à Wood's statement that Sandys held such a position[5] seems to infer that he was holding it near the end of his life, which may easily be true; but also he was an intimate of the court circle and numbered Gentlemen of the Chamber among his close personal friends at least as early as 1627.

But the first extant tangible token of the royal favour came to Sandys as poet, and with this token we return to the story of his literary career. On 24 April 1626, the King issued a patent granting to Sandys for twenty-one years the exclusive privilege of printing and selling the fifteen complete books of Ovid's *Metamorphoses* which the poet had with great care and diligence translated into English verse. This was done, said his Majesty, "the better to encourage him and others to imploie theire Labours and Studies in good Literature," though he knew that Sandys translated "rather for the Delight and Profitt of Our loving Subjects, then for the Hope of anie greate Benefitt to be by him reaped thereby."[6] The patent further stated that at great expense to Sandys the book had already been imprinted and was ready to be published. Thus the 1626 edition of the Ovid appeared with the prestigious and warning words *Cum Privilegio* across the bottom of the title-page, and an elaborate dedication to the King following on the next leaf. With the publication of this complete *Metamorphosis* and its revision six years later Sandys

5 *Athenae Oxonienses* . . . (5 vols., London, 1813–20, original ed. 1691–2), III, 97–103. Wood says that at the time of Sandys' death he was "then or lately one of the gent. of the privy chamber to K. Ch. I." For a discussion of further evidence of Sandys' connection with the Privy Chamber, see Appendix H below, and in connection with this the discussion of the Falkland circle in Chapter IX below.

6 The patent is printed in Rymer, *Foedera*, XVIII, 676–7, and in Neill, *Virginia Carolorum*, p. 44 (with modernized spelling). The original patent in the Public Record Office was checked also.

became in his own time one of the best known of Caroline poets. Here seems the proper place to consider the editions of this remarkable work, versions of which the *1626* is the focal centre, for all others lead to or from it.

Sandys' interest in translating Ovid is at least as old as the period of his preparation of *A Relation of a Journey* for the press, that is, between 1612 and 1615. Among the literary embellishments of the *Travels* are many translations from the works of Ovid, including some twenty-six from the *Metamorphoses*, ranging from one to twelve lines in length. Among them are five quotations from the first five books, which are essentially the same in couplet form, with a few changes of phrase, as the parallel passages in the 1621, 1626, and 1632 versions of Sandys' translation. One, for example, shows considerable change in phrase while retaining the couplet rhyme. The *Metamorphoses*, IV, 47–49, appears in the 1615 *A Relation* (p. 151) as

> Who with assumed wings made her ascent,
> To high-tópt towers, and there her old age spent.

while in the 1621 *Metamorphosis* (p. 89, ll. 19 ff.), the 1626 (p. 66, ll. 69 ff.), and the 1632 (p. 114, ll. 117 ff.), it reads

> Or of her daughter speake, vvith vving'd ascent
> High-pearcht on towrs: who there her old age spent.

In other cases whole lines are identical in all four versions.[7] In one passage of six lines in Sandys (the Latin *Metamorphoses*, V, ll. 386 ff.), all versions are alike except that the concluding couplet in the 1615 *A Relation* (p. 235) reads

> The boughs coole shade, the moist earth yeelds rare flowers:
> Here heate, nor cold, the death-lesse Spring deuoures.

and in the other three versions of 1621, 1626, and 1632 (1621, p. 132)

> The trees create fresh ayr, th' Earth various flowres:
> Where heat nor cold th' eternall Spring deuoures.

One cannot conclude from these comparisons that the translator had

[7] *E.g.*, in the passage in *Metamorphoses*, IV, 670 ff. (8 lines in Sandys), in 1615 *A Relation*, p. 152; 1621 *Metamorphosis*, p. 111; 1626 *Metamorphosis*, p. 83; 1632 *Metamorphosis*, p. 148. When using the title for the Latin version of Ovid's work, the spelling *Metamorphoses* is used; for Sandys' English version, the spelling *Metamorphosis* (the normal Renaissance English spelling and Sandys' own).

completed at least a rough draft of the whole fifteen books before 1615,[8] for his friend Drayton's poetical epistle to him in 1622 and his own letter to Samuel Wrote in 1623 give evidence to the contrary.[9] Sandys had probably translated appropriate passages according to his needs in embroidering his travel account, and thriftily kept these selected lines by him as he translated the whole.[10]

At any rate, at some time before 1621 he had translated and prepared for the press five entire books of the Ovid. When the first edition of these appeared we do not know—there is apparently no copy extant—but it was probably in 1621, for the work was not entered in the Stationers' Register until that year.[11] In that same year a second edition appeared, the only known copy of which re-appeared in 1947, and is now in the Folger Shakespeare Library.[12] This is a small duodecimo bearing the inscription on an engraved title-page:

[8] Though even passages from the later books (that is, VI–XV, not published until 1626) usually have their essential final form by 1615. Compare, for example, the three versions of *Metamorphoses*, XI, 50–5 (*1615*, p. 16; *1626*, p. 217, ll. 33–8; *1632*, p. 370, ll. 29–34), which show more changes between 1626 and 1632 than between 1615 and 1626, though the rhyme of two of the three couplets is the same in all three. In a longer passage, *Metamorphoses*, XIII, 595–607, though a few phrasal changes occur, the rhymes remain identical in all three (*1615*, p. 204; *1626*, p. 270, ll. 23–34; *1632*, pp. 416, ll. 47–50; 417, ll. 1–8).

[9] Of 28 March 1623. See Chapter VI above for text of letter to Wrote and the end of Chapter V for Drayton's lines. Further evidence that it was not translated before 1621 lies in the Dedication to Charles of the 1626 edition, quoted below.

[10] Evidently Ovid interested him more than the other classical authors from whom he translated. The other authors quoted most frequently in *A Relation* are Homer (28 times), Horace (22), Juvenal (22), Lucan (26), Scaliger (11), and Virgil (51).

[11] On 27 April to Matthew Lownes and William Barrett (Arber's Reprint, *S.R.*, IV, 53). For a discussion of some confusion as to this date of entry, see R. B. Davis, "The Early Editions of George Sandys' 'Ovid': the Circumstances of Production," *Papers of the Bibliographical Society of America*, XXXV (Fourth Quarter, 1941), 255–76.

[12] See James G. McManaway, "The First Five Bookes of Ovids [*sic*] Metamorphosis, 1621, *Englished by Master George Sandys*," *Papers of the Bibliographical Society, University of Virginia*, I (1948–9), 71–82, for the circumstances under which the little volume was located. Only once before, in 1808, was this second edition (perhaps the very copy the Folger now has) described by a bibliographer (Joseph Haslewood, in Sir Egerton Brydges, ed., *Censura Literaria*, VI, 132, 133, 135). Though many, including the present writer, have doubted the veracity of the Haslewood description, it turns out to be scrupulously exact

THE/ *First Five Bookes/ of/ Ovids Metamorphosis/ edit 2d/ Imprinted for W: B:/* 1621 [13]

The appearance of two editions in one year,[14] if such were the case, would indicate the book's immediate popularity. That it was highly thought of is borne out also, of course, by Drayton's poetic advice to Sandys that he continue his translation.

In 1625/6, perhaps always with an eye to the King's favour, Sandys hurried[15] his complete *Metamorphosis* through the press. It must have appeared in the bookstalls a few days after the King's patent was issued.[16] The words of the dedication indicate that the translator felt

(except for one detail of a leaf with an engraved head of Ovid, which almost surely was in the Folger copy originally).

[13] For a complete bibliographical description of the volume, see McManaway, pp. 72–3, and Bowers and Davis, *George Sandys: A Bibliographical Catalogue* pp. 26–7. The engraved title-page is a copy in reverse of that in a 12mo. Latin Ovid published in Amsterdam in 1619 by Guilielmus Ianssonius, and engraved in England by Delaram, who had done the title-page for *A Relation* (see McManaway, pp. 71–2). It will be noticed that Sandys' name does not appear on the title-page. One should recall that in his letter from Virginia to Samuel Wrote (quoted in Chapter VI, pp. 137–43 above) he refers to the Ovid as "that slotheful worke wch I was ashamed to ffather."

[14] This second edition may have been a final corrected version completed just before Sandys sailed. Dr. McManaway (p. 76) thinks that the first five books of the 1626 edition were printed from a 'corrected' copy of this 1621 edition and gives reasons for concluding that this second edition was not pirated. The fact that it is the only known edition of any of Sandys' works without a dedication to Charles makes one suspect, however, that he may not have seen it through the press. That the five books were popular is indicated further by the recently discovered 1623 edition (copy in Winchester College Library), which the present writer plans to discuss elsewhere at some future time.

[15] At least he so states in his address "To the Reader" in the 1626 edition (see below). The date of the King's patent, 24 April 1626, would bear out this hurriedness, for Sandys almost surely did not reach England until 1 September. Yet the patent suggests in April that the book is already through the press.

[16] Apparently Barrett's heirs had asserted some claim to the 1621 edition by assigning on 3 April 1626 a share to "Master Parker" (Arber reprint, *S.R.*, IV, 120). On 7 May, however, William Stansby, perhaps acting as Sandys' agent, "Entred for his Copie . . . A booke Called Ovid's *Metamorphosis XV: bookes in English verse* by GEORGE SANDYS" (Arber Reprint, *S.R.*, p. 122). Despite the *Cum Privilegio*, the book was printed in 1628 in a small duodecimo, "Printed by Robert Young, . . . to be sold by *J. Grismond*, 1628." Though the printers based their claim on some part of the former Lownes-Barrett right to the first five books, Sandys naturally regarded its publication as an infringement of his patent. He was upheld in the Stationers' Court twice (see Stationers' Court

his work to be primarily a product of America and the colony from which he had so recently returned. Briefer and more personal than the earlier inscription to his patron in *A Relation*, it is a strong bid for court favour and reward for arduous civil labours[17] faithfully performed:

To the most High and Mightie
Prince Charles, King of
Great Britaine, France, and
IRELAND

SIR,
Your Gracious acceptance of the first fruites of my Trauels, when you were our Hope, as now our Happinesse; hath actuated both Will and Power to the finishing of this Peece: being limn'd by that unperfect light which was snatcht from the howers of night and repose. For the day was not mine, but dedicated to the seruice of your Great Father, and your Selfe: which, had it proued as fortunate as faithfull, in me, and others more worthy; we had hoped, ere many yeares had turned about, to haue presented You with a rich and wel-peopled Kingdome; from whence now, with myselfe, I onely bring this Composure:

Inter victrices Hederam tibi serpere Laurus.

It needeth more then a single denization, being a double Stranger. Sprung from the Stocke of the ancient Romanes; but bred in the New-world, of the rudenesse whereof it cannot but participate; especially hauing Warres and Tumults to bring it to light in stead of the Muses. But how euer unperfect, Your fauour is able to supply; and to make it worthy of life, if you iudge it not unworthy of your Royall Patronage. Long may you liue to be, as you are, the Delight and Glorie of your People: and slowly, yet surely, exchange your mortall Diadem for an immortall.[18] *So wishes*

Your Maiesties
most humble
Seruant
GEORGE SANDYS.

Records of 8 April 1628 and 26 January 1631, reproduced in Davis, "Early Editions," pp. 220–1): Sandys always ignored the 1628 as an edition, referring to the 1632 as "the second Edition."

[17] It is interesting to note in this dedication that Sandys claims that his labours in America were in the King's service. This might only refer to the year 1624–5, after the dissolution of the Virginia Company, but it seems to cover the total period of his stay in America. If so, he must have thought of the work under the Company as primarily national service. Notice his claim of the year 1631 that he gave several of the best years of his life to the public service in the Virginia Plantation (Chapter X below).

[18] King Charles took much comfort in Sandys' *Psalms* in his last years. See below. Hooper, I, liii, suggests that Charles may have had the above words in mind when he exclaimed, "I go from a corruptible to an incorruptible crown" (cf. *I Corinthians*, XV, 42, 53).

This small folio[19] was popular at once [20] in court circles, and probably among the London learned generally. Sandys was therefore encouraged to prepare such an edition as he perhaps had originally contemplated, with elaborate commentaries and copperplate illustrations. This new version appeared in 1632, six years after the first. The 1626 edition's briefly worded title,

> OVID'S / METAMORPHOSIS / Engliſhed / by G. S. / [*ornament.*] / Imprinted at / LONDON / MDCXXVI / *Cum Privilegio*

on an engraved title-page, was replaced by two title-pages, engraved and letter-press, with the title of the latter indicating the enlarged scope of the new version:

> OVID'S / METAMORPHOSIS / ENGLISHED, / MYTHOLOGIZ'D, / *And* / Repreſented in Figures. / An Eſſay to the Tranſlation / of VIRGIL'S ÆNEIS. / *By G. S.* / IMPRINTED *An. Dom.* MDCXXXII. / *Cum Priuilegio ad imprimendum hanc Ouidij* / TRANSLATIONEM.

This large folio, printed in 1500 ordinary and 50 fine-paper copies, remains one of the handsome books of English Renaissance printing.[21] Copies were presented to the King and Queen, and to many other Caroline persons and personages including the courtier Sir Thomas Bludder, the musician Henry Lawes, the engraver Francis Clein, and perhaps Ben Jonson himself.[22] Clearly this edition presented all Sandys intended to or could do with the *Metamorphosis*. Another folio in 1640

[19] For a bibliographical description of this 1626 edition, see Bowers and Davis, pp. 27–8.

[20] Sandys' name was connected with Ovid's almost at once. See, for example, Falkland's verses sent by Ben Jonson to the Earl of Newcastle on 4 February 1631/2 (Kurt Weber, *Lucius Cary, Second Viscount Falkland* [New York, 1940], p. 284):

> Did Ouid's and high Lucan's praise display,
> Without beholdingnes to Sands or May!

[21] For a full account of the circumstances of production of this edition, see R. B. Davis, "George Sandys *v.* William Stansby: the 1632 Edition of Ovid's *Metamorphosis*," *The Library*, 5th series, III (December 1948), 193–212.

[22] See Davis, "Sandys *v.* Stansby," for a list of persons to whom special copies went. It is not entirely clear whether all of these were presentation copies or merely copies Sandys procured for friends who desired to purchase them.

is but a cheaper reprint[23] of this version. A duodecimo[24] of the Ovid text only in 1638 indicates the continuing popularity of the translation for itself alone. In the course of the century the complete translation in one of its two forms went through at least ten editions.[25]

As the titles quoted above may suggest, there is considerable difference in format and content between the editions of 1626 and 1632. The elaborate engraved title-page of 1626 by T. Cecill is replaced in 1632 by an even more elaborate title-page designed by Sandys' friend Francis Clein[26] and engraved by Salmon Savery.[27] The only other engraved illustration of 1626, the head of Ovid in an oval surrounded by mythological figures[28] is replaced in 1632 again by a more elaborate but similar engraving to which have been added a silver medal and a cornelian showing Ovid's profile.[29] In the 1632 edition appear fifteen new copperplate

23 For a bibliographical description of this edition, see Bowers and Davis, pp. 33–4.

24 For a bibliographical description of this edition, see Bowers and Davis, pp. 32–3.

25 The 1626, 1632, and 1640 were the only folios. The 1628 (unauthorized), 1638, 1656, 1664, 1669, 1678, and 1690 were duodecimos. See Bowers and Davis, pp. 26–39.

26 Clein, Cleyn, or Clen (1590?–1658; see *D.N.B.* article by Lionel Cust) had under the patronage of Charles a tapestry-making establishment at Mortlake. He was granted a pension of £100 per annum when Charles ascended the throne. Sandys may have presented a copy of the 1632 edition to him simply because he designed the plates, but the indications are that the poet knew the artist personally. For Sandys' interest in Clein's type of art, see the address "To the Reader" in the 1632 edition of the Ovid.

27 The basic designs of 1626 and 1632 are the same. The greatest difference is that the 1626 title-inscription is in an open space like a portal in the classical proscenium which is the main design of the page, while the 1632 title is engraved on a curtain placed in the open space. An engraved title-page strikingly similar to the 1632 is to be found in *Les Metamorphoses d' Ovide Trãduites en Profe Francoife, et de nouveau soigneusement reueuës, corrigees en infinis endroits, et enrichie*[*s?*] *de figures à chacune Fable. Avec XV. Discours Contenans l'Explication Morale et Historique . . . 1619, Pour l'Autheur, A Paris . . . Auec priuilege du Roy.* The engraved bust of Ovid, the dedications, and other preliminaries also remind one at once of Sandys' 1632 edition, and that his book remained in the Renaissance Ovid (Latin or vernacular) tradition.

28 Engraved by William Marshall, famous craftsman (see Sidney Colvin, *Early Engraving and Engravers in England* [London, 1905], p. 121).

29 Sandys states in his "Life of Ovid" (p. ¶, recto), in a sentence added in the 1632 edition, that he has seen a likeness of Ovid in a curious Roman ring, "a Cornelian, of exquisite workmanship" and another on a silver medal he himself owns. Both of these he reproduces in the engraving.

illustrations,[30] each summarizing in the figures presented the contents of the book of the *Metamorphosis* it introduces.[31] Preliminaries common to both complete editions, besides those mentioned above, are a poem[32] explaining the symbolism of the figures on the engraved title-page; "The Life of Ovid," a brief biographical sketch;[33] "Ovid Defended," a series of quotations from ancient authors and Renaissance editors in praise of Ovid as writer and of the *Metamorphoses* in particular;[34] and a Latin poem, "AVGVSTISSIMO CAROLO. . . . Caesar Brittanice." The 1626 edition follows the text of the fifteen books with a brief address "To the Reader," explaining the inclusion of a gloss of words unfamiliar to the "meere English Reader" which follows. The author had hoped to include them in the margins, but "the hastinesse of the Presse, and vnexpected want of leasure, haue preuented me." In the

30 And retained in the 1640 folio.

31 Each plate is marked to fit a book. The plate for Book III bears the names of "Sa:Saueri" as engraver and "F. Clein" as designer. Many of the Latin and French *Metamorphoses* include copperplate illustrations, but none so elaborate as these. The plates of Sandys' *1632* edition have a curious history. His engraved title-page, unchanged in any particular, Ovid's portrait-page engraving, and separate engravings of the fifteen books appear in a Paris Latin edition *PVB. OVIDII NASONIS METAMORPHOSEΩN LIBRI XV. AD FIDEM EDITIONVM OPTIMARUM ET CODICUM Manuscriptorum examinati, animadversi, necnon Notis illustrati. Operâ & studio THOMAE FARNABII. Editio nunc primum in Gallia & multis figuris aeneis adornata. PARISIIS* . . . M.DC. XXXVII. *Non fine Regis priuilegio.* A Latin dedication to William, Archbishop of Canterbury, is included. Since these plates were used again in the 1640 folio of Sandys, they may or may not have gone to Paris for Farnaby's edition. The latter may have had the sheets run off in England. There is a copy of the 1637 edition and of another smaller one of Farnaby's Ovid (Amsterdam, 1639, without Sandys' plates) in the Harvard University Library. The *1637* is also in the British Museum, No. 76. h. 11. Farnaby has been called the chief classical scholar as well as the chief schoolmaster of his time and was internationally known (cf. *D.N.B.* article by S. L. Lee). William Burton the antiquary, perhaps Sandys' travelling companion in the Near East, was an usher under him in 1630. The *D.N.B.* lists a London edition of 1637 of Farnaby's Ovid as the first edition by the scholar, but the staff of the British Museum informs me that its only copy is the Paris edition (letter of 9 July 1949, from H. Sellers).

32 "The Mind of the Frontispiece and Argument of this Worke," usually occupying the page opposite the title in the 1626 edition.

33 Several pages of prose including certain poetic quotations. The 1632 edition adds several new sentences to the prose.

34 These also appeared in the 1621 edition, though the group of authorities beginning with Marcus Antonius Tritonius through Antonius Muretus do not appear in 1621.

1632 edition "To the Reader" is a longer, even more detailed, explanation of the method and purpose of the newly added commentaries and illustrations. In the 1632 dedication to the King, just before "Long may you live to bee . . .," appears a sentence not present earlier:

> To this haue I added, as the Mind to the
> Body, the History and Philosophicall sence of the
> Fables (with the shadow of either in Picture)
> Which I humbly offer at the same Altar,
> that they may as the rest of my labours,
> receiue their estimation from so great an
> Authority.

Of course the great differences are (1) the added prose commentaries after each book in the 1632 edition, occupying at least as much space as the poetic text; (2) the addition in the 1632 edition, after the Ovid, of a translation in decasyllabic couplets of the first book of "Vergil's Æneis,"[35] and (3) the elaborate engraved illustrations for each book, which Sandys himself considered most significant.

Sandys' choice of Ovid's *Metamorphoses* as the focus for the great poetic work of his life is characteristic of the man and of his time. *A Relation of a Iourney* had already afforded abundant evidence of his interest in Roman and Greek fable, and in euhemeristic, scientific, and moral interpretation of them. Of all the great classical poems, the *Metamorphoses* most nearly summarized these interests. It was a work which had attracted the Western European translator as early as 1210, when it was rendered in German couplets,[36] and as Sandys showed in the "Ovid Defended," the church fathers even earlier had been able to quote or refer to the original with approval.[37] In the Renaissance proper its

[35] In a special prefatory address to the reader (p. 532) Sandys says that he had translated this first book of the *Aeneid* many years before, but finding the whole "to heavy a burthen (my minde being also diverted from these studies) I gaue it over, even in the first entrance. Yet I haue published this assay, in tender of my obedience to Soveraigne commaund. . . ." Though Dryden was to state later that had Sandys completed his translation of the *Aeneid* he himself would never have attempted it (Hooper, I, xliv), few critics then or later noticed the work. They seem to have accepted it as Sandys presented it, as a distinct afterthought not nearly so valuable as the *Metamorphosis*.

[36] See Wilmon Brewer, *Ovid's Metamorphoses in European Culture* (*Books I–II–III–IV–V*) . . . (Boston, 1933), p. 25.

[37] Among others, Sandys quotes Lactantius, St. Jerome, and St. Augustine (1626 edition, pp. b_4 r & v). Of course Ovid was the favourite Latin poet of the

influence was enormous. Elizabethan England read Ovid more than Virgil. Latin editions, varying, in quantity of annotation and commentary, had appeared in almost all the countries of western Christendom early in the sixteenth century, and had been reprinted up to Sandys' own time.[38] Before the great English Renaissance poets had appeared, Arthur Golding's remarkable translation into seven-stress ballad couplets was ready at hand, with its apology for presentation of the pagan poet, and its reconciliation of this classical mythology with Christian thought. Though Golding's metre is very different from Sandys',[39] Golding and the Renaissance Latin editors had brought to flowering a traditional attitude towards the *Metamorphoses* which Sandys in his commentaries in general followed. In certain respects Sandys in his 1632 edition is the last great representative of the tradition of allegorized interpretation which began in the Middle Ages.[40] But more of this below.

Like Golding,[41] Sandys translated and published a portion of the poem before he completed the whole. And Golding's must have been one of the books ready at hand as he translated, for he owes something of phrase and word to it. The names of the dogs in the Diana-Actaeon episode of III, ll. 245 ff. in Sandys (1626, pp. 50–1, Ovid III, ll. 206–35) are almost identical with those in Golding (pp. 67–8), homely English names like Greedigut (in Golding) and Greedy (in Sandys), or Ringwood, Kildeere, Lightfoot, Swift, identical in the two. In phraseology the indebtedness is usually not marked. The most striking

Middle Ages. For an able discussion of "The Christian Ovid," see Chapter I of Davis P. Harding, *Milton and the Renaissance Ovid* (Urbana, 1946), pp. 11–26.

[38] See Harding, pp. 18 ff. and Douglas Bush, *Mythology and the Renaissance Tradition in English Poetry* (Minneapolis, 1932), *passim.*

[39] Golding, a man of strong Puritan sympathies, prefaced his work with a long metrical explanation of his reasons for considering it a work of edification. Like his predecessors and contemporaries among editors of the Latin Ovid, he shows how the pagan machinery may be reconciled to Christian thought. Of course it was from Golding that many of the Elizabethans gained their knowledge of classical mythology (see Brewer, pp. 31–2).

[40] See Harding, p. 25, and discussion below in the present chapter. Professor Harding's statement that Sandys is "an Indian summer flowering of the allegorical tradition" must be qualified by the fact that in his commentaries he is much more than this. Even as early as "Ovid Defended," in the 1626 edition, however, he places himself in the tradition by his appeals to pagan and early Christian authority.

[41] Golding had published the first four books in 1565, and the complete fifteen two years later.

similarity observed[42] between the two poets was in Book XI (Ovid, Loeb ed., XI, ll. 482–3).

> "ardua iam dudum demittite cornua" rector
> clamat "et antennis totum subuectite velum."
> hic iubet. . . .

which in Golding (p. 230, XI, ll. 557–8), is translated

> Anon the Mayster cryed: strike the toppesayle, let
> the mayne
> Sheate flye and fardle it too the yard. Thus spake
> he, but in vayne.

and in Sandys (*1626*, p. 228, ll. 23 ff.).

> Strike, strike the Top-saile, let the Maine-sheat fly,
> And furle your sailes, the Master cry'd; his cry
> The blustring winds and roring seas suppresse.

In the first five books, the earlier extracts published in *A Relation*, and in the two complete versions, Sandys employed the decasyllabic couplet. With the increasing general interest in the development and origins of heroic verse has come a considerable attention to the possible sources, the dates of production, and specific forms of all Sandys' verses in this metre, particularly to those in his *Metamorphosis*. Since at least one full-length examination[43] of these matters has recently been made, here we shall attempt primarily to outline Sandys' place in the couplet tradition on the basis of critical materials already available, but also to clear up certain confusions and misconceptions regarding the nature of his text and its relation to his sources.

Commentators have occasionally intimated that Sandys' couplet even in the editions of the Ovid changed considerably between the 1615 excerpts, the 1626, and the 1632, changes indicative of the progress of the couplet toward the more rigid forms it was to take with Dryden and especially Pope. A line-for-line comparison of the excerpts of 1615, the

[42] My own not too detailed a comparison revealed few similarities, though one of the staff editing Dryden's *Works* at the University of California (Los Angeles) has informed me that Sandys "lifts" almost entire couplets from Golding, and that sometimes Dryden lifts them in turn from Sandys.

[43] Miss Beatrice Ingalls, under the direction of Professor Douglas Bush of Harvard, has written a dissertation on Sandys' couplet of the *Metamorphosis* and its relation to the development of that verse form. The study was incomplete and unavailable when this brief analysis was undertaken. We understand that it is to be published.

recently discovered first five books of 1621, the complete 1626, and the complete 1632 edition,[44] however, indicates that such changes are very slight. Among the three main editions, the vast majority of changes were mere re-phrasings for purposes of smoothness. On the basis of edition of first appearance of the various books of the *Metamorphosis*, there are only four examples of expansion and one of contraction in number of lines in the whole fifteen books, and in each case only two lines were added or subtracted.[45] Other changes are interesting but not pronounced or frequent. The most common type in the whole fifteen books, a replacement of one or two words, occurs relatively few times among the three versions of the first five books, but more frequently between the 1626 and 1632 editions of Books VI–XV. Fifteen such replacements are a maximum in any one of the first five books, with a total for the five books of only fifty-five. Of the fifty-five, only twenty-six occur between *1621* and *1626*. In no case do all three differ. On the other hand, there are thirty-two changes in Book VI, forty-five in VII, forty-eight in VIIII, forty-five in IX, thirty-eight in X, forty-one in XI, twenty-three in XII, fifty-five in XIII, nineteen in XIV, and twenty-two in XV.

Analysis of change of single phrase or clause within a line and of the rhymes only of a couplet, or of the reworking of a single line, of the reworking of a couplet or of two successive non-couplet lines, and of the reworking of long three-to-six line groups, shows similar tendencies among the books. For example, there is one complete change of couplet rhyme in the first five books to be compared with five in the remaining ten. A single line generally reworked occurs fourteen times in the first five, forty-nine times in the other ten. A couplet or two successive non-couplet lines have been reworked thirteen times in the first five books, 125 times in the last ten. Of the larger groups of three-to-six lines, there are no examples of reworkings in the first five books, but thirty-five in the last ten. In the whole fifteen books, there is one phrase or clause

[44] A comparison made with the assistance of Lois B. Davis.

[45] Book II, three lines in *1621* and *1626* become five in *1632* (restoring the sense of the original): *1621*, p. 56, ll. 5–7; *1626*, p. 42, ll. 5–7; *1632*, p. 62, ll. 41–45. Book III, five lines in *1621* contract to three in *1626* and *1632*: *1621*, pp. 66, ll. 31–2, 67, ll. 1–3; *1626*, p. 50, ll. 11–13; *1632*, p. 85, ll. 24–6. Book V, one line in *1621* and *1626* becomes three in *1632*: *1621*, p. 139, l. 4; *1626*, p. 104, l. 30; *1632*, p. 187, ll. 5–7. Book VII, seven lines in *1626* become nine in *1632*: *1626*, p. 144, ll. 3–9; *1632*, p. 246, ll. 12–20. Book VIII, three lines of *1626* become five in *1632*: *1626*, p. 168, ll. 22–4; *1632*, p. 281, ll. 14–18. Book XIII, six lines contract to four: *1626*, p. 266, ll. 17–22; *1632*, p. 433, ll. 25–8.

and one single line reworked twice (*i.e.*, appearing differently in each of the three editions). Among these reworkings of the first five books about half occur between 1621 and 1626. And it should be remarked that the number of run-on lines and run-on couplets remains almost exactly the same from 1621 to 1626 to 1632.

The changes Sandys made to improve all versions were, as he avowed, simply polishing—sometimes to regularize the metre, more often to improve unity, occasionally to render the Latin original's meaning more accurately. "Fruits" in 1621 (I, p. 3, l. 18) and 1626 (I, p. 2, l. 38) became "gummes" in 1632 (I, p. 2, l. 32), though what seems a move in a different direction is indicated in the change from "fluent hair" (1626, XI, p. 235, l. 32) to "flowing hair" in 1632 (XI, 385, l. 34). "Say now" in 1626 (VI, p. 112, l. 14) becomes "Behold" in 1632 (VI, p. 205, l. 26), and "The stranger thus reply'd" in 1626 (VI, p. 115, l. 42) "The *Lycian* thus reply'd" in 1632 (VI, p. 208, l. 30). These single or double-word changes rarely add or subtract a syllable. Usually they represent the poet turning his eye to the Latin and seeking a closer approximation to the original; or simply the conscious artist seeking the more felicitous expression. Changes among the larger word-groups or lines occur for substantially the same reasons. The second of these is certainly smoother:

> Now shee, a Goddesse, is ador'd by those
> That linnen weare, where sacred *Nilus* flowes.
>
> *1621*, Bk. II, p. 26, ll. 15–16.

> Now shee, a Goddesse, is ador'd by those
> That shine in linnen stoles where *Nilus* flowes.
>
> *1632*, II, p. 17, ll. 12–13.

Incidentally, this couplet is essentially an expansion of one Latin line (Ovid, I, 1. 747):

> Nunc dea linigera colitur celeberrima turba

Some changes are primarily inversions. Others, for the sake of the metre, slur, as "to a" (*1621*, III "Argument") to "t'a" (*1626* and *1632*). Between 1621 and 1626 Sandys frequently altered the spelling of a dissyllabic word to insure its pronunciation as a monosyllable.[46] Generally there is real improvement.

That there is a fairly steady increase in the number of unstopt lines in

[46] See McManaway, p. 76.

the translation from Book I to Book XV was demonstrated in a study[47] made some years ago. Of unstopt lines, the percentage in I is 14 per cent, increasing in XV to 29 per cent. Of unstopt couplets, I shows 1·8 per cent, increasing in Book XV to 10·4 per cent. This is used to make the interesting point that when Sandys was composing the first five books, he was closer in his actual contact with or in his reading of the French classical school, perhaps through his visits to Paris in 1610–12. He was therefore more conscious of the new rule for the stopt line and adhered to it more faithfully then than he did later.[48]

Though whether the rhetoric of the 1632 edition is a step on from the 1626 towards the rhetoric of the school of Pope is a question which only a detailed study can answer fairly, one can conclude at least two things from the data outlined above. (1) The first five books of 1621 were originally almost exactly what they always remained. Evidently the poet was quite satisfied with what he had written during the relative leisure of the years before he went to Virginia. And (2) because of the slightness of the changes in the last ten books between 1626 and 1632, the latter edition may safely be used as representative of Sandys' fundamental characteristics in metre and rhetoric over the whole period of his composition.

The matter of the origin of Sandys' decasyllabic couplet involves the whole question of the origins of the English heroic couplet generally and can only be touched upon here.[49] One of the most powerful direct influences in forming Sandys' verse was the Latin distich of Ovid himself,[50] an influence that the English closed couplet had felt since it

[47] H. Wood, "Beginnings of the 'Classical' Heroic Couplet in England," *American Journal of Philology*, XI, I (1890), 74–5. He uses only the 1632 edition. He gives a statistical table, showing an average of only 17.6 per cent unstopt lines in the first five books, and an average of 27.5 per cent for the last ten. Figures for unstopt couplets are similar. Actually by his figures Books XI and XII show a higher percentage of unstopt couplets than do Books XIII–XV.

[48] Wood finds that the one book of Virgil shows 32 per cent unstopt lines and 10 per cent unstopt couplets. The lack of date for this work makes any conclusion impossible, though Sandys said it had been translated many years before it was published (in 1632).

[49] The whole question of Sandys' couplet in the *Metamorphosis* is discussed by Miss Ingalls in the study mentioned in note 43 above. The present discussion is only a pointing rather than a drawing of conclusions, and is based on scholarly articles from various sources combined with a careful reading of the various editions of Sandys' work.

[50] Ruth C. Wallerstein, "The Development of the Rhetoric and Metre of the Heroic Couplet, Especially in 1625–1645," *PMLA*, L (March 1935), 166–209.

appeared in Tottel's *Miscellany* in 1557. At least partly through his travels, Sandys may also have been affected by Malherbe and the "classical" reform in French literature which forbade *enjambement*.[51] And again there is possible or probable indebtedness to Jonson,[52] Drayton,[53] and Sylvester.[54]

The metre and language of Sandys' couplet have significance in his own time and for the future. One study, concerned largely with the characteristics of the rhetoric of the classical pentameter couplet in 1625–45, assigns to Sandys an important place.[55] With a conscious technique, it is shown, Sandys translated Ovid's rhetoric into forms suited to English idiom, building upon the structure of the epigrammatic, closed couplet. In his own system of closed lines and closed couplets and medial cæsura he marks a definite advance over Drayton toward the Popean form. More completely than Drayton and effectively than Jonson, he kept his rhetorical expression in "close lock-step with the metrical units." Though his language owes something to Ovid, in his floriate expansion and in his "general, intellectualized, abstract expression inclined to periphrasis," Sandys is highly original.[56] Ovid is certainly his model in general in his rhetorical and balanced style, but the character of his rhetoric in relation to the form of the line[57] and his particular use of

[51] Wood, "Beginnings of the Classical Heroic Couplet in England," pp. 55–79. He admits that the English heroic couplet is a "thoroughly national product" but points out that "a sudden quickening of literary conscience in certain English writers, about the years 1616–26, as to the sin involved in the unstopt line, has never been explained." A statistical comparison of Waller and Sandys is part of the evidence here given that Sandys, not Waller, is the first Englishman to write uniformly in heroic couplets "on the whole in accord with the French rule. . . ."

[52] Felix E. Schelling, "Ben Jonson and the Classical School," *PMLA*, XIII (1898), 221 ff. Though only Sandys' paraphrases and occasional verse were used in making this study, the sweeping conclusion must by implication include Ovid: "there is not a tract which came to prevail in the poetry of the new classical school as practised by Waller and Dryden, and later by Pope, which is not directly traceable to the influence or to the example of Ben Jonson."

[53] W. J. Courthope, *A History of English Poetry*, III (London, 1924), 101. See also J. W. Hebel, K. Tillotson, and B. H. Newdigate, *The Works of Michael Drayton* (5 vols., Oxford, 1931–41), V, 99.

[54] Geoffrey Tillotson, *On the Poetry of Pope* (Oxford, 1938), p. 66.

[55] Ruth C. Wallerstein, *op. cit.*, in note 50 above. She includes Sandys' Ovid (*1632* only), the *Paraphrase upon Job*, and various commendatory verses for the 1638 Paraphrases in her study. See Chapter IX below.

[56] Wallerstein, pp. 188–9.

[57] *Ibid.*, pp. 189–91.

antithesis produce clearly distinguishable effects. In the couplet melody he achieved an evenness, varied by a shift of cæsura, not evident before him.

Looking back from the poetry of Pope, one may also see considerable significance in the character of Sandys' heroic couplet in the later development of the form. There are many evidences of the later "correctness" already present in Sandys.[58] Assuming that Sylvester's translation of DuBartas may begin the tradition which leads to Pope, Professor Tillotson still concludes that it was "Sylvester's imitator Sandys, who did most to fix the vocabulary of 'progressive' English poetry for more than a century."[59] Sandys' vocabulary, much more selective than Sylvester's, shows increasingly favourite words. To obtain the conciseness he desired, that is, to fulfill his aim of translating Ovid in as few lines more than the original as possible, Sandys latinized his syntax, imitated Latin use of present and past participles as adjectives, and used verbs from Latin instead of English verbs. But most important to later poetry is Sandys' group of favourite words: his use of *sad*, for example, five times in a place where Golding did not use it once,[60] anticipates Milton. Seventeenth-century poets outside the satirical and metaphysical groups based their vocabulary on Sandys and his sources.[61]

One further word on Sandys' verse in his *Metamorphosis*. He has been highly praised or severely censured for his so-called compression, his alleged desire to keep his own line within Ovid's. It has been stated that, for good or bad, he actually kept down the number of his lines almost to Ovid's. An actual count shows that compared with almost exactly 12,000 lines in Ovid,[62] Sandys shows more than 13,100. Compared with Golding's almost 14,500 lines, this is compression, but in reality it does allow more room for poetic expansion than has generally been supposed. Actually, of course, Sandys was attempting to compress, an attempt which led to certain of his rhetorical and rhythmical devices most influential on later poets.[63]

[58] Tillotson, *On the Poetry of Pope*, pp. 63–4.

[59] *Ibid.*, p. 66.

[60] *Ibid.*, p. 68. He points out (p. 70) Milton's use of *sad* and its compounds in the same situations.

[61] *Ibid.*, p. 70.

[62] I used the Loeb edition, and counted 11,994 lines. The later duodecimo editions of Sandys' Ovid frequently place the *number of the Latin lines* opposite Sandys' line. The 1669 edition, for example, does this and differs from the Loeb edition in showing 16 more lines for the Latin original.

[63] Tillotson, pp. 68–73, 152–4.

After the couplet, the second great characteristic of Sandys' *Metamorphosis* is the elaborate prose annotation or explication after each book of the 1632 edition. This also influenced his poetic successors in several ages, but for reasons opposite in many respects from those for their noticing his versification. For the "Commentaries" fascinated later generations largely because in most respects they summed up the ancient rather than anticipated the new, as his versification may be said to do.

Though the 1621 and 1626 editions give no sign of it beyond the "Ovid Defended" statements of authorities ancient and contemporary, Sandys' very choice of subject for translation almost compelled allegorical commentary. The tendency to read allegory into Ovid appears to have been well under way by the time of Charlemagne. As Ovid became steadily more popular, there was a proportionate increase in this allegorizing, the most notable mediaeval example being the *Ovide Moralisé*, a laborious attempt to reconcile the Ovidean tales with Christian theology.[64] And there are other ways through which the Christian allegories of the Roman poet reached the Renaissance.[65]

Though Caxton translated Ovid into English as early as 1480,[66] the earliest annotated European Latin edition of the *Metamorphoses* apparently was not printed until 1492. This first allegorized text "cum commentario Raph. Regii,"[67] unauthorized, was followed by dozens of Regius' editions from various European presses during the whole of the succeeding century. Sandys shows that he knew at least one Regius and several other Renaissance editions by his quotations in "Ovid Defended" and by reference to their editors as authorities in his own commentaries. He refers by name to Anulus (Barthelmi

64 See Davis Harding, pp. 13–15, for a summary of the anonymous author's method. The book was apparently written in the first quarter of the fourteenth century.

65 See Harding, pp. 16–17 and Bush, *Mythology and the Renaissance Tradition*, pp. 11–47.

66 See Harding, p. 18.

67 *Ibid.*, p. 18. The British Museum catalogue lists Regius' editions of 1497, 1505, 1509, 1513, 1526, 1527, 1543, 1586, and others. The Folger Shakespeare Library has many Regius' editions, among them those dated 1493, 1509, 1510, 1527, 1541, and 1565, examined by the present writer. The Houghton and Widener Libraries at Harvard also hold many Regius editions. Among them I have examined those of 1501, 1504, 1505, 1506?, 1510, 1512, 1526, 1543, 1574. Several of these are editions with notes by Regius emended and augmented by notes from other scholars, particularly with those of Micyllus (see note 71 below).

Aneau),[68] Hercules Ciofanus,[69] Baptistus Pius (Giovanni Battista Pio),[70] Jacobus Micyllus (Jacob Moltzer),[71] and Raphael Regius, and must certainly have known all their editions of Ovid, though one recent scholar has said that Sandys mentions only two Renaissance editors of the *Metamorphoses*.[72] The same scholar points out that some of Sandys' marginal annotations are simply unacknowledged translations from Regius, and that probably the Regius-Micyllus edition of 1543 or a reprint of it was his principal model for the form of his commentaries and notes.[73] With the two latter points in the main one must agree, but must add at the same time that Sandys certainly used the editions of the other Latin commentators he mentions and perhaps also certain Italian or French Ovids.[74]

68 His *Trois Premiers Liures de la Metamorphose d' Ouide, Traduictz en Vers Frãcois* . . . appeared in Lyon in 1556 and later. Sandys quotes and translates Anulus in 1632, p. 475 (Commentary Book XIV). See the copy of *Trois Premiers Livres* at Harvard University.

69 His *In Omnia P. Ovidius Nasonis opera observationes* . . . is dated Antwerp 1583. There is also an Ovid with seventeen books of "observationes" dated 1575, Venice.

70 *P. Ouidii Nasonis . . . Metamorphoseos Librorum XV. Opus . . . Annotationes B. Pii* exists in an edition of 1527. See Br. Mus. Catalogue. Sandys quotes him as reporting "out of Varro" of a miraculous olive tree (1632, Commentary Book VI, p. 218) in support of an Ovidean tall tale.

71 His *P. Ovidii Nasonis Metamorphoseos Libri Quindecini, cum Commentariis Raphaelus Regii. Adiectis etiam Annotationibus Iacobi Micylli* . . . appeared in Basle in 1543 and many times later. Sandys mentions both Regius and Micyllus in "Ovid Defended" as though separate editors. Professor Harding infers (pp. 21, 23) that Sandys was much indebted to this edition, and more to Regius than he admits.

72 Harding, p. 21. The inaccuracy of the statement seems obvious.

73 *Ibid.*, pp. 21–3. Actually Sandys refers in the commentaries in Books I and II to Regius by name. In his statement of his principal sources, Sandys adds that he has used many others to a lesser degree. Actually he was as scrupulous, if not more scrupulous, in his acknowledgments than most other Renaissance editors of Ovid.

74 Several of them have title-pages, preliminaries, illustrations, and commentaries in format strikingly like Sandys' own. *Le Trasformationi di M. Lodovico Dolce di Nvovo Ristampate, e da lui, & recorrette, & in diuersi luoghi ampliate*—CON PRIVILEGI. . . . *Venetia*, . . . MDLIII has a title-page bearing in its various features strong resemblances to those of 1621, 1626, and 1632. *Le Metamorfosi di Ovidio Ridotte da Cio Andrea dell' Angvillara in Ottava Rima: con le Annotationi di M. Gioseppe Horologgi . . . di M. Francesco Tvrchi* . . . [*Venice*] . . . *M.D.L. XXXIV* is a large octavo, with commentaries at the end of each book, full-page copper-plate illustration for each book, poetic "Arguments" for each book, and many other details most strongly resembling those in the 1632 Sandys. See the copy

Besides all the Latin, French, and Italian Renaissance precedents, Sandys had certain forerunners in his own language. The most conspicuous of these is Abraham Fraunce, who had published in 1592 *The Third Part of the Countess of Pembroke's Ivy Church*, sixteen Ovidean tales in verse and the most elaborate allegorical commentary in English before Sandys' own.[75] Yet Sandys' 1632 edition shows no slavish imitation of any earlier editions. The poet announces in his address "To the Reader" that this will be a fresh collection and collation of commentary, and much more. It was his purpose in this "*second Edition . . . to collect out of sundrie Authors the Philosophical sense of these fables of Ouid; if I may call them his, when most of them are more antient then any extant Author. . . .*" He calls Plato as witness to the moral and instructive value of such fables, which teach magnanimity, justice, and the truth of the immortality of the soul. And he continues:

> *In the Muthologie I haue rather followed (as fuller of delight and more usefull) the varietie of mens seuerall conceptions, where they are not ouer-strained, then curiously examined their exact proprietie; which is to be borne-with in Fables and Allegories, so as the principall parts of application resemble the ground-worke.*
>
> *I haue also endeauored to cleare the Historicall part, by tracing the almost worne-out steps of Antiquitie; wherein the sacred stories afford the clearest direction. For the first Period from the Creation to the Flood, which the Ethnickes called the Obscure, some the Emptie times; and the Ages next following which were stil'd the Heroycall, because the after deified Heroes then flourished; as also the Fabulous, in that those stories conuayed by Tradition in loose and broken Fragments, were by the Poets interwoven with instructing Mythologies, are most obscurely and perplexedly deliuered by all, but*

at Harvard University. Professor Harding in his bibliography gives a most useful list of principal early editions and commentaries of Ovid's *Metamorphoses*, nineteen in all, from 1497 to 1727. He does not include, however, several of those just noted above mentioned by Sandys in his own commentaries or in "Ovid Defended." And quite naturally Italian or French editions with commentaries were not included in his list, though Sandys must have known and have used some of them.

75 Bush, *Mythology and the Renaissance Tradition*, p. 32.

> *the supernaturally inspired* Moses. *Wherefore, not without authority, haue I here and there giuen a touch of the relation which these fabulous Traditions, haue to the diuine History, which the Fathers haue obserued, and made use of in conuincing the Heathen. By this and the rest it may appeare, that our Subiect, how euer slight in appearance, is nothing lesse both in use and substance, wherein if my Intentions faile not, the matter and deliuery is so tempred, that the ordinary Reader need not reiect it as too difficult, nor the learned as too obuious. . . .*

Thus Sandys set the tone and purpose of his work well within the allegorical tradition, for the general as well as the learned reader. The mediaeval reconciliation of Ovid and Scripture which had continued and even grown in the earlier Renaissance is still present.[76] But the new critical spirit, hardly evident in this address to the reader, is also present. Within certain prescribed limits he is, like Raleigh and others, critical.[77] Names new in allegorical commentary appear in his pages, names of contemporary scientists and literary critics. And the relish for a good contemporary tall tale or an urge to refer to his own varied personal experience enlivens the account.

Professor Bush has called this 1632 edition "the greatest repository of allegorized myth in English."[78] The list of Sandys' authorities is in itself amazing. In a kind of afterthought note at the end of Book I,[79] he names those he considers his "principall Authors." Among the Greeks he acknowledges Plato, "the poeticall Philosopher," Palaphates [*sic*], Apollidorus [*sic*], Aratus, Strabo, Diodorus, Pausanias, Plutarch, and Lucian; among the Romans, Cicero, Higinus, Pliny, and Macrobius; among the "antient Fathers," Lactantius, Eusebius, St. Augustine, and Fulgentius; and of "moderne writers," Geraldus, Pontanus, Ficimus, Vives, Comes, Scaliger, Sabinus, Pierius, "and the *Crowne of the latter*, the Viscount of St Albons: *assisted, though lesse constantly, by other authors, almost of all Ages and Arguments*."[80] These twenty-six are but a minor

76 Harding, pp. 24–5.

77 Bush, *Mythology and the Renaissance Tradition*, pp. 242, 243.

78 *Ibid.*, p. 243.

79 1632 ed., p. 18.

80 Sandys adds that the interpretations quoted were chosen because they "*either beare the stampe of Antiquity, or receive estimation from the honour of the author.*"

fraction of the almost two hundred[81] he mentions by name in the commentaries proper. Of these latter approximately one-fourth are classical Greek writers, one-fourth classical Latin, one-fourth Renaissance scholars, poets, and scientists, and the remainder Biblical prophets, mediaeval theologians, or Renaissance theologians or historians. To illustrate or compare he quotes most frequently from the poets Vergil, Seneca, Homer, Ovid, and Horace (in this descending order) and refers most frequently to Plutarch, Plato, Aristotle, and Lactantius (in the same descending order), and many times to St. Augustine, Strabo, and Pausanias. He names such miscellaneous mediaeval authority as Tzetzes, twelfth century Byzantine poet and grammarian; Suidas, Greek lexicographer; and Albumazar, Arab astronomer. Among the more interesting of his references to contemporaries, or near-contemporaries, are those to Bodin (1530–96), French political philosopher who wrote a book on witchcraft; the Scottish exile Earl Bothwell (*d.* 1595), also an authority on witchcraft;[82] Buchanan (1506–82), Scottish humanist and translator; Fabricius (1537–1619), Italian anatomist, a "chirurgeon of our times"; Peter Ramus' friend Lambinus (1520–72), French scholar and editor of many Latin classics; and several others including Montaigne, Linscot, Edward and Francis Lopez, Sannazarus, Galileo, Schmidel, Tycho Brahe, Vives,[83] and Erasmus. Sandys' acknowledged debt to Bacon is quite evident. Bacon's exposition of myths allegorically in *De Sapientia Veterum* (1609), *e.g.*, "Narcissus, or Self-Love," and his scientific comparisons in the same work Sandys follows quite closely, though of course the method is not original with Bacon.[84] The theological and euhemer-

[81] I have counted 192, of which number I have identified positively all but two or three.

[82] See *A Relation*, Book IV, p. 250 and Chapter IV above.

[83] It is interesting to note that Juan Luis Vives (1492–1540), resided at Sandys' own Corpus Christi College at one period and was in 1523 tutor to the Princess Mary.

[84] See Bush, *Mythology and the Renaissance Tradition*, pp. 240–1, and Grace Eva Hunter, *The Influence of Francis Bacon on the Commentary of Ovid's "Metamorphoses" [sic] by George Sandys* (Unpublished Doctoral Dissertation, State University of Iowa, August 1949). Miss Hunter points out that seventeen of Sandys' interpretations of myths are taken directly from Bacon, and she gives parallel text to prove her point. She also shows that Sandys followed Bacon part of the way in his reliance on the concrete rather than the abstract as a phase of the revolt against asceticism. In Bacon's attitude toward myths as examples, in his principle of "practical utility" in interpretation, and in certain other matters, was the source for a great deal, but not all, of Sandys' approach to mythology.

istic interpretations may also owe something to Bacon but have origins almost anywhere among Sandys' sources.

As we have noticed, within limits drawn by certain fundamental assumptions, Sandys is critical. The assumptions include of course primarily literal[85] acceptance of the Bible, and perhaps an acceptance of the black arts[86] and certain other general superstitions. As he stated in his address to the reader, he preferred to present a variety of interesting interpretation from several authorities to presenting dogmatically an opinion of his own. Apparently, he accepted the findings of Renaissance natural science. In his discussion of Ovid's description of the shape of the Earth and its relation to the planets in Book I, Sandys refers to the theory of Copernicus and the experiments of Galileo, then observes that Lactantius and St. Augustine deride the theory of the Earth's rotundity and the doctrine of the Antipodes. He concludes:

> *. . . but heaven is everywhere aboue vs, and upward and downeward are only words of relation in sphericall bodies, the superficies on every side, being the extreame, and the middle the Center. Yet Virgilius Bishop of Salsburg, was deprived of his Bishopricke for maintaining this opinion: now discovered by daily navigations, as long since by reason . . .*[87]

The commentaries are full of Platonism, pure and adulterated. "*True glory adheares to the Supreame goodnesse . . .*;"[88] that "*confused Masse, which the Platonists call the undigested World, as the World the digested Chaos: ordered, as they say by Loue . . . that harmony in Nature created by the Almighties Fiat . . .*"[89] "*Beauty is a quick and sprightly grace (as the Platonists hold) infused at first by a heavenly Ray; Shining in the Minde of man, the concinnitie of the body, and the harmony of the voice . . .*";[90] or "*Love is a desire of Beauty*"[91] are only a few of the evidences of idealistic philosophy. Discussions of art and morality are well balanced with earthy descriptions and narration. Sandys relishes, as he did in *A Relation*, the Renaissance traveller's tales

[85] The term *literal acceptance* must be taken to mean here acceptance of Biblical story as fundamental truth. Certainly he would admit some variety of interpretation of these same stories.

[86] One cannot be sure that he accepts witchcraft, for his statements and references are generally objective. The courtier and follower of the son of James I, however, would naturally give no evidence of actual disbelief in the existence of black magic.

[87] 1632 ed., p. 20. [88] *Ibid.*, p. 98. [89] *Ibid.*, p. 19.
[90] *Ibid.*, p. 25. [91] *Ibid.*, p. 158.

of the strange and the marvellous. An Ovidean episode may come alive when it reminds the commentator of a Bristol-ship's quartermaster's yarn of an evil curse,[92] or of rumours of satyrs seen by those who trade in "Ginny,"[93] or of a hair-raising Scottish witch-story.[94]

To illustrate Erisichthon's gastronomic capacity, Sandys tells of "Wood *of Hollingbourne in Kent . . . I have heard those say that knew him, how he eat a whole hog at a sitting: and at another time thirty dozen of pigeons.*"[95] Or an Ovid story may remind him of something in his own travels—of French love-making,[96] Levantine carrier-pigeons,[97] or Egyptian statues.[98] Another impels him to quote Plato and Homer in support of the quite normal Caroline political theory "that the Monarchicall government is of all the best."[99] Or he gives apparent evidence of his familiarity with contemporary drama by drawing a parallel with Macbeth,[100] the Duchess of Malfi,[101] or Sejanus.[102]

One is tempted to continue, for the treasures of these commentaries are almost inexhaustible. One thing more must be pointed out. Within these prose explications are hundreds of lines of translation from the classical poets into decasyllabic or octosyllabic verse. Though usually not so polished as the Ovid text, many lines possess real poetic quality. One apostrophe from Seneca has a familiar Renaissance theme:

O *Sleepe*
Thou charme to all our cares, that art
Of humane life the better part:
Wing'd issue of a peacefull mother;
Of rigid death the elder brother,
Father of things, of life the Port
The daies repose, and nights consort;
To Kings and vassalls equall free,
The labor-tir'd refresht by thee:
Who man (whom death doth terrify)
Invr'st continually to dy.[103]

92 *Ibid.*, p. 110. 93 *Ibid.*, p. 155. 94 *Ibid.*, p. 293.
95 *Ibid.*, p. 299. 96 *Ibid.*, p. 393. 97 *Ibid.*, p. 416.
98 *Ibid.*, p. 334.
99 *Ibid.*, p. 29. Sandys compares Jupiter to the King. He says the twelve greater gods and goddesses compose the upper house of their parliament, Juno being speaker. The Commons is made up of those "defiled for their vertues." This is therefore no absolute monarchy.
100 *Ibid.*, p. 356. Possibly a reference to the historical Macbeth rather than the Shakespearean. 101 *Ibid.*, p. 265. 102 *Ibid.*, p. 299.
103 *Ibid.*, p. 396. For a list of the classical authors he quoted most frequently, see the text of the present chapter above.

Sandys' theory of translation is suggested in his dedications, his prefaces on Ovid, and in his address to the reader. His modicum of fame can come only with his author's.[104] He thus makes no claim to originality. Yet like other English Renaissance translators he is, contrasted with more recent translators, a creative poet. In practice he is not nearly so free as Golding or so prescribed as Dryden. For him Ovid's creatures skip and dance and trot with Elizabethan exuberance, but always within the fence of neo-classic form. The theory that this practice illustrates is everywhere implicit and occasionally explicit. An avowed intention was to present Ovid to the whole, not merely to the learned English reading public in language it could understand. The translator would be faithful to his author, but being faithful did not suggest that the poetry might not have a flavour of its own peculiar to its rendering in the new language and in this particular age.

Through what I had composed under the sway of Ovid's muse, said Sandys, "I may modestly hope to be rescued from Oblivion." This modest bid for a modest immortality has apparently been accepted and approved by posterity. Though the exact extent and quality of the book's influence is yet to be determined, there is plenty of evidence of its use from Sandys' own time to John Keats'. Drayton's early encouragement to Sandys to continue from the first five books was succeeded a few years later by another comment from the same poet which set the tone for the Ovid's reception by most of his contemporaries.

> Then dainty *Sands* that hath to *English* done
> Smooth sliding *Ovid*, and hath made him run
> With so much sweetnesse and unusual grace,
> As though the neatnesse of the English pace,
> Should tell the Jetting *Lattine* that it came
> But slowly after, as though stiffe and lame[105]

Robert Cresswell,[106] Viscount Falkland,[107] and George Daniel[108]

[104] *Ibid.*, "To the Reader," p. π 6 v.

[105] Hebel, Tillotson, and Newdigate, edd., *The Works of Michael Drayton* . . . (5 vols., Oxford, 1931–41), III, 230 "To My Most Dearely-Loved Friend Henery Reynolds Esquire, of Poets and Poesie."

[106] Cresswell, in a poem to Falkland, refers to the "fluent Sands." See Kurt Weber, *Lucius Cary, Second Viscount Falkland* . . ., pp. 122–4.

[107] In one of his several commendatory poems prefixed to Sandys' *A Paraphrase upon the Psalmes*, 1636, he mentions Sandys' "pure phrase."

[108] In "A Vindication of Poesie" (Alexander B. Grosart, ed., *The Poems of George Daniel, Esq.* . . . [4 vols., Privately Printed, 1878], I, 26–32) he mentions Sandys in two stanzas, the first evidently written while the latter was in America, and the second after 1636.

are among those who echo in their own critical verse this idea of the "fluent Sands." The height of this extravagant contemporary praise is probably reached in the anonymous panegyric which concludes that students of art in future ages will conclude

> When Naso afterwards arrives their hands,
> Ovid hath well translated English SANDS.[109]

In the same period, however, George Wither attacks him, with Sylvester, as being a mere translator, lacking true poetic quality, "for invention is the soul of poesy."[110] Yet Wither devotes so much space relatively to the two as to indicate their considerable importance among such poets as Drayton, Beaumont, Fletcher, Davenant, Massinger, Cary, May, Heywood, and Shakespeare.[111] Thomas Fuller sums up the favourable and yet considered judgment of the next generation after Sandys' death:

> . . . as the soul of Aristotle was said to have passed into Thomas Aquinas (because rendering his sense so naturally), Ovid's genius may seem to have passed into Master Sandys. He was a servant, but no slave, to his subject; well knowing that a translator is a person in *free custody*; *custody* being bound to give the true sense of the author he translated; *free*, left at liberty to clothe it with his own expression. . . .[112]

Dryden, often quoted in regard to Sandys' Ovid, actually expressed two opinions. About 1693, commenting on what he himself wishes to do in translating Ovid, he observes that Sandys leaves Ovid prose when he found him verse; but he confesses that this judgment is based on memory, for he had not read Sandys since he was a boy.[113] Six years later, apparently after having re-read the *Metamorphosis* of 1632, he com-

[109] Bodleian, Ashmole MS. 47, No. 80; printed in Hooper, (*Works*, I, lxxiv).

[110] *The Great Assizes Holden in Parmassus by Apollo and His Assessours* . . . (London, 1645), pp. 12–14.

[111] These were the "Jurours" at the trial. Bacon, Sidney, Scaliger, Erasmus, Casaubon, Grotius, Bodin, and other familiar figures composed the "Parnassian Court."

[112] *History of the Worthies of England*, edited by P. A. Nuttall (3 vols., London, 1840), III, 434 [original ed. 1662]. Quotations from Sandys' Ovid appear frequently in the commonplace books of the period: *e.g.*, in that of Sir John Gibson, c. 1658, Br. Mus. Add. MSS. 37719. See also the 1658 allusion to him quoted in Brydges, *Censura*, VI, 226–8.

[113] Sir Walter Scott, ed., *The Works of John Dryden*, (18 vols., Edinburgh and London, 1821), XII, 56. Professor Bush refers to this and to Drayton's verses quoted just above as representative of the extremes of seventeenth century opinion concerning Sandys' Ovid, and remarks that of course neither is right.

pliments "the ingenious and learned Sandys, the best versifier of the former age," who could give to his verse the same turn it had in the original, a talent not to be found in every poet.[114]

Milton has left no recorded opinion of the Ovid, but to it and to *A Relation* he must have referred most frequently. Word and phrase of verse and curious explanation from the commentary are echoed or repeated through much of his work, early and late.[115]

In the eighteenth century Pope himself owed much of his rhetoric and diction to Sandys.[116] It has been observed that Pope gave credit to Denham and Waller as perfectors of the couplet and ignored Sandys,[117] but one should recall that his "Sandys' Ghost" is a poem ridiculing the pretensions of Garth as a translator of Ovid when compared with Sandys,[118] and that in his notes on the *Iliad* he praised Sandys as one of the "chief refiners of our language."[119] Bowles and Warburton sang the praises of the Ovid.[120] Most naturally of all Keats in the new Romantic period found in the 1632 edition many a fascinating story which he was to use in his greater poems, including "Hyperion" and "Endymion."[121]

114 *Ibid.*, XI, 206. Dryden is referring to his own translation of five passages from the Ovid such as the Hunting of the Boar, Cinyras and Myrrha, and Baucis and Philemon, which he hopes he has translated closely enough to give it "the same turn of verse which it had in the original."

115 Frank Allen Patterson, ed., *The Works of John Milton* (18 vols., New York, 1931–8), shows several such indebtednesses to *A Relation* but none to the Ovid. Professor Bush (*Mythology*, pp. 267–8, 280, etc.), Professor Harding (pp. 62–3, 64–5, 73, 97, etc.), and Professor Tillotson (p. 70) point out many parallels and probable indebtednesses to the 1632 Ovid. For a discussion of a Milton-Ovid script, on MS. poem in which Sandys' name is involved by scholars, see Appendix I below.

116 See Tillotson, pp. 63–73, 152–4, 172; and Whitwell Elwin, ed., *The Works of Alexander Pope, New Edition* (10 vols., London, 1871–89), I, 79, 104, 106–8, 143, 202, 244, 248, 316; II, 157; V, 18, 19.

117 See Elwin, ed., *Works*, II, 56. Elwin states that Pope does not do sufficient justice to Sandys.

118 Elwin, ed., *Works of Pope*, IV, 486.

119 *Ibid.*, V, 18. The editor remarks that "Sandys is praised by Dryden and Pope as one of the chief refiners of our language." Joseph Spence, *Anecdotes, Observations, and Characters of Books and Men . . .* (London, 1858), p. 209, quotes Pope as saying (in 1742–3) that when he was eight or nine years of age he enjoyed Sandys' Ovid a great deal.

120 *Ibid.*, II, 56 n. The editor refers to Ruffhead's *Life of Pope*, in which Sandys' Ovid is called an indifferent translation. Warburton in a manuscript marginal note to his copy denies this vigorously, Elwin states.

121 See E. De Selincourt, *The Poems of John Keats . . .* (London [1905]), *passim*

GEORGE SANDYS, PROBABLY IN THE 1630's

by Cornelius Janssen

From the portrait in the possession of Lord Sandys of Ombersley, Worcestershire

Thus Sandys' Ovid was used by major poets and praised by critics for almost two centuries. Whether the translation is actually the first poetry of English-speaking America is an interesting and not too easily settled matter. Of course the question of definition is involved. Professor C. M. Andrews, for example, claimed Sir William Vaughan's *The Golden Fleece* as the first "strictly original literary effort of the New World,"[122] a qualified claim which would not necessarily conflict with any made for Sandys' work and yet presumably aimed at certain claims for the *Metamorphosis*. Actually *The Golden Fleece* is not poetry and, according to the scholar[123] who has done most with Vaughan in recent years, was not even composed in America. Dr. McManaway in his article on the 1621 edition of the first five books of Sandys' Ovid nominates the recently reproduced "Good Newes from Virginia . . ." 1623, as "the first published verse in the English language which was written on the mainland of North America,"[124] another careful qualification for a work which may be verse, but is not poetry. Thomas Lodge's "A Margarite of America," 1596, and Christopher Brooke's "A Poem on the Late Massacre in Virginia . . .," 1622, have proved not to have been written on the North American continent.[125] It is entirely possible that one or more of the news-ballads concerning Virginia which appeared between 1610 and 1622 were composed in America, but again they are hardly verse, much less poetry.

It has been pointed out above that two books were translated by Sandys on the voyage over and eight in Virginia, that the dedication to Charles I claims the book's New World origin, and that the commentaries of the 1632 edition contain many references to America.[126] One must still conclude, as Professor Moses Coit Tyler did in 1878, that

> This production, handed down to us in stately form through two centuries and a half, is the very first expression of elaborate poetry, it is the first utterance of the conscious literary spirit, articulated in America. . . . This book may well have for us a sort of sacredness, as being the first monument of

[cf. index], and Claude L. Finney, *The Evolution of Keats's Poetry* (2 vols., Cambridge, Mass., 1936), *passim* [*index*].

122 *The Colonial Period in American History*, I, 307 and 307 n.

123 Dr. William F. Marquardt, who is now editing certain of Vaughan's works.

124 P. 80.

125 R. B. Davis, "Early Editions," pp. 255–6.

126 R. B. Davis, "America in George Sandys' 'Ovid,'" pp. 297–304.

English poetry, of classical scholarship, and of deliberate literary art, reared on these shores. And when we open the book, and examine it with reference to its merits, first, as a faithful rendering of the Latin text, and second, as a specimen of fluent, idiomatic, and musical English poetry, we find that in both particulars it is a work that we may be proud to claim as in some sense our own, and to honour as the morning-star at once of poetry and of scholarship in the new world.[127]

[127] *History of American Literature . . ., 1607–1676* (2 vols., New York, 1878), p. 54.

IX

COURTIER AND SACRED POET

SANDYS' LIFE from the publication of the 1626 Ovid to his death at the outbreak of the Civil War was apparently busy and happy. Not too much direct evidence as to his personal actions remains. But the surviving details pieced together with the knowledge of what his court circle was doing indicate congenial companionship and continued intellectual activity.

He had probably, as we have noted, become a Gentleman of the Privy Chamber soon after his return from Virginia, between 1626 and 1628. The duties of the Household were apparently not too arduous nor too confining,[1] and there was usually in Charles I's time a comfortable annual income of £200 connected with the position.[2] Presumably Sandys performed official duties for three months of the year and had the remaining nine to himself. Naturally the group of courtiers centred in Lord Falkland became his intimates, for they were those most interested in verse and scholarship. He probably witnessed the swearing in, as fellow-Gentlemen of the Chamber, of his friends Wintoure Graunt in 1628, Thomas Carew in 1630, and Sidney Godolphin in 1631.[3] They, with Falkland, Waller, Henry King, Sir Henry Rainsford, Sir Thomas Bludder, and his kinsmen Sir Dudley Digges, Sir Francis Wyatt, and Sir Francis Wenman, were apparently his most frequent associates.[4]

Probably even in the first years of his return from "exile," Sandys spent a portion of his time in Kent among his many maternal and several paternal relations, for Sir Francis Wyatt and Sir Edwin Sandys lived there, and Sandys before 1620 had been listed as a resident of

[1] See Appendix H, II below.

[2] See Appendix H, III below.

[3] See Chapter VIII, note 5, and Appendix H, I.

[4] All of these save Bludder and Wenman wrote commendatory verses included in one or more of Sandys' later works. For further evidence of the intimacy of this group and Sandys, see below. Sir Thomas Bludder, himself a Gentleman of the Chamber, had in his library two editions of Ovid in English, both presumably by Sandys (see John L. Lievsay and R. B. Davis, "A Cavalier Library—1643," *Studies in Bibliography*, VI [1953–4], 141–60), one of which had been presented to him by the poet.

Canterbury.[5] Also at some time after his brother Sir Edwin's death in 1629 he was guardian for the latter's younger children, and was occupied in business for them which must have required his presence in Kent. Sir Edwin, who had left nothing more to each of his brothers than a forty-shilling gold ring,[6] had not included George among the supervisors of his will. On 1 January 1637/8, however, George entered suit[7] against Sir Edwin's eldest son Henry on behalf of the latter's younger brothers and sisters, who felt that the terms of Sir Edwin's will had not been lived up to.[8] George Sandys is referred to as "of London gent guardian."[9]

Despite these ties, it is probable that before 1638 he spent much more of his time in the Midlands than in Kent. There were at least three major attractions in Oxfordshire and the neighbouring counties. One of Sandys' nieces, Lady Ann Wenman, daughter of Sir Samuel Sandys, had as husband an accomplished gentleman and scholar, Sir Francis Wenman of Carswell near Witney, Oxfordshire. Though Wenman is said to have lacked the health and ambition to play a prominent part in public affairs, no man of his quality in England was more esteemed at court. A neighbour and close friend of Lord Falkland, he was one of the influential members of the group[10] attracted to that noble man. A good

[5] See Chapter II.

[6] See the Will, Somerset House, Probate Section, 84 Ridley, 20 August 1629. The rings were only of *twenty*-shilling value, according to the abstract of the will in the *Virginia Magazine*, XXIX (April 1921), 240–2.

[7] P.R.O., C. 2/Ch. I/S125/29. The suit continued in later courts or resulted in further litigation. See P.R.O., C. 2/Ch. I; S13/45; C. 2/Ch. I/58/27 and especially C. 2/Ch. I/L49/32 dated 25 January 1643/4.

[8] It was stated that Henry had withheld the portions of the younger girls, had not endowed the metaphysical lectures at Oxford as stipulated, and otherwise had failed to live up to the terms of the will.

[9] It is barely possible that another George Sandys is referred to, but the poet's close relationship, legal training, residence in London, etc., almost ensure that he is the guardian named.

[10] For a good sketch of Wenman, see Clarendon (Edward Hyde), *Characters of Eminent Men in the Reigns of Charles I and II* (London, 1793), pp. 186–7. Wenman was an M.P. for the University of Oxford in the Parliament of 1639–40, when his friend Falkland was also a member. He died about 1642. He is not to be confused with his cousin Sir Ferdinando Wenman. For more of Wenman, see Neill, *Virginia Vetusta*, p. 75; Brown, *First Republic*, p. 393; K. B. Murdock, *The Sun at Noon* (New York, 1939), p. 151; Nash, *Collections for the History of Worcestershire* (2 vols., London, 1782), II, opp. p. 220; Weber, *Falkland*, pp. 74–5, 82, etc. Wenman is named in Suckling's "A Session of the Poets" (W. Carew Hazlitt, ed., *The Poems, Plays, and Other Remains of Sir John Suckling* [2 vols., London, 1892], I, 6) as one of the literary men of his time.

Latin scholar, something of a poet, a sharp wit and keen reasoner, Wenman would naturally have attracted Sandys for himself alone. But Carswell lay only a few miles from Burford, the one of Falkland's Oxfordshire estates at which first gathered a group of congenial spirits. And neither Burford nor Carswell was too far from Clifford in Gloucestershire, the home of another courtier and friend, Sir Henry Rainsford.

In fact, the earliest proof of Sandys' direct association with a member of the Falkland circle shows him intimate with Rainsford. The latter, son of Drayton's friend Sir Henry Rainsford[11] and Drayton's "Idea," the former Ann Goodere, himself entertained Drayton, and perhaps Sandys also, in 1631.[12] Though Rainsford's commendatory poem on Sandys' *Paraphrases* proves the intimacy of the two in 1638, there is proof that they were friends and companions as early as 1627. It begins with a letter written by a former official of the Virginia Company, Nicholas Ferrar, begging George Sandys' assistance on behalf of his younger brother, Richard. Among other things, the letter indicates Sandys' London residence and perhaps a position at court which might influence the Master of the Savoy, another courtier:[13]

> 3 Decemb. 1627.[14]
> Noble S^r.
>
> I neither know what the nature of the thing is in it selfe, nor of what weight it may bee as a Courtezy from you And Yet the Necessity and Importunity of

[11] See Drayton's "Upon the Death of His Incomparable Friend, Sir Henry Raynsford of Clifford" (Hebel, *et al*, edd. *The Works of Michael Drayton*, III, 232–4).

[12] The younger Sir Henry married Eleanor Boswell, was M.P. for Anderson, Hants, and apparently died in 1641 (see Nicholas Ransford, "British Settlers in America," *N & Q* April 4, 1925, Vol. 148, No. 14, and W. P. Phillimore and George S. Fry, edd., *Inquisitiones Post Mortem, Gloucestershire, Reign King Charles I* [London, British Record Society, 1895–], Pt. II, 12–18 Charles I, 1637–42, pp. 163–4.)

[13] The Savoy, earlier a royal palace, had become in 1505 the Hospital of the Savoy, with the Chapel which had escaped earlier destruction. The mastership was apparently a court appointment. At this time it is possible that Walter Balcanqual, later vicar of Sandys' own parish church of Boxley, and by 1617 King's Chaplain, was Master of the Savoy. He certainly held the position for some years between 1617 and 1640. See Cave-Browne, *History of Boxley Parish*, p. 93.

[14] The surviving MS. is a copy, evidently in Nicholas Ferrar's own hand, of the original and is now among the Ferrar Papers, Magdalene College, Cambridge. The letter has been reproduced in B. Blackstone, *The Ferrar Papers . . .* (Cambridge, 1938), pp. 248–9, with a few minor changes in punctuation.

a brother enforceth mee humbly to request your fauor, towards the obtayning of the masters of the Sauoy, that my Brother Richard may bee protected safe from Arrest for some twoe months tyme in the Libertys of the Sauoy—the reason of this desyre is His wyfe being greate wth child and ready to Ly downe And there being noe conveniency where she now liues for such an occasion shee hath hyred certayne Lodgings in the Sauoy I would not motion such a matter uppon a Lighter ground nor at all yf soe bee I thought it might not stand with iustice or were altogether unusuall but I am enformed that it is often doñ and for the person himselfe I assure you there cañ bee none more capable of such fauor yf any bee For hee hath at present nothing at all to satisfy his Creditors and his imprisonement would but hynder it for heerafter S^r^ I dare not press you wth many words because I am not sure of the matter & most sure of y^r^ friendly loue use it bee fit in it selfe and for you to do[15]

And to which I recommend it and my selfe to y^r^ good grace

Your faithfull serv . . . XI

N.F.

A few days later Richard Ferrar wrote to Nicholas asking for "word of Mr George Sandys' lodgings."[16] A second letter from Richard to Nicholas shows Sandys' Rainsford connection:

Good Brother:[17]

I thank you for ye letter wch you wrote to Mr Sandys; but as yett it is of noe use to me for I was yesternight—at his lodgings and hee was gonne out of Towne In ye morninge wth Sr Henery Raynsford whether or when to returne They knowe not. The M^r^ of the Savoy is In Towne and will e[?] this 3 weekes . . . for it is his wayting month. . . .

He goes on to say that Mr. Sandys cannot be of much assistance, he understands, but perhaps can vouch for his inability to pay his debts and otherwise intercede with the Master of the Savoy in his behalf. Evidently it was not Sandys' waiting month.

If one may judge by praise in verse, Sandys' most admiring friend in the court society was that ideal cavalier, Lord Falkland. Lucius Cary, second Viscount Falkland (*c.* 1610–43) had inherited his Oxfordshire estates of Burford and Tew from his maternal grandfather in 1625, married against his father's will at the age of twenty-one, and succeeded

[15] As Mr. Blackstone remarks, this sentence is difficult to decipher. I have followed Blackstone's reading here, which is essentially my own also.

[16] Ferrar Papers, No. 580, December 1627.

[17] *Ibid.*, No. 579, December 1627.

to his father's title in 1633.[18] Apparently his coterie of poets and scholars gathered at Burford only after 1631 and at Great Tew after 1633,[19] but it is most probable that the nucleus of his circle lay in the Sons of Ben[20] of whom Falkland was avowedly one, or in the loosely-knit group of courtier-men-of-letters who seasonally frequented London. Sandys and the youthful Sir Lucius may have become acquainted even before the latter's marriage in 1631.[21] In any event, Sandys was almost surely a frequent visitor or a seasonal resident of the Midlands before the famous gatherings of scholars, poets, wits, theologians, statesmen, and courtiers began at Great Tew.

Even the buildings of Great Tew have now passed away, but within its high-walled gardens and spacious library during the 1630's gathered one of the last great societies of England's golden age. Their host was, according to sophisticated courtier or pious cleric, one of the remarkable characters of the period. Falkland died at thirty-three and left no real body of writing behind him. Like the later Dr. Johnson, he is remembered more for what he was than for what he wrote. Candid and courageous, charitable and affable, tactful and mirthful, generous, wealthy, and scholarly, he attracted to himself and usually to his house and board a rare assemblage. A genius such as Ben Jonson,[22] sober scholars and theologians of the University such as William Chillingworth and Dr. John Earle, gentleman scholars and statesmen like Edward Hyde and Sir Francis Wenman, and poet-courtiers such as Sandys, Rainsford, Waller, Godolphin, and a dozen others were among them.[23] These men

18 For accounts of Falkland see Kurt Weber; Murdock; J. A. R. Marriott, *The Life and Times of Lucius Cary, Viscount Falkland* (London, 1907); John Tulloch, *Rational Theology in the Seventeenth Century* (2 vols., London, 1872), I, 76–169.

19 Tulloch, I, 92, says about 1632.

20 For Falkland's relation to Jonson and his circle, see Weber, pp. 63–5, etc.

21 Falkland mentions Sandys and his Ovid in verses addressed to Ben Jonson before 4 February 1631/2. See Weber, p. 284.

22 There is no direct evidence that Jonson ever visited Falkland in the country, though biographers of the latter have sometimes taken it for granted that he did, since the two were great friends.

23 Professor Kurt Weber, who has made the most recent and thorough study of the Falkland circle, lists the following (p. 82, alphabetical order only) as certainly visitors at Tew or Burford, though surely not all in any one season or year: Thomas Barlow, William Chillingworth, John Duncon, John Earle, George Eglionby, Charles Gataker, Sidney Godolphin, Henry Hammond, Edward Hyde, George Morley, Sir Henry Rainsford, Dr. Walter Raleigh, George Sandys, Gilbert Sheldon, Thomas Triplet, Edmund Waller, Sir Francis Wenman, and Patrick Young. Among those listed with less certainty are

rode the miles from Oxford or Carswell or even London for study and refreshing rural atmosphere. The study was sometimes among the books, but was more often in stimulating conversation. It is said that Falkland, scholar though he was, read no book during his guests' stay, for he loved company, and above all he enjoyed drawing from even the most retiring of his visitors all the power of intellect and imagination that was in him. Some of his great intellects may have needed no drawing forth, perhaps the reverse, but Falkland's ready wit was apparently equal to every situation of his symposium.

In the earlier seventeenth century in England pedant, poet, and patron formed a close-knit literary society.[24] The Great Tew circle included all these normal elements, but in many varieties. Hyde and Waller and Wenman might discourse on government, monarchical and parliamentary. Sandys might broaden their discussions by observations on the problems of colonial administration at home and abroad, for he was now a member of the Privy Council's sub-committee on the plantations, and could see both sides of the matter. The London courtiers and Oxford dons must have debated both learnedly and lightly on the beauties of the classical in contrast to their own writings. And perhaps all listened respectfully or impatiently to the Sons of Ben among them on the place and nature of English verse in the world of letters.

In all these matters and many others Sandys would have taken delight, but in two particularly he was vitally interested. Verse and religion were of fundamental concern to him throughout his life.

A study[25] noted above has already indicated the literary significance

Abraham Cowley, Robert Cresswell, Hugh Cressy, Sir Kenelm Digby, John Hales, Thomas Hobbes, Robert Sanderson, John Selden, John Vaughan, and perhaps Endymion Porter. Professor Weber (pp. 82–156) devotes considerable space to a discussion of the interests of each of these men, interests which probably supplied topics of conversation at Tew. Chillingworth is considered in a special chapter. John Aubrey (*Brief Lives* [2 vols., Oxford, 1898], I, 151), who knew personally many of the former guests at Tew, lists Rainsford, Wenman, Jonson, Waller, Hobbes, and Sandys as among them. Tulloch (I, 95) feels that Falkland's friends were in two groups chronologically, first the poets, and then scholars and theologians later. Sandys, of course, could have been a bridge between the two. That the two groups were distinct, however, is not supported by real evidence. The idea is probably based on the fact that Falkland himself did turn from poetry to theology, though even this "change" must be qualified.

24 See Murdock, p. 79.

25 Ruth Wallerstein, "The Development of the Rhetoric and meter of the Heroic Couplet," p. 166–209.

of Sandys and certain members of this group who contributed commendatory verses to the 1636 and 1638 editions of Sandys' poems. Though probably not all of these men visited Great Tew in Sandys' time,[26] it was almost certainly from the stimuli of the minds of this circle upon one another, whether in London or in Oxfordshire, that much of the metre and rhetorical forms of their couplet derived. Waller, who paid his tribute with the rest and may have owed more to Sandys' verse than is generally admitted, almost surely owed a great deal to the prosodic ideas and practice of this group[27]— especially to their characteristic balance and antithesis in the couplet.

But at least in the later years the absorbing interest of Falkland personally,[28] several of the Oxford scholars, and perhaps some of the London gentlemen, was theology. Sandys himself, as we shall see, was deeply concerned with it. This was a time when thinking men should be interested in the queen of the sciences, a time when theological extremists on two sides were racking the very foundations of the English governmental and social structure. But consideration of theological problems was for this Falkland group more than a duty and a necessity. It was stimulating intellectual exercise.

The two opposite poles of extreme Puritanism and the type of Arminianism being forced upon the English church by Archbishop Laud were bound to clash. Most patriotic Englishmen were conscious of this, and took sides according to conscientious conviction or mercenary motive.

26 Of these versifiers (Falkland, Henry King, Dudly Digges, Thomas Carew, Francis Wyatt, Henry Rainsford, Wintoure Grant, "Edward" Waller, and Sidney Godolphin), there is little indication that Digges, Wyatt, or Grant were members of the Great Tew circle. Sandys' kinsmen Digges and Wyatt, however, probably visited Sir Francis Wenman and therefore Tew in this period. Grant was a fellow-Gentleman of the Privy Chamber with Sandys and Falkland. Actually all may have written their verses after reading the manuscripts of the *Paraphrases* at Great Tew. See below.

27 See Wallerstein, pp. 186–99. Also see J. W. Hebel and H. H. Hudson, *Poetry of the English Renaissance* (New York, 1929), p. 1034, for the observation that "Waller, himself, claimed 'he derived' the harmony of his numbers from Fairfax . . ., but it is interesting to note that George Sandys presented Waller with a copy—of the first edition of his *Paraphrase upon the Divine Poems.*" See *Book-Auction Records*, XXIII, p. 285, for author's presentation copy to "E. Waller."

28 Professor Murdock, pp. 98–9, gives evidence that Falkland "turned" from interest in verse to interest in theology. That the two continued hand in hand is evidenced in Falkland's relation to Sandys. Even a worldly poet like John Suckling wrote at least one religious treatise, "An Account of Religion by Reason" (1637). (See Tulloch, I, 112).

Falkland, after years of study of church history ancient and modern, and earnest conversation with or even tutelage from scholars like Dr. John Hales or his friend William Chillingworth, had taken his stand in the middle. In other words, the dogmatists of either persuasion seemed to him mistaken and dangerous. Theological doctrine and church government were to be determined by reason, and reason only. Therefore he became, in the 1633–9 period, a champion of religious tolerance and intellectual freedom.

Falkland's rational theology never became a petrified thing. All during the period at Great Tew he and his friends debated, during the long summer evenings in the gardens or far into the night during the more austere seasons, the pressing problem. Apparently all the group believed the national church was Christ's church, and all distrusted the narrowness of the "sects," which included the Roman as well as the Puritan. To them the Anglican church in doctrine and government was based on reason, the rational test of Christianity. Much they undoubtedly owed to the Socinians,[29] and perhaps much more to the Dutch Arminians like Grotius, who had visited England in his earlier life.[30] Then and later Falkland disliked Laud and his Anglican-church-as-institution ambitions, though he must have been conscious that in matters of doctrine the prelate was one of the most tolerant churchmen of his time.[31] Falkland himself, and perhaps others of the group, developed from a mildly Calvinistic position in the early 1630's to one essentially Arminian,[32] and towards a belief with Grotius that the English church should recognize and in some respects join with certain other Protestant churches of northern Europe.

From the Great Tew discussions grew an interesting body of theo-

[29] The name as an epithet was often applied to the group, though Falkland may have been shocked to be called one. See Weber, pp. 197–205.

[30] See H. Vreeland, *Hugo Grotius, Father of the Modern Science of International Law* (New York, 1917), p. 64. Falkland was opposed to Laud and in agreement with Grotius on a union between the Anglican church and other Protestant groups on the Continent (Tulloch, I, 155).

[31] *E.g.*, see Weber, pp. 189. It should be recalled that Laud's godson the rationalist theologian Chillingworth was a principal member of the Great Tew group and influenced Falkland tremendously (cf. Weber, Chapter V, 157–212). I do not mean to imply that the Great Tew group presented a united front of theological and political opinion. Actually they differed in interpretation and detail. Some were much closer to Laud than Falkland was.

[32] At least in such essentials as the interpretation of the doctrine of predestination (Weber, pp. 193–4). In 1651 (see note 33 below) Falkland stated that in the matter of free will he had rather be called Pelagian than Calvinist.

logical prose. Partially under the influence of Chillingworth, Falkland himself composed a few tracts, the most notable of them an argument against the infallibility of the church of Rome.[33] Chillingworth produced the most famous of their treatises, his rationalistic argument, *The Religion of Protestants a Safe Way to Salvation*.[34] And there were others.

Sandys in the commentaries on the 1632 *Metamorphosis* had shown his familiarity with the church fathers and many of the Renaissance theologians,[35] Roman and Protestant, studied by the Falkland group. The crown of all his authorities, one recalls, was the rationalist Francis Bacon.[36] And the essence of Sandys' process of interpretation, the liberalism from reasoning within prescribed limits, is also the essence of the Great Tew brand of theological exposition.

Sandys is characteristic of this circle again in the choice of subject for his later poems and translations to be discussed below. But the last and crowning evidence of the essential kinship of his interests to those of Falkland is revealed in a brief account of Sandys by the antiquarian Aubrey. Sandys' niece Lady Wyatt told Aubrey, that at the time of the poet's death "he had something in divinity ready for the presse, which my lady lost in the warres—the title of it shee does not remember."[37] It would be more than interesting to know content as well as title, but one may be sure, in the light of his friends' expressed opinions of him in verse and of their own ideas in verse and prose, of his own paraphrases, and of his translation of Grotius, that it had much in common with the work of the other sojourners in the gardens of Oxfordshire. Evidently at the very last what another sojourner, Sir John Suckling, had earlier said of Falkland could with some justice be applied to Sandys:

> He was of late so gone with divinity,
> That he almost forgot his poetry[38]

[33] *Of the Infallibilitie of the Church of Rome* . . . (Oxford, 1645). For later editions see Weber, p. 334. For discussion see Tulloch, I, 157 ff.

[34] First edition, Oxford, Leonard Litchfield, 1638 [1637]. Note that the publisher is the son of the same man who printed Sandys' 1632 Ovid. See R. B. Davis, "George Sandys *v.* William Stansby," pp. 204, 207.

[35] *E.g.*, Vives. Compare with Falkland's reference to them in a selection from his *Reply* (quoted by Weber, p. 195).

[36] Of course Bacon proclaimed the divorce between philosophy and theology and would not apply philosophical reasoning to the investigation of Christian truth. See Tulloch, II, 19, and Grace Hunter.

[37] John Aubrey, *Brief Lives*, II, 212.

[38] W. Carew Hazlitt, ed., *The Poetical Works of Sir John Suckling* (2 vols., London, 1892), I, 10. Hazlitt dates the poem about 1637.

But when the Great Tew circle was most active, between 1635 and 1638, Sandys had by no means forgotten his poetry, though by now it went hand in hand with divinity. On 3 December 1635 the King's Signet Office recorded his Majesty's grant of privilege for fourteen years to George Sandys, Esq., "for the sole printing publishing and selling . . . in England and Ireland of a Paraphrase by him written on the Psalmes of David & other hymnes dispersed through the old and new Testament,"[39] provided the same be first licensed. The licence was obtained, for the modest little octavo appeared within a few months:

> *A* / PARAPHRASE / VPON / THE PSALMES / OF
> DAVID / *And* / VPON THE HYMNES /
> *Dispersed throughout* / THE OLD AND NEW /
> TESTAMENTS. / By G.S. / *LONDON* / At the
> *Bell* in St. *Pauls* / Church-yard. / CIƆ.IƆC.XXXVI.
> / *Cum Priuilegio Regiæ Majestatis.*[40]

The now customary dedicatory poems to the King and Queen preface the paraphrases. In the verses to Charles, the poet points out his new role as sacred lyrist:

> Ovr graver Muse from her long Dreame awakes,
> Peneian Groves, and Cirrha's Cares forsakes,
> Inspir'd with zeale, she climes th' Æthereall Hills

This little work is, he continues, an oblation

> To God: and Tribute to a god-like King.

The first of what is to be a series of commendatory poems by Falkland also appears among the preliminaries of this work. "To my Noble Frend, Mr *George Sandys* / upon his excellent Paraphrase on the Psalmes /," begins

> Had I no Blushes left, but were of those,
> Who Praise in Verse, what they Despise in Prose:
> Had I this Vice from Vanity or Youth;
> Yet such a Subject would have taught me Truth:

39 P.R.O., Signet Office Docquets, Index 6810, through "the Archbishop of Canterbury . . . by Mr Secretary Windebank." Rymer, *Foedera*, XIX, 708–10 gives the date as 4 December; *Calendar of State Papers, Domestic, 1635*, lists 2 December. The patent is in P.R.O., Patent Rolls, C. 66/2694.

40 The licensing by the Archbishop of Canterbury, "Summa Approbationis. *Perlegi hoc Poema Paraphrasticum in Psalmos Davidis, et alios Hymnos sacros, in quo nihil reperio S. Paginae contrarium, quo minus cum utilitate, ut et summa lectorum voluptate imprimatur,*" is dated 28 November 1635 in the printed form. Probably a lag between granting of the *Priuilegio* and its recording accounts for the discrepancy in dates.

Falkland summarizes Sandys' literary career, praising first his travels,

Teaching the frailety of all Humane things;

the terrible state of Christian churches in the East, the threat of the Turk, the disunion of Christendom. Then he mentions the Ovid, produced amid the wars and tumults of the New World, yet

The Happy Off-spring of so sweet a Muse:

The commentaries, the first book of Vergil, and even the "panegyricke" to the Queen and King receive comment. Though always the poet's muse was "Ethnically chaste," now Sandys has

Diverted to a Purer Path thy Quill;
And chang'd Parnassus Mount to Sions Hill:

In verses of great sweetness, Sandys has made clear the "darkest Texts;" and above all, he has properly ornamented the sacred. Falkland anticipates and refutes certain criticism of this last quality by asking

Yet, as the Church with Ornaments is Fraught,
Why may not that be too, which There is Taught?

Actually, such polishing may bring to the Heavenly Kingdom some of those souls who

Refuse a Cordial, when not brought in Gold.

So concludes the rationalist.

The little book, small and insignificant in format[41] in contrast with the great 1632 Ovid which preceded it, contains paraphrases of 150 psalms, and hymns from *Exodus XV*, *Deuteronomy XXXII*, *Judges V*, *I Samuel II*, *II Samuel I*, *II Samuel VII*, *Isaiah V*, *Isaiah XXVI*, *Isaiah XXXVIII*, *Jonah II*, *Habakkuk III*, *Luke I* (2 excerpts), and *Luke II*. Between the Psalms and the dispersed hymns is printed for the first time Sandys' finest original poem, his "Deo Opt. Max.," ninety lines in his favourite decasyllabic couplet. This second hymn to his Redeemer echoes Renaissance humanism and Ovidean rhetoric, and sums up the varied experiences of the poet-adventurer's life. It is a conscious swan-song, with a dignity, even a sublimity, which make us wish for more from the poet's original genius. The creation of Earth and Man, the coming of Sin and Sorrow and Death, and above all God's Mercy:

[41] The type is small and irregular and printers' errors are fairly frequent. See Bowers and Davis, pp. 39–40.

My gratefull Verse thy Goodness shall display,
O Thou who went'st along in all my way:
To Where the Morning with perfumed wings
From the high Mountaines of Panchæa springs,
To that New-found-out World, where sober Night
Takes from th' Antipodes her silent flight;
To those dark Seas, where horrid Winter reignes,
And binds the stubborne Flouds in Icie chaines:
To Libyan Wastes . . .

God's mercy and glory he has met everywhere. He lists his own narrow escapes from Simoan strife, Arab thievery, the "false Sidonian wolfe," the bloody massacre of faithless Indians, and barbarous pirates, from fever and tainted air and towering tempest. He thanks his God that he has brought him home in safety

that this Earth
Might bury me, which fed me from my Birth:
Blest with a healthfull Age; a quiet Mind,
Content with little. . . .

But this *envoi* was somewhat premature. There was yet more music in the poet, not to mention some further worldly experience. On 1 September the printer-publisher Andrew Hebb[42] entered in the Stationers' Register, "for his Copie . . . a booke called *A Paraphrase upon Job. The Psalmes. Ecclesiastes, and the Lamentacions* of JEREMIAH by GEORGE SANDES Esquire. . . ."[43] By the beginning of the next year[44] this new enlarged edition, in a small but elegant folio, was on sale among the booksellers. Its title-page is less specific than that of 1636:

A / PARAPHRASE / VPON THE / DIVINE POEMS. /
BY / *George Sandys.* / [*rule*] / [*ornament*] /
[*rule*] / *LONDON,* / At the *Bell* in S^{t}. *Pauls*
Church-yard. / CIƆ. IƆC. XXXVIII.

This time the brief dedicatory poem is replaced by a full page prose dedication and a poem. The elaborate dedicatory words refer to Charles,

42 A man Sandys trusted. See R. B. Davis, "George Sandys *v.* William Stansby," pp. 198 n., 200 n. Evidently Hebb was merely Sandys' representative here.

43 Arber, *Transcript of the S.R.*, IV, 366.

44 The title-page bears the 1638 date, but the colophon, "*London*,/ printed by Iohn Legatt./1637." would indicate its early printing. Also the license from the Archbishop of Canterbury is dated 7 November 1637.

among his other styles, as "Lord of the Foure Seas; of Virginia, the Vast Territories Adioyneng, and Dispersed Islands of the Westerne Ocean," another reminder of Sandys' own labours. And the verses following remind the King that Sandys' muse, which "from your Influence tooke her Birth," after wanderings and diverse singing,

> Now Old, hath her last Voyage made; and brought
> To Royall Harbor this her Sacred Fraught:

The subsequent octosyllabic verses "To the Queene" apparently refer to the dark times which have fallen upon the Court, for her Majesty has a cheerful "Ray" which

> Can turne the Saddest Night to Day:

This same note of comforting appears in certain additional dedicatory poems present in some copies of this edition.[45] Two brief poems "To the Queene of Bohemia," Charles's sister, the first in decasyllabic and the second in octosyllabic couplets, are tactful courtier-verses of personal praise.[46] Yet they reflect Elizabeth's own mounting troubles and indirectly those of her family in England. The beginning of the first of the two,

> Crowns are the sport of Fortune

was certainly prophetic. Another poem "To his Grace of Canterbury" may be merely a courtier's gesture towards Charles's favourite churchman, or it may indicate, as it appears to, a genuine respect and affection for Laud that Sandys' friend Falkland certainly did not share. Whatever the motives for its composition, this poem also reflects those troublous times, for Laud is the pilot.

> Who through such Rocks and Gulphes, on either side,
> So steadily the Sacred Vessel guide:[47]

[45] Actually brief lines "To the Prince" appearing in all copies do not show this "overcast spirit."

[46] For texts of the two, see R. B. Davis, "Two New Manuscripts Items for a George Sandys Bibliography," *Papers of the Bibliographical Society of America*, XXXVII (Third Quarter 1943), 220; and "George Sandys and Two 'Uncollected' Poems," *Huntington Library Quarterly*, XII (November 1948), 107–8. The Folger Shakespeare Library has the only known copy of the 1638 edition containing the two poems to Elizabeth of Bohemia.

[47] See Davis, "Two New Manuscript Items," p. 221. This poem survives, apparently, only in a manuscript with a copy of the first of the verses to Elizabeth of Bohemia, in a blank leaf of a 1638 *Paraphrase* now in the Library Company of Philadelphia. Since the companion piece to Elizabeth does appear elsewhere in print, it appears likely that this did also.

This 1638 volume is rich in commendatory verses from many of Sandys' friends. The dedicatory poems are followed immediately by two new eulogies in decasyllabic couplets from the pen of Falkland. The first praises the additions made to this edition of the *Paraphrases* and the second intimates, as Sandys had done, that these are the "last accents of a Dying muse," but insists on their immortality as art.

Henry King, later a bishop and paraphraser of the *Psalms* himself, proclaims the immortality of Sandys' verse in lines "To my much honoured friend," congratulating himself that he is like the poet a "Prelates Sonne." He praises Sir Edwin's *Europæ Speculum* as well as George's previous work:

> And scarcely have Two Brothers farther borne
> A Fathers Name, or with more Value worne
> Their Owne, then Two of you: whose Pens, and Feet
> Have made the distant Points of Heav'n to meet:
> Hee by exact discoveries of the West,
> Your Selfe by painfull Travels in the East.

Sidney Godolphin's encomium in decasyllabic triplets follows King's lines, and mentions that Sandys has not printed the Canticles because his paraphrase of them preserves too much of the author's "Strength and Light." Carew's decasyllabic couplets confess the unworthiness of his "unhallow'd feet" and "unwasht Muse" to pollute these things Divine, but Sandys' verse persuades him to turn to sacred themes. Dudly Digges,[48] scholar and traveller himself as well as merchant prince, honours his "worthy Kinsman M^{r}. George Sandys." as does Sir Francis Wyatt. Briefer pieces by Sir Henry Rainsford, "Edward" Waller, and Wintoure Grant, Sandys' fellow-courtiers, complete the parade of praises which reflects the seriousness and dignity with which this last[49] of Sandys' larger poetic undertakings was received.

The paraphrases of the *Psalms* and the songs from the Old and New Testaments which made up the 1636 volume remained essentially unchanged in text in the 1638. In all these English versions Sandys was working from a Latin original. He probably used *Biblia Interprete Sebastiano Castalione Una Cum Eiusdem Annotationibus Totum Opus Recognouit*

[48] His grandfather Leonard Digges married the sister of George Sandys' mother. See Br. Mus. Add. MSS. No. 33, 896, "Rev'd T. Streatfield, Collections Relating to Kent"; and Brown, *Genesis*, II, 879.

[49] For a discussion of the metrical forms used in these commendatory poems, see Ruth Wallerstein, pp. 194–9.

Ipse. . . .[50] This text by Castalio, the first independent version of the Bible, with learned notes referring to Ovid, would have appealed to the Protestant humanist. And it is actually mentioned in the 1638 Paraphrase in a note on one of Falkland's commendatory poems.[51] It has been suggested that Sandys may also have used *Testamenti Veteris Biblia Sacra Sive Libri Canonici Priscæ Ivdæorum . . . Scholiis illustrati ab Immanuele Tremellio & Francisco Iunio,*[52] though a comparison of a few selections only from *Job*, the *Psalms*, and the *Song of Solomon*[53] would indicate that the English verse in sense is much closer to Castalio's than to the Tremellius-Junius version.[54] But he might have used either or both.

For these paraphrases Sandys did not adhere to the heroic couplet, but used a number of metres. Thirty-five of the Psalms and four of the songs appear in varied combinations of octosyllabic lines,[55] including nine Psalms and one song in triplets. Twenty-nine Psalms and three songs are in octosyllabic couplets, and sixteen Psalms and one song in heptasyllabic couplets. Twenty-one Psalms and two songs are in the decasyllabic couplet, including two Psalms divided into quatrains. Thirty-six Psalms and four songs appear in stanzas composed of combinations of octosyllabic lines with lines of four or six syllables. Seven Psalms appear in stanzas each composed of a quatrain of six-syllable and a quatrain of four-syllable verse. The remaining six Psalms are in six-syllable couplets. The additions to the 1638 volume—the *Job, Ecclesiastes,* and *Lamentations of Jeremiah*—are in decasyllabic couplets. Thus the three long pieces, twenty-one Psalms, and two songs, show that the heroic couplet was his favourite metre here as it had been the only metre of the Ovid.

In paraphrasing the Scriptures Sandys was making his entry into the already crowded literary field of the "divine poem." For before him the Renaissance Englishman, like his Continental contemporary, had already tried his hand many times at versifying portions of the Bible or singing

[50] Basilæ. I compared the 1551 and 1556 editions. The first edition was in 1551.

[51] Falkland alludes to a translation of the Bible into Latin which was done to give the truth to the "polite-pagan-Christians."

[52] London, 1580, was the edition examined. There are many others. Hooper, *Works*, I, lxxxvii, notes that Sandys may have used Castalio but finds him very close to the London, 1593, edition of Tremellius-Junius.

[53] See discussion below.

[54] Especially is this true of *A Paraphrase upon the Song of Solomon.*

[55] Of these, several are in the stanza Tennyson was to make famous in *In Memoriam.*

original hymns to his Creator. It was as natural a direction for the Tudor or Caroline poet to take as those which led him to compose the love lyric or erotic verse narrative, to travel in the Ancient World or to explore the New.[56] The religious poems were varied in form and subject, ranging from highly original verses to faithful translations of Biblical poetry, from sonnets to long narratives. The paraphrase of the obviously lyrical portions of the Scriptures was perhaps the favourite mode and matter of expression, for it offered certain freedom from exact translation and yet did not compel original conception. Before Sandys there were almost countless paraphrases of the Psalms especially, varying from small groups of only a few Psalms to the complete Psalter. Even his brother Sir Edwin had tried his hand.[57]

But of the earlier and contemporary versions of the Psalms only a few appear to have been intended for general or private parochial use. Sternhold and Hopkins, Archbishop Parker, Sir Philip Sidney and his sister the Countess of Pembroke, Sir Francis Bacon, and John Milton more or less ambitiously undertook to produce volumes of English Psalms for private devotion or public worship.[58] That Sandys intended his at least for private devotion is evident in the new title-page for the Psalms portion of the 1638 edition. It includes the lines:

Set to new Tunes for private Devotion:
And a thorow Base, for Voice,
or Instrument.
by
HENRY LAWES Gentleman of His
Majesties Chappell Royall.

Henry Lawes was already a distinguished musician-composer. Only the year before under his own name he had published the music and

[56] The interest of the many-sided Elizabethan in religious poetry has frequently been pointed out. *E.g.*, J. J. Jusserand, *A Literary History of the English People* (3 vols., New York, 1909), II, 415–17 and note.

[57] *Sacred Hymns, Consisting of Fifti Select Psalms of David and Others, Paraphrastically turned into English Verse, and by Robert Tailour, set to be sung . . .* (London, 1615). Among others than those mentioned above who tried their hands in the earlier seventeenth century were Carew, Denham, Joseph Hall, George Herbert, King James, Henry King, and George Wither. Wyatt and Surrey in Britain and Marot in France had also earlier paraphrased Psalms in the vernacular.

[58] See the anonymous article, "Psalmody," *The Quarterly Review*, XXXVIII (July 1828), 16–53, for a survey of these early versions of the Psalms.

libretto for a masque. Since the verse was by a young unknown named John Milton, the poet's name did not appear.[59] In the case of Sandys', however, the composer was glad to increase his own prestige by having his name appear under a more famous one.

As the words of the title suggest, Lawes' music was primarily suited for private devotionals[60] and intended to please the King.[61] Sandys' dedicatory poem to Archbishop Laud may have been a bid for consideration of the volume for more general use, but there is no other indication of such an ambition. At any rate, Lawes liked Sandys' Psalms sufficiently to make new musical setting for thirty[62] of them before 1648, and print them in his *Choice Psalms Put Into Musick For Three Voices* . . .,[63] a book mentioning Sandys only in the dedication to the King but prized today especially because it contains a commendatory sonnet "To My Friend Mr. Henry Lawes" by John Milton himself. Later in the century appeared *The Psalms of George Sandys set to Music for Two Voices* . . .[64] by Walter Porter, like Lawes a Gentleman of the Chapel Royal under Charles I.

Actually Sandys' paraphrases have received more direct praise from at

[59] See Willa McC. Evans, *Henry Lawes, Musician and Friend of Poets* (New York, 1941), pp. 138–41.

[60] *Ibid.*, p. 143. See this reference for a discussion of Lawes' music in relation to the verse text.

[61] Apparently Charles did use and enjoy it. Sir Thomas Herbert, *Memoirs of the Last Two Years of the Reign of King Charles I* (London, 1839 [orig. ed. 1702]), p. 61, notes that it was one of the books Charles delighted "to read" in when he was a prisoner in the Isle of Wight.

[62] Eight of these had been originally printed as airs in 1638 and were now reconstructed as part-songs; sixteen of the earlier tunes were omitted, and twenty-two were completely new (Evans, p. 183). Lawes also used Sandys' paraphrases of at least four Psalms in *Select Psalmes Of A New Translation, To be Sung in Verse and Chorus of five parts, with Symphonies of Violins, Organ, and other Instruments, November 22, 1655. Composed by Henry Lawes, Servant to His late Majesty* (Evans, p. 211 n).

[63] London, 1648, in quarto. The four parts are found in many instances bound separately (as Br. Mus. [Music] c. 110 and Br. Mus. K. 3 h. 18; Bodleian Music Sch. E. 513 and 516, Bodleian Art. 40 p. 17 BS). For a bibliographical description of this book in its variant and divided states, see Emma V. Unger and William A. Jackson, *The Carl H. Pforzheimer Library, English Literature, 1475–1700* (3 vols., New York, 1940), II, 607–9.

[64] *Circa* 1670. I have not located a copy. It is mentioned in *Allibone's Dictionary of English Literature and British and American Authors*, II, p. 1648. Porter, the composer, also published books of airs and madrigals in 1632 and 1639, and of motets in 1657.

least fairly discriminating critics than the Ovid has.[65] In his own time Cowley, though he did not feel that Sandys had recreated the Psalms in a spirit equal to that of the originals, admitted the pre-eminence of the translation among metrical versions of the scriptures.[66] Richard Baxter in the next generation also gave these divine poems top ranking, singling out the *Job* as having restored the glory of the original, and lamenting that the Psalms had not been fitted to the usual tunes.[67] Pope thought highly of the Job especially.[68] In the early nineteenth century a *Quarterly* reviewer called Sandys' the most poetic translation of the Psalms,[69] and H. J. Todd, an authority on English psalmody, agreed, regretting that it is actually "too poetical for the comprehension of common Congregations, *into which it has therefore never found its way*."[70] In his observations on the development of the Psalter in English, Todd quotes Sandys' versions of Psalms XCI, CXXXIX, and CXLVIII. Catterwole, a contemporary of Todd, states that no other version presents "the combination of poetry with terse and correct versification, and a strict adherence to the original,"[71] that Sandys' does. Late in the nineteenth century, G. A. Simcox cites Sandys' paraphrases as maintaining the highest level of those in English, though he thinks the *Job* "appallingly tame."[72] In the last fifty years critics have generally been less enthusiastic concerning the intrinsic beauties of the paraphrases, but have given more attention to the form of their decasyllabic couplet

[65] Of course these critics are in certain cases specialists on psalmody or hymnology who did not even know the *Metamorphosis*.

[66] Abraham Cowley, *Complete Works . . .*, ed. by A. B. Grosart (2 vols. [Edinburgh], 1881), II, 4.

[67] Baxter says Herbert's and Sandys' translations are the scripture poems pleasing him best (*Poetical Fragments . . .* [London, 1681], p. A8). Sandys' are "an elegant and excellent paraphrase."

[68] See William Lisle Bowles, ed., *The Works of Alexander Pope* (10 vols., London, 1806), VI, 217, for Warton's note that "The Job of Sandys does not seem to be admired and known, in a degree equal to its merits. Harte told me how highly Pope thought of it. . . ."

[69] Anonymous, "Psalmody," *Quarterly Review*, XXXVIII (July 1828), 27.

[70] *Observations upon the Metrical Versions of the Psalms . . .* (London, 1822), pp. 70–2, 83.

[71] R. Catterwole, *Sacred Poetry of the Seventeenth Century*, Vol. I (London, 1835), pp. 47–8. He reprints Psalms XIII, XX, XXVI, XXXV, XLII, LXVI, LXXXVIII, XCII, C, and CXXXVII, one of the songs, and two of Sandys' original poems.

[72] "Sandys, Herbert, Crashaw, Vaughn" in Thomas H. Ward, *The English Poets, Selections with Critical Introductions by Various Writers* (5 vols., London, 1880–1918), II, 192–3.

and its possible significance. Actually they conclude little, but do point out such interesting things as that the heroic couplet of *Job* and the *Psalms* shows more run-on lines and run-on couplets than the Ovid,[73] a finding which bears out an earlier analysis of the Ovid showing a steady increase in run-on lines through the course of that poem.[74]

In the end, *A Paraphrase* remains far less interesting to the modern reader than the *Metamorphosis*. The influence of the couplet of these religious poems on later writers is not so evident. Though there is variety of metre, some of it, particularly the four and six-syllable lines, Sandys never fully mastered. The poet's early habit of condensation is still here, and on the whole his metre is more regular than in the Ovid. But perhaps primarily because of the difference in the originals from which he worked, the paraphrases lack the skip of joy of the Ovid and yet never quite recapture the glow of divine fervour of the scriptural source with which to replace the pagan exuberance. The paraphrases do show the influence of the Ovidean rhetoric. But most of us prefer the *Metamorphosis*, simply as poetry, to the sacred verses.

Yet Sandys is not to be judged as a sacred poet entirely by *A Paraphrase upon the Divine Poems*. As we have indicated, the swan-song implications of dedications and commendatory verses in the 1638 volume were somewhat premature. In 1640 appeared a small octavo with the title,

> CHRISTS / PASSION. / A / TRAGEDIE. / WITH / ANNOTATIONS. / / LONDON, / Printed by *Iohn Legatt*. / M. D. C. XL.[75]

This was Sandys' translation of Hugo Grotius' *Christus Patiens*, which

[73] Felix Schelling, "Ben Jonson and the Classical School," pp. 237–8, compares Sandys' use of run-on lines and other devices with those of Spenser, Marlowe, Drayton, and Chapman. He finds Sandys closer to the earliest poet, Spenser, than to the others. To make this comparison Professor Schelling used 100 lines from *Psalm LXXIII* and *Job* and compared them with 100 lines from each of the other poets. Professor Wallerstein, pp. 187–8 agrees more or less tacitly as to the run-on lines, but points out that Professor Schelling's conclusion that Sandys also shows fewer rhetorical lines must be qualified.

[74] H. Wood, pp. 74–5, shows the steady increase in unstopt lines from Books I–XV. See Chapter VIII above. Wood's explanation is that Sandys "reverted" (to earlier Renaissance freedom) as he grew farther away in time from first hand contact with the French developers of the couplet in the 1610–20 period, or from the time when he was "fresh from theoretical studies of poetics."

[75] For variant forms of this title and a bibliographical description of the volume and of later editions, see Bowers and Davis, pp. 47–52. The work had been entered in the Stationers' Register on 9 October 1639 as the copy of Master Legatt. See Arber, *S.R.*, IV, 483.

had been originally published in Latin in 1608.[76] The original had been lauded by Casaubon, and was called a perfect tragedy in the classical tradition.[77] Already inclined to scriptural themes and as a member of the Great Tew circle sympathetic with Grotius' brand[78] of Protestantism, Sandys found its subject appealing.

The dedication to the King takes cognizance of the monarch's spiritual and mental cares, for it alludes to Grotius' troubles which led the Dutch poet to such a theme.[79] And it concludes with a reflection on Sandys himself in relation to the times:

> Thus in the Shadow of your Absence, dismist
> from Arms by an Act of Time, have I, in what I
> was able, continued to serve you.[80]
>
> The humblest of your
> Majesties Servants,
> GEORGE SANDYS.

Falkland's verses "To the Author" which follow are a double tribute to Grotius and Sandys, the "great pair." They begin with Grotius:

> Our age's wonder; by thy birth the fame
> Of *Belgia*, by thy banishment the shame;

Falkland sketches Grotius' career as scholar, theologian, and statesman.

[76] Hamilton Vreeland, *Hugo Grotius*, p. 34.

[77] *Ibid.* It was perhaps well-nigh perfect as a neoclassic imitation, but imitation it distinctly is.

[78] Grotius (1583–1645) himself had been in England in 1613 as Dutch representative in a freedom-of-the-seas dispute. While there he became a friend of Isaac Casaubon. Later, imprisoned in his own land in theologico-political disputes, escaping, and living abroad, he was one of the champions of learning, the enquiring mind, and Protestantism in his age. At the time of Sandys' translation he was Sweden's ambassador in France. He had for a long time influenced certain groups of religious thinkers, including the Great Tew circle (see Weber, pp. 187 ff. for a discussion of Grotius' ideas as they are related to those of Falkland and Chillingworth). A new annotated bibliography of Grotius' works is now being prepared by Dr. Jacob ter Meulen at the Hague.

[79] In both the dedication and in a brief address to the Reader Sandys mentions that Apollinaris of Laodicea and Gregory Nazianzen had previously written on the same subject. W. S. M. Knight (*The Life and Works of Hugo Grotius* . . . [London, 1925], p. 117) denies any similarity between the work of Grotius and that of St. Gregory beyond an inevitable similarity in the names of the *dramatis personae.* He feels that the drama is remarkably indebted to Aeschylus and Euripides.

[80] Hooper, *Works*, I, xlvi, suggests that this may refer to Sandys' inability, on account of age, to join the army against the Scots.

Then he asks what England can do to match the great career of the author.

All that we can, we do: a Pen divine,
And differing only in the Tongue from thine,
Doth thy choice labours with success reherse,
And to another world transplant thy verse,
At the same heighth to which before they rose,
When they forc'd wonder from unwilling foes:
Now *Thames* with *Ganges* may thy labours praise,
Which there[81] breed Faith, and here devotion raise.
Though your acquaintance all of worth pursue,
And count it honour to be known to you,
I dare affirme your Catalogue does grace
No one who better doth deserve a place:
None hath a larger heart, a fuller head,
For he hath seen as much as you have read:
The neerer Countries past, his stepts have prest
The new found World, and trod the Sacred East,
Where his brows due the loftie Palmes doe rise,
Where the proud Pyramids invade the skies;
And, as all think who his rare friendship own,
Deserves no lesse a journey to be known.
Vlysses, if we trust the *Grecian* song,
Travel'd not farre, but was a prisoner long,
To that by Tempest forc'd; nor did his voice
Relate his Fate: His travels were his choice,
And all those numerous Realmes, returnd agen,
Anew, he travl'd over with his Pen,
And, *Homer* to himselfe, doth entertaine
With truths more usefull, then his Muse could faine.
Next *Ovids* Transformations he translates
With so rare Art, that those which he relates
Yeeld to this transmutation, and the change
Of men to Birds and Trees appeares not strange:
Next the Poetick parts of Scripture, on
His loome he weaves, and *Iob* and *Solomon*[82]
His Pen restores with all that heavenly Quire;
And shakes the dust from *Davids* solemn Lyre:
For which from all with just consent he wan
The title of the *English Buchanan*.
Now to you both, great Paire. . . .

[81] Falkland's or Sandys' own footnote says this refers to *De Veritate Religionis Christianæ*, Grotius' work intended to convert the Indians.

[82] See below in the present chapter.

The outline-structure of a classical five-act play, with chorus and a minimum of characters, Sandys found in his Latin original and followed faithfully in his translation. The English version is written in decasyllabic and octosyllabic couplets, the dialogue of the individual *dramatis personae*[83] usually appearing in the former and the Chorus of Jewish Women and characters' response to the Chorus in the latter, though there is variation. Sometimes Sandys stays close to the original as he had done in his other translations, but any attempt at compression is not so evident. In Act II, for example, Grotius has 272 lines, Sandys 334. Though perfect smoothness is not always achieved, as in the paraphrases the metre is regular. And as in the paraphrases, his rhymes are less emphatic than in the earlier Ovid.

The merit of the work as translation has been discussed at length elsewhere.[84] Sandys is in this work as much paraphraser as translator, even in the Elizabethan sense of the latter term. Though the Latin original certainly influenced the form of the English work, mere suggestion in the Latin is expanded in robust and picturesque language.

Grotius himself knew early of Sandys' translation. On 29 November 1639, presumably before the 1640 edition was published, he wrote to his brother William:

> . . . Produit in Anglia Tragoedia nostra Christus Patiens, optimis in ea lingua expressa. Vir Illustrissimus elogium proposuit cuius initum sic me aloquitur:
>
> *Our Ages Wonder, by thy birth te* [*sic*] *Fame*
> *Oft* [*sic*] *Belgia, by thy banissement* [*sic*] *the shame.*
>
> Id quid sit, Anglus tibi aliquis inter praetabitur Liber Regi dedicatus est. Addidit interpres Notas eruditas.[85]

[83] The "Persons" consist of Jesus, Chorus of Jewish Women, Peter, Pontius Pilate, Caiaphas, Judas, the Jews, first Nuncius, Second Nuncius, Chorus of Roman Soldiers, Joseph of Arimathea, Nicodemus, John, and Mary, the Mother of Jesus.

[84] Gunther Hans Grüninger, *George Sandys als Übersetzer des "Christus Patiens" von Hugo Grotius* (Tauberbischofsheim, 1927). This brief study (a doctoral dissertation) does little more than compare Latin and English lines as to poetic technique in the two. The "notes" (*i.e.*, commentaries) are not considered.

[85] *Hvgonis Grotii . . . Epistolae Quotquot repiriri potuerunt* . . . (Amstelodami . . . MDCLXXXVII), letter 473, p. 889. In another letter of 30 November 1639 to Gerardo Iounni Vossio, Grotius states: "Nescio an videris Christum patientem nostrum versum à Sandescio Anglicé, & Regi Magnae Britanniae dedicatum. Magno favore is liberi receptus est; & deliberatur de vertendis nostris illis de jure belli ac pacis. Non dubito quin omnia nostra ibi multos sint lectores inventura."

The *notas eruditas*, as Grotius remarks, are Sandys' own. Unlike the Ovid commentaries, they are actually numbered-verse annotations, explaining the meaning or origin of geographical or proper names, giving mythological backgrounds for an allusion, sketching secular or religious history, or interpreting Biblical custom. They contain the same sort of translations from the classics as the *Metamorphosis*, and allusions to such authors as Ovid, Seneca, Horace, Vergil, Cicero, Eusebius, St. Jerome, Martial, Lucretius, Statius, and Prudentius. Though brief compared with the Ovid commentaries, they have the classical-humanistic flavour, even though the text they explicate is of the very essence of the Christian religion.

Christ's Passion has been called "the least pleasing of all Sandys' works,"[86] because of its artificial form and ornate rhetoric. Yet it offers further proof of the poet's continued ability in the heroic couplet, of his basic religious interests,[87] and of his broad erudition. Perhaps the limitations of the original kept it from equalling the Ovid or even the paraphrases as poetry, for the Latin author in this case at least was not a great poet. Grotius properly was pleased by the translation, for it is better poetry than his own.[88]

Even *Christ's Passion* was not Sandys' final publication of religious poetry. A year after its appearance another slim volume bore his initials:

> A / PARAPHRASE / VPON / THE SONG OF / SOLOMON. / BY G.S. / *Cum Privilegio Regiae Majestatis.* / *LONDON,* / Printed by *Iohn Legatt.* / 1641.

[86] J. M. Attenborough, "George Sandys, Traveller and Poet," *Westminster Review*, CLXIII (June 1905), 643–5.

[87] It has been suggested that Grotius put his own strong Protestant doctrine in certain places into the mouths of his characters. Protestant or not, the subject had interested Sandys at least from the time of his visit to the Holy Sepulchre in 1611.

[88] Cf.Grüninger, p. 70, who agrees. My own comparison of Sandys, 1640 edition, was made with *Hugonis Grotii Christus Patiens* . . . (Gorlicii, 1685). Curiously Sandys, on the basis of this one work, is given a place among the English dramatic poets. See Edward Phillips, *Theatrum Poetarum* (London, 1675), ii, 56; Gerard Langbaine, *An Account of the English Dramatic Poets* (Oxford, 1691), pp. 436–8; [Charles Gildon], *The Lives and Characters of the English Dramatic Poets* (London, 1698), p. 121. T. R. Nash (*Collections for the History of Worcestershire*, 1782 ed., II, 223) and J. Nichols (*A Select Collection of Poems* . . . [8 vols., London, 1782], VIII, 238–40) speak of Lauder's charge of plagiarism against Milton as being based partly on Sandys' *Christ's Passion*.

This was almost surely a second-thought printing of a work which had been composed at about the same time as *A Paraphrase upon the Divine Poems*. It is to be remembered that in the 1638 *Paraphrase* Sidney Godolphin referred to the fact that the Canticles were not printed, giving what is probably the real reason why they were withheld—that Sandys had preserved too much of the Biblical author's "Strength and Light."

> But you so crush those odors, so dispense
> Those rich perfumes, you make them too intense
> And such (alas) as too much please our Sense.[89]

Further proof that the *Song of Solomon* was circulated in manuscript perhaps lies in the considerable number of manuscript copies surviving, one of which gives 1637 as the date of composition.[90] Some of them survive in separate sheets,[91] but at least three[92] appear in copies of the 1638 edition of *A Paraphrase upon the Divine Poems*. Of course it is possible that these latter were inserted after the printed *Song of Solomon* appeared, but it seems more likely that they were written in between 1638 and 1641 so that the owners might have the poet's paraphrases "complete." At any rate, all these copies indicate that *A Paraphrase upon the Song of Solomon* was highly popular.

Sandys wrote for this little work his last dedication[93] to his royal

[89] *A Paraphrase upon the Divine Poems*, p. (**2). That the *Solomon* existed in 1640 is of course borne out by Falkland's allusion to it in the *Christ's Passion* commendatory poem quoted above.

[90] The University of Cincinnati 1638 *Paraphrase* (PR 2338, A 68 1638, an 8-leaf MS.) contains a manuscript *Solomon* with a handwritten title-page "A PARAPHRASE/ VPON THE SONG/ OF SOLOMON/ By George Sandys/ Anno/ 1637."

[91] (1) Bodleian MSS. Ashmole 47 folio 113–14; (2) Bodleian MSS. e. Museo. 201 (S.C. 3707); (3) Br. Mus. MSS. Sloane 1009 ff. 376^{b}–85; (4) [This has the autograph of Charles Cheyney, 1643] Lansdowne 489. ff. 121. Arthur Clifford (*Tixall Poetry* [Edinburgh, 1813], pp. 335–6) says "I have in my possession a manuscript copy of this [*Song of Solomon*] . . . transcribed in the year 1638, which I have great reason to believe has never been faithfully printed."

[92] One of these appears in an "Ex dono auctoris" copy of the 1638, a book now in the Library Company of Philadelphia, the same volume in which appear manuscript dedicatory poems to Elizabeth of Bohemia and Archbishop Laud. See. R. B. Davis, "Two New Manuscript Items for a George Sandys Bibliography." The other two appear in the William A. Clark Memorial Library, Los Angeles (PR 2338. p. 21, a 6-leaf MS.), and in the University of Cincinnati Library (see note 90 above).

[93] W. Carew Hazlitt, *Handbook of the Popular . . . Literature of Great Britain . . .* (London, 1867), p. 533, describes an edition, *A Paraphrase upon the Song of Solomon. Written by G. S. and Dedicated to the Queenes Majesty*. Oxford, 1641. "4 to,"

master, pointing out that the *Song of Solomon* was a most fitting tribute to a perfect marriage such as was Charles's, and noting again the end of his own career.

To the King

SIR,

I presume to invite you to these Sacred Nuptials: the Epithalamium sung by a crowned muse. Never was there paire of so divine a Beautie, nor united in such harmonious Affections: and infinitely he deserved her love; redeemed at so dear a Price, and enriched with so invaluable a Dowry.

SIR, Let me finde your Pardon for thus long continuing to make my Allay currant by the impression of your Name. Directed by your propitious Aspect, have I safely steered between so many Rocks; and now, arrived at my last Harbor, have broken up my ruinous Vessel.

The humblest of your
Majesties Servants
GEORGE SANDYS.[94]

Whatever earlier moral or religious scruples regarding publication of the work the old poet may have had, the graceful tact of this dedication appears to indicate that he had overcome or dissipated them. That Godolphin was right in considering these love lyrics the most sensuous, if not sensual, of Sandys' verse is obvious in their first lines. As in *Christ's Passion*, Sandys was affected greatly by his desire to recreate the spirit of his original and yet at the same time show his own poetic faculty. Here his source was one of the great love poems of all literature. The result is more successful than in the Grotius drama or the other scriptural poems.

The octosyllabic couplets of *A Paraphrase upon the Song of Solomon* are

but no copy has been located. There is, however, a 1642 London edition dedicated "to the Queenes Majesty," with a text differing slightly from that of the London 1641 (perhaps because it is based on the lost Oxford 1641 edition). The *Song of Solomon* is not included in the collected *A Paraphrase upon the Divine Poems* until the 1676 edition. See Bowers and Davis, pp. 45–8.

94 A poetic dedication "To the Queene" appears neither in the London 1641 nor in the 1642 London edition "Dedicated to the Queen's Majesty." The words "To the Queene" appear in the MS. Cincinnati copy in the proper position after the title, but the space for the poem is left blank. The poem to the queen does appear in the two MS. versions in the British Museum, and both the prose dedication to the King and the Poetic dedication to the queen appear with the *Paraphrase upon the Song of Solomon* in the 1676 edition of *A Paraphrase upon the Divine Poems*. It may be presumed that the poetic dedication to the Queen appeared in the unlocated Oxford edition of 1641 of the *Song of Solomon*.

in rhetoric and spirit much closer to the Elizabethan lyrics than to the heroic verses the poet had shaped elsewhere. They seem nearer to Marlowe than to Dryden or Pope. Keats should have enjoyed this verse as much as or more than the Ovid he so extensively used. One can imagine his delight in these lines on love in spring:

Lo, the sharp Winter now is gone,
The threatning Tempests over-blown;
Harke, how the Aires Musicians sing,
And carrol to the floury Spring,
Chast Turtles, hous'd in shady Groves,
Now murmur to their faithfull Loves:
Green figs on sprouting trees appear,
And Vines Sweet smelling Blosomes bear.
Arise my Love, my Faire one Rise,
O Come! delay our Ioy envies.[95]

Or these,

My Love, by mutuall vous assur'd,
A Garden is with strength immur'd:
A Christall Fountain, a cleare Spring
Shut up and sealed with my Ring:
An Orchard stor'd with pleasant Fruits;
Pomgranat Trees, there spread their roots,
Where sweetly smelling Camphire blows,
And never dying Spiknard grows;
Sweet Spiknard, Crocus newly blown,
Sweet Calamus and Cinamon:
Those Trees which sacred Incense shed,
The Teares of Myrrh, and Aloes bled
From bitter wounds; with all the rare
Productions which perfume the Aire.[96]

With the publication of such verse a literary career of almost thirty years was concluded. The author's *A Relation* had by 1642 gone through five editions, the *Metamorphosis* through six,[97] and the various sacred paraphrases and translations were with the earlier works to appear again several times in the course of the century. Sandys might well break up his ruinous vessel with the comfortable knowledge that in his own century

95 "Sponsa," pp. 8–9, 1641 London ed.
96 "Sponsus," p. 16.
97 Including the 1621 edition of the first five books and the unauthorized 1628 edition.

at least his fame was secure. Dryden's judgment of him—"the best versifier of the former age"— perhaps summarizes the later seventeenth century's feeling about Sandys. In other words, he was the ablest poet between Ben Jonson and Dryden and Milton.

Succeeding generations have hardly agreed with this verdict. When considered at all, Sandys has been placed rightly below some of his contemporaries and wrongly below others. He is by no means a major writer. But when his accomplishments are added up the result is impressive. (1) A sophisticated, accurate, and basically entertaining travel account in a distinctive prose style. (2) A translation of a Roman classic in language and tone somewhere between the Elizabethan Golding and the Augustan Pope, in a closed and balanced yet flexible couplet[98] in itself a genuine contribution to the development of the heroic metre. This work in rhetoric and metre directly influenced Dryden, Milton, Pope, and Keats. In its prose commentaries the *Metamorphosis* was a mine of materials on a romantic stimulus to many literary generations. (3) A paraphrase of the Scriptures and a translation of a Renaissance Christian poem, renderings distinguished for regularity of form and felicity of phrase among the many others of the *genre* of their time, and in some places really fine poetry. (4) And finally, a handful of original poems, many of them dedicatory verses, but in some instances, as in the "Hymn to the Redeemer" and "Deo. Opt. Max.," deeply sincere expressions of religious feeling, the dignity of man, and the magnificent adventure which was life in the English Renaissance. With all these works goes a consistently straight-forward and intelligible style, at times strongly colloquial. These are no trivial accomplishments.

Sandys preserved much of the ebullient imagination of the Elizabethans in the very forms in which he prepared the way for the neoclassical age. He is clearly not of the school of Donne or Herbert, nor of his friends Carew and Lovelace,[99] though with them all he shares many qualities. He is more the scholar-poet than any of them. Perhaps this phrase "scholar-poet" is the key to his weakness and his strength.

[98] See A. H. Thompson, "Writers of the Couplet," *Cambridge History of English Literature* (15 vols., New York, 1907–33), VII, 59.

[99] Though in at least one instance he writes in their tradition. In addition to his published original poems mentioned in the chapters above, another original poem almost surely is his:—"A Dreame," reprinted for the first time in R. B. Davis, "George Sandys and Two Uncollected Poems," *Huntington Library Quarterly*, XII (November 1948), 109–11, from a Folger MS. commonplace book. It is a light, erotic, court-circle poem, much inferior in quality to "Deo. Opt. Max." or the "Hymn to the Redeemer."

X

COLONIAL EXPERT: LAST YEARS

POETRY, the Great Tew circle, and the royal court did not occupy all of Sandys' time after his return from Virginia. We have noticed already that he acted as guardian and legal counsel for his brother Sir Edwin's younger children in litigation involving their inheritance. On his own account he appeared in law chambers to defend his sole-publication privilege for the Ovid against a piratical private printer,[1] and to sue another printer-publisher who had, he thought, been unfair or dishonest in handling the sale of the 1632 *Metamorphosis*.[2] From the documents of the last we learn that he was in London and Oxford at least several times between 1632 and 1635, that he took a great personal interest in the printing of the 1632 Ovid, that he was well acquainted among London printers and booksellers, and that he presented copies of the edition to many of his friends, who are named.[3]

Sandys sat at least twice for the fashionable court-painter Cornelis Janssen, or Cornelius Jonson, for the portraits survive today.[4] His

[1] See the excerpts from the Stationers' Court Book, under the year 1628, quoted in R. B. Davis, "The Early Editions of George Sandys' Ovid," pp. 270–1.

[2] See R. B. Davis, "George Sandys *v.* William Stansby." The documents in this suit throw considerable light on printing and publishing procedures in the period.

[3] Apparently the single copies listed were largely presentation copies. They include copies for the King and Queen, for Sandys' nephew and namesake George Sandys, and for such people (tentatively identified by surname given) as John Payne, well-known engraver; Ben Jonson; Charles Butler, philologist and author; Sir Thomas Bludder, Gentleman of the Privy Chamber; a Lady Wingfield; Francisco Clein the etcher; and John Barnard, musician. For the names of others who received copies, see Davis, "George Sandys, *v.* William Stansby," pp. 198–9.

[4] One of them (reproduced opposite p. 224), in the possession of Lord Sandys at Ombersley, has been copied in engravings since the eighteenth century. It represents the poet in court dress, with greying or powdered hair. Apparently it was painted at some time after 1632, for it represents a much older man than does the second portrait, which bears the date 1632 on the back. Copies of this first portrait are in the possession of Colonel George O. Sandys of Graythwaite Hall and of the University of Virginia. The second original portrait,

interest in the illustrative arts is perhaps suggested in his friendships with Thomas Howard, Earl of Arundel, the great collector[5] of his generation, and with Clein of Mortlake,[6] and certainly by his remarks on illustration in the address to the reader at the beginning of the 1632 *Metamorphosis*. And the names of the musicians Henry Lawes and John Barnard among his acquaintance, not to mention all sorts of allusions to music in his *Travels* and in the Ovid commentaries, must represent other personal interests.

But the major non-literary interest of these later years was the colony of Virginia. Evidently he departed hurriedly from America and at first expected to or was expected to return. The Virginia Council's minutes for two or three years continued to contain references to him as official and as individual planter. Some of the former Treasurer's indentured servants wished to buy their freedom or claimed that the period of service was over.[7] Certification had to be secured from him in England that certain property such as cattle had been turned over by him as Treasurer to other officials,[8] or that payment had been made for the passage of a servant evidently sent to his private plantation after his

now in the possession of Colonel George O. Sandys of Graythwaite Hall, represents the poet (see frontispiece) as a dark-haired man with a melancholy, dreaming face. This portrait, which came to Colonel Sandys from members of the family living in Cornwall, bears the inscription on the back of the canvas: "G.S. C.J. Pinxit 1632." One of the engravings of the Ombersley portrait appears in Nash, *Collections for a History of Worcestershire*, II, 223. Cornelius Janssen [Jonson, or Johnson] (1593–1664?) was a London-born painter of Dutch ancestry who from 1618 to 1636 was the fashionable depicter of the court and nobility. In 1636 he moved from London to Bridge, near Barham Downs, near Canterbury, where he painted the Kentish families of Digges, Aucher, and Hammond, the two former at least being Sandys' relatives. It seems possible that the Ombersley portrait was painted in Kent after Sandys' retirement to Boxley. Janssen liked to use cool, subdued colouring, black dress especially. Both the Sandys portraits, particularly that of 1632 in which the costume is apparently black velvet, are good examples of Janssen's colour technique.

5 See R. B. Davis, "Two New Manuscript Items for a George Sandys Bibliography," p. 217. The Library Company of Philadelphia copy of the 1638 Paraphrase contains an "ex dono auctoris" inscription to Arundel.

6 See R. B. Davis, "George Sandys *v.* William Stansby," and the illustrations in the 1632 Ovid.

7 "Minutes," *Virginia Magazine*, XXV (October 1917), 338, and McIlwaine, ed., *Minutes*, p. 179.

8 McIlwaine, ed., *Minutes*, pp. 118, 161. On 12 October 1626 and 6 February 1627, Dr. Pott was ordered to procure evidence from George Sandys or Sir Francis Wyatt that the Treasurer had delivered certain kine to the physician; for William Claiborne, official surveyor, claimed an unfair distribution. On

departure.[9] It was necessary that he clear up the accounts of properties formerly under the control of the Treasurer as Company official.[10] All these were more or less routine matters.

But characteristically, Sandys was involved in litigation regarding his personal affairs in Virginia. In this case because of its connection with his former office, the suit was carried through the Privy Council at home and the Governor and Council in the colony rather than through ordinary courts. Sandys had learned that the Virginia Council was planning to levy on the servants and perhaps other items of his personal estate[11] in the colony to obtain compensation for the spoliage of tobacco one of his deputies, Captain Whitaker, had collected while Sandys was Treasurer. Sandys appealed to the Privy Council. That body on 25 July 1627 addressed letters to the Governor and Council in Virginia declaring that, after a thorough investigation of Sandys' claims, they must require the colony to restore and continue him in the "quiett possession of all such Tenants and Servants, togeither with the profitt of theire labours past and to come"[12] and directed that the matter of the tobacco be not passed upon until the full proceedings were transmitted to England for the Privy Council to review. A reply from Governor Francis West and the Virginia Council, dated 4 March 1627/8, stated that while Sandys complained of the loss of four tenants taken by the Council's order, actually in 1623 Sandys "took to himself sixteen tenants without any order from the Virginia Company."[13] High-handed though such a

22 June 1638 he was witness in a suit regarding properties of Sir Thomas Gates in Virginia. His address is given as "of Whitefriars' London." See P.R.O., C. 24/629/32.

9 McIlwaine, ed., *Minutes*, pp. 144. March 12, 1626/7.

10 See W. L. Grant and James Munro, edd., *Acts of the Privy Council of England, Colonial Series, 1613–1680* . . . (Hereford, 1908), p. 118 [Item 192]. Sandys had left the properties of the shipyard, then dismantled and sold in part to private persons, and also tobacco due the old Company, in the hands of Sir Francis Wyatt. Wyatt in turn had left them in the care of Abraham Peirsey, cape merchant, when he came away in 1626.

11 Apparently the colonial Council's action was aimed partly or wholly at recovering the services of tenants whose terms of service had been "awarded" to Sandys, in 1624, when (as Sandys stated) his term as Treasurer was up, in recompense for the insufficient number (when compared with the number promised) which had come to him at the beginning of his term of office. These "Tenants and Youthes" were working on Sandys' personal estate.

12 Grant and Munro, edd., *Acts of the Privy Council, Colonial*, pp. 116–17 [Item 190].

13 W. N. Sainsbury, ed., *Calendar of State Papers, Colonial Series, 1574–1660*

procedure may have been, Sandys was almost surely justified[14] in taking the sixteen to make up something of the number promised by his original commission. Sir Francis Wyatt as governor must have consented in the matter. At all events, there is no evidence of further action by Privy Council or by colony in the case.

This reply from Governor West and the Council, received in July and written in March 1628, mentions Sandys' two years' absence from the colony and his purpose not to return. On 22 March, however, he had been re-appointed to the Virginia Council under Governor Harvey, as he had been re-appointed under Governor Yeardley on 4 March 1626. This royal commission of 1628 may be merely a renewal of that of 1626, substituting Harvey for Yeardley, but the continued presence of Sandys' name may indicate that he still considered, or pretended to consider in order to safeguard his property, the possibility of returning to the colony.

Whether he ever really meant to return or not, Sandys' interest in the colony remained. The accession of Charles had revived the hopes of some members of the old Virginia Company, for the new king was favourably disposed toward Sir Edwin Sandys, Sir John Danvers, the two Ferrars, and other leaders of the Sandys faction in the Company,[15] and had asked their advice concerning the future government of the colony. It was upon this occasion that the Sandys faction submitted its great propaganda document, its *apologia*, the "Discourse of the Old Company,"[16] in an attempt to revive the charter. The Privy Council, to which the matter was submitted, would not consent to political powers for such a company,[17] and left the whole matter unsettled. Apparently inspired by persons who wanted some action, on 17 June 1631 the King appointed a new commission "to consider how the estate of the Colony of Virginia has been . . . and to present their proceedings [*i.e.*, recommendations] from time to time."[18] The commission was to continue in force indefinitely.[19] Headed by the Earl of Dorset, who was

(London, 1860), p. 88, and partially in Sainsbury, "Virginia in 1628," *Virginia Magazine*, VII (January 1900), 259. The Virginia reply was received in July.

[14] See note 11 above.

[15] Cf. George Louis Beer, *Origins of the British Colonial System, 1578–1660* (New York, 1908), p. 309.

[16] Kingsbury, *Records*, IV, 490.

[17] Rymer, *Foedera*, XVIII, 72.

[18] Abstract by Sainsbury, "Virginia in 1631," *Virginia Magazine*, VIII (July 1900), 33, and in full in Rymer, *Foedera*, XIX, 301.

[19] Actually it was superseded by Laud's commission in 1634.

Lord Chamberlain to the Queen, its membership included Danvers, Wyatt, Sir Dudley Digges, John and Nicholas Ferrar, and George Sandys,[20] apparently as its Secretary.[21] Though by no means all of the committee were of the old faction, none of their leading opponents served.[22] The result might have been expected. The commissioners' report was in favour of reincorporating the Virginia Company, though this time as a trading body only, the government being reserved for the Crown. The King was to appoint a "President and Council" to govern the plantation from England, much as the Company's Council had done, though with appeal to the King or Privy Council much more easily made. Also there was to be a Governor and Council in Virginia as heretofore, again to be nominated by his Majesty. The report asked finally for "recompense" for the governing body and permission to confer at once with his Majesty's Attorney-General for the legalizing of the measure.[23] The recommendations are signed by eleven men, George Sandys' signature appearing last.

The matter was considered seriously. But the opposition was still very much alive. Among the surviving papers on the subject is a list of seven considerations against the proposal. Most of them appeal to the King's fears of such things as loss of revenue or spirits refractory to "monarchicall government." And there is what now seems the absurd contention that since Ireland had no corporation government, Virginia should not.[24] This last seems especially fallacious when one recalls that the Bermuda Company still existed and that the Massachusetts Bay colony charter of 1629 was in essence the same as the old Virginia charter.[25] The most nearly valid objection, that the planters themselves opposed a new charter, is open to grave doubt, certainly as to how the majority of the colonists felt.

At any rate, the commission's proposal was rejected. Apparently at about the same time, in 1631, the King considered the governing of Virginia and other plantations by a sub-committee of the Privy Council, an idea actually put into effect a few years later. It seems to have been in

20 Sainsbury, "Virginia in 1631," p. 33.

21 See below.

22 Though Samuel Wrote was a member. See Chapters V and VI above.

23 Sainsbury, "Virginia in 1631," pp. 38–9.

24 *Ibid.*, pp. 41–3.

25 W. F. Craven, *The Southern Colonies in the Seventeenth Century* ([Baton Rouge,] 1949), p. 151 admits this, and suggests also that but for the "bitter factionalism" still dividing the Virginia adventurers the charter might have been renewed.

1631 that Sandys, who probably knew of the King's thoughts on the colonial situation through his own Court connections, petitioned[26] his Majesty that he might be appointed Secretary to this proposed committee.[27] For, said Sandys, his ripest years had been spent in Virginia in the public service under King James. He called attention to the fact that already he had received a favourable answer to his petition to be nominated Secretary "when the King heretofore appointed a President and Council for the affairs of that colony."[28] With the new position he would be glad, he assured his sovereign, to accept any monetary allowance the King chose to make.

The position of Sandys' name at the end of the report of 1631 commission recommending restoration of the Company perhaps indicates that he had been secretary of the group, as the personal petition also seems to suggest. There is no evidence that Sandys' request was complied with in 1631, for there was no such committee then appointed. In 1634, however, the famous Laud commission for the government of the plantation was chosen. Its personnel was identical with that of a standing committee of the Privy Council for the plantations appointed the same year,[29] composed of the highest officials of church and state. Since all these people were busy with many affairs other than colonial, a number of men of lower rank but greater experience, as had been customary in the government at least since 1622,[30] were appointed as a subordinate advisory body. These men were known as the "subcommissioners," or sometimes as "the subcommittee for foreign plantations." To this working board George Sandys was appointed, again probably as secretary. He signed its extant reports of 15 and 27 July 1638,[31] and of 30 July[32] and 18 August 1639,[33] dealing with such

[26] Abstracts of his petition appear in Sainsbury, "Virginia in 1631," p. 43, and Sainsbury, *Calendar State Papers*, p. 138. The two abstracts include somewhat different valuable details. The date is questioned in the *Calendar* but given quite simply as 1631 in the *Virginia Magazine*.

[27] Or to any other body of government officers subordinate to them, Sandys says.

[28] Sainsbury, *Calendar of State Papers*, p. 138.

[29] Beer, *Origins*, pp. 214–15.

[30] *Ibid.*, p. 315 n.

[31] Sainsbury, "Virginia in 1638," *Virginia Magazine*, X (April 1903), 428 and XI (July 1903), 46–7.

[32] Sainsbury, "Virginia in 1639–40," *Virginia Magazine*, XIII (April 1906), 375.

[33] Grant and Munro edd., *Acts of the Privy Council, Colonial, 1613–1680*, I, 263–4.

problems as adequate storehouses at Jamestown, the Virginia estate of Sir Thomas Gates,[34] and the advisability of selling the Northern Neck of Virginia to the Bermuda Company. In the first three of these documents his name appears last, in the fourth next to last.[35]

At about the time Sandys was signing the last of these extant documents, his old friend Sir Francis Wyatt was appointed Governor of Virginia for a second term. Always popular in the colony, Wyatt was welcomed especially following the scandalous and troubled governorship of Sir John Harvey.[36] Wyatt assumed office in November 1639, exactly eighteen years after the beginning of his first term. The wheel of fortune had again turned, for Harvey, one of the commissioners to investigate Virginia affairs in 1624, had remained a symbol of the anti-Company faction in the affairs of the colony. With Wyatt the atmosphere at least of Virginia under the Company returned. Vigorous measures were taken to limit the growing of tobacco,[37] an Old Company policy, and to render powerless the Harvey "old Commission" faction.[38]

[34] See note 8 above. The only known signatures of Sandys at this period other than on the committee reports are those appearing on his answers to queries in the lawsuit regarding Gates's property. See Dawber *vs.* Clayborne, P.R.O., C. 24/629/32, 22 June 1638. Sandys recounted what he remembered of Captain Roger Smith's enjoyment of the Gates property. Wyatt was also a witness.

[35] These were small working committees. The report of 15 July 1638 was signed by Lord Goring, Sir William Becher [*sic*], Joseph Jacob, Sir Abraham Dawes, Edward Nicholas, and George Sandys, in this order. That of 27 July was signed by the same people, omitting Nicholas and Dawes and adding Sir Dudley Carleton and T. Meautys, Sandys again being last signer. Sir William Becker [*sic*], Abraham Williams, Sir Francis Wyatt, and George Sandys, in this order, signed the report of 30 July 1639. Lord Goring, Sir William Becher, Sir Abraham Dawes, Sir Abraham Williams, George Sandis, Esqr., Tho. Meautys Esqr., in this order, signed the report of 18 August 1639. Nicholas and Meautys were clerks of the Privy Council (Beer, *Origins*, p. 315 n.).

[36] Sainsbury, "Virginia in 1639–40," *Virginia Magazine*, XIII (April 1906), 381 n.

[37] *Ibid.*, pp. 381–2. Letter of 25 March 1640 from Sir Francis Wyatt to ——.

[38] *Ibid.*, pp. 382–3. Letter of 20 March 1639 from Richard Kemp, Secretary of the colony under Harvey and for a time under Wyatt. Kemp charges that "Since ye late change by ye arrivall of new Govr was Sir Francis Wiate, They of the old Commission have bene persecuted with much malice, the weight whereofe hath hitherto principallye fallen upon Sr John Harvey whose estate is wholly sequestered att p^{r}sent and att the next Court now approaching will assuredly be swept away." Harvey and his Council had defended Kemp in a delicate matter (see *ibid.*, pp. 386–7) and Kemp and Harvey were close personal friends. Kemp "escaped" to England in 1640 (see Grant and Munro, edd.,

Wyatt called a General Assembly soon after his arrival.[39] Both Governor and representatives realized that the Harvey-Kemp faction had friends at Court. Desiring themselves to have a personal representative in England who was well acquainted in the Privy Council, the General Assembly elected, or chose in some other fashion, George Sandys as agent for the colony. Of course the appointment must have been largely at Wyatt's suggestion. From the Governor's point of view it could hardly have been bettered. Perhaps Sandys did not even find it necessary to resign from the subcommittee on the plantations. At any rate, he knew Virginia and the Privy Council and the King.

The new agent was to be paid liberally. Good Virginia tobacco to the amount of 4,102 pounds[40] was authorized as his remuneration for his trouble. Evidently the Assembly expected Sandys to earn his salary, for it knew the political pot was boiling. The anti-Company faction in England, listening to the disgruntled comments of former Governor Harvey and former Secretary Kemp, was determined to get rid of Wyatt almost as soon as he assumed office. They were at least partially successful. As early as August 1641 a patent had been issued for Sir William Berkeley to succeed to the governorship.[41] This was followed on 30 October, however, by a strong petition to the House of Lords from the Reverend Anthony Panton, minister from Virginia and agent for the church in the colony, begging that Berkeley be held in England until the complaints against Harvey *et al.* be satisfied. Panton further claimed that machinations against Wyatt and in favour of Berkeley were all the work of the Harvey faction, which did not want the Wyatt government to complete its task of cleaning house and restoring property.

Acts of the Privy Council, Colonial, I, 284). For a good survey of Harvey's terms in Virginia see Wertenbaker, *Virginia Under the Stuarts*, pp. 64 ff.

39 There were Assemblies in October 1639 and in January 1639/40 (McIlwaine, ed., *Journal*, p. xxxvii). Though it has been suggested (*ibid.*) that Sandys was appointed by the October group, it is more likely, if Sir Francis Wyatt did not assume office until November, that Sandys was chosen by the January group. The record of the proceedings of the latter do not survive (except for a brief list of 34 "Acts" in W. W. Hening, *Statutes at Large*, I, 225–9) and only a few references to the former's records remain. Allusions to Sandys' appointment mention only 1639 (McIlwaine, ed., *Journal*, p. 66). An entry of 14 October 1640 (McIlwaine, ed., *Minutes*, p. 472) states that Sandys' "pay" was "given unto him by the last Grand Assembly."

40 McIlwaine, ed., *Minutes*, p. 472. The "levy" of tobacco was to be collected by the high sheriff of Charles River County.

41 Leo Francis Stock, ed., *Proceedings and Debates of the British Parliaments respecting North America* (5 vols, Washington, D.C., 1924–41), I, 125 n.

Berkeley was stayed by order of the Lords.[42] Appearing before the upper house on 3 November, Berkeley claimed that his commission was not an evidence of prejudice against Sir Francis Wyatt, the latter's "time being near expiring."[43] Also he asserted that he had entered into an agreement with George Sandys, as Sir Francis' representative, to protect the interests of Wyatt and his friends.[44] The Lords ordered both Berkeley and Sandys to appear before them the next day with the documents of the case.[45] Actually counsel for both sides was heard on 5 November,[46] Sandys representing Wyatt.[47] Berkeley was allowed to proceed. His principal arguments had been that he had obtained letters patent from his Majesty, and that Wyatt's patent was "but *durante beneplacito.*" Berkeley assumed office in Virginia in February 1641/2.[48]

For the remainder of Sandys' activity as Virginia agent the evidence is indirect and confusing. His actions themselves and his motives for them have never been exactly explained. Apparently at some time in 1640 he presented a petition to the House of Commons, *not* to the King, requesting a renewal of the colony's rights enjoyed under the old Company and making the petition also a request for the restoration of the charters of incorporation of the Company. The first General Assembly under Berkeley, meeting in 1641/2, addressed a "Declaration against the Company"[49] to "authorities" in England, declaring that Sandys

[42] Leo Francis Stock, ed., *Proceedings and Debates of the British Parliaments respecting North America* (5 vols., Washington, D.C., 1924–41), I, 125 n.

[43] *Ibid.*

[44] *Ibid.*, and Wertenbaker, *Virginia Under the Stuarts*, p. 86.

[45] Stock, ed., *Proceedings*, I, 126, 128.

[46] *Ibid.*, p. 128.

[47] Evidently Sandys was counsel, not simply witness, for Wyatt. If so, of course, here is further indication of Sandys' legal training and practice as a lawyer. In the entry of 5 November (Stock, p. 128) Sandys is not mentioned by name. The order for the hearing dated 4 November, reads: "the cause between Sir William Berkeley and Sir Francis Wyatt shall be heard by their counsel tomorrow, when this house [the Lords] sits; and that Mr. George Sandys (appearing on the behalf of the said Sir Francis Wyatt) shall be heard what he can say in his behalf. . . ."

[48] Sainsbury, "Virginia in 1639–40," p. 381 n.

[49] McIlwaine, ed., *Journals*, pp. 66–9, and W. W. Hening, *Statutes at Large*, I, 230–6. This is the only evidence of Sandys' presentation of the petition. Unfortunately Sandys' instructions do not survive. One should note that Wyatt, waiting for his return home, appears as one of the signers of this document as a member of the Council under Berkeley. Of course the signature by no means indicates personal agreement. Ella Lonn, *Colonial Agents of the Southern Colonies* (Chapel Hill, 1945), p. 14 and Alexander Brown, *English Politics in*

had mistaken his instructions, for neither Assembly nor "inhabitants" wished the Company in any sense.

This "Declaration" has resulted in many surmises as to what Sandys actually did, and, in case he was in deliberate error, in some attempt at interpretation of his motives. The situation appears complex. Loyal courtier that he was, Sandys apparently was being supported in this appeal to Parliament rather than to King by the Pym political group[50] in the House of Commons. No one can say, however, that this appeal and its supporters showed Sandys as anti-royalist. For that Cavalier of Cavaliers, Lucius Cary, was also at this period still working whenever possible with Pym.[51] No, Sandys was almost surely representing the feelings of Sir Francis Wyatt, old Virginia Company adventurers in England, himself, and perhaps also the particular Virginia Assembly which had authorized his appointment as agent. One must remember that it is Berkeley's, not Wyatt's, Assembly which repudiated his action. And at the same time one should recall from the chapters above discussing the Sandys-Wyatt 1621–5 Virginia years, that the General Assembly apparently took its tone or direction, if not what is tantamount to orders, from the Governor and the key figures of his Council.[52] In other words, the Assembly of 1641/2 may have repudiated the action of the Assembly of 1639/40, which action Sandys had merely presented, and to avoid further enquiry simply charged Wyatt's agent with a mistake. That the legislature was not and had not always been of one mind is admitted by Berkeley's Assembly in the second paragraph of the "Declaration," a section which mentions that the present (*i.e.*, 1641/2) Assembly has "full debated and maturely considered the reasons on both sides. . . ."

Undoubtedly there were strong convictions among the planters from both points of view. Certainly many colonists feared for their private land patents under a corporation, and feared monopolies on trade and

Early Virginia History (Boston, 1901), pp. 102–3 state that the Commons actually passed a resolution authorizing revival of the patent rights of the London Company. Perhaps Brown is Professor Lonn's source. His source is not clear.

50 Craven, *Southern Colonies*, pp. 225–6. And perhaps also, as may be indicated by Panton's petition regarding Wyatt in office, by the established church in Virginia.

51 Murdock, *The Sun at Noon*, pp. 149 ff.

52 The fight for a freedom of Assembly by the colonists, though supported by Berkeley and certain other governors, was most strongly urged in Wyatt's first administration (see Chapter VII above), as was the limitation of tobacco planting. For the acts against tobacco in 1639/40, see Hening, *Statutes at Large*, I, 225–9.

provisions. The "Declaration" seems also a Royalist hit at "popular" or parliamentary government in the controls exercised over the colony from the mother country. In certain clauses it attacks the democratic dissensions of the old Company. If the Company be restored, it declares:

> We shall degenerate from the condition of our birth being naturalized under a monarchical government and not a popular and tumultuary government,[53] depending upon the greatest number of votes of persons of several humours and dispositions as this of a company must be granted to be from whose general quarter courts all laws binding the planters here did and would again issue. . . .[54]

On the other hand, as further evidence that a strong group of planters were in favour of a Company, the same document declares that hereafter any planter advocating such a corporation shall be held as an enemy to the colony and shall forfeit his estates within its boundaries.[55] Strong measures come only to repress strong convictions.

One cannot say, however, that Sandys or any other old Company adherent might not have deliberately and wrongfully interpreted a petition for the privileges enjoyed under the former corporation just as Sandys did. Whether deliberately or inadvertently mistaken, or not mistaken at all, Sandys took a step entirely consistent with his political and colonial attitude during the two decades of his close relation to the colony. Devoted personal servant of the King that he was, he had independence[56] and strength of mind enough, in his old age when his body was failing, to make one more strong move for his idea, perhaps ideal, of colonial government. His brother Sir Edwin had been dead almost a dozen years, but the Sandys faction still thought it knew how Virginia should be governed. Its members may have been thinking primarily of

[53] These same arguments had been used, at least by implication, against the Company and Sir Edwin Sandys' ideas of government in the period of the "dissolution," and one must admit with considerable justice.

[54] McIlwaine, ed., *Journal*, p. 67. Lonn, *Colonial Agents*, p. 14, says flatly that the Assembly yielded to "Berkeley's strong influence" in declaring its opposition to the renewal of the old charter. On the other hand, the passage quoted above, however much of the tone of English politics of the year 1640 it may have, would have represented equally well some of the 1623–4 arguments against the Company.

[55] McIlwaine, ed., *Journal*, p. 68.

[56] Charles I, of course, had finally decided that he was opposed to the re-establishment of the Company. Perhaps he may always have been. See Lonn, *Colonial Agents*, pp. 15 and 15 n.

THE PARISH CHURCH AT BOXLEY, IN KENT, IN WHICH GEORGE SANDYS IS BURIED

Through the courtesy of the Rev. Thomas E. Prichard, formerly Rector

their own purses, but a survey of the careers of Edwin Sandys and Francis Wyatt and George Sandys does not so indicate.

For another reason it is unfortunate that most of the records of this second Wyatt administration have disappeared. The "liberal" inclinations or actions of the Wyatt faction in matters of freedom of assembly and self-government might then be considered in some detail. One can point out only that thirty-five years later, although certain conditions may have changed considerably, it was opposition to this same Governor Berkeley and his policies that produced the "Torchbearer of the Revolution,"[57] Nathaniel Bacon.

At any rate George Sandys, America's first poet writing in English, was a public servant in or for the colony of Virginia for twenty years. Resident official, expert adviser on colonial affairs to the Privy Council, agent for Virginia, he was one of England's first civil servants who were specialists in the affairs of a particular colonial territory.

By 1639 Sandys was spending most of his leisure months of the year in Kent rather than in the Midlands. The growing political troubles had disrupted the Falkland group. And perhaps Sir Francis Wyatt had asked his trusted friend and relative to assume charge of his family while he was in America. Whitefriars probably continued to be his London address.[58] Thomas Fuller, preaching in the Savoy in 1641, saw the poet, "a youthful soul in a decayed body,"[59] in his congregation. But Boxley Abbey in Kent, the Wyatt family seat, became his refuge after the London season. The rest-and-rural period must have extended over a great proportion of the year as civil troubles mounted and Sandys' own health declined. The decayed body would certainly have been more comfortable at his niece's house than in lodgings in town.

Boxley Abbey is one of the quiet and beautiful spots in the garden of England. A few years after the poet's death, the clergyman Richard Baxter was shown by Lady Wyatt, on "the old Stone Wall in the Garden a Summer-house with this inscription in great golden Letters, that in that place Mr. G. Sandys *after his Travels over the World, retired himself for his Poetry and Contemplations*. And none are fitter to retire to God then such

57 See T. J. Wertenbaker, *Torchbearer of the Revolution, the Story of Bacon's Rebellion and Its Leader* (Princeton, 1940).

58 See Dawber *vs.* Clayborne, P.R.O., C. 24/629/32, dated 22 June 1638 for this address for Sandys.

59 *History of the Worthies of England*, ed. by P. A. Nuttall (3 vols., London, 1840), III, 434.

as are tired with seeing the vanities on Earth."[60] The frailty of man and the permanence only of God: these had been the poet-adventurer's themes during a varied life. Here at Boxley probably it was that he translated *Christ's Passion* and prepared *The Song of Solomon* for the press, and almost surely it was here that he completed his book on divinity.[61]

From this quiet place he looked out on the strife of his time and his younger relatives growing up in the midst of it. In these last years he saw one nephew, his namesake George Sandys, son of his brother Thomas, become rector of Willersley in Gloucestershire.[62] Two Sandys relatives, perhaps also his nephews, became Gentlemen of the Privy Chamber.[63] And he saw the sons of Sir Edwin and Sir Samuel dividing the family allegiance between Parliament and King on the field of battle. He must have been shocked at the behaviour of Colonel Edwin Sandys. For this son of Sir Edwin, with his Parliamentary followers, burst into Canterbury Cathedral and on leaving the precincts shot at the statue of Christ at the South-Gate.[64] And certainly he was grieved when the same Edwin was fatally wounded in a skirmish with Prince Rupert's troops at Powick Bridge near Worcester a few months later.[65] But he probably approved the raising of regiments of horse and foot for the King by other nephews, including another son of Sir Edwin and sons and grandsons of Sir Samuel.[66] For "dismissed from arms by an act of time," he had avowed his intention of serving his King as he was able.

In 1642 Sir Francis Wyatt returned home. The two men, aged not in

60 *Poetical Fragments* . . . (London, 1681), p. [A_8].

61 John Aubrey, *Brief Lives*, II, 212.

62 See *Historical Manuscript Commission, Fourth Report* (London, 1874), p. 110. Date 1641.

63 See Chapter VIII, note 5 above. "Robert Sandes" was sworn in 4 February 1639 and "William Sandes" on 2[5?] June 1640. Though there are several Sandyses with these Christian names eligible according to age, George's brother Sir Samuel had a son William (see Sandys, *The Family of Sandys*, II, Pedigree C) and his brothers Sir Edwin, Sir Myles, and Thomas each had a son Robert (*ibid.*, Pedigrees C and D) who seem the most likely candidates.

64 Dorothy Gardner, ed., *Oxinden Letters* (London, 1933), pp. 230 n and 256. See also Brown, *Genesis*, II, 994–5.

65 Murdock, *The Sun at Noon*, p. 226.

66 C. E. Long, *Diary of the Royal Army during the Great Civil War Kept by Richard Symonds* (Camden Society, 1859), pp. 11–12. All Sir Edwin's sons save one were on the Parliamentary side. See Brown, *Genesis*, II, 994.

years so much as in hard service, sat out the brief time yet allotted to them. Nearby as Dean of Rochester, and a frequent visitor as vicar of the Boxley church, was the scholar Walter Balcanqual, formerly King's chaplain and Master of the Savoy, evidently an old friend. Other cultivated gentlemen lived in the neighbourhood. The summer house at Boxley was perhaps not equal to the gardens of Great Tew, but there must have been good talk there.

But Time's winged chariot hurried even in quiet Kent. In his simple room[67] in the great manor house

> Blest with . . . a quiet mind,
> Content with little

George Sandys breathed his last in March 1643/4. On 7 March[68] he was buried in Boxley Church within the chancel near the door on the south side, a grave unmarked in his own century by any monument.[69] Sir Francis followed him within the chancel exactly five months later. The two empire-builders sleep together.

Since 1848 a handsome monument and a beautiful memorial window to the poet have been erected in the church.[70] Quite respectable verses on his death appeared in his own time, containing the usual flowery encomiums and the declaration that "His Memory" would come

> To be adored of all posterity.[71]

Of this the poet would rightly have been sceptical. He would probably much have preferred, after proper discounting, the simple but firmly asserted claim made in the Boxley parish register just above the date of

[67] The inventory of the will of Sir Francis Wyatt, taken on 17 September 1644 (Inventory of the Archdeaconry of Canterbury, Maidstone County Record Office, Book 70, Class 11, Box 11, ff. 640) lists as contents of "Mr. Sands his chamber a Bed—a chaire, a cupboard, a pair of andirons—tongs, & firepan."

[68] J. Cave-Brown, *History of Boxley*, p. 172 (entries in the Parish Register) and "Wyatt MSS.," no. 37, Earl of Romney, deposit in the British Museum.

[69] Aubrey (*Brief Lives*, II, 212) laments that "so sweet a swan should lie so ingloriously."

[70] Colonel George O. Sandys of Graythwaite Hall erected the window in 1911 under a bequest from Colonel Miles Sandys of Graythwaite. The monument was erected by a Mr. Matthew Montague in 1848. The complete inscription on it appears in Cave-Brown, p. 125 and in Hooper, I, xlix.

[71] Phillpot's Poems, 1646 (included in Hooper, I, lxviii–lxx).

his interment. It is in the hand of a parish clerk or perhaps of his friend Walter Balcanqual:

Georgius Sandys, *Poetarum Anglorum sui saeculi facile princeps*[72]

[72] Not Dryden alone of the next generation agreed with this. In the [anonymous] *Compleat History of Europe* (London, 5? vols., 1701–5?), II, 564, the writer closes his second volume (ending about 1642) with "Two Remarkables only," the death of "that Excellent Mathematician *Galilæi*" and the "other is the Death of George Sandys . . .," recognition of the two great men of Europe who died at this period.

APPENDIX A

George Sandys at Corpus Christi, Oxford

THAT George Sandys was associated with Corpus Christi College as well as St. Mary's Hall was suggested by Anthony à Wood (*Athenae Oxonienses* [London, 1817], III, 98 [original ed., 1691–2] but never made clear by him or other biographers. The present writer while visiting in Oxford in 1947 pursued the matter and made a few discoveries which appear to prove that Sandys was a scholar of Corpus Christi.

The battell, or buttery, books of neither St. Mary's nor Corpus Christi for this period seem to have survived. The records of St. Mary's Hall (later absorbed by its larger neighbour Oriel) largely disappeared with the disestablishment of the foundation (according to a letter to the present writer from Mr. J. W. Gough, Treasurer of Oriel, 23 May 1947. Mr. Gough does state that the register of matriculates and degrees with the Henry and George Sandys entries noted above in Chapter II survives). Mr. J. W. Wallace-Hudrill, Librarian of Corpus Christi, has assured me that in his college no battell-books prior to 1600 are known. Mr. Wallace-Hudrill very kindly, however, made available the seventeenth-century manuscript history of Corpus Christi by William Fulman. Fulman (Vol. II, n.p.) seems to have been working from battell-books then extant (see Thomas Fowler, *The History of Corpus Christi College* [Oxford, 1893], p. 434). He lists under "Diſcipuli" (as opposed to "Socii"): Edwin Sands Com̃on 1585./Sam. Sands Com̃on. 1580./ Henry Sands Com̃on. 1589./George Sands Com̃on 1589./Edwin Sands Comon [*sic*]. The date for the first Edwin Sandys, if it be the archbishop's son, is curious for he had received most of his degrees several years earlier. Fowler, p. 434–5, explains the date by saying he was either there as "an independent Master of Arts" or was "only battelling temporarily." Also, if Sir Samuel, the eldest son, did attend Oxford (he is not mentioned by J. Foster, *Alumni Oxonienses . . ., 1500–1714*, IV [Early Series, Oxford, 1892] nor by A. Clark. *Register*, II, Pt. IV) it would seem likely that he should have preceded Sir Edwin, who received his B.A. in 1579. The second Edwin is evidently the son of Myles Sandys of Latimer's and matriculated in 1609. Two leaves below, on the verso, Fulman gives a similar list. In the margin in what appears a late seventeenth-century hand (Fowler called it "Fulman's note"), opposite the names of Henry and George Sandys, are the words "Matric. of. S. Marie/Hall Dec. 5, 1589." Later in his biographical sketches of Corpus men, Fulman (Vol. III, folio 37, just below his notice of Sir Edwin) gives data on George Sandys, especially concerning his parentage, burial place at Boxley, and the Boxley Register burial entry regarding him. Then he writes:

> P. Matric. p. 641. Aul. B. Mar.
> Dec. 5, 1589
> Henr. Sands, Londinensis, Archi[*sic*] Episcopi fil. aet. 16.
> Georg. Sands. Eboracensis Archiep. fi . . aet. 11.
> But it seems they were Comm. at C.C.C. at
> lest had their tutor and Educat. there.
> *Ibid.* p. 221 C.C.C. [This may refer to the Buttery Book or to the entry of Nov. 13, 1609 for another Edwin Sandys immediately below.]

As Fowler, p. 435, points out, they may have originally matriculated at St. Mary's either because rooms were not yet available at Corpus, or because the number of Gentlemen-Commoners, limited by the Statutes of the Founder to six (Fowler, p. 43) was already full (there actually were at least six others who had matriculated in 1589 alone; see Fowler, p. 435). It is interesting that one President of Corpus, excusing himself for admitting more Commoners than the Statutes allowed, said that the extension was made "in favour of Lord Sondes" [perhaps of the Sondes, not Sandys, family]. The Gentlemen-Commoners, still limited to six and originally the sons of nobles or lawyers, were abolished as a class for admission in 1851 (see Fowler, p. 321).

Of the activities at St. Mary's Hall in this period little is known, although for a few years after 1579 it was the most popular Hall in the university (see C. E. Mallet, *A History of the University of Oxford*, Vol. II [London, 1924], p. 291), as indicated by the number of matriculates.

APPENDIX B

Sandys' Marriage

I. *Earlier statements regarding Sandys' marital status:*

From Anthony à Wood in *Athenae Oxonienses* to Sidney Lee in the *D.N.B.* biographers have either ignored the matter or stated that he was not married. Wood in *Athenae* (1817 ed., III, 97–103), Thomas Fuller in *Worthies* (1840 ed., III, 434), John Aubrey in *Brief Lives* (1898 ed., II, 212) ignore the matter. Henry J. Todd in *Selections from the Metrical Paraphrases* . . . [London, 1839], p. 38), J. Hall Pleasants, "Sandys of Furnace Fells," and Sidney Lee in *D.N.B.* mention the marriage contract drawn up by the parents (see below) but say the marriage did not take place (Todd says because Sandys refused to marry the lady). The Rev. Joseph Hunter in his MS. "Chorus vatum Anglicorum" (Pt. I, Br. Mus. Add. MSS. 24489 ff. 122b–3b), basing his statement on the "Torre MSS." states that Sandys married *Mary*, daughter of John Norton of Ripon (see below). The Rev. Richard Hooper (*The Poetical Works of George Sandys* [2 vols., London, 1872], I, li note), who used Hunter, still did not believe that Sandys ever married. The one positive statement that "he married and had two daughters" appears in *The New and General Biographical Dictionary* (1762, X, 250–1), and is probably based on a confusion of George Sandys with Sir George Sondes, or Sandes, K.B., who had two daughters, and was raised to the peerage in 1676 (see *Harleian Miscellany*, 1813 ed., X, 23–67). In 1937, however, Mr. Alexander McElwain of Needham, Massachusetts (now of the faculty of Boston University), in making some investigations regarding Sandys' life, noticed in the Yorkshire Archaeological Series (*Yorkshire Stuart Fines*), the names of "George Sandys and his wife Elizabeth" in the conveyance of several land titles. He saw the originals in the Public Record Office and certain other documents in the York Probate Registry and became convinced that this George Sandys was the poet. Since that time the present writer has been able to locate other documents which *prove* that this Sandys was the poet and that the marriage took place, as will be brought out in the discussion below.

II. *Absence of record of the marriage:*

The parish registers at Ripon, Richmond, Wath, Hutton Longvilliers, and Bishopthorp have been examined (the first by the present writer, the others by the clergymen in charge of the respective parishes). Usually there are no extant records of the period, and it is therefore quite possible that they were married in one of these places in which they owned property. Of course there is always the possibility of confusion of one George Sandys with another. For example, in the Registry of the Bishop of London for 13 May 1598 is the entry of intention to marry of a "George Sandys of St. Mary Woolchurch, London [Yeoman], & Millicent Gouldsburne, of Hackney, Mdx., widow . . ." (see R. Glencross, *Calendar of Marriage License Allegations in the Registry of the Bishop of London, 1597–1648* [London, 1937], p. 2, or George J. Armitage, ed. *Allegations for Marriage Licenses Issued by the Bishop of London* [2 vols., London, 1887], I, 249.)

III. *Legal documents other than those discussed in text* (see pp. 34–41 above) *affording proof of Sandys' marriage to Elizabeth Norton before 1602*: (These documents also offer evidence of George Sandys' whereabouts in the 1602–9 period.)

(1) Conveyance, Easter Term 44 Eliz. [1602] (P.R.O., Yorkshire Feet of Fines, C.P. 25[2]/258), showing "George Sandes, gentleman, & Elizabeth his wife" making over 2 messuages and various other lands "with appurtenances" in Memerley, Wath, and Hutton to Richard Manne and Christopher Walker, the consideration being £120 sterling to George and Elizabeth.

(2) Conveyance, 3 Jas. I [10 June 1605] (P.R.O., Close Roll, 3 Jas. I, Pt. 17. C. 54/1815) by "George Sandys of London, esq." and Sir Myles Sandys to Salomon Browne of Clyffordes Inn of the messuage in the parish of Rypon, co. York, late in the occupation of Christofer Bawcome or Bateman, now in the occupation of George Mallory or Anthony Taylor. George promises to keep the property free of all charges and grants. He only, not Sir Myles, receives £130.

(3) Indenture, 3 Jas. I [24 June 1605] (P.R.O. Close Roll, 3 Jas. I, Pt. III, m. 2d.), made between Thomas Spencer and Thomas Porter on the one part and Sir Myles Sandys and "George Sandys of Ripon co. York esq." on the other. Spencer and Porter, in performance of a trust from the late Archbishop Sandys, confirm to Myles and George, and to the heirs of George, the "three messuages . . . [etc. etc.] in Rippon, Gyvendale and Sawley which late were the inheritance of John Norton." They had been conveyed by John Sawmon [Salmon] and Anne his wife to Spencer and Porter. Spencer and Porter also convey a messuage in Thorpe near Ripon, formerly in the possession of Thomas Markenfield

attainted for treason. Grant made to the use of Myles and George Sandys and of the heirs of George for ever.

(4) Conveyance, Trin. Term 4 Jas. I [1606] (*Yorkshire Fines for the Stuart Period*, LIII, p. 53), of two messuages of land in Thorpe, Rippon, and Bondgate to John Watson by Myles and George Sandys and Elizabeth, George's wife.

(5) Conveyance, 5 Jas. I [25 November 1607] (P.R.O., Close Roll, 5 Jas. I, Pt. 9. C. 54/1886) from "George Sandys of London esquire and Elizabeth his wife" to Cuthbert Best and Cuthbert Pudsey of Stapelton, co. York. For "a certain sum" all capital messuage or tenement in Gyvendale formerly in occupation of George and Elizabeth his wife, Sir William Gascoigne K^t^, and William Norton and William Calverley, and also messuages in Rippon, co. York, formerly in tenure of Raphe Hutchinson, and also all buildings, lands, etc., appertaining to them "in Gevendale, Thorpe and Rippon, which premises are now the inheritance of George and Elizabeth or one of them."

(6) Final concord, Trin. Term. 6 Jas. I [1608] (P.R.O. and *Yorkshire Stuart Fines*, LIII, p. 87), between Cuthbert Best and Cuthbert Pudsey on the one hand and Georges Sandes gent. and Elizabeth his wife on the other, of lands, etc., in Gevendale and Rippon. George and Elizabeth acknowledge the right of Best and Pudsey and quit-claim them, etc. For this acknowledgment, remission, quit-claim, warranty, fine and agreement, they gave George and Elizabeth £100 sterling. (That George and Elizabeth were acting together does not indicate necessarily or at all that they were still living together.)

IV. *Legal documents proving that Elizabeth Sandys was alive and active in litigation in 1662:*

As late as this year 1662, Elizabeth Sandys was involved in chancery, this time with the descendants of her relatives and friends, regarding the income from the same property she had sued her husband for a half-century and more earlier. It is a long story. In 1614, to Christopher Aiscoughe, quer., by Francis Tunstall, Cuthbert Pudsey, Cuthbert Best, def., a messuage, watermill and lands in Geevendale and Thorpe were transferred (Easter Term, *Yorkshire Fines for the Stuart Period*, LVIII [1917], p. 13). In the same year the manor of Hutton Longvilliers and 10 messuages, etc., were transferred from Nichs. Girlington to Francis Tunstall (Michaelmas Term, *Yorkshire Fines*, LVIII, p. 23). This is made clear in an indenture of 4 April 1617 (P.R.O., Close Roll, Tunstall *vs.* Mallory & others, C. 54/2325), in which the story is retold of how the messuage in Gevendale, watermill near Ripon, etc., passed through the hands of George Sandys, to Sir William Gascoigne, William Norton, and William Calverley, to Christopher Aiscoughe (in return for "£600 paid to Francis Tunstall"). Tunstall, for the £600 and £400 more paid by Gascoigne, Norton, and Calverley, granted to William Mallory and William Staveley (Elizabeth Norton Sandys' kinsmen) "a yearly rent of £100 issuing from the manor of Huton [*sic*] Longvilliers . . . and from the lands ∝ c. there to hold immediately after the death of Francis Tunstall for eighty years for the maintenance ∝ livelihood of the said Elizabeth Sandes if she so long live." The money was to be paid twice yearly to "Mallorie" and Staveley at Trinity Church, Richmond. Mention is made specifically that Gascoigne, Norton, and Calverley had secured the property "by Indenture of demise to them made by George Sandes, late of Ripon, co. York, Esq."

In 1618 Elizabeth Norton added to her capital by quit-claiming the Sawley property (for which George had years earlier sued her relatives, as noted in Chapter II, above) to her cousin William Norton for £500. It is not entirely clear whether this is in addition to the £600 Norton had been bonded to pay her earlier. This 1618 document is "A Final Agreement" (P.R.O., Feet of Fines, Yorkshire, 16 Jas. I, File I, C.P. 25[2], Bundle 382), which seems to imply that Elizabeth had gone to court to squeeze an additional return from the property.

In 1662 Elizabeth found herself again involved in none too savoury a fashion. William Tunstall, grandson of Francis, complains (P.R.O., Chancery Proceedings, Bridges Division, C. 5/634/81, 19 June 1662) that Elizabeth continues to demand the £100 yearly according to the agreement made in his grandfather's time, even though for a consideration of £500 from the late Marmaduke Tunstall, son of Francis, she had signed a deed of release on 6 March, 14 Charles I. "Elizabeth Sandes in the lifetime of Francis Tunstall got many of the deeds in her hand, including the said release, but has offered to deliver the said statute for £10, 'to relieve her present necessity.'" Now she combines "with one Richard Taylor" to have the statute acknowledged. The complainant begs that they may be caused to appear and answer the same.

APPENDIX C

Belon as a Typical Example of Sandys' Use of Sources in *A Relation*

(For the first reference to Belon above, see Chapter III, note 30.)

Pierre Belon was one of several French sixteenth-century commentators on the Near East. His *Les Observations de plusieurs singularitez & choses memorables trouvees en Grece, Asie, Indee, Egypt, Arabie, & autres pays etranges, redigées en trois livres* . . . appeared in Paris in 1553 (1554, 1555, etc.). Sandys in Book I of *A Relation*, as always when he could, probably used the Latin version (he uses the Latin form of the author's name, Bellonius, though this may mean nothing), which appeared in 1589 and 1605 as . . . *Plurimarum singularum & memorabilum rerum in Græcia, Asia, Aegypto* . . . [Antwerp]. Belon affords a good example of Sandys' use of sources. Sometimes Sandys makes reference to Belon by name and sometimes he does not acknowledge his indebtedness in any way. Belon is probably a direct source for the Hero and Leander reference (*A Relation*, p. 25; Belon, French version of 1554, p. 77); the costumes of the Merry Greekes (*A Relation*, p. 74; Belon, p. 83); and possibly (in part) for the discussion of the pirates (*A Relation*, p. 89; Belon, p. 84); the crocodile (though there are also other sources, *A Relation*, p. 101; Belon, p. 103); pyramids, sphinx, etc. Sandys acknowledges "Bellonius" as a source for the description of the later Troy (as noted above, Belon, pp. 80–2), and of one account of the number of doors on the mosque of Sancta Sophia (*A Relation*, p. 31). In this early section of the book also Sandys admits his indebtedness to Eusebius Pamphili, Pausanias, and Zuallardo. In the same section he uses without acknowledgment such authors as Busbecq, Botero, Dousa, Gillius, Pliny, and Strabo. His authors in turn use more ancient authority. For further details of his sources, see text and notes on Chapters III and IV above.

APPENDIX D

Sandys' Travelling Companions from Cairo to Jerusalem

Though Sandys does not mention the names of any of his party (see Chapter III, text and note 110 above)—they have recently been published from an unexpected source, along with undeniable proof that Sandys himself visited Jerusalem. In 1938, in *Palästina-Hefte, Des Deutschen Vereins vom HL. Lande*, XII–XIV, under the title "Navis Peregrinorum, Ein Pilgeiverzeidnis au Jerusalem vom 1561 bis 1695," P. D. D. Zimolong published from the register of the monastery of San Salvatore at Jerusalem, the list of pilgrims who rested there. In 1611, under entry of 1 April (evidently the date of departure rather than arrival—see Chapter IV), are the names of the seven (in this order),

D. Mattheus Carbonus Medicus territorii Pashue.
R. D. Renaldus de Tortis a Mola Apuliae Sac.
Annibal Albinellus de Mutina.
D. Georgius Sandys.
D. Nathaniel Butler.
D. Gulielmus Burton.
D. Georgius Perch.
} Angli

The record transcribed was in a later seventeenth century hand (probably beginning about 1633—see Zimolong, p XI) from an earlier copy. Therefore there is a possibility of error in spelling. George Perch has not been even conjecturally identified. Nathaniel Butler may possibly be Sandys' later successful rival for the governorship of Bermuda, a man who also visited Virginia in Sandys' time (see above, and *D.N.B.* and Brown, *Genesis*, II, 836). Butler was at one period a captain in the Royal Navy. William Burton may be the older brother (1575–1645) of Robert Burton (who used Sandys' *Relation* frequently in his *Anatomy of Melancholy*), and himself author of the *Description of Leicestershire* (1662). William Burton was admitted to the Inner Temple in 1593. He was a good Royalist, and an antiquarian friend of Sir Robert Cotton. Such a tour as this to Jerusalem is not mentioned in the published accounts of the lives of either Butler or Burton, however.

The "Navis Peregrinorum" is one of two external proofs that Sandys made his tour. In his own century, one antiquary expressed in a letter some doubt that Sandys made this journey at all, basing his disbelief on the derivative plates in Book III, and certain sections of the texts of which the doubter possessed the Latin and Italian sources. See E. M. Thompson, ed., *Letters of Humphrey Prideaux . . . to John Ellis* (Camden Society, 1875), pp. 19–20. The date of Prideaux's letter was 17 September [16]74.

APPENDIX E

The Will and Epitaph of Cicely Sandys

A brief printed abstract of Cicely Sandys' will appears in *Virginia Magazine*, XXIX (April 1921), 234–5. The will is undated, but a codicil is dated 17 January 1610/11, and it was probated 12 February 1610/11. Edwin and Myles Sandys, favoured (next to Samuel, the oldest) legatees of the Archbishop himself, received from their mother only £100 each. Thomas and Henry, as George, received £200, and later in the codicil another £100 each was added to the portions of Thomas and Henry. Among other beneficiaries were Dame Katherine, wife of Sir Edwyn; Dame Anne Barne, Cecily Sandys' daughter; Mary, daughter of Sir Samuel; and Anne Barne and Margaret Aucher, also granddaughters; Sir Anthony Aucher, her grandson; Bridget Sandys, who waited on Cecily Sandys, her son Henry's daughter; and several servants. Cicely mentions that she has brought up several of her grandchildren. If the letter of this will was adhered to, it is possible that George did not receive the £200 (see Chapter V, text and note 1 above) for his return may have been later than February 1612. In all probability, however, he was back in England by this time. Sir Samuel Sandys in 1619 erected a monument to his mother (see E. S. Sandys, *The Family of Sandys*, I, 181), with an epitaph beginning:

> "Cecilie Sandys, daughter of Thomas Wilford, of Cranbrook in Kent, Esqre,. sister to ye worthie souldiers Sir James Wilford and Sir Thomas Wilford, was wife to Edwin Sandys, Archbishop of Yorke, who died in great honour on the year 1588, when he had lived full 70 yeares. . . . She bore 7 sons and 2 daughters. She led a most Christian and holy life, carefully educated her children, wisely governed hir familye, charatably relieved the poore, and was a true mirror of a Christian matron. She dep'ted this life constant in Christian faith, ye 5th Feby 1610. At the rising of the sun her blessed soule ascended to the consort of the blessed, and hir bodie lyeth heer interred, expecting the joyful resurrection."

APPENDIX F

Sir Edwin Sandys and the Virginia Company

The relation of Sir Edwin Sandys to the development of the Virginia Company is discussed primarily in C. M. Andrews, *Colonial Period in American History* (4 vols., New Haven, 1934), I, 98–109, and in W. F. Craven, *Dissolution of the Virginia Company* (New York, 1932). Professor Craven's able study appears to be slightly coloured by a leaning over backward to correct the belligerent-"patriotic" interpretations of Brown in *Genesis of the United States* and other works. Professor Craven's interpretation remains primarily an economic one, though he himself insists that the whole "failure" of the enterprise is not to be explained purely in economic terms. To one who is fresh from re-examining all of his cited primary sources in England and America, Professor Craven appears to allow Sir Edwin Sandys too little credit in motives and methods. Though one must agree that Sir Edwin and his friends the Ferrars were over-hasty colonizers, Professor Craven is severe on them personally in many places where their mistakes would appear more reasonably to be charged to lack of experience (on the part of all Englishmen) in colonial enterprise. The student of the colonial problem will often be baffled in reading the *Dissolution* by the frequent failure to give references in support of many statements highly significant in "proving" the ineptitude of the Sir Edwin Sandys' administrative group. Professor Andrews agrees generally with Professor Craven as to the causes of the failure of the Company, but places less personal blame. Perhaps because it was so much over-emphasized elsewhere, neither of these scholars appears to have taken sufficiently (if at all) into consideration "seventeenth-century liberalism" (see Chapter VII, above, notes 69, 70, and text and Appendix G below) as a major factor in the determination of colonial policy under the Sandys administration. A fresh study of the same primary documents available to Professors Craven and Andrews, plus a thorough investigation of the so-called "liberalism" among certain groups in parliament, particularly the "liberalism" of Sir Edwin Sandys and others, as a vital factor in the story, might alter at least the picture of certain individuals and their relation to the enterprise. The present biographical study could not undertake such a task without exceeding its physical limit and announced purpose. The present note is designed to indicate only that such a study might be profitable.

APPENDIX G

"Liberalism" in the Virginia Company and Colony

Certain questions regarding the so-called "liberal movement" in the Virginia colony have been suggested in the text of Chapter VII above (pp. 175–9). Despite the discussions of Professors Andrews and Craven, many of these questions remain unanswered. Alexander Brown, now generally discredited, belligerently and rather naively had asserted before the work of Craven and Andrews that Sir Edwin and the Virginians held well-developed liberal ideas of the nineteenth-century brand. Professor Craven brushes Brown's claims aside on various grounds, partially through economic interpretation, and admits little or no "liberalism" in any recent sense of the term. He offers no real explanation, however, of Sir Edwin's or the General Assembly's constant struggle for a free government in the New World. Professor Perry Miller, in "The Religious Impulse in the Founding of Virginia: Religion and Society in the Early Literature" (*William and Mary Quarterly*, 3rd series, V [October 1948], 492–522, VI [January 1949], 24–41) gives a thoughtful and stimulating reappraisal partly based on his own studies of seventeenth-century religious ideas, but unfortunately relying too heavily on Professor Craven instead of the primary source materials, such as those available in Kingsbury, III and IV. "Religion . . . was the really energizing power in this settlement, as in others," is Professor Miller's thesis. Like New England, Virginia was the legatee of the Reformation. Professor Miller notes that Virginia, more "low" than "high" church, was close to the spirit of what is called Puritan, and one agrees wholeheartedly with his survey of the kind and extent of the piety of colonial Virginia, as with his conclusion at the end of the first half of his study (V, 522): "Just as religion and economics were fused into one conception in statements of the Company's aim, so within the original Virginia—the first permanent English settlement in the New World—the government was formed by a conscious and powerful intention to merge the society with the purposes of God." The statement that the General Assembly became "a republican and even a democratic engine . . . in spite of themselves [the Company and Sir Edwin Sandys' faction]" is more doubtful, and is presumably the result of Professor

Miller's avowed reliance on Professor Craven's and Professor Andrews' studies. One must agree that, though the reasons given (in the present text) for the continued request for liberty of the assembly were usually economic ones, it is not the first time that theories of liberty have been supported by or have sprung from economic factors. When the Virginia Assembly speaks of rights, it refers, Professor Miller says, to "the organized rights of Englishmen, exercised and protected in an elective assembly." This is the one experiment of the Virginia Company which could survive and be found useful after 1624, Professor Miller feels (though one may challenge this statement by a look at Virginia history in its relation to Sandys-faction agricultural policies). One does agree that it is the most important to the whole picture of American history.

No one of these three historians gives any weight to (only Craven really considers, and discredits to his own satisfaction) Captain John Bargrave's conversation with Sir Nathaniel Rich, of 16 May, 1623 (Kingsbury, IV, 194): ". . . there was not any man in the world that carried a more malitious hart to a Gouern^{t} of a Monarchie then ~~he~~ § S^{r} Ed. Sandys § did: for Capt. Bargrave had heard him say that if eu^{9} God from heaven did . . . constitute and direct a . . . forme of Gouern^{t} it was that of Geneua: And he hath oft tymes reprehended § Capt § Bargrave that in some § written § tractates of his, and his discourses [Bargrave was a notorious Divine-Right man] he seemed to dislike the constitution and frame of the § p∫̃nt § Gouern^{t} . . . of Virginia . . . as that w^{c}h inclines § vnto § if not directly beeing a popular Gouerm^{t}. he telling Capt. Bargraue that his intent was to erect a free state in Virginia and other wordϱ to that purpose . . . [to that intent Sir E.S. persuaded Achley Carterly to allow Brownists etc. to order] . . . and his other proceedinge in those businesses of the Plantac̃ons (especially such as concern gouerm^{t}) were looked vnto it would be found that he aymed at nothing ~~el~~ more then to make a free popular state there. . . ." The point here is not the trustworthiness of Bargrave's testimony, but the very fact that Sir Edwin is accused of such ideas shows how much they were in the air in 1621–5 and how they had been connected directly with the policies of the Virginia Company under the Sandys-Southampton regime. One must repeat that this is not nineteenth-century liberalism nor Jeffersonian democracy that Bargrave speaks of, but it certainly appears a step towards either or both. Because Alexander Brown assumed too much from this Bargrave testimony does not warrant its being cast entirely aside.

And, as suggested above (Chapters VII, X, pp. 174–85, 260–4), the part of Sir Francis Wyatt and George Sandys in supporting requests for freedom of assembly and/or for charter rights over a twenty-year period, in the colony and in England, remains to be explained fully in the light of their possible relationship to Sir Edwin Sandys and his career as a "liberal" member of Parliament. In other words, either more than "the natural rights of Englishmen" are involved, or Brown is more nearly right than Craven in believing that these "rights" and theories of right were the forerunners of a later liberalism.

APPENDIX H

Sandys and the King's Privy Chamber

I. *Was Sandys actually a Gentleman of the Chamber?*

That Sandys actually ever held the formal position of Gentleman of the King's Privy Chamber may perhaps be questioned on the basis that there is a scarcity of direct evidence. As far as the present writer is able to find, the only nearly-contemporary statement to this effect is made by Anthony à Wood (*op. cit.*, see Chapter VIII, note 5, above) late in the seventeenth century, that Sandys at the time of his death was "then or lately one of the gent. of the privy chamber to K. Ch. I." Eighteenth- and nineteenth-century writers seem merely to follow Wood. Earlier seventeenth-century biographers or commentators, as John Aubrey (*Lives*, [2 vols., Oxford, 1898, orig. ed. 1684?], II, 212), Thomas Fuller (*Worthies*, [3 vols., London, 1840, orig. ed. 1662], III, 434), and Richard Baxter, *Poetical Fragments* . . . (London, 1681), Introd., p. [A_8?]) do not mention that Sandys was ever officially connected with the Court.

A fairly thorough study of the records of the Royal Household in the Public Record Office fails to reveal Sandys' name. No official or unofficial list of the Gentlemen of the Chamber was discovered, however. There are records of the "swearing" [oath-taking] by certain new Gentlemen and of payments to some of them. These are among the Lord Chamberlain's Accounts. Unfortunately the 1626–8 volume of these accounts is missing. At the beginning of the next volume [for 1628–34] an entry of 28 March 1628 (P.R.O., L.C. 9/132/p.8) records the swearing of Sandys' friend "Wintoure Graunt Esq" as "A gent of ye Privy Chamber extraordinary." Similarly on 6 April 1630 his friend Thomas Carew was sworn (P.R.O., L.C. 5/132/p. 181); on 5 May 1631 his relative Richard Lovelace (P.R.O., L.C. 5/132/p. 24) a "gent waytor extraordinary"; on 26 February 1634/5 his friend Sidney Godolphin (P.R.O., L.C. 5/134/p. 45). Other names familiar in seventeenth-century history, as those of Sir Peter Killigrew, William Killigrew, and Sir John Suckling appear on this list. The names of others known to have been Gentlemen of the Chamber, as Lucius Cary, Lord Falkland, were not found, however.

On 4 February 1638/9 "Robert Sandes" was sworn a Gentleman of the Chamber (P.R.O., L.C. 5/134/p. 307) and on [25?] June 1640 "Wm. Sandes" (P.R.O., L.C. 5/134/p. 404) in the same capacity. Though the name of either might have been confused by Wood with George Sandys, there is every probability that George was a Gentleman of the Chamber. All his known friends at this period (see Chapter IX above) were members of the court circle, and as we have noted many others than those revealed by the records are known to have been Gentlemen of the Chamber.

II. *Duties of Gentlemen of the Chamber*

Charles I's "New Household Book" (P.R.O., L.C./5/180) dated in the 1620's, sets very definite regulations as to the duties of the members of the Royal Household. The Gentlemen were the only persons below the degree of Baron or Privy Councillor who might come within the King's "inner closett." They were required "to wait" during one of the four quarters of the year. During their waiting time they brought in the King's "meate," and four of them by turn lodged each night within the Privy Chamber. They might amuse themselves with chess or cards in the Presence Chamber, but were not to play "within the Privy Chamber." There were two sorts of Gentlemen of the Chamber, "in ordinary" and "extraordinary." Most of Sandys' friends belonged to the latter group. It has been claimed that "extra-ordinary" meant more-or-less honorary, and that the Gentlemen under this classification did not have to wait regularly. A list of the "in ordinary" group, P.R.O., S.P. 16/2/No. 118 (May–June 1625) shows out of 39 that 31 were knights. Three earls were sworn "of the bedchamber" before 21 July 1626 (Birch, *Court and Times of Charles I*, I, 132). Most of the "extra-ordinary" group were commoners without any titles whatsoever. This 1625 list also groups them by the quarters of the year in which they serve, as 1 January to 31 March, etc.

III. *Emoluments of Gentlemen of the Privy Chamber*

£200 per annum was probably the maximum "fee" paid to Gentlemen of the Chamber during Charles's reign. It appears in a Br. Mus. Add. MSS. 12, 512 "fee to every of them—200[ll] per Ann." In 1626 one list states specifically (Br. Mus. MSS., 12, 508–12,) that for the "Gentellmen of the privie Chamber . . . Noe fee nor allowance of the King," and somewhere between 1626 and 1636 another list (Br. Mus. MSS., Harleian 4706) shows their fee as £50 (though perhaps by quarter instead of year). The Gentlemen Ushers received only £30 per year, even according to the lists which show £200 for the Gentlemen of the Chamber. About 1624, in James's reign, the Gentlemen of the Chamber received £50, the Gentlemen Ushers £30 (Br. Mus. Miscellaneous Tracts, Sloane, 72 ff., 119).

APPENDIX I

Sandys and the Milton-Ovid Script

The matter of a "Milton-Ovid script," a problem in which Sandys' name was involved, was introduced by H. C. Candy in the *Times Literary Supplement* for 26 January 1922. His studies were set forth at length in *Notes and Queries*, ser. 12, XI and XII, beginning 9 September 1922. In 1924 appeared a book summarizing these studies as *Some Newly Discovered Stanzas written by John Milton on Engraved Scenes illustrating Ovid's Metamorphosis this Milton-Ovid Script was written, circa 1623; discovered 1922–3*. Shortly after the publication of the book, C. W. Brodribb, in *Notes and Queries*, 2 August 1924 (CXLVII, 77–8) stated his belief that the stanzas were written by someone who had read the 1632 edition of Sandys' version of the *Metamorphoses*, or even by Sandys himself. A review of Candy's book, *TLS*, 14 August 1924, is apparently from the same source. Mr. Candy replied in *N & Q*, 16 August 1924, disagreeing with the attribution to Sandys and reaffirming his belief in Milton as author. Candy's argument is far-fetched; especially are his arguments for handwriting not convincing. On the other hand, Sandys' known 1623 hand is not at all like the plates of this Ovid text. I agree generally with Mr. Brodribb that it shows knowledge of Sandys. But it is probably not at all by either Sandys or Milton.

BIBLIOGRAPHY

I. PRINTED EDITIONS OF THE WRITINGS OF GEORGE SANDYS

A. *Editions in England before 1700.* For a chronological listing and complete bibliographical description, with an introduction on "The Man and His Work" and "The Plan and Method [of the bibliography]" see Fredson Bowers and Richard Beale Davis, George Sandys: A Bibliographical Catalogue of Printed Editions in England to 1700, New York Public Library, 1950. The short titles and dates of these editions are:

1. A Relation of a Journey Begun Anno Dom. 1610. Folios: 1615, 1621, 1627, 1632, 1637, 1652, 1658, 1670, 1673.
2. Ovid's Metamorphosis. Folios: 1626, 1632, 1640. Duodecimos: 1621, 1623 (5 books), 1628 (unauthorized), 1638, 1656, 1664, 1669, 1678, 1690.
3. A Paraphrase upon the Psalmes of David. Octavo: 1636.
4. A Paraphrase upon the Divine Poems. Folios: 1638. Octavos: 1648, 1676.
5. Christs Passion [translated from Grotius]. Octavos: 1640 (2 issues), 1687, 1693.
6. A Paraphrase upon the Song of Solomon. Quartos: 1641, 1642.

Sandys' Psalms were also the verse-text in whole or part of: Henry Lawes, Choice Psalmes Put Into Music For Three Voices . . ., London 1648 (quarto).

Henry Lawes, Select Psalmes Of A New Translation, To be Sung in Verse and Chorus of five parts, with Symphonies of Violins, Organ, and other Instruments . . ., [London?] 1655.

Sandys' A Relation appeared in part in:

Purchas His Pilgrimes . . ., 4 vols., London 1625, pp. 1,274–1,333.

B. *Foreign Editions before 1700.* Some of these editions have engraved title-pages varying in wording from the letter-press title-page. The short titles here given are letter-press only.

1. Sandys Voyagien, Behelsende Een Historie van de Oorspronkelÿcke, Amsterdam 1653 (quarto).
2. Sandys Voyagien, Behelsende Een Historie van de Oorspronkelÿcke, Utrecht 1654 (quarto).
3. Sandys Voyagien, Behelsende Een Historie van de Oorspronckelÿcke, Amsterdam 1665 (quarto).

4. Sandys Reisen Inhaltende Die Histori von dem ursprünglichen, Frankfurt 1665 (duodecimo).

C. *Excerpts from His Writings, or Selections, in the Eighteenth and Nineteenth Centuries*

1. John Harris, Navigantium atque Itinerantium Biblioteca: or, A Compleat Collection of Voyages and Travels, 2 vols., London 1705 (folio). Lib. III, pp. 783–8, etc.
2. Henry John Todd, Selections from the Metrical Paraphrases on the Psalms and other . . . Portions of Holy Scripture, by G. Sandys, with a Memoir, London 1839.

D. *The Only Modern Edition of Sandys' Poems*, with a useful introduction and compilation of poems to and concerning him, omits the text of the *Metamorphosis*. Spelling has been modernized throughout.
Richard Hooper, The Poetical Works of George Sandys, 2 vols., London 1872.

E. *"Uncollected" Original Poems.* These have been printed with commentaries by the present writer in two articles:

1. "Two New Manuscript Items for a George Sandys Bibliography," Papers of the Bibliographical Society of America, XXXVII (3rd Quarter 1943), 215–22.
2. "George Sandys and Two Uncollected Poems," Huntington Library Quarterly, XII (November 1948), 105–11.

F. *Letters.* The only known letters from Sandys are reprinted in the present work from Susan Myra Kingsbury, ed., Records of the Virginia Company, 4 vols., Washington, D.C. 1906–35, IV, *passim.*

II. SIXTEENTH AND SEVENTEENTH CENTURY MANUSCRIPT MATERIALS RELATING TO SANDYS' LIFE AND/OR WORK

A. *Bodleian, Oxford.* Two poems to Sandys (Ashmole MS. 47, folio 113; and Ashmole MS. 38, folio 138) and two versions of his Paraphrase upon the Song of Solomon (MS. e. Museo. 201[S.C. 3707]; and MS. Mus. c. 16[S.C. 16693]).

B. *British Museum.*
Additional MSS.:

15891	Correspondence between Elizabeth's ministers concerning Archbishop Sandys' blackmail case.
33894–6	Digges-Sandys relationship: "The Rev. T. Streatfield's Collections Relating to Kent."

24489 Joseph Hunter's "Chorus Vatum Anglicorum," especially ff. 122^b–3^b.
37719 Sir John Gibson's Commonplace Book.
12508–12 Fees paid the Gentlemen of the Privy Chamber.
12496 John Martin Affair in Virginia: Papers of Sir Julius Caesar.
5808 ff. 113, 115. Extracts of Letters of Sir Myles Sandys to Sir Thomas Josselyn: William Cole Papers.

Harleian MSS.:

4706 f. 24 Fees paid the Gentlemen of the Privy Chamber.
6930 Davison's translation of the Psalms.
7000 ff. 308–88. Letters of John Pory.

Lansdown MSS.:

50 f. 34 Lord Burghley's notes on Archbishop Sandys' grants to his sons: 31 May 1586.
28 f. 80 Archbishop Sandys' letter to Burghley saying there would be no reconciliation with the Earl of Huntington.
489 ff. 131–7 Version of Paraphrase upon the Song of Solomon.

Sloane MSS.:

1009 ff. 376^b–85 Version of Paraphrase upon the Song of Solomon.
72 ff. 119 Fees paid the Gentlemen of the Privy Chamber.
758 Nathaniel Butler papers.

Wyatt MSS. [on deposit by permission of the Earl of Romney]:

Entry of Sandys' burial and miscellaneous papers of Sir Francis and George Wyatt.

C. *Cincinnati, University of.* Manuscript version of A Paraphrase upon the Song of Solomon in a copy of the 1638 Paraphrase (PR 2338, A 681638). An 8-leaf MS.

D. *William A. Clark Library, University of California, Los Angeles.* Manuscript version of A Paraphrase upon the Song of Solomon in a copy of the 1638 Paraphrase (PR 2338. P21). A 6-leaf MS.

E. *Corpus Christi College, Oxford.* A three-volume seventeenth century manuscript history of Corpus Christi college by William Fulman.

F. *Henry E. Huntington Library.* The Hastings Papers contain information on the Sandys family friend, the Earl of Huntington.

G. *Library Company of Philadelphia.* A manuscript of two dedicatory poems and of A Paraphrase upon the Song of Solomon in a copy of the 1638 Paraphrase.

H. *Library of Congress.* Jefferson Library items from the seventeenth century described in Susan M. Kingsbury, Records of the Virginia Company, Washington, D.C., 1906, I, 41–54. These include contemporary copies of court books of Colonial Virginia and records of the Company.

I. *Magdalene College Cambridge.* The Ferrar Papers, about 1,200 items in all, include 78 which are either records of the Virginia Company or vitally concern it (1617–23). Of the remainder, most are concerned with family matters, including one addressed to George Sandys and two mentioning him (see Chapter IX above). The collection is described in Kingsbury, Records, I, 59–61, though since this account was written the papers have been re-indexed.

J. *Maidstone County Record Office, Kent.* Under Inventory of the Archdeaconry of Canterbury, MCRO, Book 70, Class 11, ff. 640, is the "Inventory of the Will of Sir Francis Wyatt," taken on 17 September 1644.

K. *Public Record Office, London.*

Chancery Proceedings:

C. 2/Charles I/G. 61/138	[*c.* 1609?] William Gascoigne, William Norton, and William Calverley *v.* George Sandys.
C. 8/15/92	3 November 1609. George Sandys *v.* Gascoigne, Norton, Calverley, and Pudsey.
C. 2/Charles I/S125/29 C. 2/Charles I/S13/28 C. 2/Charles I/S13/45 C. 2/Charles I/S8/27 C. 2/Charles I/L49/32	These suits from 1 January 1637/38 to 25 January 1643/44 concern George Sandys or other Sandyses *v.* Henry Sandys.
C. 3/382/50	November 1622. Sir Myles Sandys *et al* *v.* Sir Thomas Josselyn.
C. 24/629/32	22 June 1638. Dawber *v.* Clayborne.
[Town Depositions] C. 5/634/81	19 June 1662. Tunstall *v.* Elizabeth Sandys.

Close Rolls:

C. 54/1801, 3 James I, Pt. III, m. 2d	1605 Indenture. Spencer and Porter; Sir Myles Sandys and George Sandys.
C. 54/2325, 15 James I	4 April 1617 Indenture. Tunstall *v.* Mallory.

C. 54/1815, 3 James I, Pt. 17 10 June 1605 Conveyance. George Sandys and Sir Myles Sandys to Salomon Brown.

C. 54/1886, 5 James I, Pt. 9. 26 November 1607 Conveyance. George Sandys and Elizabeth Sandys to Best and Pudsey.

Inquisitions Post Mortem, Court of Wards:

Inquisitions, Wards 7/21/39 Will of John Norton of Ripon. December 1584/85; another copy in C. 142/208/236.

Lord Chamberlain's Accounts:

L.C. 5/180 [1620's?] Charles I's New Household Book.

L.C. 5/132/p. 181 6 April 1631. Swearing of T. Carew as a Gentleman of the Privy Chamber.

L.C. 5/132/p. 24 5 May 1631. Swearing of R. Lovelace. . . .

L.C. 5/134/p. 45 26 February 1634/35. Swearing of S. Godolphin. . . .

L.C. 5/134/p. 307 4 February 1638/39. Swearing of R. Sandes. . . .

L.C. 5/134/p. 404 25? June 1640. Swearing of William Sandes. . . .

L.C. 9/132/p. 8 28 March 1628. Swearing of W. Grante. . . .

Patent Rolls:

C. 66/2013, [11 James I, Pt. 36] no. 77 18 June 1613. Pardon of Alienation to George and Sir Myles Sandys.

C. 66/2694 December 1635. Patent for George Sandys' Paraphrase.

State Papers:

S.P. 12/255/ no. 34 1595. Grant to G. Sandys of keeping of the Blockhouse at Gravesend.

S.P. 16/2/no. 118 May–June 1625. List of the Gentlemen in Ordinary of the Privy Chamber.

S.P. 105/109/no. 49 September 1625. Letter in Levant Company's Papers.

Yorkshire, Feet of Fines:

C.P. 25(2)/258 Easter 1602. Conveyance: George and Elizabeth Sandys to Manne and Walker.

C.P. 25(2)/382 Trinity 16 James I. Quitclaim: Elizabeth Sandys to William Norton.

Miscellaneous:

E. 334/19	4 January 1630/31. Book of First Fruits.
S.P. 14/109, 18	8 May 1619. Letter from John Chamberlain to Sir Dudley Carleton.
G.D. 15/1/284	23 October 1620. Letter from Nathaniel Butler to Sir Nathaniel Rich.
Signet Office Docquets, Index 6810	3 December 1635. Grant to George Sandys for the sole printing of A Paraphrase.

L. *Ripon Cathedral Register.*	30 October 1580. Entry of the baptism of Elizabeth Norton.
M. *Somerset House, London.*	Will of Cicely Sandys, widow of Archbishop Sandys (Prerogative Court of Canterbury, 15 Wood, Probated 12 February 1610/11); and will of Sir Edwin Sandys (Probate Section, 84 Ridley, 20 August 1629).
N. *Virginia Historical Society.*	The Randolph MSS., three volumes of an eighteenth century copy of the [Library of Congress] court books of the Virginia colony (see Kingsbury, I, 48–51).

O. *York.*

District Probate Registry	Will of John Norton (12 December 1584) and a caveat against it (10 January 1584/85). See Craven Act Books, 1579–88, Exchequer Court of York.
Diocesan Registry	Copy of the will of Archbishop Sandys (1 August 1587).
York Minster Library	Torre MSS.

III. A SELECTION OF SOURCES, PRINCIPALLY RENAISSANCE, AND CRITICAL WORKS USEFUL IN A STUDY OF *A RELATION OF A JOURNEY*

Adrichomius [Adrichem], Christian. A Briefe Description of Hierusalem and of the Suburbs thereof, as it florished in the time of Christ . . . Translated . . . by Thomas Tymme. . . . London 1595.

—. Theatrum Terrae Sanctae et Biblicarum Historiarum. . . . Coloniae Agrippinae 1593.

Ausonius, Decius Magnus. De Magni Ausonii . . . Opera. . . . Lugduni 1575.

Belon, Pierre. Les Observations de Plusieurs Singlaritez & Choses Memorables. . . . . Paris 1554.

—. Portraits d' Oyseaux, Animaux, Serpens, Herbes, Arbres, Hommes et Femmes d' Arabie et Egypte. . . . Paris 1557.

Biddulph, William. The Travels of certain Englishmen into Africa, Asia . . . Palestina, Jerusalem. . . . London 1609.

—. The Travels of Foure English Men and a Preacher into Africa, Asia . . . [edited by T. Lavender]. London 1612.

Boemus, Johannes. The Fardle of Faccions conteining the aunciente maners, customes, and Lawes . . . of . . . Affrike and Asie. London 1555.

—. The Manners, Lawes, and Customes of All Nations . . . now Newly translated into English. By Ed. Aston. . . . London 1611.

Botero, Giovanni. Le Relationi Universali Di Giovanni Botero Benese. . . . Venetia 1596.

Braun, G. et Fr. Hohenberg. Civita Orbis Terrarum. . . . 6 vols. Cologne and Anvers 1579–1618.

Busbecq, A. Gislenii. A. Gislenii Busbequii omnia quae extant. Lugd. Batavorum 1633.

Cadoux, C. J. Ancient Smyrna: A History of the City from the Earliest Times to 324 A.D. Oxford 1938.

Calendar of State Papers, Venetian, 1610–1613. Edited by Horatio Brown. London 1905.

Capacius, J. C. [G. C. Cappacio]. Neapolitanae historiae . . . tomus primus. Neapoli 1607.

—. La Vera Antichita Di Pozzuolo. . . . Napoli 1607.

Carr, R., translator. The Mahumetane or Turkish Historie, containing three Bookes. . . . London 1600.

Cawley, Robert R. "Burton, Bacon, and Sandys." Modern Language Notes LVI (April 1941), 271–3.

—. Unpathed Waters: Studies in the Influence of the Voyagers on Elizabethan Literature. Princeton 1940.

—. The Voyagers and Elizabethan Drama. London 1938.

Chew, S. C. The Crescent and the Rose: Islam and England During the Renaissance. New York 1937.

Clarke, E. D., ed. Travels in Various Countries of Europe Asia and Africa. 6 vols. London 1810–23.

Coryate, Thomas. Crudities. . . . [orig. ed. London 1611]. 2 vols., Glasgow 1905.

Corpus Omnium Veterum Poetarum Latinorum. . . . Secundum Seriem . . . Secunda Editio. . . . Geneva 1611.

Cox, E. G. A Reference Guide to the Literature of Travel. . . . 2 vols. Seattle 1935–8.

Delitiae. CC. Italorum Poetarum, Huius Superiorisque Aevi illustrum, Collectore Ranutio Ghero. . . . 2 vols. Francofurti 1608.

De Mun, Gabriel. Deux Ambassadeurs a Constantinople 1604–1610. Paris 1902.

Dousae, Georgii. De Itinere Suo Constantinoplitano, Epistola. . . . Lugduni 1599.

Evelyn, John. John Evelyn in Naples. Edited by H. M. Smith. Oxford 1941.

Gyllius [Gilles], Pierre. De Bosporo Thracio. . . . Lugduni 1562. Another edition, 1632.

—. De Constantinopoleos Topographia. . . . Lugduni 1632.

Harris, John. Navigantium atque Itineratum Biblioteca. . . . 2 vols. London 1705.

Helvicus, Christophorus. Theatrum Historicum Sive Chronologiae Systema Novum. . . . Giessae Hessorum 1609.

Howard, Clare M. English Travellers of the Renaissance. London and New York 1904.

Ibrahim-Hilmy, Prince, ed. The Literature of Egypt and the Soudan. . . . 2 vols. London 1886–7.

Knolles, Richard. The Generall Historie of the Turkes. . . . London 1603.

Leo Africanus. The History and Description of Africa . . . by Leo Africanus . . . Done into English in the Year 1600, by John Pory. . . . Edited . . . by Dr. Robert Brown. 3 vols. London [for the Hakluyt Society] 1896.

Letters Received by the East India Company from Its Servants in the East. Edited by Sir William Foster. Volume II, London 1897.

Lithgow, William. A Most Delectable and True Discourse of the Admired and Painefull Peregrination . . . to . . . Asia and Affrica. . . . London 1623.

—.The Totall Discourse, of the Rare Adventures, and Painefull Peregrinations . . . to the most Famous Kingdomes in Europe, Asia, and Affrica. . . . London 1632.

—. The Totall Discourse of the Rare Adventures. . . . Glasgow 1906.

Mazzella, Scipio. Descrittione del Regno Di Napoli. . . . Napoli [1586].

—. Sito, et Antichita della Citta Di Pozzuolo. . . . 1606.

Menavimus, Antonius [Menavino, Antonio]. Trattato Di Costumi et Vita de Turchi. . . . Firenze 1548.

Moryson, Fynes. An Itinerary. . . . [orig. ed. 1617]. 4 vols. Glasgow 1907.

Mundy, Peter. The Travels of . . . in Europe and Asia. . . . Edited by Sir Richard C. Temple. 5 vols. London [for the Hakluyt Society] 1907.

Nashe, Thomas. The Works of. . . . Edited by R. B. McKerrow. 5 vols. London 1904–10.

Pancirolus, Guidon [Panciroli, Guido]. Rerum Memorabilium Iam Olim Deperditarum. . . . Ambergae 1599.

Parks, George B. Richard Hakluyt and the English Voyages. New York 1928.

—. "John Evelyn and the Art of Travel," Huntington Library Quarterly, X (May 1947), 251–76.

Plinius, Caecilius Secundus. The Historie of the World. Commonly Called, The Naturall Historie . . . Translated into English by Philemon Holland. . . . 2 vols. London 1601.

Purchas, Samuel. Purchas His Pilgrimes. . . . 4 parts. London 1625.

Schottus, Franciscus. Itinerarium Nobiliorum Italiae Regionum. . . . Vicentiae 1610.

Sanderson, John. The Travels of John Sanderson in the Levant 1584–1602 With his Autobiography and Selections from his Correspondence. Edited by Sir William Foster. London [for the Hakluyt Society] 1931.

Smith, Logan P. The Life and Letters of Sir Henry Wotton. 2 vols. Oxford 1907.

Strabo. The Geography of. . . . Edited by Horace L. Jones. 8 vols. London 1917–32.

—. . . . Strabonis Rerum Geographicarum . . . Isaacus Casuaubonus Recensuit . . . Genevae 1587.

Timberlake, Henry. A True and Strange Discourse of the Travailes of Two English Pilgrimes . . . in their Journey to Jerusalem, Gaza, Grand Cayro, Alexandria, and other places. . . . London 1608.

Turlerus, Hieronymus. De Peregratione. . . . Argentorati 1574.

Vautrollier, Thomas. The Auncient Ecclesiastical Histories. . . . 1585.

Ventura, C., ed. Thesoro Politico cioè Relationi. . . . Colonia 1589.

Webbe, Edward. The Rare and Most Wonderfull Things Which E. W. . . . Hath Seene and Passed in his Travailes. . . . London 1590.

Wright, Thomas. Early Travels in Palestine. . . . London 1848.

Zappullo, Michele. Historie Di Quattro Principali Città del Mondo, Gerusalemme, Roma, Napoli, e Venetia. . . . Vicenza [1603].

Zimolong, Bertrand. Navis Peregrinorum Ein Pilgerverzeichen aus Jerusalem von 1561 bis 1695. . . . Köln 1938. In Palästina-Hefte Des Deutschen Vereins Vom HL. Lande, Hefte 12–14.

Zosimus, Panopolitanus. Zosimi, Comitis et Exadvocati Fisci- Historiae. . . . Basilae [1576?].

Zuallardo, Giovanni. Il Devotissimo Viaggio Di Gerusalemme. . . . Roma 1587.

IV. A SELECTION OF RENAISSANCE EDITIONS OF OVID'S *METAMORPHOSES* IN ENGLISH, ITALIAN, FRENCH, AND LATIN WHICH MAY HAVE INFLUENCED THE FORMAT AND CONTENT OF THE 1626 AND 1632 EDITIONS OF SANDYS' TRANSLATION

Anguillara, Giovanni Andrea dell'. Le Metamorfosi di Ovidio Ridotte da Cio Andrea dell' Anguillara . . . [Venice] 1584.

Anulus [Barthelmi Aneau]. Trois Premiers Livres de la Metamorphose d'Ovide, Traduictz en Vers Frãcois. . . . Lyon 1556.

Ciofanus, Hercules. In Omnia P. Ovidius Nasonis Opera Observationes. . . . Antwerp 1583.

Dolce, Lodovico. Le Trasformati di . . . di Nuovo Ristampate. . . . Venetia 1553.

Farnaby, Thomas. Pub. Ovidii Nasonis Metamorphoseon Libri XV. . . . Notis Illustrati Opera & Studio Thomae Farnabii. . . . [Paris] 1637.

Golding, Arthur. The. XV. Bookes of P. Ovidius Naso, entytled Metamorphosis, translated oute of Latin into English Meeter. . . . [London 1567 orig. ed.] Edited by W. H. D. Rouse. London 1904.

Micyllus, Jacobus [Jacob Moltzer]. P. Ovidii Nasonis Metamorphoseos Libri Quindecim, cum Commentariis Raphaelis Regii. Adiectis etiam Annotationibus. . . . Basle 1543.

Pius, Baptistus [Giovanni Battista Pio]. P. Ovidii Nasonis . . . Metamorphoseos Librorum XV. Opus. . . . 1527.

Renouard, N. Les Metamorphoses d'Ovide Traduites en Prose Francoise, et de Nouveau Soigneusement Reveuës . . . Avec XV Discours Contenans l'Explication Morale et Historique. . . . Paris 1619.

V. GENERAL CRITICAL AND BIOGRAPHICAL SOURCES, INCLUDING PERIODICALS AND WORKS QUOTED OR REFERRED TO BY SANDYS IN HIS LETTERS. All items are listed alphabetically by title or author. Items of anonymous authorship both in periodical and book form are here listed by title. Critical and creative works are listed by author. Publications of the Public Record Office, the Historical Manuscripts Commission, and other British government agencies are listed by title. Other edited historical documents appear under the name of the editor, except that in certain situations items which are parts of series are listed under the title of the series. The edited works of individual authors, including letters, appear under the names of the authors.

Acts of the Privy Council of England. Colonial Series. Vol. I, A.D. 1613–1680. Edited by W. L. Grant and James Munro. Hereford 1908.

Aikin, Lucy. Memoirs of the Court of King Charles the First. 2 vols. London 1833.

Alciati, Andreas. Sacra Emblemata. . . . Venice 1546. Another edition Patavii 1621.

Allibone, S. Austin. A Critical Dictionary of English Literature and British and American Authors. . . . 3 vols. London 1900.

Andrews, Charles McL. The Colonial Period of American History. 4 vols. New Haven 1934–8.

Andrews, Matthew Page. The Soul of a Nation: the Founding of Virginia and the Projection of New England. New York 1943.

Andrews, William Loring. Jacob Steendam Noch Vaster; a Memoir of the First Poet in New Netherland. . . . New York 1908.

Arber, Edward, ed. A Transcript of the Registers of the Company of Stationers of London; 1554–1640 A.D. 5 vols. London 1875–7.

Archaeologia Cantiana: Being Transactions of the Kent Archaeological Society. Volume XV. London 1883.

Armitage, George J., ed. Allegations for Marriage Licenses Issued by the Bishop of London. Harleian Society. 2 vols. London 1887.

Attenborough, J. M. "George Sandys, Traveller and Poet." Westminster Review, CLIII (June 1905), 643–55.

Aubrey, John. 'Brief Lives,' Chiefly of Contemporaries, Set Down by John Aubrey. . . . Edited by Andrew Clark. 2 vols. Oxford 1898.

"Bacon, Shakespeare and George Sandys' 'Journey' (1615)," Baconiana, 3rd Series, XXVII (July 1943), 142–3.

Bailey, John E. The Life of Thomas Fuller, D.D. . . . London 1874.

Baker, David E. Biographia Dramatica. . . . 2 vols. London 1782.

Barker, Russell H. "George Sandys' [*sic*] Relation." Transactions of the Wisconsin Academy of Sciences, Arts and Letters, XXX (1937), 253–73.

Baxter, Richard. Poetical Fragments. . . . London 1681.

Beer, George L. The Origins of the British Colonial System 1578–1660. New York 1933.

Besant, Sir Walter. London in the Time of the Stuarts. London 1903.

Beverley, Robert. The History and Present State of Virginia. . . . London 1722. Another edition Chapel Hill 1947, edited by Louis B. Wright.

Birch, Thomas. The Court and Times of Charles the First. . . . 2 vols. London 1848.

—. The Court and Times of James I. . . . 2 vols. London 1849.

Book-Auction Records. . . . Volume I, 1902– London.

Bredvold, Louis I. The Intellectual Milieu of John Dryden. . . . Ann Arbor 1934.

Brewer, Wilmon. Ovid's Metamorphoses in European Culture (Books I–II–III–IV–V). . . . Boston 1933.

Broadribb, C. W. "Ovid, Sandys, and Milton." Notes and Queries, CLVII (2 August 1924), 77–8.

Brown, Alexander. English Politics in Early Virginia History. Cambridge, Mass. 1901.

—. The First Republic in America. . . . Cambridge, Mass. 1898.

—. The Genesis of the United States. . . . 2 vols. Cambridge, Mass. 1897.

Browne, Sir Thomas. The Works of. . . . Edited by Geoffrey Keynes. 6 vols. London 1928–31.

Bruce, Philip A. Economic History of Virginia in the Seventeenth Century . . . 2 vols. New York 1896.

—. Institutional History of Virginia in the Seventeenth Century. . . . 2 vols. New York 1910.

Brydges, Sir Egerton. The British Bibliographer. 4 vols. London 1810–14.

—. Censura Literaria. . . . 10 vols. London 1805–9.

Burk, John. The History of Virginia from Its First Settlement to the Commencement of the Revolution. 3 vols. Petersburg, Virginia 1822.

Bush, Douglas. Mythology and the Renaissance Tradition in English Poetry. Minneapolis 1932.

Calendar of State Papers, Colonial Series, 1574–1660. Edited by W. Noel Sainsbury. London 1860.

Calendar of State Papers, Domestic Series, of the Reign of Elizabeth, 1595–1597. Edited by Mary Anne E. Green. London 1869.

Calendar of State Papers, Domestic Series, of the Reign of Charles I., 1635. Edited by John Bruce. London 1865.

Calendar of State Papers, Domestic Series, of the Reign of Charles I., 1641–1643. Edited by William D. Hamilton. London 1887.

Campbell, Charles. History of the Colony and Ancient Dominion of Virginia. Philadelphia 1860.

Candy, Hugh H. C. Some Newly Discovered Stanzas written by John Milton on Engraved Scenes illustrating Ovid's Metamorphoses. . . . London [1924].

Carew, George. Letters from Lord George Carew to Sir Thomas Roe . . . 1615–1617. Edited by John MacLean. London [for the Camden Society] 1860.

Carew, Thomas. The Poems of Thomas Carew Sewer in Ordinary to Charles I, and a Gentleman of his Privy Chamber. Edited by W. Carew Hazlitt. [London?] 1870.

Cary, Lucius, 2nd Viscount Falkland. Of the Infallibilitie of the Church of Rome. . . . Oxford 1645.

Castalio, Sebastian [Sebastien Chateillon]. Biblia Interprete . . . Una Cum Eiusdem Annotationibus Totum Opus Recognovit Ipse. . . . Basiliae 1551.

Cattermole, R. Sacred Poetry of the Seventeenth Century. . . . 2 vols. London 1836.

Cave-Browne, J. The History of Boxley Parish . . . Including An Account of the Wiat Family. . . . Maidstone 1892.

Chamberlain, John. The Letters of. . . . Edited with an Introduction by Norman E. McClure. 2 vols. Philadelphia [Memoirs American Philosophical Society] 1939.

Charles I. The Letters, Speeches and Proclamations of. . . . Edited by Sir Charles Petrie. London [1935].

Chester, Anthony. Scheeps-Togt van Anthony Chester na Virginia, gedaan in het jaar 1620. . . . Leyden 1707.

Cibber, Theophilus. The Lives of the Poets of Great Britain and Ireland, to the Time of Dean Swift. . . . 4 vols. London 1753.

Claiborne, J. H. William Claiborne of Virginia. . . . New York 1917.

Clark, Andrew, ed. Register of the University of Oxford, Vol. II, (1571–1622). . . . 4 vols to Parts I–IV. Oxford 1887.

Clark, G. N. The Seventeenth Century. Oxford 1929.

Clifford, Lady Anne. The Diary of. . . . Introductory Note by V. Sackville-West. London 1923.

Clifford, Arthur, ed. Tixall Poetry. . . . London 1813.

Cokain, Sir Aston. Small Poems of Divers Sorts. London 1658.

C[okayne], G[eorge] E., ed. The Complete Peerage of England, Scotland, Ireland, Great Britain and the United Kingdom. . . . 13 vols. London 1926.

Colonial Records of Virginia. Richmond, Virginia 1874.

Colvin, Sidney. Early Engraving and Engravers in England (1575–1695). . . . London 1905.

A Compleat History of Europe . . . from the Year, 1600, to the Treaty of Nimeguen. . . . 5 vols. [?] London 1701–5?

Copland, The Rev. Patrick. Virginia's God be thanked, or A Sermon of Thanksgiving for the happy success of affairs in Virginia this last year. . . . April 1622. London 1622.

Courthope, W. J. A History of English Poetry. Vol. III. The Intellectual Conflict of the Seventeenth Century. . . . London 1924.

Cowley, Abraham. The Complete Works in Verse and Prose of. . . . Edited by A. B. Grosart. 2 vols. [Edinburgh] Privately printed 1881.

Craven, Wesley Frank. Dissolution of the Virginia Company. . . . New York 1932.

—. The Southern Colonies in the Seventeenth Century, 1607–1689. Vol. I. of A History of the South. [Baton Rouge] 1949.

Cunningham, G. C., ed. Lives of Eminent and Illustrious Englishmen from Alfred the Great to the Latest Times. . . . 8 vols. Glasgow 1835–7.

DaCosta, Joseph. The Natural & Moral History of the Indies . . . Reprinted from the English Translated Edition of Edward Grimston, 1684. Edited by Clements R. Markham. London [for the Hakluyt Society] 1880.

Daniel, George. The Poems of. . . . Edited by A. B. Grosart. 4 vols. Privately printed 1878.

Davis, Richard B. "America in George Sandys' Ovid." William and Mary Quarterly, 3rd Series, IV (July 1947), 297–304.

—"The Early Editions of George Sandys' Ovid: the Circumstances of Production." Papers of the Bibliographical Society of America, XXXV (4th Quarter 1941), 255–76.

—. "George Sandys and Two 'Uncollected' Poems." Huntington Library Quarterly, XII (November 1948), 105–11.

—. "George Sandys, Poet-Adventurer." Americana, XXXIII (April 1939), 180–95.

—. "George Sandys *v.* William Stansby: the 1632 Edition of Ovid's Metamorphosis." The Library, 5th Series, III (December 1948), 193–212.

—. "Two New Manuscript Items for a George Sandys Bibliography." Papers of the Bibliographical Society of America, XXXVII (3rd Quarter 1943), 215–22.

deBeer, Esmond S. "Edward Barton." Bulletin of the Institute of Historical Research, University of London, XIX (November 1942), 158–60.

deBeer, Esmond S. "George Sandys's Account of Compania." The Library, 4th Series, XVII (March 1937), 458–65.

DeBry, Theodore, *et al.*, edd. Historia Americae . . . in XIII. distinctis partibus. . . . Francofurti 1634.

D'Ewes, Sir Symonds. College Life in the Time of James the First, as Illustrated by an Unpublished Diary of Sir Symonds D'Ewes. . . . Edited by John H. Marsden. London 1861.

Drayton, Michael. The Bataile of Agincourt . . . Elegies upon sundry occasions. . . . London 1627.

—. The Works of. . . . Edited by J. W. Hebel *et al.* 5 vols. Oxford 1931–41.

Dryden, John. The Works of. . . . Edited by Sir Walter Scott. 18 vols. Edinburgh 1821.

"Earliest Extant Land Patents of the Colony of Virginia." The Researcher, I (January 1927), 92 etc.

Elton, Oliver. The English Muse. . . . London 1933.

Evans, Willa McClung. Henry Lawes, Musician and Friend of Poets. New York 1941.

Ferrar, Nicholas, *et al.* The Ferrar Papers. . . . Edited by B. Blackstone. Cambridge 1938.

Finney, Claude L. The Evolution of Keats's Poetry. 2 vols. Cambridge, Mass. 1936.

Fitz-Herbert, Nicholas. . . . Oxoniensis in Anglia Academiae Descriptio. . . . Romae 1602.

Force, Peter, ed. Tracts and Other Papers, Relating Principally to the Origin, Settlement, and Progress of the Colonies in North America. . . . 4 vols. Washington 1836–8. Reprinted New York 1947.

Forman, Henry C. Jamestown and St. Mary's, Buried Cities of Romance. Baltimore 1938.

Foster, Joseph, ed. Alumni Oxonienses: the Members of the University of Oxford, 1500–1714. . . . 4 vols., Early Series. Oxford 1891–2.

—. Pedigrees of the County Families of Yorkshire. 3 vols. London 1874.

Fowler, Thomas. The History of Corpus Christi College. . . . Oxford 1893.

Fuller, Thomas. Anglorum Speculorum or the Worthies of England, in Church and State. . . . London 1684.

—. The History of the Worthies of England. Edited by P. A. Nuttall. 3 vols. London 1840.

Fulton, John F. Sir Kenelm Digby, Writer, Bibliophile, and Protagonist of William Harvey. New York 1937.

Gardiner, Samuel R. History of England from the Accession of James I. to the Outbreak of the Civil War, 1603–1642. 10 vols. London 1904–9.

Garrett, Christina H. The Marian Exiles: A Study in the Origins of Elizabethan Puritanism. Cambridge 1938.

Gayley, Charles M. Shakespeare and the Founders of Liberty in America. New York 1917.

Gildon, Charles. The Lives and Characters of the English Dramatic Poets. . . . London 1698.

Glencross, Reginald, ed. A Calendar of the Marriage Licence Allegations in the Registry of the Bishop of London . . . 1597 to 1648. The Index Library. London [British Record Society] 1937.

Godfrey, Elizabeth [pseud.]. Home Life under the Stuarts, 1603–1649. London 1903.

Godolphin, Sidney. The Poems of. . . . Edited by William Dighton. Oxford 1931.

"Good Newes from Virginia." Broadside of March 1623. Reproduced in facsimile in A Selection of Extremely Rare and Important Printed Books and Ancient Manuscripts, Catalogue 77, Wm. H. Robinson, Ltd., London 1948. Also printed in William and Mary Quarterly, 3rd Series, V (July 1948), 351–8.

Gordon, Armistead C. "George Sandys." Dictionary of American Biography.

Grierson, H. J. C. The First Half of the Seventeenth Century. Edinburgh 1906.

Grotius, Hugo. . . . Epistolae Quotquot repiriri potuerunt. . . . Amstelodami 1687.

—. . . . Christus Patiens. . . . Gorlicii Lusatorum [1685].

Grüninger, Gunther H. George Sandys als Übersetzer des "Christus Patiens" von Hugo Grotius. Inaugural-Dissertation zur Erlangung der Doktor würde einer hohen Philosophischen Facultät der Albert-Ludwig-Universität zu Freiburg i. Br. vorlegt von. . . . Tauberbischofsheim 1927.

Harding, Davis P. Milton and the Renaissance Ovid. Urbana 1946.

Hart, Mrs. E. P., ed. Merchant Taylors' School Register 1561–1934. . . . 2 vols. London 1936.

Hatch, Charles E. "Glassmaking in Virginia, 1607–1625." William and Mary Quarterly, 2nd Series, XXI (April and June 1941), 119–38, 227–38.

—. A Preliminary Historical Study of Glass House Point, with Special Emphasis on the First Attempts at Glassmaking in Virginia. U.S. Department of the Interior, National Park Service, Colonial Historical Park, Yorktown, Virginia . . . December 4, 1940. Typescript.

Hazlitt. W. Carew. Handbook of the Popular, Poetical, and Dramatic Literature of Great Britain. . . . London 1867.

Hebel, J. W., and Hudson, H. H., edd. Poetry of the English Renaissance. New York 1929.

Hening, William W. Statutes at Large . . . of Virginia. 13 vols. Richmond and New York 1810–23.

Henrietta Maria, Queen. Letters of . . . . Edited by Mary Anne E. Green. London 1857.

Herbert, Sir Thomas. Memoirs of the Last Two Years of the Reign of King Charles I. . . . Fourth Edition [orig. ed. 1702]. London 1839.

Hervey, Mary F. S. The Life Correspondence and Collections of Thomas Howard Earl of Arundel "Father of Vertu in England." Cambridge 1921.

Hiden, Mrs. P. W. "Education and the Classics in the Life of Colonial Virginia." Virginia Magazine of History & Biography, XLIX (January 1941), 20–8.

Historical Manuscripts Commission. Eighth Report of. . . . Appendix, Part II. London 1881.

—. Fourth Report of. . . . Part I. London 1874.

Holdsworth, W. S. A History of English Law. 12 vols. Boston 1927.

Hotten, John C., ed. The Original List of Persons of Quality; Emigrants; Religious Exiles; Political Rebels; Serving Men Sold for a Term of Years . . . and Others Who Went from Great Britain to the American Plantations, 1600–1700. . . . London 1874.

Howe, Henry. Historical Collections of Virginia. . . . Charleston, S. C. 1845.

Hume, Martin A. S. The Great Lord Burghley, a Study in Elizabethan Statecraft. London 1898.

Hunter, Grace Eva. The Influence of Francis Bacon on the Prose Commentary of Ovid's "Metamorphoses" by George Sandys. Unpublished Doctoral Dissertation, State University of Iowa, 1949.

Hyde, Edward. Characters of Eminent Men in the Reigns of Charles I. and II. . . . London 1793.

Jacob, Giles. The Poetical Register: or, the Lives and Characters of All the English Poets. . . . 2 vols. London 1723.

Jones, E. Alfred. American Members of the Inns of Court. London 1924.

Jones, Howard M. "The Colonial Impulse, an Analysis of the Promotion Literature of Colonization." Proceedings of the American Philosophical Society, XC (May 1946), 131–61.

—. The Literature of Virginia in the Seventeenth Century. In Memoirs of the American Academy of Arts and Sciences, XIX, Part 2. Boston 1946.

Jusserand, J. J. A Literary History of the English People. 3 vols. New York 1906–9.

Keats, John. The Poems of. . . . Edited by E. De Selincourt. London [1905].

King, Henry. The English Poems of. . . . Edited by Lawrence Mason. New Haven 1914.

Kingsbury, Susan M., ed. Records of the Virginia Company of London. 4 vols. Washington, D.C. 1906, 1933, 1935.

Knappen, M. M. Tudor Puritanism, a Chapter in the History of Idealism Chicago 1939.

Knight, W. S. M. The Life and Works of Hugo Grotius. . . . London 1925.

Land, Robert H. "Henrico and Its College." William and Mary Quarterly, 2nd Series, XVIII (October 1938), 453–98.

Langbaine, Gerard. An Account of the English Dramatic Poets. . . . Oxford 1691.

Leach, Arthur F. Early Yorkshire Schools. 2 vols. Yorkshire Archaeological Society, Record Series, XVII and XXXIII, 1899 and 1903.

Lefroy, Sir J. Henry, ed. The Historye of the Bermudaes or Summer Islands. . . . London [for the Hakluyt Society] 1882.

—. Memorials of the Discovery and Early Settlement of the Bermudas or Somers Islands 1515–1685. . . . 2 vols. London 1877–9.

Lemmi, Charles W. The Classic Deities in Bacon. Baltimore 1933.

Letters Received by the East India Company from Its Servants in the East. . . . Vol. I, introd. by Frederick C. Danvers, London 1896. Vol. II, introd. by Sir William Foster, London 1897.

Lievsay, John L., and Richard B. Davis, "A Cavalier Library—1643," Studies in Bibliography, VI (1953–1954), 141–160.

[Longueville, T.?] The Life of Sir Kenelm Digby by One of His Descendants. London 1896.

Lonn, Ella. The Colonial Agents of the Southern Colonies. Chapel Hill 1945.

Mallet, Charles E. A History of the University of Oxford. 3 vols. London 1924–1927.

Manahan, John E. The Cavalier Remounted, a Study of the Origins of Virginia's Population, 1607–1700. Unpublished Dissertation, University of Virginia, 1946. Also see Abstracts of Dissertations, 1945–1947, University of Virginia, Charlottesville 1948, pp. 68–72.

Marriott, J. A. R. The Life and Times of Lucius Cary Viscount Falkland. London [1907].

McCabe, W. Gordon. "The First University in America, 1619–1622." Virginia Magazine of History & Biography, XXX (April 1922), 133–56.

McEuen, Kathryn A. Classical Influence upon the Tribe of Ben. . . . Cedar Rapids, Ia., 1939.

McIlwaine, H. R., ed. Journals of the House of Burgesses of Virginia 1619–1658/59. Richmond, Virginia 1915.

—. Minutes of the Council and General Court of Colonial Virginia 1622–1632, 1670–1676. . . . Richmond, Virginia 1924.

McManaway, James G. "The First Five Bookes of Ovids Metamorphosis, 1621, Englished by Master George Sandys." Papers of the Bibliographical Society, University of Virginia, I (1948), 71–82.

Martin, Charles T., ed. Minutes of Parliament of the Middle Temple. . . . 4 vols. London 1904–5.

Mathew, David. The Jacobean Age. London [1938].

Matthiessen, F. O. Translation, an Elizabethan Art. Cambridge, Mass. 1931.

Maycock, A. L. Nicholas Ferrar of Little Gidding. London [1938].

Mead, William E. The Versification of Pope in its Relations to the Seventeenth Century. Doctoral Dissertation, University of Leipzig. Leipzig 1889.

Miller, Frank J., ed. Ovid's Metamorphoses. 2 vols. Cambridge, Mass. 1916.

Miller, Perry. "The Religious Impulse in the Founding of Virginia: Religion and Society in the Early Literature." William and Mary Quarterly, 3rd Series, V (October 1948), 492–522; VI (January 1949), 24–41.

Milton, John. The Works of. . . . Edited by Frank A. Patterson. 18 vols. New York 1931–8.

Murdock, Kenneth B. The Sun at Noon. . . . New York 1939.

Nash, Treadwell R., ed. Collections for the History of Worcestershire. 2 vols. London 1782.

Neill, Edward D. The Earliest Contest in America on Charter-Rights, Begun A.D. 1619. . . . St. Paul, Minn. 1890.

—. The English Colonization of America during the Seventeenth Century. London 1871.

—. History of the Virginia Company of London with Letters to and from the First Colony Never Before Printed. Albany 1869.

—. Memoir of the Rev. Patrick Copland. . . . New York 1871.

—. Virginia Carolorum: the Colony under the Rule of Charles the First and Second. . . . Albany 1886.

—. Virginia Governors under the London Company. St. Paul, Minn. 1889.

—. Virginia Vetusta, During the Reign of James the First, Containing Letters and Documents Never before Printed. . . . Albany 1885.

A New and General Biographical Dictionary; Containing an Historical and Critical Account of the Lives and Writings of the Most Eminent Persons in Every Nation; Particularly the British and Irish. . . . 12 vols. London 1761–7.

Newdigate, Bernard H. Michael Drayton and His Circle. Oxford 1941.

N[ichols], J. "Brief Memoirs of George Sandys." Gentleman's Magazine, LII (July 1782), 368.

Nichols, J., ed. A Select Collection of Poems. . . . 8 vols. London 1780–2.

Nicolas, Sir N. Harris. Memoirs of the Life and Times of Sir Christopher Hatton, K.G. . . . . London 1847.

Norcliffe, C. B., ed. Visitation of Yorkshire in the Years 1563 and 1564. London [Harleian Society] 1881.

Northup, C. S. A Register of Bibliographies of the English Language and Literature. New Haven 1925.

A Note of the Shipping, Men, and Provisions, Sent and Provided for Virginia, by the Right Honorable, the Earle of Southampton, and the Company, this Yeare, 1620. [London 1620.]

Nugent, Nell M. Cavaliers and Pioneers, Abstracts of Virginia Land Patents and Grants, 1623–1800. 5 vols. Richmond, Virginia 1934–.

Oldys, W. and Park, Thomas, edd. The Harleian Miscellany. . . . 10 vols. London 1808–13.

The Oxinden Letters 1607–1642 Being the Correspondence of Henry Oxinden of Barham and His Circle. Edited by Dorothy Gardiner. London. 1933.

Palaser, Thomas. Sacra Ritum Congregation Sectio Historica Westmonasterien Beatificationis seu Declarationis Martyrii Venerabilium Servorum Dei Thomae Palaser, Sac. Saec. Jonnis Norton, Laici, Jonnis Talbot Laici in

Odium Fidei, Uti Fertur, Dunelmi in Anglia Die 9 Aug. 1600 Interfectorum. [Br. Mus. no. 20010.i.8.]

Peckard, Peter. Memoirs of the Life of Mr. Nicholas Ferrar. Cambridge 1790.

Penrose, Boies, II. "Some Jacobean Links between America and the Orient." Virginia Magazine of History & Biography, XLIX (January 1941), 51–61.

—. Urbane Travelers 1591–1635. Philadelphia 1942.

Phillimore, W. P. and Fry, George S., edd. Inquisitions Post Mortem, Gloucestershire, Reign King Charles I. British Record Society. Part II, London 1895.

Phillips, Edward. Theatrum Poetarum. . . . London 1675.

Pickel, Margaret B. Charles I as Patron of Poetry and Drama. London 1936.

Pinto, V. DeSola. The English Renaissance 1510–1688. New York [1938].

Pleasants, J. H. "Sandys of Furnace Fells, Lancashire." Virginia Magazine of History & Biography, XXIX (April 1921).

Plummer, Charles, ed. Elizabethan Oxford: Reprints of Rare Tracts. Oxford 1887.

Pope, Alexander. The Works of . . . in Verse and Prose. Containing the Principal Notes of Drs. Warburton and Warton. Edited by the Rev. William Lisle Bowles. 10 vols. London 1806.

—. The Works of . . . New Edition . . . Collected in Part by the Late Rt. Hon. John Wilson Croker. Edited by the Rev. Whitwell Elwin. 10 vols. London 1871–89.

Powell, Chilton. English Domestic Relations 1487–1653. . . . New York 1917.

Powell, William S. "Books in the Virginia Colony before 1624." William and Mary Quarterly, 3rd Series, V (April 1948), 177–84.

—. John Pory: His Life, Letters and Work. Unpublished M.A. Thesis, University of North Carolina. Chapel Hill 1947.

Prideaux, Humphrey. Letters of Humphrey Prideaux Sometime Dean of Norwich to John Ellis Sometime Under-Secretary of State 1674–1722. Edited by Edward M. Thompson. [London? For the Camden Society] 1875.

Prouty, C. T. George Gascoigne, Elizabethan Courtier, Soldier, and Poet. New York 1942.

"Psalmody." The Quarterly Review, XXXVIII (July 1828), 16–53.

Purchas, Samuel. Hakluytus Posthumus or Purchas His Pilgrimes. . . . 20 vols. Glasgow 1905–7.

Raine, Angelo. History of St. Peter's School, York. . . . London 1926.

Ransford, Nicholas. "British Settlers in America." Notes & Queries, CXLVIII (4 April 1925), 237–40 etc.

[Review of] "Henry Ellis' Original Letters Illustrative of English History," Edinburgh Review, XLVI (June 1827), 195–217.

Rice, Warner G. "Early English Travelers to Greece and the Levant." Essays and Studies in English and Comparative Literature . . . University of Michigan, Ann Arbor 1933. University of Michigan Publications, Language and Literature, X, 205–60.

Rich, R. Newes from Virginia, the Lost Flocke Triumphant. London 1610.

Ripley, William Z. The Financial History of Virginia 1609–1776. Studies in History, Economics, and Public Law . . . of Columbia College, IV, No. 1. New York 1893.

Robinson, Conway, and Brock, R.A. edd. Abstract of the Proceedings of the Virginia Company of London, 1619–1624. . . . 2 vols. Richmond 1888–9.

Robinson, Hastings, ed. The Zurich Letters. . . . Cambridge 1846.

Rymer, Thomas, and Sanderson, Robert, edd. Foedera, Conventiones, Literae, . . . Acta Publica. . . . 20 vols. London 1704–35.

St. George, Sir Henry, and St. George, Sir Richard, gen. edd. The Visitation of London, Anno Domini 1633, 1634, and 1635. Edited by Joseph J. Howard. 2 vols. London 1880–3.

Saintsbury, George. A History of English Prosody. . . . 3 vols. London 1906–10.

Sandys, E[dward] S[eton]. History of the Family of Sandys of Cumberland, afterwards of Furness in North Lancashire. . . . 2 vols. Barrow-in-Furness 1930.

Sandys, Archbishop Edwin. Sermons Made by the Most Reverend Father in God, Edwin, Archbishop of Yorke. . . . London 1585.

—. The Sermons of Edwin Sandys, D.D. . . . Archbishop of York. . . . Edited by the Rev. John Ayre. Cambridge [for the Parker Society] 1842.

Sandys, Sir Edwin. Europae Speculum, or, a View or Survey of the State of Religion in the Westerne Parts of the World. . . . Hagae-Comitis 1629.

—. A Relation of the State of Religion . . . in the severall States of these Westerne Partes of the World. London 1605.

—. Sacred Hymns, Consisting of Fifty Select Psalms of David and Others, Paraphrastically Turned into English Verse. . . . London 1615.

Sandys, Sir Miles. Prudence, the First of the Foure Cardinall Virtues. . . . London 1634.

Schelling, Felix E. "Ben Jonson and the Classical School." PMLA, XIII (No. 2 1898), 221–49.

Scott, William R. The Constitution and Finance of English, Scottish and Irish Joint-Stock Companies to 1720. 3 vols. Cambridge 1910–12.

Slingsby, Sir Henry, Bart. The Diary of Sir Henry Slingsby, of Scriven, . . . Edited by the Rev. Daniel Parson. London 1836.

Smith, Captain John. The Generall Historie of Virginia, New England, & the Summer Isles. . . . 2 vols. Glasgow 1907.

—. . . . Works, 1608–1631. Edited by Edward Arber. Birmingham 1884.

Smith, Logan P. The Life and Letters of Sir Henry Wotton. 2 vols. Oxford 1907.

Spelman, Henry. Relation of Virginia . . . by . . . 1609. Edited by J. F. Hunnewell. London 1872.

Spence, Joseph. Anecdotes, Observations, and Characters, of Books and Men. . . . London 1858.

Stith, William. The History of the First Discovery and Settlement of Virginia. . . . . Williamsburg, Virginia 1747.

—. History of the First Discovery and Settlement of Virginia. Reprinted for J. Sabin. New York 1865.

Stock, Leo F., ed. Proceedings and Debates of the British Parliaments respecting North America. Volume I, 1542–1688. Washington, D.C. 1924.

Strachey, William. The Historie of Travaile into Virginia Britannia. . . . Edited by R. H. Major. London [for the Hakluyt Society] 1849.

Strype, John. Annals of the Reformation. . . . 4 vols. Oxford 1824.

—. The Life and Acts of Matthew Parker. . . . 3 vols. Oxford 1821.

—. The Life and Acts of John Whitgift, D.D. . . . 3 vols. Oxford 1872.

Suckling, Sir John. The Poems, Plays and Other Remains of. . . . Edited by W. Carew Hazlitt. 2 vols. London 1892.

Symonds, Richard. The Diary of the Marches of the Royal Army during the Great Civil War; Kept by. . . . Edited by Charles E. Long. Cambridge [for the Camden Society] 1859.

Tawse, George. "George Sandys." American Historical Record, I (May 1872), 193–8.

Thompson, A. H. "Writers of the Couplet." Chapter III of Vol. VII, 55–81, Cambridge History of English Literature, 15 vols. New York 1907–27.

Tillotson, Geoffrey. On the Poetry of Pope. Oxford 1938.

Todd, Henry J. Observations upon the Metrical Versions of the Psalms. . . . London 1822.

Townsend, Dorothea. George Digby, Second Earl of Bristol. London [1924].

—. Life and Letters of Mr. Endymion Porter. . . . London 1897.

Tradescant, John, the Younger. Musaeum Tradescantium. . . . London 1656.

Traill, Henry D., ed. Social England. . . . 6 vols. London 1894–8.

Tremellius, Immanuel, and Junius, Francis. Testamenti Veteris Biblia Sacra sive Canonici Priscae Iudaeorum . . . Scholiis illustrati . . . ab. . . . Londini 1580.

Trevor-Roper, H. R. Archbishop Laud, 1573–1645. London 1940.

Tulloch, John. Rational Theology and Christian Philosophy in England in the Seventeenth Century. 2 vols. Edinburgh 1874.

Turner, Edward R. The Privy Council of England in the Seventeenth and Eighteenth Centuries, 1603–1784. 2 vols. Baltimore 1927–8.

Tyler, Lyon G. The Cradle of the Republic: Jamestown and James River. Richmond, Virginia 1900.

—. ed. Encyclopedia of Virginia Biography. . . . 5 vols. New York 1915.

—. ed. Narratives of Early Virginia 1606–1625. New York 1907.

Tyler, Moses C. A History of American Literature . . . 1607–1765. 2 vols. New York 1878.

Unger, Emma V., and Jackson, William A., edd. The Carl H. Pforzheimer Library, English Literature, 1475–1700. 3 vols. New York 1940.

Usher, James. A Collection of Three Hundred Letters [of]. . . . Edited by R. Parr. London 1686.

Venn, John, and Venn, J. A., edd. Alumni Cantabrigienses. . . . Part I, Vol. IV. Cambridge 1927.

The Virginia Historical Register and Literary Advertiser. Edited by William Maxwell. 6 vols. Richmond 1848–53.

Virginia State Library Calendar of Transcripts. . . . Richmond, Virginia 1905.

Vivian, Comley. Some Notes for a History of the "Sandys" Family of Great Britain, Ireland, and the (Former) Colony of Virginia. . . . London 1907.

Vreeland, Hamilton. Hugo Grotius, the Father of the Modern Science of International Law. . . . New York 1917.

Walker, John, ed. Letters Written by Eminent Persons of the Seventeenth and Eighteenth Centuries. . . . 2 vols. London 1813.

Waller, Edmund. The Works of . . . in Verse and Prose. Edited by E. Fenton. London 1730.

Wallerstein, Ruth. "The Development of the Rhetoric and Metre of the Heroic Couplet, Especially in 1625–1645." PMLA, L (March 1935), 166–209.

Walton, Izaak, and Cotton, Charles. The Complete Angler. . . . Edited by John Major. Philadelphia [1881].

Walton, Izaak. The Life of Mr. Rich. Hooker. . . . London 1665.

Ward, Sir A. W. Shakespeare and the Makers of Virginia. London 1919.

Ward, Thomas H., ed. The English Poets, Selections with Critical Introductions by Various Writers. . . . 4 vols. London 1880–1.

Waterhouse, Edward. A Declaration of the State of the Colony and Affairs in Virginia [after the massacre]. . . . London 1622.

Weber, Kurt. Lucius Cary Second Viscount Falkland. New York 1940.

Wertenbaker, Thomas J. The First Americans 1607–1690. New York 1929.

—. Patrician and Plebeian in Virginia. . . . Charlottesville, Virginia 1910.

—. Torchbearer of the Revolution, the story of Bacon's Rebellion and Its Leader. Princeton 1940.

—. Virginia Under the Stuarts 1607–1688. Princeton 1914.

Whitaker, Alexander. Good Newes from Virginia. . . . London 1613.

Whiting, George W. Milton's Literary Milieu. Chapel Hill 1939.

Williamson, G. C. George, Third Earl of Cumberland . . . His Life and His Voyages. . . . Cambridge 1920.

Williamson, J. Bruce. The History of the Temple, London, from the Institution of the Order of the Knights of the Temple to the Close of the Stuart Period. . . . London 1925.

Willis, Leota S. Francis Lenton, Queen's Poet. Philadelphia 1931.

Wilson, Malcolm Sands. Descendants of James Sands of Block Island. Privately printed. New York 1949.

Winsor, Justin, ed. Narrative and Critical History of America. 8 vols. Boston 1884–9.

[Wither, George?]. The Great Assises Holden in Parnassus. . . . London 1645.

Wood, Anthony à. Athenae Oxonienses. . . . 5 vols. London 1813–20.

Wood, Henry. "Beginnings of the 'Classical' Heroic Couplet in England." American Journal of Philology, XI (No. 1 1890), 55–79.

Wright, Louis B. Middle-Class Culture in Elizabethan England. Chapel Hill 1935.

—. Religion and Empire: the Alliance between Piety and Commerce in English Expansion 1558–1625. Chapel Hill 1943.

Yardley, J. H. R. Before the Mayflower. New York 1931.

Yonge, Samuel H. The Site of Old "James Towne" 1607–1698. . . . Richmond, Virginia 1907.

The Yorkshire Archaeological and Topographical Association. Record Series.

Feet of Fines of the Tudor Period. Part IV . . . Vol. VIII [1890].

Index of Wills in the York Registry A.D. 1568 to 1585 . . . Vol. XIX [1895]

Index of Wills in the York Registry A.D. 1585 to 1594 . . . Vol. XXII-[1897].

Yorkshire Fines for the Stuart Period . . . 1603–1614 . . . Vol. LIII [1915].

Yorkshire Fines for the Stuart Period . . . 1614–1625 . . . Vol. LVIII [1917].

INDEX

Names of authors used as sources by Sandys, or of authors who used his writings as sources, are followed before the appropriate page numbers by a capital or an abbreviation in parentheses which refers to Sandys' particular work. *E.g.* (O) refers to the Ovid's *Metamorphosis* with its prose commentaries, (R) refers to *A Relation of a Journey*, and (ParaDivPoems) to *A Paraphrase upon the Divine Poems*. Persons with identical names in the Sandys' family have been distinguished as clearly as possible. Though the letter "n" after a page number indicates that the entry is referred to in a note, no additional page number is given if the same entry is also referred to in the text. Titles of books, poems, written documents, etc., are given in *italic* type. Main references in CAPITALS and **bold type.**

Adrichomius, Christianus (R) 69n–70n, 70–1, 74n
Aeschylus (R) 61n
Agathius (R) 86
Aiscoughe, Christopher 273
Albinellus, Annibal 276
Albumazar (O) 219
Alcadinus (R) 82n, 86n
Alciatus, Andreas (R) 51, 86; quote from in ltr., 140n
Allen, Cardinal 84n
Alphaeus (R) 86
Alpinus (R) 60n
Altius, Gabriel (R) 82n, 86
Anaxagoras (R) 61n
Andrews, C. M., on founding of Va., 280–1
Aneau Anulus, Barthelmi (O) 215n–6n
Angello a Negar 153n
Appian of Alexandria (R) 76n, 82n
"Apollidorus" [Apollodorus] (O) 218
Aquinas, Thomas 223
Aratus (O) 218
Archimedes 79
Argall, Governor Samuel 182
Aristotle (O) 219
Arundel, Thomas Howard, Earl of 255
Arundle, Peter 129n, 154n, 191
Athenaeus (R) 82n
Aubrey, John 232n, 235n
Aucher family 255n
Aucher, Sir Anthony 278
Aucher, Dame Margaret (Sandys) 278
Augerianus (R) 82n
Ausonius (R) 65n, 76n, 82n
Avicenna (R) 86

Bacon, Sir Francis 92, 223n, 235n, 242; (R) 58, 66n, 79n, 89n; (O) 218, 219n
Bacon, Nathaniel 265
Bailiffe, George 187n
Bainham, Mr. 186n
Balcanqual, Walter 229n, 267–8
Baldwin, John 170n, 187n
Banks' horse 64n
Barclay, John 90
Bargrave, Capt. John 109n–10n, 143n, 281
Barlow, Thomas 231n
Barnard, John 254n, 255
Barne, Dame Anne (Sandys) 278
Barne, Sir William 25n
Barnes, Richard 172
Barrett, William 201n, 202n
Barton, Edward 52n–3
Barwick, Capt. 134n, 164n
Bawcome (or Bateman), Christopher 272
Baxter, Richard 244n, 265–6n, 283
Baynam (see also Bainham) 181n, 187n
Beaumont, Francis 223
Becher, Sir William 260n
Belon (R) 51n, 55n, 60n, 85, 275
Benge, William 187n
Benlowes (R) 90n
Berkeley, John 122n, 124n, 126n, 164
Berkeley, Sir William 261n–2n, 264n
Bermuda Company of London (or Summers Island Co.) 93, 98n, 105, 258, 260
Bernardo 165n, 187n, 196n
Bernardo, Mrs. 165n, 187n
Best, Cuthbert 273
Biddulph, William 45n, 70; (R) 69n
Blaney (or Blayney or Blaine), Edward, 150n, 153n, 158n, 188n
Blaney, Mrs. 171n
Blount, Sir Henry 90
Bludder, Sir Thomas 204, 227n, 254n
Bodin, Jean (O) 219; 223n
Bolton, The Rev. Francis 115, 192n
Bonoeil, John 143n
Borgius (R) 82n
Botero, Giovanni (R) 59n, 85, 275

Bothwell, Francis Stewart Hepburn, 5th Earl of 81n; (O) 219n
Bourne, Sir John 22n
Bowles, William Lisle 224n
Brahe, Tycho (O) 219
Braun, G., and F. Hohenberg, *Civitas orbis terrarum* (R) 82n
Brooke, Christopher, *A Poem on the Late Massacre in Virginia*, as the first American poetry 225
Browne, Saloman 272
Browne, Sir Thomas (R) 68n, 79n, 89n
Browning, William 186n
Buchanan, George (O) 219
Buck, Mara 171n
Buck, The Rev. Richard 171n, 192n
Buckingham, Marquis of 105n, 137n
Burghley, William Cecil, Lord 23, 24n
Burton, Robert (R) 58, 89n
Burton, William 206n, 276
Busbecq (R) 85, 275
Butler, Charles 254n
Butler, Capt. Nathaniel 99n–100, 106, 155n, 178–81, 182n, 184, 189, 276; *The Vnmasked face of Or Colony in Virginia . . . 1622*, 179–81; as GS' travelling companion in Palestine 276

Caesar, Sir Julius 173n
Callimachus (R) 86
Calthropp (or Colthorp), Capt. Christopher 142n
Calverley, Walter 38n
Calverley, William 37n, 39n, 273–4
Cambridge University, graduates of among Virginia colonists 190n–3n
Caninge, William 154n
Cant, Hadrian 56n
Capacius, J. C. (or G. C. Cappacio) (R), 81n, 86
Capps, William 128n, 170n
Carbonus, Mattheus 276
Carew, Thomas 227, 233n, 242n, 253, 283; verses on *ParaDivPoems*, 240
Carleton, Sir Dudley 85n, 100, 260n
Carter, Rosamus 187n
Cartwright, John 45n
Cary, [Thomas? also see Falkland] 223
Casaubon, Isaac (R) 61n, 86; 223n, 246
Cassiodorus (R) 86
Castalione, Sebastiano (*ParaDivPoems*), 240–1
Catterwole, R. 244
Cavalieri, G. B. de, engraving of (R), 61n, 83n
Cecill, T. 205
Chamberlain, John 100–1
Chambers, James 187n
Charles I 66n, 227, 236, 257n, 263–4, 283–5; as Prince, 93, 137n; coronation of, 198; comfort in *ParaPsalms*, 203n, 243; GS' dedications of works to, 45–6, 198, 203, 238, 246, 251n
Chillingworth, William 231n, 234, 235n
Choerilus (R) 60n, 86
Christophorus Helvicus (R) 60n, 68n, 86
Cicero (R) 82n; (O) 218
Ciofanus, Hercules (O) 216n
Claiborne (or Clayborne or Cleburne), William 115, 120n, 151n, 186n, 190n, 195n, 256n
Claudianus (R) 86
Claudius Ptolemaeus (R) 60n
Claxon, John 187n
Clein, Francis 204, 205n, 206n, 254n, 255
Clifford, Anne, Countess of Dorset 27n, 69
Clifford, George (see Earl of Cumberland)
Cole, William 20n, 29n, 31n
Collinwood, Edward 106n
Comes, John (O) 218; 187n
Comon, Nicholas 187n
Conquest, Edmund 32n
Conway, Secretary of Privy Council 159n, 184, 197
Copernicus (O) 220
Copland, The Rev. Patrick, *Virginia's God be thanked*, 102n, 124n
Coptic Christians 62, 73n
"Corona Pighius" [S. V. Pighius] (R) 82n, 83n
Coryat, Thomas (R) 45n, 47n, 51n, 90
Cotton, Sir Robert 276
Cowley, Abraham (R) 89n; 232n, 244n
Cox, Richard 21
Cranfield, Lionel, Earl of Middlesex 137n
Crashaw (or Croshaw), Capt. Rawley 133n, 166n
Craven, W. F., on Virginia Co. and Colony 280–2
Cresswell, Robert 222n, 232n
Cressy, Hugh 232n
Cripps, Zachary 188n
Cumberland, George Clifford, Earl of 19, 25n–7

Dale, Governor Sir Thomas 95, 148
Dallington, Sir Robert (R) 47n
Dameron, John 133n
Dancy (or Daunsey), John 187n
Dancy (or Daunsey), Thomas 187n
Daniel, George 222n
Danvers, Sir John 97, 106n, 113, 152n, 257, 258
Darbie, Thomas 36n
Davenant, William 223

Davison, Christopher 112, 115, 117n, 122n, 142n, 157, 168n, 172, 179, 190n
Davison, Mrs. 153n
Davison, Francis 112n-3
Davison, Walter 113
Dawes, Sir Abraham 260n
De Bry, Theodore, engraving of Jamestown massacre 120n
Dekker, Thomas (R) 90n
Delaram, F. 202n
de la Warr, Lady 114
De la Warr, Lord, governor of Va. 95, 194
Denham, Sir John 242n
Dering, the Puritan 22n
Dictys Cretensis (R) 86
Digby, Sir Kenelm 66n, 232n
Digges family 255n
Digges, Sir Dudley 24n, 66n, 113, 198n, 227, 233n, 258; verses on *ParaDivPoems* 240
Digges, Leonard 24n, 240n
Diodorus Siculus (R) 60n, 79n, 86; (O) 218
"Dion." (R) 82n
"Dionysus" (R) 86; 76
Ditchfield, tobacco commissioner 169
Donatus Franciscus (R) 82n
Donne, John, school of 253
Dorset Earl of 257-8
Dousa, Georgii (R) 56n, 85, 275
Drayton, Michael 201, 202, 213n, 222, 223n; verses of 93; lines to GS 118n
Dryden, John, on GS' Ovid 209, 222, 223-4, 252-3; on GS, 268n
du Bartas, Guillaume Salluste 214
Duncon, John 231n
Duppa (or Dupper), his "stinking beer" 136n, 139n, 155n

Each, Capt. 148n, 155n, 161n
Earle, Dr. John 231n
Eden, Luke 171n
Edmunds, Robert 187n
Edwards, John 187n
Eglionby, George 231n
Egypt, descriptions of 60-7
Elizabeth, Queen of Bohemia 48, 239n, 250n
Elizabeth, Queen of England 23-4, 31
Empedocles 79
Epicharmus 79
Erasmus, Desiderius (O) 219; 223n
Euclid 79
Eure, Mary, Lady 26n
Eure, William, Lord 25n, 26n
Euripides (R) 61n, 86
Eusebius Pamphili (R) 275; (O) 218
Eustatius (or Eustathius) (R) 82n, 86
Evans, John 187n
Evelin, George 186n
Evelin, Marjoy 186n
Evelyn, John 90
Ewens, William 115
Eyres, Nicholas 187n

Fabricius, Hieronymus (O) 219
Falkland, Lucius Cary, 2nd Viscount 59n 66n, 222n, 227, 228, 230n-4, 233n, 263, 283; commendatory verses on GS' *Ovid*, 204n; on *Para Psalms*, 236-7; on *ParaDivPoems*, 239n; on *Christ's Passion*, 246-7; his theology, 234
Farnaby, Thomas 206n
Ferrar, John 97, 100, 103, 108n, 109, 131n, 157, 160-1n, 163n, 164n, 165n, 168n, 189, 191n, 257, 258; ltrs. to from Va., 132-7, 150-8; as Va. landowner, 152n
Ferrar, Nicholas 97, 103, 132, 160n-1, 191n, 229n, 257, 258
Ferrar, Richard 229n-30n
Ferrar, William 171n, 191n
Ficinus (O) 218
Finch, Sir John 198n
Fitzherbert, Nicholas 84n
Flaminius (R) 82n, 86
Fletcher, Giles 90, 223
Fletcher, Phineas (R) 90n
Franciscus Vivius (R) 82n, 86
Franklin, Mr 146
Fraunce, Abraham (O) 217
Freethorne, Richard 128n, 156n
Fulgentius (O) 218
Fuller, Thomas 223n, 265n, 283; (R) 89n; opinion of GS' *Ovid*, 223n

Galilei, Galileo (O) 219, 220; 268n
Gascoigne, Sir William 37n, 39n, 273-4
Gataker, Charles 231n
Gates, Sir Thomas 95, 256n, 260
Gaudentius, Pater-Guardian of Holy Sepulchre 73, 74
Gentlemen of the King's Privy Chamber, duties 284; emoluments, 284-5
Geny, Mrs. 171n
Geraldus (O) 218
Gibbs, Thomas 113n, 143n
Gibson, Sir John 223n
Gillius (or Gyllius), Petrus (R) 51n, 56n, 85, 275
Girlington, Nicholas 273
Glover, Sir Thomas 52n-4
Godolphin, Sidney 227, 231, 233n, 250n, 283; verses on GS' *ParaDivPoems*, 240
Golding, Arthur (O) 208n-9n, 214, 222, 253
Good Newes from Virginia (1623), by John Trundle, as first American poetry 225; 102n-3n, 129-30n

Gookin, Daniel 127
Goring, Lord 260n
Graunt (or Grant), Wintoure 227, 233n, 283; verses on GS' *ParaDivPoems*, 240
Great Tew Circle of Wits, Poets, and Theologians 213n–5, 246
Greeks, their character in GS' time 59
Gresham, English merchant 80
Grey, Lady Jane 26
Grindal, Archbishop Edmund 21
Grindon, Edward 186n
Grismond, J. 202n
Grotius, Hugo 223n, 234n, 235; his *Christus Patiens* transl. by GS, 245–8n
Grotius, William 248n

Hales, John 232n, 234
Hall, Joseph 242n
Hall, Thomas 187n
Hamer (or Hamor), Capt. Ralph 122n, 130n, 131n, 157n, 190n
Hammond family 255n
Hammond, Henry 231n
Harmer, Charles 191n
Harmon, Mathew 188n
Harriott, Thomas 125
Harrison, John 189n
Harvey, Governor Sir John 181, 184, 195n, 257, 260n
Harwood, Capt. 122n
Hastings, Henry, Earl of Huntingdon 26n
Hawkeshead Grammar School 19n
Hebb, Andrew 238
Henry, Prince, son James I 140n
Herbert, Lord, of Cherbury (R) 47n
Herbert, George 106n, 242n, 253
Herbert, Thomas 90
Hermesianax (R) 86
Herodotus (R) 60n, 61n
Haynes, William, Jr. 186n
Heywood, Thomas 223
Higinus (O) 218
Hilliard, Nicholas 27n
Hobbes, Thomas 232n
Holgate Grammar School, York 28n
Holland, Philemon (R) 64n
Homer (R) 51, 56n, 77n, 82n, 86n, 201n; (O) 219, 221
Hooker, Richard, 23, 29, 31
Horace (R) 50n, 82n, 84, 201n; (O) 219
Hudson, Fretum, *A Treatise on the North-west Passage . . .* 156n
Hutchinson, Raphe 273
Huntingdon, Catherine, Countess of 25, 26n
Hyde, Edward 231n, 232
Hyde, Sir Nicholas 32n

INDIANS OF VIRGINIA, **massacre by,** 125–8; campaigns against, 168n; **colonists' revenge on, 128–31**; treachery of, 139, 147; sue for peace, 149; "Laughing King," 127; Nenemathanewes, 130n; Opechancanough, 126, 131. **Tribes**: Anacostan, 154n; Chickahominies, 179; Pamunkeys, 166; Potomackes, 166; Tappahannas or Tappahanncoks, 129, 187
Inns of court, former students of among Va. colonists 190n–3n
Isocrates (R) 60n

Jacob, Joseph 260n
James I 47, 53, 74n, 105, 118n, 172n, 195, 242n; assumption of control of Va. colony (1624), 196; death of, 198
Janiculo, Stefano 53n–4
Jansen, Cornelis (Cornelius Jonson) 254n–5n
Jefferson, John 182n
Johnson, Alderman Robert 97n, 104, 106, 138n, 177–8, 179, 181, 182n, 184
Jones, Sir William 178, 182n
Jonson, Ben 82n, 89n–90, 204n, 213, 231n, 232n, 254n
Jordan, Cicely 171
Josephus (R) 68n, 86
Josselyn, Sir Thomas 146n, 147n
Jourdan, Samuel 127n
Juvenal (R) 82n, 201n; 136n

Keats, John (O) 224n
Kemp, Richard 260n
Kendall, Miles 154n, 181n
Killigrew, Sir Peter 283
Killigrew, William 283
King, Henry 227, 233n, 242n; verses on *ParaDivPoems*, 240
Kithly, Philip 188n
Knolles, Richard (R) 57n; 90

Lactantius (O) 207n, 218, 219, 220
Lambinus, Dionysius (O) 219
Lapworth, Michael 122n, 190n
Laud Commission for government of foreign plantations, 259
Laud, Archbishop William 29n, 66n, 206n, 239n, 243, 250n
Lawes, Henry 204, 242n–3, 255
Leate, The Rev. William 192n
Leech, Capt. 122n
Legatt, John 238n
Lello, Henry 53
Leo Africanus (R) 61n, 86
Liberalism in Va. colony in 1639-42, 263n–5; in England and America in 17th century, 280–2

Linscot (or Linschoten), Jan Huyghen van (O) 219
Lithgow, William 52n, 54n, 60n, 69n, 70, 72n, 82n, 83n
Lodge, Thomas, *A Margarite of America* as first American poetry, 225
Long, Jane 187n
Longe, Elias 187n
Lopez, Edward (O) 219
Lopez, Francis (O) 219
Lovelace family and Sandyses 25
Lovelace, Richard 253, 283
Lower, Sir William 90n
Lownes, Matthew 201n, 202n
Lucan (R) 61n, 76, 82n, 201n, 204
Lucian (O) 218
Lucretius (R) 61n, 80, 86
Lucy, Sir Thomas 19n

Macbeth 221
Macrobius (O) 218
Malfi, Duchess of 221
Mallory, George 272
Mallory, William 273–4
Mandeville, Lord President of Privy Council 159n
Maninus (R) 86
Manne, Richard 272
Mansfield, David 187n
Mantuanus (R) 86
Markenfield, Thomas 272
Marlowe, Christopher 252
Marshall, William 205n
Marson, Thomas 146
Marston, John (R) 90n
Martial (R) 82n
Martin, Capt. John 173–5, 185, 191n, 195n
Martin, Thomas 146n
Martyr, Peter 21n
Mary, Queen of Scots 24n
Mary, Queen of England 21, 26n
Massachusetts Bay Colony charter of 1629 258
Massacre of 1622, engraving of, description 120n
Massinger, Philip 223
Matthews (or Mathew), Capt. Samuel 158n, 167, 181, 184n, 188n, 195n
May, Thomas 204, 223
Maycock (or Macocke), Samuel 122n, 126n, 190n
Mazzella, S. (R) 81n, 82n, 86
Meautys, Thomas 260n
Mediterranean, islands of visited by GS, 60
Melling, Thomas 143n, 149
Menander (R) 86
Menavimus Antonius (R) 55n
Merry, Sir Thomas 184n
Middlesex, Earl of (see Cranfield)
Middle Temple, curriculum of 33–4
Miller, Perry, on religious impulse in founding of Va. 280–2
Milton, John (R) 90n, 214, 224n, 242, 243; charge of plagiarism against, 249n; Milton-Ovid script, 286
Minter, Richard 164n
Moltzer, Jacob (or Jacobus Micyllus) (O) 216n
Montaigne, Michel de (O) 219
Morley, George 231n
Moryson, Fynes 44n, 54n, 71n, 82n, 83n, 90n
Mott, John 187n
Mundy, Peter (O) 55n, 90
Muretus, Antonius (R) 86; (O) 206n

Newce, Thomas 115n, 122n, 151n
Newce, Mrs. Thomas 151n
Newce (or Nuce), Capt. Sir William 111n–12, 115n, 117n, 122n, 133n, 150n, 165
Nicholas, Edward 260n
Northumberland, John Dudley, Duke of 21
Norton, John 34, 41n; will of, 34n–5n, 38, 39
Norton, Margaret (Redshaw) 35n
Norton, Richard 35n
Norton, William 35n, 37n, 39n, 273–4
Norton, Capt. William (of Va.) 113n, 114n, 124, 135
Nunne, Thomas 152n

Ombersley Court 25n, 149n
Ovid (R) 49n, 51, 82n
Ovid's *Metamorphosis* 140n; GS' editions of (see GS)
Oxford, University of curriculm in Elizabethan period, 30–1; Corpus Christi College, life in, 29n–31, 267–70; St. Mary's Hall, 29n, 269–70; graduates among Va. colonists, 190n–3n

Pace (Va. settler) 126
Palaphates (O) 218
Palaser, Thomas 41n
Palestine, history and descriptions of 68ff.
Pancirollus (R) 86
Panton, The Rev. Anthony 261
Parker, Archbishop Matthew 22n, 242
Parker, Master 202n
Parsons, leader of English Jesuits in Rome 84n
Parsons, John 187n
Paulet (or Pawlet), Thomas 122n
"Paul. Partaroll." (R) 86
Paulus Marcitus 63

Pausanias (R) 55n, 60n, 275; (O) 218, 219
Payne, John 254n
Peirce (or Perce, etc.), Mrs. Jane 150n–151n, 153n
Peirce, Jane (dau.) 150n, 157n
Peirce (or Perse, Pierce, Perce), Capt. William 150n, 153n, 157n, 158, 193
Peirsey, Abraham 181, 256n
Pembroke, Mary Herbert, Countess of 242
Perch, George 276
Percy, Capt. George 95
Persius (R) 86
Petronius (R) 82n
Pierius (O) 218
Pilkington, Margaret 187n
Pilkington, William 187n
Pio (or Pius Baptistus), Giovanni Battista (O) 216n
Plato (O) 217, 218, 219, 220n, 221
Pliny 60n; (R) 61n, 275; (O) 218
Plutarch (R) 49, 60n, 86; (O) 218, 219
Pomponius Laetus (R) 82n, 86
Pontanus (R) 82n; (O) 218
Poole, Daniel and family 187
Poole, Robert 166n
Pooley, The Rev. Greville 171, 192n
Pope, Alexander (O) 209, 212, 213n, 214, 252–3; and GS, 224n, 244n
Pope John XXII (R) 86
"Portacel" (R) 82n
Porter, Endymion 232n
Porter, Thomas 36–7, 272
Porter, Walter 243n
Pory, John 112n, 125, 163, 172, 181, 182n, 184, 191n; (R) 61n; as man of letters, 191n–3n
Pott, Dr. John 115, 117n, 122n, 142n, 153n, 157n, 171, 190n, 255n
Pountis, Vice-Admiral John 115n, 122n, 131n, 154n, 157n, 172, 184
Powell, Capt. Nathaniel 122n, 126n, 130n, 134n, 179, 190n
Powell, Capt. William 134n
Prideaux, Humphrey 277
Privy Council 169, 174, 181, 256; appoints Va. Commissioners, 181–2n; subcommittee on Plantations, 176, 232
Propertius (R) 82n
Prudentius (R) 82n
Pudsey, Cuthbert 39n, 273–4
Pullen, John 28
Purchas (*his Pilgrimage*) 90
Pym faction in Parliament 263n

Rainolds, John 31
Rainsford, Lady Ann (Goodere) 229n
Rainsford, Lady Eleanor (Boswell) 229n
Rainsford, Sir Henry, the elder 229n
Rainsford, Sir Henry 227, 229n, 230, 231, 232n, 233n; verses on GS' *ParaDivPoems*, 240
Raleigh, Dr. Walter 231n
Ramus, Peter (O) 219
Regius, Raphael (O) 215n–16
"Relationi di Napoli" (R) 81n
Renaldus de Tortis 276
Rich, Sir Nathaniel 106, 132n, 138n, 143n, 158, 159, 160n, 184, 281
Rich, R., *Newes from Virginia* (1610) 122n
Right, William 186n
Roe, Sir Thomas 110
Rolfe, Jane (Peirce) 150n–1n
Rolfe, Capt. John 114, 122n, 133n, 157n, 190n
Rota (R) 82n
Russell, Lady Margaret 19n
Rutilius Numantianus (R) 82n

Sabinus (O) 218
St. Augustine (O) 207n, 218, 219, 220
St. Jerome (R) 74n, 86; (O) 207n
St. Peter's School, York 28n
Salanicus (R) 60n
Salmon, Ann Norton 35, 36n, 272
Salmon (or Sawman), John 35n, 36n, 39n, 272
Sanderson, Robert 232n
Sandys family Bible at Hawkeshead 19n, 25n
Sandys, Anne (see Barne, Wenman) 19n, 25n
Sandys, Anthony 32n
Sandys, Arthur Hill, Lord 254n
Sandys, Bridget (dau. Myles S. of Latimers) 32n
Sandys, Bridget (dau. Henry S. and niece of GS) 278
Sandys, Cicely (Wilsford or Wilford) 22n, 24, 25n, 42n; bequest to GS, 91n; will and epitaph, 278
Sandys, The Rev. David 108n, 171n, 188n, 192n
Sandys, Archbishop Edwin 19–24, 32n, 38, 41, 42n, 91n, 149n, 272, 278; appetite for "fruits and fees," 20, 22; early life and education, 20–1; academic career, 21, 26n; exile in Switzerland, 21–2; stormy ecclesiastical career, 21–4; learning, 23; regarding GS' marriage, 35–7; legacy to GS, 36n
Sandys, Sir Edwin (d. 1607–8) 32n, 269
Sandys, Sir Edwin (1561–1629) 19n, 20n, 23n, 24n, 29n, 32n, 42n, 91, 93, 94, 95n, 96, 97n, 107n, 108n, 112n, 113, 114n, 117n, 132, 137n, 141n, 143n, 154n, 159n, 160, 168n, 169, 174, 177, 184n, 185, 189, 198, 227, 254, 257, 264, 266n, 278, 279; work for reform in Va. Co.

London, 97; and Bermuda Co. compromise, 99–100; elected Treasurer Va. Co. London, 100; activities in Va. and Bermuda Cos., 101n–5n; plans for agriculture and industry in Va., 103; accuses Smith faction, 105n; his conscious personal rectitude, 105n, 106; his "liberalism," 176, 282; death, 228n; at Oxford, 269–70; and the Va. Co., 279; his *Europae Speculum*, 44n, 47, 90, 240; his *Sacred Hymns*, 242n

Sandys, Colonel Edwin (d. 1642) 266n

Sandys, Elizabeth (Norton) (1580–1662?) wife of GS 35n–43, 271; documents relating to, 272–3; marriage to GS, 272–4

Sandys, Elizabeth (m. Edmund Conquest) 32n

Sandys, Lady Elizabeth (Cooke) 25n

Sandys, George (*fl.* 1509) 19n

Sandys, George (d. 1547) 19n

Sandys, Sir George (d. 1618?) 32n

SANDYS, GEORGE (1578–1644) 15–17, 39, 41n

Early Life (1578–1610) parentage 19–24; godparents, 25–7, education: at Oxford, 29–33, 269–70, Middle Temple, 33–4; marriage, 34–43, 271–4; litigiousness, 33n, 39n

Travels (1610–1612) 44–90; France to Constantinople, 47–53; Constantinople, 53–60; Egypt, 60–7; Palestine, 68–75; travelling companions in, 276–7; Phoenicia, 76; Mediterranean voyage to Malta, 78–9; Sicily, 78–80; Calabria, 80; Naples, 81–4; Rome, 84

Virginia Adventure (1612–1621) bequest from mother, 91, 278; Va. Co. stockholder, 91–118; candidate for governorship Bermuda, 99n; attendance at Va. Co. Courts, 101n, 104n, 106, committees of, 109–10; propaganda writer for Va. and Bermuda Cos., 106–7; friendship with Sir Francis Wyatt, 109n; elected resident Treasurer for Va., 111n; perquisites of office, 111n; duties, 116n–117n; preparations for voyage, 113–14; embarkation, 115–17; "servants" carried by GS, 115n; verses addressed to GS by Drayton, 118n

Virginia Years (1621–1625) colonial official, 119–62, 255; arrival, 119; early troubles, 123n; duties as director of industry, 123–5; collector of revenue, 163–4; report to Va. Co. London concerning massacre, 127; leads avenging expedition against Indians, 129n; letters to friends and relatives, 132–58; critic of Va. Co. London policies, 132–58; plantations of, 144–7, 185n–9n; residence, 153n; wishes to seek NW Passage, 156n; estimate of Va. Council of State, 157n–8n; "indiscretions" in ltrs. home, 159–61; "servants" of in Va., 164n, 169n, 187n–8n, 189; makes treaty with Indians, 166n; duties as member Va. Council of State, 166–75; acting Secretary Va. colony, 168n; as author Va. General Assembly's "Answer" to N. Butler, 180n; Butler's attacks on, 180n–1; as "liberal," 185, 280–2; as model farmer, 188; translates Ovid, 193n; ltrs. to Tradescant, 193n; appointment by James I to Council in 1624 after "Dissolution" of Va. Co., 195n; return to England, 195–7n

Courtier and Poet (1625–1644) reappointment to Va. Council (1626, 1628), 198n; Gentleman of Privy Chamber, 199n, 227, 283–5; circle of friends among, 227; life in Kent, 227–8, 267–8; in Oxfordshire and Gloucestershire, 228–36; Great Tew circle, 231–6; residence in Whitefriars (1638), 256n; suit against "pirates" of Ovid's *Metamorphosis*, 254n; appeals to Privy Council for protection of Va. property, 256–7; petitions for position as Secretary of subcommittee on foreign plantations, 259–60; Secretary of new commission for Va., 258; agent for Va. colony, 261–5; final years at Boxley Abbey, 265–8; death, 267; monuments to, 267–8

Portraits of 254n–5n. **Bibliographies** 287–309

Works (1) *A Relation of a Journey* (1615): 117n; dedication, 45–6; use of sources in, 48, 85ff.; style and other literary qualities, 87–8; verses incorporated in, 87; editions of, 89; authors most frequently quoted, 201n. (2) Transl. *Ovid's Metamorphosis* (1621, 1626, 1632): 75n, 87n, 253; *1621*: 117n–8n, 200n–2n; *1626*: 119, 193n, 199ff.; Charles I grants patent for, 199n; dedication, 203n; *1632*: 204n, 204–7; commentaries on, sources, 207n, 217–9, 220–1; allegory in, 215–21; development of couplet in, 209–13; debt in format to Italian and French Ovids, 216n–17n; influence of book on later poets, 222–5 critical opinions of, 222–4; as first

SANDYS, GEORGE—*contd.*
Works—*contd.*
American poetry, 225n; lawsuits regarding, 39n, 202n, 204n, 254n. (3) Lost work in theology, 235n. (4) *A Paraphrase upon the Psalms* (1636): 236–45; royal licence for, 236; dedication, 236; commendatory poems upon, 236–7. (5) *A Paraphrase upon the Divine Poems* (1638): 238–45; Latin sources, verse forms, 240–2, 241, 245. (6) *Christ's Passion* (1640): 245n–9. (7) *A Paraphrase upon the Song of Solomon* (1641): 249–52; MS. versions of, 250n; dedications, 251n; versification, 251–2. (8) "*Deo. Opt. Max.*", 253. (9) "*A Dream,*" 253. (10) "*Hymn to the Redeemer,*" 73, 253
Learning from education, 30n, 31n; acquired during travels, 85
Sandys, George, of St. Mary Woolchurch, "yeoman," 272
Sandys, George (nephew GS) 25n, 92n, 266n
Sandys, Lt.-Col. George Owen 254n–5n, 267n
Sandys, Henry (b. 1572) 20n, 23n, 25n, 29n, 32n, 91, 93n, 149n, 198, 269–70, 278
Sandys, Sir Henry (m. 1602) 32n
Sandys, Henry (1606–1636) 228n
Sandys, Hester 32n
Sandys, James 20n
Sandys, Dame Katherine 278
Sandys, Margaret (m. Sir A. Aucher) 19n, 25n
Sandys, Mary (1st wife Archbishop) 20n
Sandys, Mary (b. 1595) 278
Sandys, Myles (d. 1601) 19n, 24n, 32n
Sandys, Sir Myles (d. 1636) 24n, 145n
Sandys, Sir Myles, 1st Bart. (1563–1644) 19n, 23n, 24n, 25n, 32n, 38, 39, 40, 41n, 92, 143n, 146n, 159n, 198, 266n, 272–3, 278
Sandys, Myles (d. 1651) 145n
Sandys, Myles (baptized 1582) 145n
Sandys, Sir Myles, 2nd Bart. (1593–1653–4) 145n
Sandys, Richard 93
Sandys, Robert 25n, 266n, 283
Sandys, Sir Samuel 19n, 20n, 23n, 24n, 25n, 29n, 32n, 91, 92n, 93, 107n, 141n, 144; 147–9; 159n, 266n, 269, 278
Sandys, Thomas 23n, 25n, 32n, 91, 92, 93n, 107, 108n, 149n, 266n, 278
Sandys, William (father of Archbishop) 32n
Sandys, William (1565– d. young) 20n, 25n
Sandys, Sir William (d. 1641) 32n, 145n
Sandys, William (GS' "servant" in Va.) 188n
Sandys, William (Gentleman of Privy Chamber) 266n, 284
Sannizarius (Jacopo Sannazaro) (R) 82n; (O) 219
Sarpi, Fra Paolo 47
Savery, Salmon 205n–6n
Scaliger, J. C. (R) 51, 79n, 82n, 86n, 201n; (O) 218
Schmidel (O) 219
Schottus, Franciscus (R) 81n
Sejanus, 221
Selden, John 232n
Seneca 79n; (R) 82n; (O) 219, 221
Shakespeare, William 223
Sharpless, Edward 153n, 168–9, 172n, 184
Sheapard, Robert 187n
Sheldon, Gilbert 231n
Sheppard 165n
Ships: mentioned in *A Relation*: *Armado*, 50; *Great Exchange*, 49; *Little Defence*, 48; *Trinity*, 60, 75; on Virginian voyages: *Abigail*, 134, 143n, 148n, 155n, 159; *Bona Nova*, 187n–8n; *Charles*, 115n; *Duty*, 133n, 187n; *Elizabeth* (pinnace), 166n; *Flying Hart*, 115n; *Furtherance*, 188n; *George*, 119, 122, 185, 187n; *Guift*, 187n; *Hopewell*, 150; *James*, 188n; *Margaret and John* 188n; *Marmaduke*, 115n, 189n; *Marygold*, 187n; *Sea Flower*, 115n, 127, 154n; *Temperance*, 115n; *Tyger*, 115n, 153, 170n, 186n, 187n; *Warwick*, 115n
Shirley, Sir Anthony 45n; (R) 90n
"Sibylline Prophecies" (R) 86
Sidney, Sir Philip 223n, 242
Sidonius (R) 82n
Silius Italicus (R) 80, 82n
Simcox, G. A., on GS' *Psalms* 244n
Smith, Jane (Peirce Rolfe) 157n
Smith, Capt. John 93n, 113n, 173n
Smith, Capt. Roger 122n, 131n, 133n, 148–9, 151, 153n, 157n, 188n, 190n, 260n
Smith, Sir Thomas 95–6, 97n, 98, 100n, 102n, 104n, 105n, 178, 181, 183
Smith, William 186n
Sondes, Lord 270
Sondes, Sir George, K.B. 271
Southampton, Earl of 96, 103, 106, 107, 114n, 116, 132, 141n, 281
Southwell, Capt. 99
Sparks, John 187n
Spelman, Capt. Henry 154n, 191n
Spelman, Sir Henry 154n
Spencer, Thomas 36–7, 272
Stansby, William, 39n, 202n, 204n, 254n
Statius Pomponius (R) 60n

Staveley, William 274
Sternhold and Hopkins, version of *Psalms* 242
Stone, John 187n
Strabo (R) 60n, 61n, 64n, 65, 79n, 275; (O) 218, 219
Strachey, William 120n, 194n–5
Suckling, Sir John 235n, 283
Suidas (O) 219
Sweete, Robert 180n–1
Swifte, Thomas 164n, 166n, 187n
Sylvester, Joshua 213n, 223

Tarborer, Richard 165n
Taylor, Anthony 272
Taylor, Richard 274
Temple, Sir Thomas 32n
Thomas 90
Thompson, Nicholas 187n
Thorpe, George 108n, 115n, 122n, 165, 190n; slain in massacre, 126n–7n
Timberlake, Henry 45n, 60n, 64n, 69n
Tobacco, grant of sole importation of to Va. and Bermuda Cos., 130, 138; sent to England by GS, 146n; as payment for transportation, 163; monopoly and contracts for, 169, 181; as rent, 171; taxes agreed on by General Assembly, 174
Todd, H. J., on GS' *Psalms* 244
Tradescant (or Tredescant), John 66n, 193n
Tremellius, Immanuel (*ParaDivPoems*) 241
Triplet, Thomas 231n
Tritonius, Marcus Antonius 206n
Trundle, John, *Good Newes from Virginia* (1623) 129–30n
Tucker, Daniel 98
Tucker, Capt. William 129n, 133n, 158n, 167n
Tuke (or Tucke), Capt. John 143n, 146, 155n
Tullius Laura (or Laurea) (R) 82n
Tunstall, Francis 42n, 273–4
Tunstall, Marmaduke 274
Tunstall, William 42n, 274
Turks, life and government of 57ff.
Turlerus, Hieronymus (R) 44n
Turner, Martin 187n
Tyas, Robert 25n
Tyler, Moses Coit, opinion of GS' Ovid 225–6n
Tymme, T. (R) 69n–70n
Tyos, John 187n
Tzetzes (R) 86; (O) 219

Utie, John 187n

Vaccaria, L. della (R) 61n
Valerius Flaccus (R) 86
Vaughan, John 232n
Vaughan, Sir William 225n
Vergil (R) 49, 51n, 77n, 80, 82n, 201n; (O) 219
Vincentio (or Vincencio) 165n, 187n, 196n
VIRGINIA COLONY: **agriculture** in, 103; **college** at Henrico, 107, 127, 130, 135n–136, 164n–5; **colonists**: origins, 121n, revenge on Indians, 128–31, losses of, 136; **commissioners** for the affairs of (in London), 169; **new commission** for appointed by Charles I, 257–8; commission to investigate, 138n, 172, 175, 181–2; **constitution** for (1621), 122n; **Convention of 1625**, 185; **Council of State** in: 97, 255, 256–7, personnel, 122n, report of massacre, 127–8, ltrs. to England, 131n, functions of, 166–7, crimes tried before Court of, 171–2, secrets of sold, 172, Governor and Council, 173n–4n, handling of Martin affair, 174–5; **education and culture** of chief men of, 189n–93n; **General Assembly** (House of Burgesses): 97, 122, 123, 263–5, secrets of sold, 172; actions, 177–85, vs. Nathaniel Butler, 181–4, petition for freedom to convene, 183–4, 263n; called by Wyatt in 1639–40, 261n, "Declaration against the Company," 262–3; **Indians** (see separate entry); **industry** in: 103; glassworks, 103, 113n, 134–5, 153, 165–6n, ironworks, 130, 164n, sawmills, 164, shipyard, 134, 164, silkworm culture, 135, 166, vineyards, 135, 143n, 152, 164n, 166; **Jamestown**, 153n, 194–5, appearance of (1621–1624), 119n–21; **joint-stock companies** operating in, 150n; **"liberalism"** in, 175–7, 280–2; **maids** sent to, 104; **massacre** (1622), 120n, 125–8; **situation** after, 144–5, 149; natural resources, 164; **revenue** from farms, 163–4: from Company lands, 172; **Society of Martin's Hundred,** 156n; **tobacco** (see separate entry)
Virginia Company of London, 93–118, 129–31; attempts to renew charter (1639–40), 257–65; Brewster-Argall affairs of, 105n; charters of, 93, 95, 97n, 106; Courts of, 152nff.; criticism of Va. Council by, 129–32; "Discourse of the Old Company," 169, 257; early history, 93–5; factions: Smith-Warwick, 109n, 132n, 137n, 149n, 159, 160, 177, 179–81, 185, Sandys-Southampton, 111, 137n, 149n, 159n, 177, 183, 263n–4, 280–2, responsibility for colonial policy, 161n–2; "Instructions to Governour

Virginia Company of London—*contd.* and Council of State in Virginia" (1621), 115n; joint-stock companies of, 112–4n; letters to colony, 130–1; "liberalism", in, 280–2; lotteries of abolished, 112
Vives, Luis 235n; (R) 55n, 86; (O) 218, 219n

Walker, Christopher 272
Waller, Edmund (sometimes Edward), 213n, 227, 231, 232n, 233n; verses on GS' *ParaDivPoems*, 240
Warburton, John, on GS' Ovid 224n
Warwick, Earl of 98n
Washington, Alice 25n
Waterhouse, Edward, *A Declaration of the State of the Colony and Affaires in Virginia (1622)*, 102n, 124n, 126n, 156n
Watson, John 273
Webbe, Edward (R) 60n, 69n
Wenman (or Weneman, Wayneman), Lady Anne (Sandys) 92, 107n, 149, 228
Wenman, Sir Francis 92, 107n, 227n, 228n, 231n, 233n
West (see also de la Warr)
West, Anthony 188n
West, Capt. Francis (later Lt.-Governor of Va.) 66n, 116n, 122n, 177, 190n, 196n, 198n, 256, 257
Whitaker, The Rev. Alexander, *Good Newes from Virginia (1613)* 102n, 103n, 142n
Whitaker, Capt. Jabez 142n, 151n, 164n, 171n, 256
White, Edward 188n
White, The Rev. Thomas 192n
Whitgift, Archbishop John 22n
Wilcocks, Capt. John 133n, 151n
Wilford (or Wilsford), Elizabeth (Sandys) 42n
Wilford, Sir James 22n, 278
Wilford, Thomas 22n, 278
Wilford, Sir Thomas 22n, 24n, 42n, 198n, 278
Willet, Andrew 140n
Williams, Sir Abraham 260n
Wingfield, Lady, 254n
Wither, George 223n, 242n
Wood, Anthony à 29n, 31n, 283
Wood, Roger 170n
Wotton, Sir Henry 47n, 84n, 90
Wrote, Samuel 113n, 119n, 159n, 201, 202, 258n; GS' ltr. to, 137–43
Wyatt, Sir Francis 91n, 107n–8n, 109, 112n, 113, 114, 115n, 118n, 121–2n, 126, 131n, 132, 141n, 142n, 147, 159–160, 165n, 166n, 167, 168n, 174, 175, 179, 181, 182, 184–5, 186, 190n, 195, 197, 227, 233n, 255n–6n, 257, 263, 266–267, 281–2; house in Jamestown, 153n; defends GS, 160; use of Va. Co. tenants, 169n; as "cypher," 170n; **"liberalism,"** 176–7; verses on GS' *ParaDivPoems*, 240; second term as Governor in Va., 260–5
Wyatt, George 108n, 160n, 191n
Wyatt, The Rev. Haut 115, 192n
Wyatt, Lady Margaret (Sandys) 91n, 92, 108n, 115n, 145n, 149, 153n, 160n–1n, 235n, 265
Wyatt, Sir Thomas 108

Yeardley, Sir George 97, 98, 107, 108n, 112n, 116n–17n, 121, 122n–3n, 126, 130, 131n, 134, 142n, 157, 158, 167, 172, 177, 182, 183, 185, 187, 191n, 195n, 196–7, 257
Young, Patrick 231n
Young, Robert 202n

Zappullo, Michele (R) 71n
Zonaras, Joannes (R) 60n
Zosimus (R) 55n
Zuallardo, Giovanni (R) 48n, 70n–1n, 74, 86, 88n, 275